TRANSFORMING THE POLICE

TRANSFORMING THE POLICE

THIRTEEN KEY REFORMS

EDITED BY

CHARLES M. KATZ
ARIZONA STATE UNIVERSITY

EDWARD R. MAGUIRE
ARIZONA STATE UNIVERSITY

Long Grove, Illinois

For information about this book, contact:
Waveland Press, Inc.
4180 IL Route 83, Suite 101
Long Grove, IL 60047-9580
(847) 634-0081
info@waveland.com
www.waveland.com

Cover design: Betty Fernandes

10-digit ISBN 1-4786-3998-9
13-digit ISBN 978-1-4786-3998-5

Printed in the United States of America

7 6 5 4 3 2 1

Contents

Acknowledgments

We are grateful to many friends, colleagues, and students for helping to make this book a reality. Thanks to Chief Charlie Beck for writing the Foreword and starting the book off on the right note. Thanks to the chapter authors for contributing their time, energy, and expertise. A special thanks to the response essay authors—an amazing roster of innovative police executives—for taking time out of their busy lives to contribute their valuable perspectives.

Dean Jonathan Koppell urged us to take on this project, and we are grateful for his support. We are also grateful to Cassia Spohn, former director of ASU's School of Criminology and Criminal Justice, for supporting this project from the outset.

Thanks to Mike and Cindy Watts for their contributions to ASU's Center for Violence Prevention and Community Safety. Their generosity helped make this book possible.

Kristin Walinski and Sandy Hausrath at Scribe on Demand copyedited the book manuscript. Their keen eyes and sharp pens made this a better product. Megan Oakley served as project manager for this book, coordinating with the authors, copy editors, and publishers to help get the manuscript across the finish line. We are grateful for her many contributions. Thanks also to Betty Fernandes for designing the cover of the book.

Finally, thanks to Neil and Carol Rowe and the team at Waveland Press for their support and for making the publication process so pleasant.

Foreword

Chief Charlie Beck (Ret.)
Los Angeles Police Department

American policing is at a crossroads. The choices we make at this critical historic juncture will define who we are and how we police for generations of police officers who follow us. It is important that we pick our course wisely and with the prudence required for decisions of this gravity.

Make no mistake: a new course will be plotted for law enforcement. The forces involved that are calling for change are too powerful to be ignored, and there can be no doubt that change will come. The only real questions are: Who will design the change, and what will the new standard be for policing? I believe professionals on both the practitioner and academic sides must define our new course; this is the only way that rational and valuable progress can be made. The alternative is change for change's sake designed by those less qualified and certainly less tied to the success of their product. Therefore, we must be involved in picking the path forward, or we are doomed to have it selected for us.

So, how did we arrive at this point in history? What caused this urgent call for change coming from all of our major groups of influencers? How is it that the public, the press, and the politicians have come to the same conclusion: "We want cops to police differently. We're not sure exactly what that looks like, but we know that we don't like what we see now."

As with any question of this depth, multiple converging forces are responsible. The first is a point in history that needs to be viewed as a watershed moment: Ferguson. Ferguson, Missouri, is a small town that has had a huge impact on how people currently view policing. We are all judged through the lens of the police shooting of Michael Brown and the response of local law enforcement to the public outcry over his death. This is not a judgment on my part of the propriety of the actions taken. It is merely a matter of fact.

The second force in the call for change is one of our own making. Video and the release of video have brought the violence inherent in policing into the living rooms of America. Just as the then-groundbreaking news camera coverage of the Vietnam War caused many Americans to question their military, body-worn video and in-car cameras are causing some Americans to question their police.

And, lastly, we are heavily influenced by technology, or, more specifically, the speed at which information now travels. When a law-enforcement shooting or other high-profile incident occurs, it is immediately in the public eye, and conclusions are often drawn long before the facts are known and often before investigations are even started.

All of this has combined to create a crisis in policing. It is a crisis of public trust. Even though it certainly isn't universal, it is prevalent to the degree that it demands our attention and action.

That brings us back to our two big questions. Who will design the path forward, and how do we chart it? That's why this book is so important. It brings together the two ablest groups to lead the discussion: the finest and most experienced police professionals and qualified academics. The combination represents our best efforts to suggest solutions—and not just the theory behind solutions but real-world practices that can make real-world differences. Best of all, those who choose our path forward will also be the ones who have to walk it.

About the Authors

ASU Affiliates

A. Johannes Bottema is a doctoral student in the School of Criminology and Criminal Justice at Arizona State University. His primary research interests are evidence-based policing and the utilization of intelligence within law enforcement.

Scott H. Decker is emeritus foundation professor of Criminology and Criminal Justice at Arizona State University. His primary areas of research include gangs, criminal justice policy and police accountability.

Michaela R. Flippin is a doctoral student and research assistant at Arizona State University in the school of Criminology and Criminal Justice. Her research interests primarily focus on procedural justice.

Janne E. Gaub is an assistant professor of criminal justice at the University of North Carolina at Charlotte. Her research focuses on police technology, use of force, misconduct, and the intersection of gender and policing.

Jessica Huff is a doctoral candidate in Criminology and Criminal Justice and a research assistant in the Center for Violence Prevention and Community Safety at Arizona State University. Her research interests revolve around policing, race/ethnicity, neighborhoods, and research methods and design.

Charles M. Katz is a professor in the School of Criminology and Criminal Justice and is Watts Family Director of the Center for Violence Prevention and Community Safety at Arizona State University. His research primarily involves collaborating with agencies to increase their organizational capacity to identify and strategically respond to crime and violence affecting local communities.

Natasha Khade is a doctoral student in the School of Criminology and Criminal Justice at Arizona State University. Her research focuses on the rehabilitation of offenders, desistance from crime, disengagement from gangs, and cross-cultural applications of criminological theory.

Brooks Louton is a police planning and research supervisor with the Tempe Police Department, as well as an adjunct faculty member at Arizona

State University. She received her PhD in Criminology and Criminal Justice from Arizona State University in 2016. Her current research interests include policing and police technology.

Edward R. Maguire is a professor in the School of Criminology and Criminal Justice at Arizona State University, where he also serves as an associate director of the Center for Violence Prevention and Community Safety. His research focuses primarily on policing and violence.

Victor Mora is a doctoral student in the School of Criminology and Criminal Justice at Arizona State University. His primary areas of research include policing, with a focus on training, gangs, and group processes.

Carlena Orosco is an analyst in the Strategic Planning, Analysis and Research Center (SPARC) at Tempe Police Department, as well as a doctoral student in the School of Criminology and Criminal Justice at Arizona State University. Her research interests include discretion and decision-making in policing, the role of police dispatchers, gangs, and the neighborhood and spatial dynamics of crime.

Kathleen E. Padilla is a doctoral student in the School of Criminology and Criminal Justice at Arizona State University. Her primary research interests involve policing, including officer stress and stress interventions, mental health and wellness, public perceptions of law enforcement, particularly among youth, and the application of criminological theory to police work.

Michael D. Reisig is a professor in the School of Criminology and Criminal Justice at Arizona State University. His research focuses on the nature of social control (formal and informal), the neighborhood context of policing, and the measurement of criminological concepts.

Michael S. Scott is a clinical professor at Arizona State University's School of Criminology and Criminal Justice and the director of the Center for Problem-Oriented Policing, a research center that produces and disseminates information about how police can effectively and fairly address specific public-safety problems. Scott holds a law degree from Harvard Law School and a bachelor's degree from the University of Wisconsin, Madison.

John A. Shjarback is an assistant professor in the Department of Law and Justice Studies at Rowan University. His research interests center on policing, specifically environmental and organizational influence on discretionary officer behavior and current issues and trends.

Logan J. Somers is a doctoral student in the School of Criminology and Criminal Justice at Arizona State University. His primary research interests are police experience, use of force, and culture.

Cassia Spohn is a foundation professor of Criminology and Criminal Justice at Arizona State University. Her research interests include prosecutorial and judicial decision-making, the intersections of race, ethnicity, gender, crime and justice, and sexual assault case processing decisions.

Suzanne St. George is a doctoral student in the School of Criminology and Criminal Justice at Arizona State University. Her research focuses broadly on sexual violence, particularly how incidents of rape and sexual assault are perceived, and to what extent these perceptions affect decision-making. She is also interested in neighborhood dynamics, especially ways to promote informal social control and collective efficacy among disadvantaged communities.

Cody W. Telep is an associate professor in the School of Criminology and Criminal justice at Arizona State University. His research interests include synthesizing research to assess what works in policing, examining the impact of police practices on crime and citizen perceptions of legitimacy, and examining and increasing receptivity to research and evidence-based practice in policing.

William Terrill is interim associate dean in the Watts College of Public Service and Community Solutions and a professor in the School of Criminology and Criminal Justice at Arizona State University. His primary research interests center on police use of force, police culture, and organizational policy.

Natalie Todak is an assistant professor of Criminal Justice at the University of Alabama at Birmingham. She studies policing, corrections, race and gender in criminal justice, and qualitative and mixed research methods.

Rick Trinkner is an assistant professor in the School of Criminology and Criminal Justice at Arizona State University. Broadly speaking, his research seeks to understand why people follow rules and defer to authority and how regulatory agencies can best foster support from those they serve.

David H. Tyler is a doctoral student in the School of Criminology and Criminal Justice at Arizona State University. His research explores organizational change within police departments, crowd dynamics and protest policing, and quantitative methods.

Danielle Wallace is an associate professor in the School of Criminology and Criminal Justice at Arizona State University. Her research involves understanding disparities in policing and creating practitioner-friendly methods of identifying whether bias is occurring within law enforcement agencies.

Vincent J. Webb recently retired as a professor of practice in the School of Criminology and Criminal Justice and the Center for Violence Prevention and Community Safety at Arizona State University. His research relies on collaborations with criminal justice agencies and communities to generate empirical evidence that can be used to inform the development of effective policies and practices to improve community safety.

Michael D. White is a professor in the School of Criminology and Criminal Justice at Arizona State University and associate director of ASU's Center for Violence Prevention and Community Safety. His primary research interests involve the police, including use of force, technology, and misconduct.

Police Practitioners

Art Acevedo is chief of police for the Houston Police Department's 5,200 sworn officers and 1,000 civilian personnel. He previously served as chief of the California Highway Patrol and Austin (TX) Police Department. Acevedo is a proponent of "relational policing" and emphasizes that every interaction is an opportunity to develop or strengthen a relationship of trust. He is currently president of the Major Cities Chiefs Association and has also held leadership roles with the International Association of Chiefs of Police.

Charlie Beck was appointed chief of the Los Angeles Police Department in November 2009, a position he held until his retirement in 2018. During his time with the LAPD, Chief Beck led the third largest police department in the United States, managing 10,000 sworn officers and 3,000 civilian employees. Most recently, Chief Beck was assigned as interim superintendent of the Chicago Police Department. Chief Beck is renowned for his ability to forge community outreach programs tempered with the input of diverse stakeholders to form enduring crime abatement programs.

Theron Bowman has over 35 years of public service as a police and city executive. He is president and CEO of The Bowman Group, an expert police practices consulting firm. He has received multiple federal court appointments to oversee consent orders, teaches and trains across the United States, and is a published author and an inductee into the George Mason University Evidence-Based Policing Hall of Fame. He holds a doctorate degree in Urban and Public Administration from the University of Texas at Arlington.

Mike Brown has served in the Salt Lake City Police Department since 1991. He was appointed chief of police in May 2016. Chief Brown's experience has been focused on a number of specialty functions to address community needs, participation and management of special events and demonstrations, serious collision investigations, and coordination with federal and municipal agencies. As the Special Operations Bureau commander, he oversaw SWAT, Safe Streets Gang FBI Task Force, DEA Metropolitan Narcotic Task Force, Organized Crime Unit, Hazardous Device Unit, Motorcycle Squad, Public Order Unit and Accident Investigation.

Michael "Mike" L. Brown has 43 years of public service and nearly four decades of experience in law enforcement, safety oversight, and public policy. He was appointed as the chief of police for the Alexandria (VA) Police Department in January 2017. From 2010 until his appointment as chief in Alexandria, Brown served as Director of the Office of Impaired Driving and Occupant Protection at the National Highway Traffic Safety Administration (NHTSA). He also devoted 31 years of service to the California Highway Patrol, culminating in his appointment as commissioner from 2004 to 2008.

Jim Bueermann was chief of police in the Redlands, CA Police Department until his retirement in June 2011. He had worked for the Redlands Police Department since 1978, serving in every unit within the department. He was appointed police chief and director of housing, recreation and senior services in May 1998. Most recently, he served as president of the Police Foundation in Washington, D.C. He holds a bachelor's degree from California State University at San Bernardino and a master's degree from the University of Redlands.

Edward A. Flynn led the Milwaukee Police Department for ten years, preceded by service as police commissioner in Springfield, MA; secretary of public safety in Massachusetts, and as police chief in Arlington, VA. His early career was spent in the Jersey City Police Department. George Mason University inducted him into its Evidence Based Policing Hall of Fame, and he now consults for the Major Cities Chiefs Association.

Margo L. Frasier is nationally known as an expert in law enforcement and corrections, having served as a subject matter expert for the U. S. Department of Justice, Special Litigation Section. She also serves as a court-appointed monitor over the reform provisions contained in the consent judgments regarding Orleans Parish, Louisiana and Bernalillo County, New Mexico jail system. She previously served as the police monitor for the City of Austin, where she successfully advocated for the expansion of the powers of the Office of Police Monitor to provide greater accountability and transparency. She also served as the elected sheriff of Travis County (TX), as a civil rights attorney and as president of the Major County Sheriffs of America. She received her undergraduate degree from Sam Houston State University and her law degree from Florida State University.

Eric Jones is police chief of the Stockton Police Department. He developed and led "Principled Policing" with the California State Department of Justice for statewide training. He led Stockton to be one of only six sites for the National Initiative for Building Community Trust and Justice. His work was profiled in *The New York Times* in July 2016, and in *USA Today* in June 2017.

David W. McGill is a recently retired law enforcement executive. He has worked in three police departments in two states, including 25 years with the Los Angeles Police Department in patrol, investigations, specialized divisions, and as an adjutant for two deputy chiefs. He also held appointments with the Newport Beach (CA) Police Department as the first assistant police chief and served as chief of police in Sedona, Arizona. McGill earned a bachelor of science degree in biology/pre-medicine at the University of California at Irvine and holds a master's degree in public administration from the California State University at Long Beach.

Steven Pitts has 40 years of policing experience with the Reno Police Department and advising U.S. programs overseas. This experience includes over 30 years of training and program development, 25 years of tactical operations, and 15 years of executive level experience. Steve has been nationally recognized as an innovator, educator and practitioner in intelligence-led policing, community oriented policing and problem solving, and many other nationally recognized policing initiatives. He is adjunct faculty at the University of Nevada-Reno where he teaches leadership, multi-culturalism, community policing and problem solving, homeland security, and terrorism.

Ivonne Roman is a police executive with 25 years of experience, serving in every rank from police officer to police chief. She is an executive board member of the National Police Foundation and the American Society for Evidence-Based Policing and earned fellowships with the National Institute of Justice LEADS program and TED Talks. She is a PhD student at Rutgers-Camden studying women in policing and organizational legitimacy.

Owen West was born and bred in Yorkshire to a policing family. His father, brother, and wife are retired West Yorkshire officers. Owen joined the force in 1989 and retired in 2019. Since 2000 Owen has held a range of specialist portfolios in public order policing. Owen served as an advanced silver commander for WYP, leading large scale events and acting as operational commander during events such as national English Defence League demonstrations and counter demonstrations. He also served as director of corporate services. Owen holds a master's degree with distinction from Cambridge University in Applied Criminology and Police Management and is a research fellow at Keele University.

Calvin Williams is the City of Cleveland's 40th chief of police. Chief Williams was appointed to the Division of Police in February 1986. In 1989, he was assigned to the SWAT unit and then promoted to sergeant in July 1997, becoming the SWAT unit supervisor. Chief Williams has also served as the supervisor of both the vice unit in the Fourth District and the fugitive unit. In 2005, Chief Williams became the Cleveland Police Liaison to the US Marshal's Fugitive Task Force and was promoted to commander of the Third District in March 2006. In September 2011, he was promoted to deputy chief of field operations. Most recently, Chief Williams completed his bachelor's degree in Public Safety Management at Cleveland State University.

Introduction

Edward R. Maguire
Charles M. Katz
Arizona State University

Policing in the United States is currently in a profound state of uncertainty. In the fifty years of police reform since the creation of the Law Enforcement Assistance Administration (LEAA) in 1968, police across the country have experimented with and implemented a wide variety of reforms.[1] On certain measures, evidence that important reforms have taken place could not be clearer. For instance, police agencies in the United States are more diverse and more educated than ever.[2] Technological advancements have also had a profound influence on numerous policing functions.[3] At the same time, police continue to be embroiled in controversy, particularly with regard to issues surrounding race, use of force, and police-community relations.[4] Critics argue that police continue to be heavy handed, particularly when dealing with minorities.[5] Police and certain pundits counter that the job of policing has become much more difficult in recent years, especially post-Ferguson. Indeed, some claim that there is now a "war on cops" in the United States.[6]

During this same time, a robust and growing industry of police research has emerged.[7] That industry consists of social scientists from a variety of disciplines who specialize in the study of police and policing. Most of these policing specialists are employed in universities and think tanks. Based on their efforts, there is now a considerable body of research on policing and on issues of concern to police. That body of research has led to the emergence of the "evidence-based policing" movement, which seeks to apply social science research evidence to decisions about police administration, strategies, and tactics. Just as physicians can now draw on a massive body of research evidence when considering the best treatment options for their patients, police leaders can now draw on research evidence in deciding how to police their communities.[8]

The School of Criminology and Criminal Justice at Arizona State University (ASU) has invested heavily in recruiting faculty with expertise in policing and police research in its efforts to deliver policy-relevant or "use-inspired" research that makes a difference—not just in the ivory tower of academia but also in the real world. By way of background, ASU, which consists of four campuses in the Phoenix metropolitan area, is a public institution with a current enrollment of approximately 100,000 students across 250 majors and more than 1,000 graduate programs. In 2018, its annual research expenditures totaled over $600 million. It is ranked as the most innovative university in the country, ahead of Stanford and MIT. More directly, ASU's School of Criminology and Criminal Justice has substantial experience working with senior-level law enforcement executives from around the world. The school offers bachelor's, master's, and Ph.D. programs. It currently has one of the largest criminology and criminal justice faculties in the nation, with twenty-six tenured and tenure-track faculty members; nineteen research professors, clinical professors, professors of practice, lecturers, and instructors; and fifty-eight faculty associates. Collectively, this faculty is responsible for teaching about 2,530 undergraduate students, 287 master's students, and thirty-eight Ph.D. students. Because of its commitment to teaching, research, and service, ASU's School of Criminology and Criminal Justice is currently ranked as one of the best criminology programs in the nation, according to the most recent *U.S. News and World Report*.[9]

With one of the largest and most respected faculties in the world, focused on criminology in general and policing specifically, we at ASU view the current crisis in American policing as an opportunity to take stock of policing and police reform in the United States, drawing on the expertise of our faculty, alumni, and doctoral students. Our review, fifty years after the creation of the LEAA, focuses on making practical and policy-relevant recommendations that police agencies can rapidly implement to see immediate improvements in policing in their communities.

In thirteen concise and definitive chapters, the authors in this volume—all of whom are affiliated with ASU's School of Criminology and Criminal Justice in one way or another—highlight a specific problem area in policing, review the research evidence on potential solutions, and recommend specific reform measures. Following each chapter is a response essay written by a current or former police leader. Taken together, these chapters and response essays represent an important step forward in thinking about the police, their problems, and the reforms that every police agency should consider adopting.

This book was written for everyone interested in the future of policing, including mayors, city and county managers, other elected officials, police leaders, students of policing, scholars, and the general public. Although the primary focus is on policing in the United States, the book also has significant implications for policing elsewhere in the world. Indeed, several of the chapter authors have carried out significant research on police not only in the United States but also in other regions around the world.

■ Police Reform in the United States

The 1960s was a turbulent period in the United States. The decade was marked by a number of key historical events and social changes, including the war in Vietnam, the civil rights movement, the riots that engulfed numerous U.S. cities, rising crime rates, the emergence of a powerful countercultural movement, and the assassinations of John F. Kennedy, Robert Kennedy, and Martin Luther King Jr. The police played an important role in many of these historical developments, with serious questions raised about their fairness, legitimacy, and effectiveness. As policing scholar Samuel Walker noted, events in the 1960s "created a national crisis that provoked a sweeping reconsideration of the basic role of the police, the conduct of police officers, and—in particular—the role of the police in African-American communities. The reconsideration of policing included fundamental challenges to the existing norms of police professionalization."[10]

President Lyndon Johnson formed the President's Commission on Law Enforcement and Administration of Justice in 1965 to examine, in part, the role of the police. In 1967, the Commission released its landmark final report, *The Challenge of Crime in a Free Society*. The report articulated a new vision for policing in the United States. The Commission's recommendations focused on several key themes that remain relevant today: police-community relations, controlling police discretion, staffing (including racial and gender diversity), and the appropriate role of police in a democratic society.[11] The Commission also highlighted the importance of carrying out research on the police, emphasizing "the urgent need for research into every aspect of police work, by the police and by scholars working with the police."[12]

In 1968, President Johnson signed into law the Omnibus Crime Control and Safe Streets Act. The Act established the LEAA, which provided financial assistance to "state and local governments to improve all aspects of their criminal justice systems—police, courts, and corrections."[13] The LEAA experienced significant controversy associated with both its mission and its methods.[14] It was disbanded in 1982, but two of its lasting legacies included improving and expanding criminal justice education at the university level and establishing the importance of the federal government's support for high-quality research on criminal justice issues.[15] Many of the

LEAA's functions were folded into the Office of Justice Programs, which continues to fund research and evaluation on policing and other criminal justice issues today.[16]

In spite of all the energy invested in police reform in the United States during the 1970s and 1980s, a 1990 review of changes in policing concluded that "based upon the slow pace at which street level policing has changed in the past, the safest prediction undoubtedly is that the patrol officers of today can be expected to do their work by and large as they did a decade ago and as they will do a decade hence."[17] Nearly two decades later, another review of changes in policing reached a similar conclusion, noting that "[f]or all the strategic innovation that has been introduced to the American police field over the past four decades, one can still reasonably conclude that conventional policing strategies—and the organizational systems, structures, and cultures that support them—predominate."[18]

In spite of these pessimistic appraisals, strategic reforms in policing have taken place since the 1960s. These reforms may have been limited in scope or only implemented in certain jurisdictions. Nonetheless, police agencies have experimented with a variety of strategic reforms aimed at curbing crime and violence, such as problem-oriented policing, "hot spots" policing, and focused deterrence interventions, as well as reforms aimed at enhancing police accountability, such as civilian review, body-worn cameras, and early intervention systems. To be sure, policing has evolved and has improved tremendously over the past fifty years, but, as recent events illustrate very clearly, there is still significant room for improvement in American policing.

■ Organization of This Book

The first two chapters make recommendations related to the crime-control function in policing. Chapter 1, by ASU professor Cody Telep and doctoral student A. Johannes Bottema, outlines evidence-based policing (EBP) and its implications for the crime-control strategies used by police agencies. A response essay by Jim Bueermann, the recently retired president of the National Police Foundation and former police chief in Redlands, California, discusses the benefits of EBP and the real-world challenges to its implementation and presents various strategies to overcome those challenges. Chapter 2, by ASU professor Charles Katz and doctoral student Jessica Huff, recommends that police engage in collaborative strategic crime control, presents the fundamental principles of a strategy for police-led collaborative strategic crime control, and provides examples of its utility in addressing deeply rooted problems within communities. Houston police chief Art Acevedo responds to chapter 2 by discussing the finite resources available to the police and the simultaneous need for more comprehensive data-driven responses to community problems. He provides an example of his agency's implementation of strategic crime control through the Comprehensive Gang Model to address gang violence in Houston.

The next three chapters recommend police strategies for enhancing police fairness and legitimacy. These issues have received significant attention in recent years and formed the core of the recommendations issued by the President's Task Force on 21st Century Policing in 2015.[19] Chapter 3, by ASU professor Michael Reisig, recommends that the police institutionalize procedural justice and legitimacy, two key concepts in recent police reform debates. A response essay by Theron Bowman, former police chief of Arlington, Texas, supplements Professor Reisig's suggestions, making several concrete recommendations for implementing procedural justice reforms and enhancing legitimacy in police agencies. Chapter 4, by ASU interim associate dean and professor William Terrill, recommends that police further reduce unnecessary use of force and provides seven specific actions they should take. A response essay by Chief Michael Brown of the Alexandria, Virginia, Police Department highlights the importance of use of force and its impact on a police agency's relationship with the community and discusses the significance of professor Terrill's recommendations. Chapter 5, by ASU professor Danielle Wallace, doctoral student Carlena Orosco, and Brooks Louton (police planning and research supervisor with the Tempe Police Department and an ASU alumna), recommends reducing racial disparities in police practices by implementing a number of organizational reforms. Calvin Williams, chief of police for the Cleveland Division of Police, responds by discussing his efforts, in combination with a settlement agreement with the U.S. Department of Justice, to make procedural changes to address systemic racial inequalities promulgated by police in the past.

Chapters 6 and 7 address police accountability issues. In chapter 6, ASU professor emeritus Scott Decker and Rowan University professor (and ASU alumnus) John Shjarback discuss the role of civilian oversight in policing and provide options for refining the oversight model in American police agencies, including the need for best practices in police oversight. Margo Frasier, the former sheriff of Travis County, Texas, and current vice president of the National Association for Civilian Oversight of Law Enforcement, responds with a thoughtful discussion on the benefits and limitations of civilian oversight agencies for improving police accountability. In chapter 7, ASU professor Michael White and two ASU alumnae—East Carolina University professor Janne Gaub and University of Alabama professor Natalie Todak—recommend several principles for adopting body-worn cameras (BWCs) and outline the steps to properly plan, implement, and manage a successful BWC program. A response essay by former Milwaukee police chief Ed Flynn reflects on some of the implementation and technical issues his agency faced in adopting BWCs.

Two chapters then examine organizational learning in policing. Chapter 8, by ASU clinical professor Michael Scott, recommends the use of "sentinel event reviews" following critical incidents as a means of enhancing organizational learning. A response essay by David McGill, former chief of the Sedona, Arizona, Police Department, reflects on his career working in Sedona and Los Angeles and the importance of critical incident reviews for preventing police-involved harm. Chapter 9, by ASU professors Vincent Webb (retired) and Charles Katz and doctoral student Michaela Flippin, examines the importance of police partnerships with universities and makes recommendations on how to institutionalize these relationships. Captain Ivonne Roman with the Newark Police Department reflects on the consequences of prior policies and programs that were not rooted in evidence and discusses the value of embracing data, research, and evidence in contemporary policing.

Next, two chapters examine reforms intended to improve the workplace environment and quality of life for police employees. Chapter 10, by ASU professor Rick Trinkner and doctoral student David Tyler, focuses on "organizational justice" and the use of procedural fairness by supervisors, managers, and administrators when interacting with police employees. A response essay by Stockton, California, police chief Eric Jones reflects on his agency's efforts to adopt "principled policing" strategies that help to establish a healthier internal organizational climate. Chapter 11, by ASU professor Edward Maguire and doctoral students Logan Somers and Kathleen Padilla, examines efforts to improve physical and emotional health and wellness among police officers. A response essay by former Reno, Nevada, police chief Steve Pitts reflects on these issues and discusses the changes his agency made to improve the physical and mental health of Reno police officers.

The last two chapters examine contemporary issues in policing. Chapter 12, by ASU professor Edward Maguire and doctoral students Natasha Khade and Victor Mora, explores the police handling of protests. A response essay written by former Chief Superintendent Owen West from the West Yorkshire Police in the United Kingdom reflects on the British experience of policing protests. Finally, chapter 13, by ASU professor Cassia Spohn and doctoral student Suzanne St. George, focuses on the police response to sexual assaults. In the wake of scandals associated with the rape kit backlog in the United States, this chapter examines an important and timely issue. A response essay by Chief Mike Brown in Salt Lake City describes how his agency responded to the problem through a change in police culture, a revamped training curriculum, and evidence-based policy changes.

In short, this volume features essays written by twelve professors, four PhD program alumni, and ten doctoral students from the School of Criminology and Criminal Justice at Arizona State University. It also features reflections from fourteen current or former police executives. Taken together, the 40 authors featured in this volume represent the vanguard of current thinking about policing and police reform. Their collective voices provide a compelling road map for charting out the future of policing.

NOTES

[1] Wesley G. Skogan, "The Commission and the Police," *Criminology and Public Policy* 17, no. 2 (2018): 379–396.

[2] David L. Carter, Allen D. Sapp, and Darrel W. Stephens, *The State of Police Education: Policy Direction for the 21st Century*, (Washington, DC: Police Executive Research Forum, 1989); Randa Embry Matusiak and Matthew C. Matusiak, "Structure and Function: Impact on Employment of Women in Law Enforcement," *Women & Criminal Justice* 28, no. 4 (2018): 313–335; Brian A. Reaves, "Local Police Departments, 2013: Personnel, Policies, and Practices, *Bureau of Justice Statistics Bulletin,* NCJ 248677 (May 2015): 1–21.

[3] James Byrne and Gary Marx, "Technological Innovations in Crime Prevention and Policing: A Review of the Research on Implementation and Impact," *Journal of Police Studies* 3, no. 20 (2011): 17–40.

[4] Sue Rahr and Stephen K. Rice, "From Warriors to Guardians: Recommitting American Police Culture to Democratic Ideals," *New Perspectives in Policing*, (Washington, DC: National Institute of Justice, John F. Kennedy School of Government, 2015).

[5] Rod K. Brunson, "Police Don't Like Black People": African-American Young Men's Accumulated Policing Experiences," *Criminology and Public Policy* 6, no. 1 (2007): 71–101.

[6] Heather Mac Donald, *The War on Cops: How the New Attack on Law and Order Makes Everyone Less Safe*, (New York: Encounter Books, 2016).

[7] Jack R. Greene, "New Directions in Policing: Balancing Prediction and Meaning in Police Research," *Justice Quarterly* 31, no. 2 (2014): 193–228; Darrel W. Stephens, "Enhancing the Impact of Research on Police Practice," *Police Practice and Research: An International Journal* 11, no. 2 (2010): 150–154.

[8] Cynthia Lum and Christopher S. Koper, *Evidence-Based Policing: Translating Research into Practice*, (Oxford, UK: Oxford University Press, 2017); Lawrence W. Sherman, "The Rise of Evidence-Based Policing: Targeting, Testing, and Tracking," *Crime and Justice 42*, no. 1 (2013): 377–451.

[9] U.S. News & World Report, "Best Criminology Schools," Accessed September 1, 2019, https://www.usnews.com/best-graduate-schools/top-humanities-schools/criminology-rankings

[10] Samuel E. Walker, "Governing the American Police: Wrestling with the Problems of Democracy," *University of Chicago Legal Forum* Vol. 2016, Article 15 (2016): 631.

[11] Wesley G. Skogan, "The Commission and the Police," *Criminology and Public Policy* 17, no. 2 (2018): 379–396.

[12] Ibid, 3.

[13] Charles H. Rogovin, "Achieving Criminal Justice Reform," *Judicature* 53, no. 3 (1969): 104–107, 104.

[14] Malcolm M. Feeley and Austin D. Sarat, T*he Policy Dilemma: Federal Crime Policy and the Law Enforcement Assistance Administration*, (Minneapolis: University of Minnesota Press, 1981); Charles H. Rogovin, "The Genesis of the Law Enforcement Assistance Administration: A Personal Account," *Columbia Human Rights Law Review* 5, (1973): 9–26; Jay N. Varon, "A Reexamination of the Law Enforcement Assistance Administration," *Stanford Law Review* 27, no. 5 (1975): 1303–1324; Susan O. White and Samuel Krislov, *Understanding Crime: An Evaluation of the National Institute of Law Enforcement and Criminal Justice* (Washington, DC: National Academy of Sciences, Committee on Research on Law Enforcement and Criminal Justice, Assembly of Behavioral and Social Sciences, 1977).

[15] Charles Weirman and William G. Archambeault, "Assessing the Effects of LEAA Demise on Criminal Justice Higher Education," *Journal of Criminal Justice* 11, no. 6 (1983): 549–561.

[16] Michael Tonry, "Evidence, Ideology, and Politics in the making of American Criminal Justice Policy," *Crime and Justice* 42, no. 1 (2013): 1–18.

[17] Stephen D. Mastrofski, "The Prospects of Change in Police Patrol: A Decade in Review," *American Journal of Police* 9, no. 3 (1990): 1–79, 62.

[18] Michael S. Scott, "Progress in American Policing? Reviewing the National Reviews," *Law and Social Inquiry* 34, no. 1 (2009): 171–185, 177.

[19] President's Task Force on 21st Century Policing, *Final report of the President's Task Force on 21st Century Policing*, (Washington, DC: Office of Community Oriented Policing Services, 2015).

1

Adopt Evidence-Based Policing

Cody W. Telep
A. Johannes Bottema
Arizona State University

Background

The term *evidence-based policing* (EBP) generally refers to police strategies and tactics that are guided by scientific evidence of their effectiveness. In his landmark work, Sherman first discussed the concept 20 years ago, arguing that "police practices should be based on scientific evidence about what works best."[1] More recently, Lum and Koper refined their definition of the concept, describing evidence-based policing as "a law-enforcement perspective and philosophy that implicates the use of research, evaluation, analysis, and scientific processes in law-enforcement decision-making."[2] The idea that research should play a role in policing has gained traction in recent years. As Sherman notes, "examples of the growth of evidence-based policing abound"[3] and scholars have pointed to the growth and development of EBP in the U.S. and abroad.[4] The creation of the *Cambridge Journal of Evidence-Based Policing* in 2017 demonstrates the growing interest in research on the topic.[5]

Government and professional societies now also emphasize the important role of research in policing practice. For example, former Acting Director Howard Spivak argued in the National Institute of Justice's (NIJ) strategic plan for policing research that, "the challenges facing police officers today require evidence-based research that will advance police operations and practices."[6] Chief Terrence Cunningham, 2015–2016 President of the International Association of Chiefs of Police (IACP), argued "We need to fully embrace evidence-based policing and best practices" when outlining his priorities as president.[7] The IACP has a Research Advisory Committee, and *The Police Chief* magazine includes a "Research in Brief" section quarterly. Practitioners founded the American Society of Evidence-Based Policing in 2015 and have held three conferences highlighting police-led research projects.

This chapter is titled "Adopt evidence-based policing" because of a large and growing body of research suggesting that police can be more effective and efficient when they use research to guide policy and practice.[8] EBP does not dictate a singular intervention that the police must implement but rather emphasizes that strategies should have evidence that they work. This chapter reviews multiple strategies that can be considered evidence based. The "evidence" in "evidence-based policing" has often focused on findings from methodologically rigorous work and in particular randomized experiments and quasi-experiments that can provide the most convincing answer to questions of whether a strategy or tactic works.[9] However, a variety of methods, both quantitative and qualitative, can be used to generate evidence.[10] Regardless of methodology, EBP emphasizes that policing practice should be guided, at least in part, by science and empiricism, rather than anecdotes, untested traditions, or hunches.[11] Officer experience remains an important part of the equation and ideally complements research findings so that practices are evidence based and agency appropriate.[12]

In the next section, we review the research evidence related to EBP. We focus in particular on police effectiveness, with an emphasis on crime-control effectiveness, because the evidence here is strongest.[13] For a recommendation for police to be more evidence based, there must be a sufficiently large evidence base on which to draw. The Evidence-Based Policing Matrix, a collection of rigorous policing studies evaluating impacts on crime, now includes more than 160 studies, close to 60 percent of which were published in the last 15 years.[14]

After reviewing the research evidence, we turn to solutions for agencies interested in being more evidence based. These solutions focus on implementing effective strategies, as well as developing the organizational capacity to be an evidence-based agency.[15] This requires both an emphasis on providing officers knowledge about what works and developing the analysis and evaluation capabilities to systematically assess department practices. In addition to police practice being guided by research, evidence-based policing emphasizes that police departments must consistently evaluate their own practices. Sherman argued that evidence-based policing combines research on what works with "ongoing outcomes research about the results each unit is actually achieving by applying (or ignoring) basic research in practice."[16] This requires a strong emphasis on analysis and data to guide decision-making.

Research Evidence

In this section, we review the large body of studies examining the crime-control effectiveness of policing, focusing on strategies for which there is strong evidence of crime reduction effects. We view these strategies as evidence based and suggest in the next section that they should be prioritized in police decisions about crime control. We also more briefly review the evidence on police efforts to improve relationships with the community. The evidence here is not as extensive as it is for crime control, although police legitimacy is a key concern of many agencies nationwide.[17] Finally, we also provide an overview of research on officer receptivity to evidence-based policing. Here, we describe existing survey research exploring how open officers are to research and evidence-based policing, which also informs our suggested solutions in the next section.

Police Effectiveness

We focus on three strategies for which there is strong evidence of crime-control effectiveness.[18] While hot spots policing, problem-oriented policing, and focused deterrence strategies have different emphases, these strategies share in common a reliance on data and analysis to appropriately focus police resources to maximize effectiveness.[19] These evidence-based approaches also all take a more targeted approach to crime problems and all have been rigorously evaluated in multiple contexts.[20]

Hot spots policing. Hot spots policing involves focusing greater police resources on small units of geography with high levels of crime to reduce crime and disorder problems in those places. The exact size of a hot spot varies across studies, but overall the units tend to be significantly smaller than the police beats traditionally used in allocating resources.[21] A number of studies find that crime of all types is highly concentrated at a small number of places, suggesting that crime hot spots are responsible for a sizable proportion of a jurisdiction's crime problem. Across cities of different sizes and in different countries, 50 percent of crime is typically found at 5 percent or fewer places.[22]

A series of rigorous studies find evidence that hot spots policing can reduce crime. As a result, a recent National Academies of Sciences review of proactive policing concluded that "hot spots policing interventions generate statistically significant crime-reduction impacts without simply displacing crime into areas immediately surrounding the targeted locations."[23] A systematic review of hot spots policing studies by Braga and colleagues found an overall modest but significant effect of hot spots policing on crime when synthesizing 78 tests of hot spots policing from 65 experimental and quasi-experimental studies.[24]

The specific tactics police use to address crime hot spots vary across studies.[25] At its simplest, hot spots policing can entail increasing the amount of time officers spend in high crime places. This increased presence alone is associated with crime declines.[26] More complex strategies seem to be even more effective. Combining problem solving (discussed below) with hot spots policing can be particularly effective. Braga and colleagues found problem-oriented hot spots studies tend to have, on average, somewhat greater impacts on crime than hot spots interventions focused on simply increasing presence.[27]

Problem-oriented policing. Problem-oriented policing (POP) is a strategy to address problems by learning as much as possible about the underlying causes of the problem and then developing a response tailored to that analysis.[28] The SARA model (scanning, analysis, response, assessment) is widely used as a framework for implementing POP projects.[29] An agency facing a burglary spike, for example, might first scan by precisely specifying the scope of the problem (e.g., repeat residential burglaries in a precinct). The analysis phase entails learning as much as possible about the problem and its causes, drawing upon a variety of data sources (e.g., incident reports, interviews with former burglars, resident surveys). The response should be targeted at the causes uncovered in the analysis phase and may include enforcement but often involves police expanding their toolkit and considering a variety of options, including efforts to address situational dynamics contributing to crime. Finally, the impact of the response on the problem should be assessed. A systematic review by Weisburd and colleagues found a modest but statistically significant decline in crime resulting from POP interventions that utilized the SARA model.[30] The 2017 National Academies of Sciences report echoes these findings about overall effectiveness but laments the small number of rigorous evaluations of POP.[31]

As noted above, POP seems to work especially well in concert with hot spots policing. One example is an experiment in Jacksonville, FL, which directly compared increasing presence to conducting problem solving in hot spots. Taylor and colleagues found saturation patrols were associated with reduced crime during the intervention, but the effects dissipated quickly after.[32] In the POP hot spots, there was not a significant crime decline during the intervention period, but in the 90 days after the experiment, street violence declined 33 percent.

Focused deterrence. Focused deterrence strategies attempt to maximize the deterrent effects of police and the criminal justice system by communicating directly to offenders the risk of increased certainty, swiftness, and severity of punishment.[33] Many of these interventions employ the "pulling levers" framework popularized in Boston with Operation Ceasefire, in which gangs were notified that violence would no longer be tolerated and if violence did occur, every available legal lever would be pulled to bring an immediate and certain response.[34] This message is delivered at a call-in forum by a multiagency group of stakeholders, generally representing law enforcement, prosecutors, probation, and community leaders. Additionally, focused deterrence strategies rely on an analysis of violent crime problems to tailor the intervention to community dynamics, which links the approach to POP.

In a systematic review of quasi-experimental focused deterrence interventions, Braga and colleagues found such approaches have significant beneficial impacts on crime, particularly violent crime.[35] Nineteen of the 24 studies found impacts on crime, and meta-analyses showed an overall significant impact of such strategies on reducing crime. Programs focused on gang violence tended to be more successful than those focused on drug market violence (commonly called drug market initiatives or DMI). While noting concerns about the lack of randomized trials, the National Academies of Sciences review also concluded that focused deterrence approaches can lead to significant reductions of crime in treatment areas.[36]

While focused deterrence strategies concentrate on particular offenders or groups of offenders, there is still a place-based component, as these interventions tend to focus on individuals operating in particular geographic areas. In a study in Philadelphia, Groff and colleagues similarly found benefits in focusing on high-rate offenders in particular geographic areas in the context of hot spots.[37] Although they were not testing focused deterrence, they did examine the benefits of an offender-focused hot spots treatment, which involved using intelligence analysts and tactical squad officers to identify and make frequent contact with repeat offenders. The offender-focused treatment was associated with a 42 percent decline in violent crime and a 50 percent drop in violent felonies relative to control hot spots. The results suggest the benefits of focusing in on "hot people" living in and committing criminal acts in "hot places."

Police Fairness

We recognize that crime control is not the only outcome of interest for policing agencies, although it has been the focus of much of the evaluation literature. We briefly describe the evidence here on police strategies to improve relationships with the community and to build legitimacy, although these important issues are the focus of other chapters in this volume. Police fairness is an important focus in democratic policing.[38] Ideally, police can implement effective strategies in fair ways so that fairness and effectiveness are mutually reinforcing.[39] Many recent discussions about police fairness have focused on influential work by Tyler, suggesting the importance of procedural justice in building legitimacy and enhancing citizen views of the police.[40] We view these efforts as important but note that the evidence base for procedural justice training and other efforts to build legitimacy remains small.[41]

There is a larger body of research on community policing programs, which also focus on improving citizen views of police plus an emphasis on problem solving and community involvement in crime fighting. We have already described the effectiveness of problem solving but note here that while community policing programs have been popular since the 1980s and early 1990s, they remain difficult to evaluate because they have encompassed a wide variety of strategies and interventions. A systematic review by Gill and colleagues found community policing programs tended to have greater impacts on citizen satisfaction and perceptions of legitimacy than on crime control, although such improvements in citizen views of the police could have long-term impacts on crime control.[42]

Receptivity to Evidence-Based Policing

A small but growing number of recent studies have focused not on what works in policing but rather on the extent to which practitioners understand what works.[43] Research on receptivity to research and EBP in the United States, Canada, and the United Kingdom is largely consistent. There is general support from practitioners for EBP, particularly from high ranking officers, but there are also gaps in officer understanding of the evidence base and concerns about successful implementation.[44]

Findings from multiple agencies suggest variability by rank and agency in the extent to which officers are familiar with the term *evidence-based policing*.[45] Higher-ranking officers are generally more familiar with the term, but officers across ranks tend not to define the term in the same way that academics do.[46] In an analysis of officer-provided definitions of evidence-based policing, Telep and Somers found that definitions most commonly included mentions of statistics or data but less often mentioned analysis or science.[47] In terms of openness to research and researchers, officers generally see the value of research evidence and partnerships with researchers. They also tend to be open to engaging in research, with more hesitance toward conducting randomized trials.[48]

Officer views about the policing evidence base are somewhat mixed. Officers tend to recognize the effectiveness of strategies that work. Telep and Lum found the majority of officers across multiple agencies viewed POP as effective.[49] Officers also typically view hot spots policing as an effective way to reduce crime but tend to be less familiar with focused deterrence approaches. Respondents also frequently expressed agreement that less effective, more traditional strategies, such as random preventive patrol and rapid response to 911 calls for service, are useful for reducing crime.[50] Telep found the views of officers with advanced degrees were generally more in line with research.[51]

■ Solutions

Based on our review of research, we present four solutions and recommendations for agencies interested in being more evidence based. We draw here from prior discussions of implementing EBP, including work by

Sherman and a recent book by Lum and Koper.[52] We recognize there is not universal agreement in policing scholarship that evidence-based policing should be adopted. We acknowledge these debates, which often surround the value of officer experience and the role of different types of evidence in informing policing practice, and have tried to incorporate critiques about EBP into our suggested solutions.[53]

1. Adopt Strategies with Evidence of Effectiveness

We focused in the previous section on three crime-control strategies with strong evidence of effectiveness. Our first solution here is perhaps not surprisingly a recommendation for agencies to implement these and other evidence-based strategies. We note that these strategies are often evaluated as special projects with a specific intervention period (in part because of grant funding cycles), but hot spots policing, POP, and focused deterrence approaches could all be integrated long-term into a police agency's crime prevention portfolio.

To what extent are agencies already using these strategies? This is difficult to answer, because national-level data collection efforts on police agencies ask only a few questions about strategies. The most recent Law Enforcement Management and Administrative Statistics (LEMAS) data provide little information on hot spots policing and focused deterrence strategies but suggest about 40 percent of agencies had officers engaged in problem solving using the SARA model.[54] The National Academies of Sciences 2017 report examined data from multiple surveys of larger agencies, finding that 80 percent or more of departments reported using POP and hot spots policing.[55] Departments also reported commonly adopting directed patrols/focused deterrence, although it is not clear the extent to which these departments implemented pulling-levers-style focused deterrence. Such approaches have been adopted in at least 84 cities that have worked with the National Network for Safe Communities, a group led by David Kennedy that assists cities in implementing violence reduction initiatives.[56]

While the results are promising in terms of diffusion of evidence-based practice (at least in larger cities), a challenge with all of these surveys is limited knowledge about the dosage and intensity of adoption of evidence-based approaches. That is, even if an agency reports using problem-oriented policing, it is not clear how widespread its adoption is across the department. We suspect that in many departments these approaches are being utilized infrequently or only by special units, although more systematic research on this is needed. We also argue that while most police agencies are stretched thin when it comes to manpower, these evidence-based approaches are especially useful in this context, because they target crime problems effectively and efficiently and make the most of limited resources. Such approaches should help reduce heavy emergency call loads in high crime locations that are often a major drain on patrol resources.

Problem-oriented policing and hot spots policing in particular have the potential to be implemented by patrol officers. Hot spots patrols could be integrated into regular officer duties, as they were in Sacramento when officers visited hot spots for about 15 minutes at a time during their downtime[57] or in Portland when officers were dispatched to visit hot spots, similar to a regular radio call.[58] Problem-solving projects could also be implemented at the patrol level if officers are given the time and discretion to do so, although prior studies examining POP in action found challenges in adoption (even in departments committed to the approach) along with a general lack of emphasis on thorough problem analysis and assessment.[59] While focused deterrence strategies tend to involve special units and multiple agencies, patrol officers could still play a role, particularly in ensuring strong deterrent messages are acted upon if necessary.

We also suggest further utilization of translation tools as one way for agency leaders and frontline staff to learn more about the effectiveness of these evidence-based practices and how to implement them. While journal articles are still frequently challenging for practitioners to access without a university library subscription, there are a number of other ways for police to learn about what works. The Campbell Collaboration was founded in 2000 to help advance knowledge about what works in social policy, and the Crime and Justice Group now includes more than 15 systematic reviews on policing topics, all of which are free and most of which have plain language summaries available.[60]

Other examples include NIJ's CrimeSolutions.gov, a "what works" clearinghouse with information and effectiveness ratings for more than 100 programs in law enforcement. All studies on CrimeSolutions.gov are reviewed by multiple researchers and categorized as effective, promising, no effects, or inconclusive evidence. The What Works Centre for Crime Reduction in the UK College of Policing has a similar Crime Reduction Toolkit.[61] The Evidence-Based Policing Matrix[62] and the What Works in Policing site, both housed in the Center for Evidence-Based Crime Policy (CEBCP) at George Mason University, are designed to help synthesize the rigorous crime-control evaluation literature.[63] The What Works site focuses on reviewing the evidence for particular strategies and providing quick summaries and freely available resources on how to implement effective approaches. Material from both sites is available through the Police Foundation's free Evidence-Based Policing App, which can be downloaded to smartphones and used by officers in the field.[64]

2. Dedicate Resources to Crime (and Intelligence) Analysis

A fundamental way to facilitate EBP is to invest resources in crime analysis. Findings from analyses can be utilized for target identification, strategy implementation, and project evaluation.[65] We briefly describe the benefits of analysis here; see the informative volume by Santos for more detail and distinctions between criminal intelligence analysis, tactical crime analysis, and strategic crime analysis.[66]

Agencies should prioritize investment in crime analysts. Smith, Santos, and Santos found the most significant predictor of crime analysis integration in an agency was having a primary crime analyst dedicated to conducting analysis.[67] In a national survey of U.S. police agencies, however, only 57 percent of departments met this criterion, suggesting gaps in many agencies.[68] In a survey of Oregon police executives, Telep and Winegar found chiefs in departments with less than 50 officers almost universally did not have an analyst on staff, and 83 percent of chiefs overall said they needed more analysts in their agency.[69]

Agencies must also be more cognizant of how analysts are being utilized. Crime analyst duties are driven by command staff, and analysts are often expected to cover large areas and assist police personnel in investigations, typically in ways that reinforce reactive policing approaches.[70] To transcend this and move toward a more proactive EBP framework, analysts should be given the opportunity to shift their focus to more long-term considerations. For example, Piza and Feng found analysts are infrequently involved in program evaluation and suggest that analysts should receive more training and play a key role in future evaluations, which could help ensure police play a leadership role in producing scientific knowledge.[71]

Crime analysts must also be provided with the support and tools they need to be effective. The variety and complexity of analysis that can be conducted by analysts has been linked to the training, availability of hardware and software, and the structure of an agency.[72] In terms of structure, one of the key components predicting integration of crime analysis is the prioritization of accountability throughout an agency.[73] More specifically, increased accountability leads to greater utilization of analytic products by patrol officers. One way to facilitate such accountability throughout a policing organization is by using the stratified policing model,[74] which incorporates problem solving and analysis into an agency's structure at all ranks and uses meetings to ensure follow-through on responding to prioritized problems.[75]

In addition, crime analysis would also benefit from efforts by leadership to educate all agency employees on the value of crime analysis and crime analysts. One method for accomplishing this would be to incorporate training about analysts into the academy and even to have analysts make presentations to new recruits.[76] Agencies should acknowledge the myriad of ways analysts can contribute. In particular, their role as bridges to other organizational partners[77] as well as translators of research should be recognized.

Crime analysis is vital to the implementation and evaluation of all of the strategies discussed previously. Hot spots policing cannot take place without the identification of crime hot spots. This requires the aggregation of police data and crime mapping to choose target areas. Crime analysis is particularly crucial in this regard as research has suggested that police are typically unable to identify hot spots accurately or consistently.[78] In addition to identifying hot spots, crime analysts can provide guidance on the type and magnitude of issues occurring within a small geographic area. This assists in making decisions about appropriate responses.

Crime analysis is also essential for POP. Analysts are not only useful for identifying problems but obviously are also a valuable resource for problem analysis. Analysts can assist in determining the scope of the problem, people involved, and the environment and social context. Analysts can also play a role in assessing the success of problem-solving responses. Similarly, analysts can play a key role in helping the multiagency working group in focused deterrence projects develop a tailored response. As an example, Braga and colleagues describe how careful analysis of gang dynamics led to a different response in Lowell, Massachusetts, than with Operation Ceasefire, because of the nature of the city's gang dynamics.[79]

3. Conduct Rigorous Evaluations

A third solution is for agencies to continue to add to the policing evidence base through rigorous evaluations. These could be done either in-house or in conjunction with research partners. We should note that this is not an either/or proposition. In-house evaluations can involve consultation with academics, and studies led by researchers should involve close collaboration with police partners in design and implementation.

In-house evaluations could be led by research and planning units.[80] Bond and Gabriele found that about 43 percent of larger agencies had a separate research and planning unit and that agencies with such a unit tended to engage in more innovative practices.[81] Haberman and King, however, found that such units are often tasked with administrative work and are less frequently involved in evaluation studies.[82] An additional option is for particular officers to take the lead in an in-house evaluation. This approach has been increasingly common in recent years with the rise of "pracademics," generally defined as serving officers who also have an advanced degree and some training in research methodology.[83]

The American Society of Evidence-Based Policing has showcased a number of innovative research projects led by practitioners and pracademics at their conferences. One example comes from the Vallejo, CA, Police Department, where Potts ran a three-month experiment on license plate reader technology.[84] He did so in collaboration with BetaGov, a nonprofit research organization that provides free technical assistance to interested agencies.[85] Potts is also a NIJ Law Enforcement Advancing Data and Science (LEADS) program scholar.[86] The program provides funding for conferences and professional development for sworn personnel interested in improving their research expertise and better integrating science into their agency.

Mitchell, who founded the American Society of Evidence-Based Policing, led a hot spots experiment in Sacramento while she was the crime analysis sergeant without any outside funding.[87] She collaborated with researchers from George Mason University on the evaluation. In-house research thus can include collaboration between academics and practitioners. In contrast to more traditional partnerships, the Sacramento Police Department took the lead in designing and implementing the study rather than simply being a study site for a researcher.[88] Mitchell used the experiment as the basis for her dissertation and also led the writing of a guide for officers interested in doing in-house experiments.[89]

We have emphasized agency-led experiments but also note the value of projects led by researchers. Indeed, much of the existing rigorous policing evidence base comes from police-researcher partnerships where researchers led an evaluation study. These partnerships frequently rely on external funding and have traditionally led to primarily scholarly products.[90] Such partnerships will be more successful to the extent that they are mutually beneficial for both police and researchers.[91] In particular, such collaborations should address questions that are of interest to police and do so in a timely fashion.[92] Fortunately, the federal government in recent years has invested more heavily in randomized experiments and rigorous research.[93] Additionally, private foundations such as Arnold Ventures have dedicated major resources to randomized experimental evaluations of policing and other criminal justice topics. While experiments can often be done in-house inexpensively, external funding remains very useful, particularly when data collection is extensive.

4. Build Receptivity to Research

Our final solution focuses broadly on efforts to build receptivity to research and EBP. As we noted in our review of research, officers tend to be open to working with researchers. Frequently, however, they are not familiar with the term "evidence-based policing" and often have views about what works that do not align with research, particularly when it comes to more traditional strategies. Within this solution, we consider two broad ways to build receptivity, focusing on both individual officers and agency processes. We recommend Lum and Koper's comprehensive volume on implementing evidence-based policing for more information.[94]

At the individual officer level, education and training could be useful tools in building officer exposure to the concepts of EBP. Telep found that officers with at least a Master's degree tended to have higher levels of openness to EBP, and these highly educated officers can often serve in pracademic roles, where they act both as generators of research and champions for using research in practice.[95] Thus, agency efforts to recruit highly educated new officers or incentivize higher education for current officers may pay dividends in terms of increased interest and openness to research.

We suspect that EBP is infrequently covered in training academies and suggest efforts to expose new recruits and current officers to the value of research and knowledge about what is effective in reducing crime.[96] We are not aware of any evaluations of EBP training in the United States, although the CEBCP has a free four-module course that could be adapted into an academy setting.[97] There has been some recent international work evaluating training and workshops. In Australia, Cherney and colleagues surveyed officers about receptivity to research, finding that officers who had attended an evidence-based policing workshop were generally more open to research and reported using more innovative practices.[98] In the United Kingdom, Fleming and Wingrove reported on a pilot training program designed to improve officers' understanding of evidence-based approaches, facilitating use of evidence in their work.[99] Participants generally found the training useful and found value in the College of Police Crime Reduction Toolkit. They also, however, were concerned about the time and resources needed to implement EBP and whether adoption would be feasible for their organization, suggesting the need for individual-level efforts to build receptivity to be closely aligned with agency-level efforts.

At the agency level, we recommend agencies think creatively about efforts to build receptivity and, in particular, to institutionalize research into practice. Here we are guided by work done by Lum and Koper on the Matrix Demonstration Project, a series of projects funded by the Bureau of Justice Assistance designed to institutionalize research into practice in ways that would not be highly disruptive to existing agency structures.[100] As one example, Koper, Egge, and Lum describe a "case of places" approach implemented in Minneapolis, MN.[101] The project integrates what is known about the concentration of crime to focus the work of detectives on problem places. Detectives worked to build cases on places, instead of suspects, trying to identify the drivers of problems at chronic problem locations. These drivers could be people or might have to do with particular features of the physical environment. The goal was to think of ways to integrate research on proactive, place-based efforts and to apply it to detective work, which has traditionally been very reactive and person based.

■ Next Steps

This chapter has focused on the benefits of agencies adopting evidence-based policing. While we have discussed primarily research on crime control, we recognize that crime control is not the only or even always the most important outcome for policing and emphasize the need for police to consider fairness alongside effectiveness in developing their portfolio of tactics and strategies. The ability of police to reduce crime efficiently and effectively are of concern to policy makers and the public, and we suggest that police will be more successful when they draw lessons from prior research in developing interventions.

Strategies that are focused rather than general and proactive rather than reactive are more likely to be effective, as are place-based approaches and those that emphasize police expanding their toolbox and working with outside partners.[102] Agencies should also cultivate partnerships to help evaluate the effectiveness of their efforts and further build the evidence base for what works in policing. Departments should also invest in analysis capabilities to effectively guide crime-control initiatives and to ensure practice is appropriately guided by data. Finally, to build a culture of evidence-based policing, agencies should think about education, training, and ways to institutionalize research into practice.

NOTES

[1] Lawrence W. Sherman, "Evidence-Based Policing," *Ideas in American Policing* (Washington, DC: Police Foundation, 1998): 2.

[2] Cynthia Lum and Christopher S. Koper, "Evidence-Based Policing," in *Encyclopedia of Criminology and Criminal Justice*, eds. Gerben Bruinsma and David Weisburd (New York: Springer, 2013), 1426–1437, 1426.

[3] Lawrence W. Sherman, "The Rise of Evidence-Based Policing: Targeting, Testing, and Tracking," *Crime and Justice* 42, no. 1 (2013): 377–451, 379.

[4] Cynthia Lum and Christopher S. Koper, *Evidence-Based Policing: Translating Research into Practice* (New York: Oxford University Press, 2017).

[5] Lawrence W. Sherman, "Editorial Policies," *Cambridge Journal of Evidence-Based Policing* 1, no. 1 (2017): 1–4.

[6] National Institute of Justice, *Policing Strategic Research Plan 2017–2022* (Washington, DC: National Institute of Justice, U.S. Department of Justice, 2017), iii.

[7] Terrence M. Cunningham, "The Year Ahead: President's Message," *The Police Chief 82*, no. 11 (2015): 6.

[8] Jim Bueermann, "Being Smart on Crime with Evidence-Based Policing," *National Institute of Justice Journal* 269 (2012): 12–15.

[9] See Lawrence W. Sherman, "Misleading Evidence and Evidence-Led Policy: Making Social Science More Experimental," *Annals of the American Academy of Political and Social Science* 589 (2003): 6–19.

[10] Jack R. Greene, "New Directions in Policing: Balancing Prediction and Meaning in Police Research," *Justice Quarterly* 31 (2014): 192–228.

[11] See Cynthia Lum, "Translating Police Research into Practice," *Ideas in American Policing* (Washington, DC: Police Foundation, 2009).

[12] See James J. Willis and Stephen D. Mastrofski, "Improving Policing by Integrating Craft and Science: What Can Patrol Officers Teach Us About Good Police Work?" *Policing and Society: An International Journal of Research and Policy* 28, no. 1 (2018): 27–44.

[13] Cody W. Telep, "Expanding the Scope of Evidence-Based Policing," *Criminology and Public Policy* 15, no. 1 (2016): 243–252.

[14] Cynthia Lum, Christopher Koper, and Cody W. Telep, "The Evidence-Based Policing Matrix," *Journal of Experimental Criminology* 7, no. 1 (2011): 3–26. See an updated interactive version at George Mason University's Center for Evidence-Based Crime Policy website, http://www.policingmatrix.org

[15] Lawrence W. Sherman, "A Tipping Point for 'Totally Evidenced Policing': Ten Ideas for Building an Evidence-Based Police Agency," *International Criminal Justice Review* 25, no. 1 (2015): 11–29.

[16] Sherman, "Evidence-Based Policing," 4.

[17] See National Academies of Sciences, Engineering, and Medicine, *Proactive Policing: Effects on Crime and Communities* (Washington, DC: National Academies Press, 2017).

[18] See Cody W. Telep and David L. Weisburd, "What Is Known of Police Practices in Reducing Crime and Disorder?" *Police Quarterly* 15, no. 4 (2012): 331–357.

[19] Sherman, "The Rise of Evidence-Based Policing."

[20] For a summary of all policing systematic reviews, see Cody W. Telep and David L. Weisburd, "Policing," in *What Works in Crime Prevention and Rehabilitation: Lessons from Systematic Reviews*, eds. David P. Farrington, David L. Weisburd, & Charlotte E. Gill (New York: Springer, 2016), 137–168.

[21] See Lawrence W. Sherman, and David L. Weisburd, "General Deterrent Effects of Police Patrol in Crime Hot Spots: A Randomized Controlled Trial," *Justice Quarterly* 12, no. 4 (1995): 625–648.

[22] See David L. Weisburd, "The Law of Crime Concentration and the Criminology of Place," *Criminology* 53, no. 2 (2015): 133–157.

[23] National Academies of Sciences, Engineering, and Medicine, *Proactive Policing*, 129.

[24] Anthony A. Braga, Brandon S. Turchan, Andrew V. Papachristos, and David M. Hureau, "Hot Spots Policing and Crime Reduction: An Update of An Ongoing Systematic Review and Meta-analysis," *Journal of Experimental Criminology* 15, no. 3 (2019): 289–311.

[25] Cody W. Telep and Julie Hibdon, "Understanding and Responding to Hot Spots," *Problem-Oriented Guides for Police, Problem-Solving Tools* No. 14 (Phoenix, AZ: Center for Problem-Oriented Policing, 2019).

[26] See Sherman and Weisburd, "General Deterrent Effects of Police Patrol in Crime Hot Spots," and Cody W. Telep, Renée J. Mitchell, and David Weisburd, "How Much Time Should the Police Spend at Crime Hot Spots?: Answers From a Police Agency Directed Randomized Field Trial in Sacramento, California," *Justice Quarterly* 31, no. 5 (2014): 905–933.

[27] Braga, Turchan, Papachristos, and Hureau, "Hot Spots Policing and Crime Reduction."

[28] See Herman Goldstein, *Problem-Oriented Policing* (New York: McGraw-Hill, 1990).

[29] See John E. Eck and William Spelman, *Problem Solving: Problem-Oriented Policing in Newport News* (Washington, DC: Police Executive Research Forum, 1987).

[30] David Weisburd, Cody W. Telep, Joshua C. Hinkle, and John E. Eck, "Is Problem-Oriented Policing Effective in Reducing Crime and Disorder? Findings from a Campbell Systematic Review," *Criminology and Public Policy* 9, no. 1 (2010): 139–172.

[31] National Academies of Sciences, Engineering, and Medicine, *Proactive Policing.*

[32] Bruce G. Taylor, Christopher S. Koper, and Daniel Woods, "A Randomized Controlled Trial of Different Policing Strategies at Hot Spots of Violent Crime," *Journal of Experimental Criminology* 7, no. 2 (2011): 149–181.

[33] Anthony A. Braga and David L. Weisburd, "The Effects of Focused Deterrence Strategies on Crime: A Systematic Review and Meta-analysis of the Empirical Evidence," *Journal of Research in Crime and Delinquency 49, no. 3* (2012): 323–358.

[34] Anthony A. Braga, David M. Kennedy, Elin J. Waring and Anne Piehl, "Problem-Oriented Policing, Deterrence, and Youth Violence: An Evaluation of Boston's Operation Ceasefire," *Journal of Research in Crime and Delinquency* 38, no. 3 (2001): 195–225.

[35] Anthony A. Braga, David Weisburd, and Brandon Turchan, "Focused Deterrence Strategies and Crime Control: An Updated Systematic Review and Meta-analysis of the Empirical Evidence," *Criminology & Public Policy* 17, no. 1 (2018): 205–250.

[36] National Academies of Sciences, Engineering, and Medicine, *Proactive Policing.*

[37] Elizabeth R. Groff, Jerry H. Ratcliffe, Cory P. Haberman, Evan T. Sorg, Nola M. Joyce, and Ralph B. Taylor, "Does What Police Do at Hot Spots Matter? The Philadelphia Policing Tactics Experiment," *Criminology* 53, no. 1 (2015): 23–53.

[38] Cynthia Lum and Daniel S. Nagin, "Reinventing American Policing," in *Reinventing American Criminal Justice, Crime and Justice: A Review of Research* 46, eds. Michael Tonry and Daniel S. Nagin (Chicago: University of Chicago Press: 2017), 339–393.

[39] National Research Council, *Fairness and Effectiveness in Policing: The Evidence* (Washington, DC: National Academies Press, 2004).

[40] Tom R. Tyler, *Why Do People Obey the Law?* (Princeton, NJ: Princeton University Press, 2006).

[41] See Daniel S. Nagin and Cody W. Telep, "Procedural Justice and Legal Compliance," *Annual Review of Law and Social Science* 13 (2017): 5–28.

[42] Charlotte Gill, David Weisburd, Cody W. Telep, Zoe Vitter, and Trevor Bennett, "Community-Oriented Policing to Reduce Crime, Disorder, and Fear and Increase Legitimacy and Citizen Satisfaction in Neighborhoods," *Journal of Experimental Criminology* 10, no. 4 (2014): 399–428.

[43] Cynthia Lum, Cody W. Telep, Christopher Koper, and Julie Grieco, "Receptivity to Research in Policing," *Justice Research and Policy* 14, no. 1 (2012): 61–95.

[44] See Laura Huey, Brittany Blaskovits, Craig Bennell, Hina Jawaid Kalyal, and Thomas Walker, "To What Extent Do Canadian Police Professionals Believe That Their Agencies Are 'Targeting, Testing, and Tracking' New Policing Strategies and Programs," *Police Practice and Research: An International Journal* 18, no 6. (2017): 544–555; Gillian Hunter, Alexandra Wigzell, Bina Bharwa, Tiggey May, and Mike Hough, *An Evaluation of the 'What Works Centre for Crime Reduction.' Year 2: Progress* (London: Institute for Criminal Policy Research, Birkbeck, University of London, 2016); and Jeff Rojek, Geoffrey Alpert, and Hayden Smith, "The Utilization of Research by the Police," *Police Practice and Research: An International Journal* 13, no. 4 (2012): 329–341.

[45] Cody W. Telep and Cynthia Lum, "The Receptivity of Officers to Empirical Research and Evidence-Based Policing: An Examination of Survey Data from Three Agencies," *Police Quarterly* 17, no 4. (2014): 359–385.

[46] Ian Palmer, Is the United Kingdom Police Service Receptive to Evidence-Based Policing? Testing Attitudes Towards Experimentation, Master's thesis (University of Cambridge, 2011); Cody W. Telep and Steve Winegar, "Police Executive Receptivity to Research: A Survey of Chiefs and Sheriffs in Oregon," *Policing: A Journal of Policy and Practice* 10, no. 3 (2016): 241–249.

[47] Cody W. Telep and Logan J. Somers, "Examining Police Officer Definitions of Evidence-Based Policing: Are We Speaking the Same Language?" *Policing and Society: An International Journal of Research and Policy* 29, no. 2 (2019): 171–187.

[48] Palmer, Is the United Kingdom Police Service Receptive to Evidence-Based Policing?; Telep and Lum, "The Receptivity of Officers to Empirical Research and Evidence-Based Policing."

[49] Telep and Lum, "The Receptivity of Officers to Empirical Research and Evidence-Based Policing."

[50] See David Weisburd and John E. Eck, "What Can Police Do to Reduce Crime, Disorder, and Fear?" *Annals of the American Academy of Political and Social Science* 593 (2004): 42–65.

[51] Cody W. Telep, "Police Officer Receptivity to Research and Evidence-Based Policing: Examining Variability Within and Across Agencies," *Crime & Delinquency* 63, no. 8 (2017): 976–999.

[52] See Sherman, "The Rise of Evidence-Based Policing," and "A Tipping Point for 'Totally Evidenced Policing'"; and Lum & Koper, *Evidence-Based Policing,* 2017.

[53] See, for instance, Greene, "New Directions in Policing"; Malcom K. Sparrow, *Handcuffed: What Holds Policing Back, and the Keys to Reform* (Washington, DC: Brookings Institution Press, 2016).

[54] Brian A. Reaves, *Local Police Departments, 2013: Personnel, Policies, and Practices* (Washington, DC: Bureau of Justice Statistics, U.S. Department of Justice, 2015).

[55] National Academies of Sciences, Engineering, and Medicine, *Proactive Policing.*

[56] See the National Network for Safe Communities website at https://nnscommunities.org/

[57] Telep, Mitchell, and Weisburd, "How Much Time Should the Police Spend at Crime Hot Spots?"

[58] Greg Stewart, Kris Henning, and Vivian Elliott, "SPI Case Study: Portland, Oregon," *Smart Policing Initiative Quarterly Newsletter* XVI (2015): 2–4.

[59] See Gary Cordner, and Elizabeth Perkins Biebel, "Problem-Oriented Policing in Practice," *Criminology & Public Policy* 4, no. 2 (2005): 155–180; Edward Maguire, Craig D. Uchida, and Kimberly D. Hassell, "Problem-Oriented Policing in Colorado Springs: A Content Analysis of 753 Cases," *Crime & Delinquency* 61, no. 1 (2015): 71–95.

[60] Telep and Weisburd, "Policing."
[61] For the Crime Reduction Toolkit website, see http://whatworks.college.police.uk/toolkit/About-the-Crime-Reduction-Toolkit/Pages/About.aspx
[62] Lum et al., "The Evidence-Based Policing Matrix."
[63] Cody W. Telep and Claudia Gross Shader, "Creating a 'What Works' Translation Tool for Police: A Researcher-City Government Partnership," *Police Practice and Research: An International Journal* 20, no. 6 (2019): 603–616. For the What Works in Policing website, see http://cebcp.org/evidence-based-policing/what-works-in-policing/
[64] For the Evidence-Based Policing App, see http://www.evidence-basedpolicing.org/about/
[65] International Association of Crime Analysts, *Definition and Types of Crime Analysis*, Committee White Paper (2014-02).
[66] Rachel B. Santos, *Crime Analysis with Crime Mapping* (Los Angeles, CA: Sage Publications, 2017).
[67] Justin J. Smith, Rachel B. Santos, and Roberto G. Santos, "Evidence-Based Policing and the Stratified Integration of Crime Analysis in Police Agencies: National Survey Results," *Policing: A Journal of Policy and Practice* 12, no 3 (2018): 303–315.
[68] Bruce Taylor and Rachel Boba, *The Integration of Crime Analysis into Patrol Work: A Guidebook* (Washington, DC: Office of Community Oriented Policing Services, U.S. Department of Justice, 2011).
[69] Telep and Winegar, "Police Executive Receptivity to Research."
[70] Lum & Koper, *Evidence-Based Policing.*
[71] Eric L. Piza and Shun Q. Feng, "The Current and Potential Role of Crime Analysts in Evaluations of Police Interventions: Results from a Survey of the International Association of Crime Analysts," *Police Quarterly* 20, no. 4 (2017): 339–366.
[72] Timothy O'Shea and Keith Nicholls, "Police Crime Analysis: A Survey of U.S. Police Departments with 100 or More Sworn Personnel," *Police Practice and Research* 4, no. 3 (2003): 233–250.
[73] Smith et al., "Evidence-Based Policing and the Stratified Integration of Crime Analysis in Police Agencies."
[74] See Rachel Boba and Roberto Santos, *A Police Organizational Model for Crime Reduction: Institutionalizing Problem Solving, Analysis and Accountability* (Washington, DC: Office of Community Oriented Policing Services, U.S. Department of Justice, 2011).
[75] Santos, *Crime Analysis with Crime Mapping.*
[76] Lum & Koper, *Evidence-Based Policing.*
[77] Scott Keay and Stuart Kirby, "The Evolution of the Police Analyst and the Influence of Evidence-Based Policing," *Policing: A Journal of Policy and Practice* 12, no 3 (2018): 265–276.
[78] Gisela Bichler and Larry Gaines, "An Examination of Police Officers' Insights into Problem Identification and Problem Solving," *Crime & Delinquency* 51, no. 1 (2005): 53–74; Jeremy H. Ratcliffe and Michael J. McCullagh, "Chasing Ghosts? Police Perception of High Crime Areas," *British Journal of Criminology* 41, no. 2 (2001): 330–341.
[79] Anthony A. Braga, Glenn L. Pierce, Jack McDevitt, Brenda J. Bond, and Shea Cronin, "The Strategic Prevention of Gun Violence Among Gang-Involved Offenders," *Justice Quarterly* 25, no. 1 (2008): 132–162.
[80] John Kapinos, "Building Planning and Research Capacity in Police Agencies," *International Association of Law Enforcement Planners Exchange* 58, no. 1 (2016): 4–6.
[81] Brenda J. Bond and Kathryn R. Gabriele, "Research and Planning Units: An Innovation Instrument in the 21st-Century Police Organization," *Criminal Justice Policy Review* 29, no. 1 (2018): 67–88.
[82] Cory P. Haberman and William R. King, "The Role of Research and Planning Units in Law Enforcement Organizations," *Policing: An International Journal of Police Strategies and Management* 34, no. 4 (2011): 687–698.
[83] Laura Huey and Renée J. Mitchell, "Unearthing Hidden Keys: Why Pracademics are an Invaluable (If Underutilized) Resource in Policing Research," *Policing: A Journal of Policy and Practice* 10, no. 3 (2016): 300–307.

[84] Jason Potts, "Police Research on the Front Lines," *Translational Criminology* 12 (2017): 24–25.

[85] See the BetaGov website, http://www.betagov.org/.

[86] See the NIJ LEADS page at: https://www.nij.gov/topics/law-enforcement/Pages/law-enforcement-advancing-data-and-science-program.aspx.

[87] Telep, Mitchell, and Weisburd, "How Much Time Should the Police Spend at Crime Hot Spots?"

[88] Renée J. Mitchell, "Frequency Versus Duration of Police Patrol Visits for Reducing Crime in Hot Spots: Non-Experimental Findings from the Sacramento Hot Spots Experiment," *Cambridge Journal of Evidence-Based Policing* 1, no. 1 (2017): 22–37.

[89] Renée J. Mitchell, Cody W. Telep, and Cynthia Lum, *The Ten-Step Guide for Conducting In-House Experimental Evaluations* (Fairfax, VA: George Mason University, Center for Evidence-Based Crime Policy, 2017).

[90] Julie Grieco, Heather Vovak, and Cynthia Lum, "Examining Research–Practice Partnerships in Policing Evaluations," *Policing: A Journal of Policy and Practice* 8, no. 4 (2014): 368–378.

[91] Robin S. Engel and James L. Whalen, "Police-Academic Partnerships: Ending the Dialogue of the Deaf, the Cincinnati Experience," *Police Practice and Research: An International Journal* 11, no 2. (2010): 105–116.

[92] Michael E. Buerger, "Policing and Research: Two Cultures Separated by an Almost-Common Language," *Police Practice and Research: An International Journal* 11, no. 2 (2010): 135–143.

[93] Cody W. Telep, Joel H. Garner, and Christy A. Visher, "The Production of Criminological Experiments Revisited: The Nature and Extent of Federal Support for Experimental Designs, 2001–2013," *Journal of Experimental Criminology* 11, no. 4 (2015): 541–563.

[94] Lum and Koper, *Evidence-Based Policing*.

[95] Telep, "Police Officer Receptivity to Research and Evidence-Based Policing."

[96] Lum and Koper, *Evidence-Based Policing*.

[97] See the curriculum at http://cebcp.org/evidence-based-policing/the-matrix/matrix-demonstration-project/academy-curriculum/

[98] Adrian Cherney, Emma Antrobus, Sarah Bennett, Bevan Murphy, and Mike Newman, *Evidence Based Policing: Queensland Police Technical Report* (Brisbane, Australia: University of Queensland, 2018)

[99] See Jenny Fleming and Jennifer Wingrove, "'We Would If We Could . . . But Not Sure If We Can': Implementing Evidence-Based Practice: The Evidence-Based Practice Agenda in the UK," *Policing: A Journal of Policy and Practice* 11, no 2 (2017): 202–213.

[100] See Lum and Koper, *Evidence-Based Policing*. For the Matrix Demonstration Project, see http://cebcp.org/evidence-based-policing/the-matrix/matrix-demonstration-project/

[101] Christopher S. Koper, Jeffrey Egge, and Cynthia Lum, "Institutionalizing Place-Based Approaches: Opening 'Cases' on Gun Crime Hot Spots," *Policing: A Journal of Policy and Practice* 9, no. 3 (2015): 242–254; See http://cebcp.org/evidence-based-policing/the-matrix/matrix-demonstration-project/case-of-places/ for resources on implementing a case of places approach

[102] See Lum et al., "The Evidence-Based Policing Matrix"; Cody W. Telep and David L. Weisburd, "What Is Known of Police Practices in Reducing Crime and Disorder?"

1

Response Essay

Chief Jim Bueermann (Ret.)
President, National Police Foundation

At no time in this country's history has the need for evidence-based approaches to policing and the control of crime and disorder been more apparent. The cost of policing has continued to escalate. Increasing proportions of local government budgets are being shifted to public safety, away from needed community services like after-school programs, parks and recreation, libraries and infrastructure repair. In addition, the political shift in America has renewed calls for more traditional, suppression-oriented policing strategies without any consideration for the effectiveness, unintended consequences, or potential harm-inducing nature of these approaches. All of this has occurred against the backdrop of national protests demanding police reform, leaving many to question whether anything has really changed.

Historically, the responsibility for advancing evidence-based policing frameworks has lain at the feet of academics. More recently, practitioners have engaged in not only the discussion of evidence-based policing (EBP) but also active involvement in the production of policing or crime research. In many cases they have actually led research efforts. These advances in evidence-based policing research aside, one group of stakeholders, largely ignored in advancing the use of science to enhance the safety of our communities, are local policy makers and elected officials. To continue ignoring them places the EBP movement in peril of becoming just another policing fad.

The individuals who make decisions about who is hired to be the chief of police and what gets funded in the public safety budget are the city managers, city council members, and the mayors of American communities. In theory, their decisions should reflect the needs and desires of their constituents—the people of their communities. If using evidence-based approaches to controlling crime and disorder and addressing the wide breadth of issues that make up policing (e.g. use-of-force, staffing and deployment, officer safety and wellness, etc.), makes sense, then identifying which "levers" to pull within the city government "system" is crucial to achieving the desired outcomes of creating safe communities. One of the most significant of these levers—largely unpulled—is the use of the police chief hiring process to advance evidence-based policing. The appointment of a police chief is one of the most important responsibilities these officials have. And their decision will have significant consequences for their community for many years.

Leadership counts in policing. Who is chosen to be a community's police chief has everything to do with the direction the police department takes in terms of controlling crime, interacting with the community, and the manner in which the police workforce is treated. The process by which police budgets are approved links directly to the level of crime and police legitimacy in communities. When crime-control strategies being considered for funding have been evaluated for effectiveness and are subject to a cost-benefit analysis, everybody wins—cops, victims of crime, policy makers, and taxpayers.

Most American police chiefs are appointed by, and work directly for, city managers. These managers are typically appointed by, and work for, city councils or mayors. When a city council, mayor and city manager all agree with, and are committed to, the notion that their police department should follow evidence-based practices, the chief they appoint will be well grounded in their vision for EBP. In addition, they will hold the chief accountable for implementing evidence-based strategies. By doing so, they create an environment in which positive policing outcomes are more likely to occur. They can assure their constituents they are being good stewards of the taxpayer investment in policing and will see crime more effectively controlled. Moreover, they are more likely to witness a reduction in the level of police-community tension when the community is asked to coproduce decisions about crime-control strategies that are grounded in scientific evidence and are not biased or capricious in nature or simplistically based on "the way we've always done it."

As long as this direction to the police chief is done with an outcomes-based emphasis, it can be accomplished without inappropriate political influence into the operations of the police department. Linking evidence-based policing, community safety, and police legitimacy outcomes to expenditures does not adversely affect the autonomy of the police. This is fundamental to a democratic form of local government. This direction simply says to the police: "These are the public safety outcomes, and the type of policing, we want in our community (e.g., effective, responsive, empathetic, credible, trustworthy, etc.), and we expect you to achieve them."

One of the challenges in implementing the framework just described is the fact that so few policy makers and elected officials have even heard of evidence-based policing (much less understand it enough to identify followers of this philosophy or to provide direction to police chiefs). Generally, they lack exposure to crucial EBP ideas or principles such as hot spots, directed patrol, focused deterrence, targeted vs general policing strategies, the importance of "place" in crime control, the importance of evaluation, and the importance of randomized controlled trials.

There are few, if any, training classes for these officials to help them understand the basic tenets of evidence-based policing and its value to their communities. Presentations are not made at their professional conferences on this topic, and there is a dearth of articles on EBP in their professional publications. If such learning opportunities were available to them (and to police chiefs for that matter) policy, practice, and culture in police departments—and local government—would reflect evidence-based approaches. The following lists a few areas of focus.

- Basic, advanced, and police leadership training programs would reflect developmentally appropriate EBP principles woven throughout the fabric of the policing culture.
- In their executive searches for police chiefs, cities would require candidates to demonstrate a deep and practical knowledge of evidence-based policing and require the successful candidates to regularly demonstrate the implementation of EBP concepts as well as the anchoring of EBP to the culture of the organization.
- Policing organizations would make it clear that EBP is an organizational philosophy—not "a program."
- The annual reports routinely published by policing organizations would include demonstrable proof of the use of EBP principles and evidence of effectiveness.
- Police employee evaluations would have a component requiring the evaluation of the employees' use of EBP principles.
- Internal police promotional processes would include a component requiring candidates to demonstrate a practical understanding of EBP.
- Community presentations made by the police would include sections designed to help community members understand EBP and its rationale.
- Cities would employ criminologists in their police departments (or shared regionally) to help analyze their crime environment, suggest evidence-based strategies, evaluate strategies as they are employed, and link the departments to other behavioral science experts who could assist the police in their mission (e.g. mental health experts).
- The cities' budgetary processes would include an assessment of programs and strategies framed around evidence of effectiveness and a cost-benefit analysis.

To address the lack of knowledge, there must be a concerted effort on the part of EBP-committed practitioners and academics alike to teach these forgotten stakeholders the requisite concepts of EBP and work to gain their commitment to EBP that is compatible to their own. Helping them understand "what's in it for them (WIIFM)" will be crucial to gaining their acceptance and allegiance to EBP and the organizational practices necessary to support it.

The benefits of moving policing toward evidence-based policing are multi-faceted. Some of these benefits include, but are not limited to:

- more effective control of crime and disorder;
- more cost-effective use of policing resources;
- the creation of a policing philosophy that is more easily defended when complaints of politics are made; crime-control strategies that are rigorously evaluated for effectiveness are neither conservative nor progressive—they are either effective or ineffective (bias can be evaluated too);
- a reduction in taxpayer concern about policing strategies being wasteful;
- safer and healthier police officers; and,
- police using EBP will be less likely to inflict unintended harm to the community.

When the advocates of evidence-based policing begin focusing significant efforts on helping elected officials, policy makers, and police leaders understand EBP and how to implement it, local government and policing will become more effective, responsive, and legitimate (in the eyes of the community). And American communities will be safer. What better justification can there be?

2

Implement Collaborative Strategic Crime Control Initiatives

Charles M. Katz
Jessica Huff
Arizona State University

Background

For more than forty years, we have known that generalized, unfocused, reactive policing relying on preventative patrol, reactive criminal investigations, and rapid response to calls for service has a minimal impact on controlling crime. In response, policing has adapted and become much more proactive and targeted. Problem-oriented policing (POP) and hot spot policing, for example, have become commonplace in medium to large police agencies and are part of a small number of policing practices known to be evidence based. Prior research has shown, for example, that hot spot policing and POP significantly reduce crime.[1] These practices, however, are often limited in scope and rarely call for resource allocations beyond that of patrol officers, a sergeant, and a crime analyst.[2] Cordner and Biebel's analysis of the implementation of POP in San Diego emphasized this limitation; they reported that POP projects typically focus on "one person, one address, one building, one parking lot, or one intersection."[3] This is not to imply that these tactics are not important—they are vital—but it suggests that these practices have their limitations and should be thought of as one of several evidence-based tactics that can be used as part of an agency's larger strategic crime-control efforts.

Police-led strategic crime-control initiatives frequently seek to address large-scale, complex problems. The model emphasizes collaborative strategic planning by policy makers who have the capacity to allocate resources, create (or change) policy, and influence relevant stakeholders. Strategic planning is guided by comprehensive community-wide problem-solving analyses that seek to understand the scope and contributing conditions associated with crime problems in a community. In turn, the problem-solving analyses provide the information necessary to implement targeted responses that address both the proximate and root causes of large, complex problems. Unlike POP and hot spot strategies, strategic crime control involves personnel at all levels of a police organization, in addition to representatives from other criminal justice and community agencies, to address a broader range of problems continually contributing to crime in a community. Responses included as part of strategic crime-control efforts are evidence based and subjected to ongoing assessment that holds managers and leaders accountable for their implementation and measures whether their efforts are effective.

This chapter describes the fundamental principles of strategic crime control and provides examples of contemporary strategic crime-control efforts. In the next section, we discuss the five principles of strategic crime control: (1) community-wide problem analysis; (2) targeted, evidence-based responses; (3) collaborative partnerships; (4) strategic planning; and (5) accountability. We then provide three examples of strategic crime-control initiatives: pulling levers, Project Safe Neighborhoods (PSN), and the Richmond, California, Homicide Initiative. Pulling levers and PSN are large-scale national programs that have been implemented in response to diverse crime problems across the United States. The Richmond, California, Homicide Initiative offers an example of strategic crime-control efforts at the local level to address homicide.

■ Defining Characteristics of Strategic Crime Control

Community-Wide Problem Analysis

The goal of community-wide problem analysis is to understand not only what the community's problems are but also why they are occurring. The principles of strategic crime control require community-wide problem analysis beyond the exclusive use of police data. If communities in general, and the police specifically, are going to solve crime problems, data from other criminal justice agencies and community services (such as local and federal law enforcement, county and state courts, local and federal prosecutor offices, and jails and corrections) are necessary. Data from these partners help police leaders understand the depth and contributing conditions associated with crime problems and provide the details necessary for them to lead the development of strategic responses that address both the proximate and root causes of a problem. These data allow for a more comprehensive, strategic approach to crime and allow for the coordination of diverse resources to address identified problems.

The community-wide approach requires strong and responsive partnerships among agencies that contribute their data for analysis. These data could include crime reports and requests for service from the police, case-processing information from courts, risk assessments from correctional agencies, and information regarding resource availability and usage from service providers. The purpose of such analyses is twofold. The first is to identify the most serious crime problems and the factors contributing to those problems (e.g., people, places, weapons, and proximate and root causes). The second purpose is to examine the community's capacity to address its crime problems. This can be done by reviewing existing data, which can identify inefficiencies within agencies (e.g., low clearance rates and low convictions) and process-oriented issues that occur due to fragmentation and "lack of integration across the system [that] allows adaptation to special problems."[4] It can also require the inventory of existing prevention, intervention, and suppression strategies for identifying where resources are under- or overdeveloped. The outcome of the community-wide problem analysis is to build a consensus on the crime problems to focus on and to align the necessary community resources to respond to the identified problem.

To facilitate data analysis, crime analysts and local research partners, who are often university-based researchers, have become essential components of police-led strategic crime-control efforts. They are relatively inexpensive when compared to sworn officers and serve as a force multiplier by providing police leaders with information that permits them to understand the people, places, times, and crime types that pose the greatest threats so they can allocate their limited resources effectively. A research partner not only leads the primary data-collection effort but also serves as the "conductor" of the community-wide problem analysis and evaluates the impact of responses to the identified problems. The research partner is responsible for isolating the data sources and data elements needed to assess community crime problems and diagnosing the community's capacity to respond to the identified problems. They can analyze the data themselves (if needed), or they can coordinate data-analysis activities across stakeholder agencies to ensure synchronization among partners. Regardless, they ensure that analysis is comprehensive enough to be inclusive of many potential problems but also detailed enough that the information can be used to accurately diagnose crime problems. The research partner also ensures that the information is communicated effectively, with the purpose of creating a consensus among stakeholders.

Targeted, Evidence-Based Responses

The second principle of strategic crime control is the use of targeted, evidence-based responses. Over the last twenty years, innovative police leaders relying on empirical research have begun to focus their scarce resources on targets identified through the use of data.[5] In the problem-analysis phase, data is used to identify community crime problems and inform the development of targeted responses to the identified problems. More specifically, data is used to determine the mechanisms responsible for producing crime (e.g., social, geographic area, situational, family, interpersonal, peer groups), and the police create responses to target these mechanisms.[6] The scope of the targeting can vary considerably from individuals and groups to microplaces, neighborhoods, jurisdictions, and even nation-states. After targets are prioritized and responses are implemented, the police continue to review and refine their targeting techniques to understand those targets that are useful for identification and response. Internal performance measures are used to track whether responses have been implemented and to understand the impact of the responses.[7]

Targeted responses employed through strategic crime-control efforts are to be evidence based, if possible. As noted in the previous chapter, evidence-based strategies are those that have been shown to have strong evidence of effectiveness. Evidence of effectiveness, however, can mean different things to different people. Here, by evidence-based strategies, we mean the intentional, conscious use of practices that are fundamentally rooted in high-quality science. This requires not only that the police are well versed in the science of best practices but also that they are actively involved in generating use-inspired research—and that use-inspired research is deeply embedded in the day-to-day decision-making of police officers, managers, and leaders. It also means that when collaborating with external stakeholders (e.g., courts, corrections, and community service organizations), police leadership emphasizes to partners that they should adopt and use evidence-based practices.

Evidence-based practices have grown substantially over the past few decades, and a number of tools have been developed to accelerate and improve the dissemination of, awareness of, and accessibility to these practices. One of the first efforts to do this was the 1997 University of Maryland report funded by the Department of Justice and led by Larry Sherman and Doris MacKenzie.[8] The report relied on a five-point scale to rate the quality of an evaluation and the evidence it produced. To be labeled as an evidence-based practice, a practice must have been evaluated by a minimum of two high-quality studies (experimental or quasi-experimental) and had to show evidence of impact. Since 1997, there have been a number of efforts to identify evidence-based best practices, including the following:

- Lawrence W. Sherman, Doris L. MacKenzie, David P. Farrington, and Brandon C. Welsh, eds., *Evidence-Based Crime Prevention* (London, England: Routledge, 2002).
- National Research Council, *Fairness and Effectiveness in Policing: The Evidence* (Washington, DC: The National Academies Press, 2004).
- National Institute of Justice, CrimeSolutions.gov
- College of Policing, "Welcome to the Crime Reduction Toolkit."
- Center for Evidence-Based Crime Policy, "Evidence-Based Policing Matrix."

CrimeSolutions.gov is the most widely known and most comprehensive toolkit that reviews and distributes information on evidence-based best practices. CrimeSolutions.gov has reviewed more than 200 law enforcement "programs."[9] Of these programs, the majority were screened out and did not qualify for further review because the quality of the research did not meet the standards of CrimeSolutions.gov. Among the seventy-six programs reviewed, fewer than twenty have been identified as effective. Some of those identified as evidence based include disorder policing, hot spot policing, POP, focused deterrence, foot patrol, homicide review teams, drug abatement response teams, and the Integrated Ballistics Identification System.[10]

Collaborative Partnerships

The police frequently discuss the many partnerships that they have with other agencies and community organizations, and many of these partnerships, if not most, are advisory in nature or involve the exchange of information. These are what we call "parallel partnerships." Parallel partnerships are those where the police meet with their partners and network in a perfunctory manner and then typically go their separate ways and act on the information shared, if deemed appropriate.

Here, we are speaking about partnerships that are conscientiously symbiotic and collaborative to achieve strategic crime control. Collaborative partnerships are typically formed in response to a specific problem such as gangs, violence, and disorder. Strategic crime-control efforts, however, seek to routinize interorganizational partnerships where there is an intersection of mandates and where a common goal cannot be attained when acting alone.[11] Collaborative partnerships in strategic crime control involve coordination and cooperation in the pursuit of a shared goal. Coordination involves organizations making substantial adjustments to preexisting operations and organizational structures to find ways to improve each other's efficiency and effectiveness. Cooperation requires sharing resources, whether personnel, funding, or office space, and aligning policies to allow for greater cooperation to achieve shared prioritized goals.

Strategic crime-control efforts require the police to collaborate with a wide number of partners that have a mandate related to the prevention, intervention, and suppression of crime and violence. Prevention programming improves the overall health of a community and reduces its risk of violence and other problems. These types of programs and activities focus on the causes of crime and seek to reduce the factors that generate crime. They address structural factors that are well-known to cause crime (such as poverty, poor educational performance, and dysfunctional families) and are implemented by community-based agencies, grassroots organizations, faith-based organizations, schools, politicians, the police, and a variety of government social service agencies. Intervention programming focuses on those people and places at the highest risk for violence and other problems. These types of programs and activities intervene at the early stages of more serious and chronic behavior. For example, they disrupt cycles of retaliatory violence, provide crisis intervention services to families in need, deliver mediation services to those in conflict, and provide counseling and other services to high-risk youth. Such personnel as violence interrupters, counselors, employment service providers, and treatment specialists provide intervention services. Suppression programming typically focuses on offenders after a crime has occurred and seeks to prevent reoffending. Suppression strategies include such activities as investigating; gathering and distributing intelligence; conducting surveillance; and arresting, prosecuting, supervising, and imprisoning offenders; suppression strategies involve local, county, state, and federal law enforcement, courts, and corrections agencies.

Strategic Planning

Strategic planning is an essential part of police-led strategic crime-control efforts. It often requires the creation of a police-led, executive-level, community-wide steering committee that consists of leaders from partner agencies who are charged with developing objectives and goals for community safety. As noted above, community-wide problem analysis is typically conducted by local researchers. The researchers present their results (and sometimes recommendations) to the executive committee, which is ultimately responsible for identifying common goals and generating high-level strategic plans. Those strategic plans are implemented by interorganizational subcommittees that are charged with coordinating efforts, developing recommendations for allocating resources, and ensuring that their agencies are following through with agreed-upon responsibilities. As such, strategic planning attempts to address problems through organizational relationship-building and problem-solving tactics to more effectively focus community resources.

It is important to acknowledge that strategic planning that involves multiple agencies with multiple mandates will encounter a number of challenges, regardless of good intentions. Different agencies have different goals or rely on different means to achieve similar goals. For example, though the police, correctional officers, and community members all strive to reduce crime, they do so in different ways. The police often emphasize suppression efforts, community-based corrections emphasize treatment and rehabilitation, and community stakeholders emphasize prevention programs. These conflicting purposes inherently cause tension among stakeholders.[12] Regardless, many organizations share core concerns and subsequently seek to solve like problems. Strategic planning requires agencies to identify and target problems of common concern and to design a plan that solves the problems. Strategic crime-control efforts result in the identification and selection of a broad number of goals that are specified by the executive committee. These goals must be measurable and evaluable. Accountability mechanisms should be implemented, including a timeline of when the agency should accomplish tasks and the performance measures that the executive committee will use to monitor the agency's progress.

As part of the strategic-planning process, required resources are identified and plans are developed to either obtain or reallocate resources to respond to the problem. While strategic plans are often developed and based on existing capacity, it is important to identify gaps in capacity and to determine the best strategy to fill those gaps. The executive committee should be well versed in evidence-based strategies so that they have the opportunity to integrate them into the plan as early as possible. This might require executives to receive training on evidence-based strategies and to be provided with resources to help them acquire information on an as-needed basis.

Accountability

The fifth principle of strategic crime control is accountability. As noted above, strategic crime control requires extensive strategic planning that thoroughly details stakeholder responsibilities, timelines, and expected outcomes. Accountability needs to penetrate throughout and among stakeholder organizations so that administrators at the executive level through line-level managers are held responsible for carrying out elements of the strategic plan. Accountability measures are vital to strategic crime-control efforts due to the breadth of operational and tactical activities that are often carried out in coordination with multiple stakeholder organizations. The breadth of operational and tactical activities involved in strategic crime control requires continuous accountability checks to ensure that all agencies and aspects of the intervention are being implemented and functioning according to the strategic plan.

Internal accountability within the police organization can often be achieved through traditional strategies such as performance evaluations,

COMPSTAT, and auditing mechanisms (e.g., internal reports). Strategic crime-control efforts led by the police, however, require broad coalitions of partners that engage, participate actively, and influence the response to crime problems at multiple levels (e.g., policy, strategy, and tactics). As such, external accountability is needed and requires holding organizations outside of the police accountable, which is obviously much more difficult and complex because of the lack of formal and administrative oversight. Transparency mechanisms that place informal institutional-level peer pressure on partner agencies are frequently used as a method of accountability. These mechanisms typically involve the routine collection and reporting of implementation data to ensure that all stakeholders are informed about what, when, and how often activities have been carried out. They allow partners to quickly identify urgent implementation problems, prioritize tasks, informally reward partners that complete activities, and isolate partners that are not upholding their responsibilities so they can work through the problems. They also help determine whether a new partner is needed to replace a nonproductive partner. This approach requires patience, tact, and frequent yet gentle nudging.

This information can also be useful for formal evaluations of strategic crime-control efforts that assess the dosage of interventions and determine the effectiveness of efforts. A cornerstone of strategic crime control is the continuous evaluation and review of efforts to determine whether they are addressing the identified problem. Impact evaluations conducted by the research partner identify short- and long-term changes and assess whether the changes are a consequence of implemented responses. They seek to determine whether the intervention had a significant impact on a specified outcome measure. These evaluations are interested not only in direct program effects (e.g., decreases in a particular crime) but also in indirect program effects (e.g., a change in residents' satisfaction with the police). In other words, they are also interested in identifying any unanticipated consequences as a result of the intervention.

These impact evaluations typically require measuring what level of services are delivered and how services are delivered. Measuring and assessing how programs are implemented is often referred to as a process evaluation, which is important for several reasons. Perhaps the most important reason is that it is essential to know that the intervention has been fully carried out and that the field implementation accurately reflects the program blueprint. Unless activities are carried out according to plan, it cannot be stated with certainty that the program's success or failure can be attributed to the intervention. Another reason for describing and measuring the intervention is that "treatments" can be administered in an uncontrolled and nonstandardized manner. This, in turn, can result in varying impacts, depending on the type and amount of "treatment" administered. Consequently, it is important to measure the dosage of an intervention to fully understand its impact.

Last, program failure is often the consequence of administering the wrong treatment. Using a process evaluation is helpful in identifying these inconsistencies between program design and program implementation. The continual use of process evaluations to recognize these gaps can assist in pinpointing problematic plan components and improving program design. Given the complexity of programs designed to reduce crime, implementation failure is not uncommon. Describing the qualities (and quantity) of an intervention using a process evaluation can help the researchers and practitioners understand the true impact of the intervention and its components on targeted crime problems.[13]

■ Strategic Problem-Solving Projects as Proof of Concept

We are unaware of any community that has fully embraced strategic crime control to the point that its principles permeate a police organization. Instead, there have been several attempts to implement strategic problem-solving projects that exhibit all or many of the characteristics of strategic crime control but are restricted to addressing one problem type for a limited period, usually the duration of a federal grant. Below are examples of strategic problem-solving projects that we believe serve as "proof of concept" of what strategic crime-control efforts might look like. The first two examples, pulling levers and PSN, are large, federally funded programs that were implemented in agencies throughout the United States to address a variety of crime problems. The third example, the Richmond Homicide Initiative, is an example of a strategic-planning effort created to address factors contributing to local homicide problems in Richmond, California. These examples detail the processes used to implement strategic crime control and the effectiveness of these efforts. We emphasize, however, that strategic crime control involves a diffusion of the five principles of strategic crime control throughout a police organization where a multitude of problems are addressed, and the analysis leads to a continually evolving, multidisciplinary, targeted response to community problems.

Pulling Levers

Based on the recognition that most crime is committed by a small group of serial offenders, pulling-levers strategies (also known as focused deterrence) seek to stop the individuals who contribute most to general crime problems from offending.[14] Pulling-levers strategies include several components: (1) problem identification, (2) interagency collaboration, (3) research relating to the problem, (4) a response to the problem that includes a variety of sanctions (levers that can be pulled), (5) services focused toward targeted offenders, and (6) direct and repeated communication with offenders regarding the program's purpose.[15]

Pulling-levers strategies accomplish both specific and general deterrence.[16] Specific deterrence is achieved through directly informing targeted offenders about the program. This ensures that offenders are aware of the sanctions that will be applied if they offend, understand that offending will be met with a swift criminal justice response, and realize that the sanctions they receive will be severe.[17] As most of the offenders targeted by these initiatives are involved in a range of criminal activities, pulling levers capitalizes on the multifaceted vulnerabilities that active offenders have to prosecution.[18] General deterrence is achieved through informing the community at large about the project, the costs of crime, and the actions that will be taken if criminal activity is discovered.

Pulling levers initially emerged as a part of the Boston Gun project, a POP initiative to reduce gun violence among youth in Boston.[19] The Boston Gun Project was designed to be a citywide intervention, with spillover effects for gangs and individuals not directly targeted by the program.[20] Research conducted as a part of the project indicated that youth homicides were generally committed by and against gang-involved youth who were often involved in numerous offenses. The interagency collaboration created to respond to this issue included representatives from the Boston Police Department; probation and parole agencies; the Bureau of Alcohol, Tobacco, and Firearms; the Massachusetts U.S. Attorney; the Suffolk County District Attorney; Boston School Police; Boston youth outreach workers; and a research team from the Harvard Kennedy School of Government.[21] The collaboration wanted to communicate that no form of offending would remain unpunished; thus, the intention was to prosecute offenders fully using all available levers, including warrants, parole and probation violations, and truancy.[22] Offenders were directly notified about their inclusion in the program and the services available to them at notification meetings, where representatives of each agency in the collaboration spoke about their role in the project.[23]

In addition to addressing gangs and gun violence, pulling-levers strategies have been applied to repeat offenders and open-air drug markets. A meta-analysis revealed that interventions addressing criminal groups were the most successful, followed by drug market interventions and repeat offender programs,[24] though an updated version of the study found that programs targeting repeat offenders were more effective than those targeting drug markets.[25] Of eleven pulling-levers strategies in the original analysis, ten had noteworthy crime reductions; nineteen of the twenty-four studies in the updated review identified notable crime reduction benefits. Consistent with these findings, CrimeSolutions.gov rates pulling levers as a promising crime-reduction strategy.[26]

Pulling levers encompasses the principles of effective community crime control. Community-wide problem analysis is a crucial component in the design of pulling-levers interventions. The effectiveness of pulling levers often traces back to the quality of crime analysis used to identify target individuals and places for intervention.[27] Similarly, pulling-levers strategies rely on collaborations between law enforcement, other criminal justice agencies, service providers, and community members.[28] Unsurprisingly, pulling-levers strategies are more successful in cities that have previous experience with multiagency collaborations.[29] Given requirements for organizational change and competing organizational goals, strategic planning and continued attention to processes are required for pulling levers to succeed,[30] highlighting the importance of ongoing process evaluations to facilitate accountability. As crime varies between communities, addressing specific problems with the assistance of external research partners using focused, targeted responses is imperative.[31] Finally, performance and accountability measures under pulling levers emphasize crime reduction as opposed to agency activity levels.

Project Safe Neighborhoods (PSN)

PSN is a federally funded initiative implemented in U.S. Attorneys' Offices and was designed to promote collaborations between federal, state, and local agencies to develop site-specific, strategic gun reduction strategies and to effectively prosecute gun cases.[32] Grounded in policing strategies that proved promising in the reduction of gun violence (such as Operation Ceasefire in Boston), PSN incorporates strategic problem solving, interagency partnerships, community involvement, training, and accountability elements.[33] PSN emphasizes deterrence and incapacitation through community-wide and offender-specific notification programs and federal prosecutions. It also includes a procedural justice component that uses transparent, nonadversarial communications with offenders.[34]

McGarrell and his colleagues examined the impact of PSN and PSN "dosage" on changes in violent crime in 252 U.S. cities with more than 100,000 residents.[35] Their findings indicated that PSN cities experienced significantly greater reductions in violence compared to non-PSN cities. Further, higher levels of PSN dosage (measured using indicators of collaboration, research-based strategic planning, and enhanced federal prosecution) were associated with significantly greater reductions in violent crime. Similarly, CrimeSolutions.gov rates PSN strategies as promising.[36]

An evaluation of PSN in Chicago demonstrated that the strategy significantly reduced homicides, gun homicides, and aggravated assaults and batteries.[37] Papachristos and his colleagues further examined the impact of four components of the Chicago PSN strategy: federal prosecution, increased sentence length, policing the supply side of firearm markets, and deterrence marketing through offender notification meetings. The PSN dimension associated with the greatest reduction in homicide rates was the percentage of offenders who attended a notification meeting. The number of gun seizures was associated with a significant reduction in gun homicides, and the number of federal prosecutions was associated with significantly lower homicide and gun homicide rates. Using a quasi-experiment to assess the effect of notification forums on individual offender recidivism, Wallace and her colleagues reported that those who attended a PSN notification meeting were less likely to recidivate and took longer to recidivate than offenders who did not attend a meeting.[38]

The Eastern Missouri PSN problem identification process revealed that most gun violence is perpetrated by a small group of individuals in a small number of neighborhoods.[39] This analysis further identified gaps in coordination between local and federal prosecutors in case processing. Interviews with task force members indicated that PSN successfully improved collaboration and case processing for gun-involved incidents, and interviews with targeted offenders suggested that PSN increased perceptions of the certainty and severity of sanctions associated with gun crime.

Like pulling levers, PSN contains all the elements of strategic crime control. One defining feature of PSN is the central role of a research partner to guide and evaluate the intervention.[40] This community-wide strategic planning intends to provide context-specific responses to causes of gun crime in different jurisdictions.[41] Further, the receipt of federal PSN funds depends on the development of a collaborative task force.[42] Strategic planning plays a central role in PSN due to the recognition that local and state laws vary, requiring the adaptation of these programs to their local context.[43] The flexibility of PSN to be modified to fit local conditions as part of focused interventions is one of the program's strengths.[44] In terms of accountability, the Department of Justice emphasized that it would judge program success based on reduced gun crime as opposed to arrests or prosecutions.[45]

Richmond (CA) Comprehensive Homicide Initiative

Traditional police wisdom held that homicide was often caused by factors beyond police control (e.g., social structural factors), as police could not change the underlying social conditions contributing to homicide.[46] However, the development of community-oriented policing (COP) and POP strategies have led the police to view crime in a broader context and to ask what they can do to effectively reduce homicide.[47] A Murder Summit hosted by the International Association of Chiefs of Police in 1995 made thirty-nine recommendations to reduce homicide, largely centered on the use of community-wide, collaborative strategies. Afterward, the Bureau of Justice Assistance deployed a Comprehensive Homicide Initiative to test multifaceted responses to homicide through emphasizing prevention, intervention, enforcement, and prosecution. Richmond, California, was selected as one of the first pilot sites.[48]

Like many cities at the time, Richmond had experienced an increase in gun killings, drug- and gang-related killings, and drive-by shootings.[49] To respond to these issues, community-based nonenforcement strategies were developed, including collaborations with Public Works and the Housing Authority to improve the community's appearance, job skills training, mentorship programs in elementary schools, probation officers in high schools, a youth court, and domestic violence support programs. Investigative and enforcement strategies were also used, such as a team approach to information gathering in high-profile homicides; working with the FBI on unsolved homicides; working with the DEA, FBI, and the California Bureau of Narcotics Enforcement to target the drug culture; assigning an evidence technician to the detective bureau, and improving information sharing and technology.

The Richmond project began with an in-depth analysis of homicide trends to evaluate contributing factors.[50] Guided by these analyses, Richmond focused on high-crime areas and homicides occurring outdoors involving gangs, guns, and drugs. In an evaluation of homicides in Richmond from 1985 to 1998, gun and drug-related homicides declined substantially after the intervention; homicides occurring outdoors and drive-by homicides also decreased. Comparing homicide trends in Richmond to other California cities suggested that the changes in Richmond were unique and likely due to the Comprehensive Homicide Initiative. Consistent with these results, CrimeSolutions.gov rated the Richmond Comprehensive Homicide Initiative promising.[51]

The Comprehensive Homicide Initiative also incorporated prevention and intervention strategies aimed to reduce violence more broadly, including the development of a School-Community Police Truant Recovery Program to keep students in school and off the streets.[52] Eight police departments participated in the program with the school district and assigned patrol cars to conduct truancy sweeps. Baseline analyses found that many truants were struggling in school, had low attendance, and experienced high numbers of disciplinary infractions. An evaluation of the School-Community Police Truant Recovery Program suggests that the program did lead to some improvement in truant behavior and attendance in school, but it did not impact criminal justice contacts or grades.

Like the previous examples, the Comprehensive Homicide Initiative encompasses many of the principles of strategic crime control. COP and POP were used to treat individual incidents as parts of larger community patterns in the problem-analysis phase, leading the police to identify root causes of violence.[53] These analyses were also used to develop targeted responses, such as the use of restraining orders barring known gang members and drug dealers from going to public housing and high-crime streets and neighborhoods. The Richmond Police recognized they would be better able to prevent violence by collaborating with community institutions and did so in a variety of ways to develop prevention and intervention programs. Strategic planning was used to examine factors contributing to homicide and to develop a multifaceted strategy to address those underlying causes.

Conclusion

This chapter proposed that the police should lead strategic crime-control efforts in their communities. Strategic crime-control initiatives are characterized by community-wide problem analysis; targeted, evidence-based responses; collaborative partnerships; strategic planning; and accountability. The model builds on prior strategic problem-solving projects and calls for the integration and replication of their key principles throughout a police organization. The idea is to empirically identify the most pressing problems in a community and focus the limited resources available on those problems and locations that need them the most. While we recognize that there are many impediments to implementation and that its adoption and institutionalization will take decades, not years, the model offers a framework that brings the best of a community together, led by the police, to comprehensively respond to its problems.

NOTES

[1] David L. Weisburd, Cody W. Telep, Joshua C. Hinkle, and John E. Eck, *Effects of Problem-Oriented Policing on Crime and Disorder* (Washington, DC: National Institute of Justice, Office of Justice Programs, U.S. Department of Justice, 2008); Anthony A. Braga, Andrew V. Papachristos, and David M. Hureau, "The Effects of Hot Spots Policing on Crime: An Updated Systematic Review and Meta-Analysis," *Justice Quarterly* 31, no. 4 (2014): 633–663.

[2] Rachel Boba and John P. Crank, "Institutionalizing Problem-Oriented Policing: Rethinking Problem Solving, Analysis, and Accountability," *Police Practice and Research* 9, no. 5 (2008): 379–393.

[3] Gary Cordner and Elizabeth P. Biebel, "Problem-Oriented Policing in Practice," *Criminology & Public Policy* 4, no. 2 (2005): 155–180, 164.

[4] John Klofas, Natalie K. Hipple, and Edmund McGarrell, *The New Criminal Justice* (New York: Routledge, 2010), 5.

[5] Lawrence W. Sherman, "The Rise of Evidence-Based Policing: Targeting, Testing, and Tracking," *Crime and Justice* 42, no. 1 (2013): 377–451.

[6] Cynthia Lum, Christopher S. Koper, and Cody W. Telep, "The Evidence-Based Policing Matrix," *Journal of Experimental Criminology* 7, no. 1 (2011): 3–26, 11.

[7] Sherman, "The Rise of Evidence-Based Policing."

[8] Lawrence W. Sherman, Denise C. Gottfredson, Doris L. MacKenzie, John Eck, Peter Reuter, and Shawn D. Bushway, *Preventing Crime: What Works, What Doesn't, What's Promising* (Washington, D.C., National Institute of Justice, Office of Justice Programs, U.S. Department of Justice, 1998).

[9] Edward R. Maguire, *A Review of Law Enforcement Programs in CrimeSolutions.gov* (Arlington, VA: National Institute of Justice Research Conference, June 20, 2011).

[10] National Institute of Justice, "All Programs & Practices," accessed July 18, 2019, https://crimesolutions.gov/programs.aspx

[11] Meghan E. Hollis, "Community-Based Partnerships: Collaboration and Organizational Partnerships in Criminal Justice," *Journal of Family Strengths* 16, no. 2 (2016): 1–17.

[12] Kevin N. Wright, "The Desirability of Goal Conflict within the Criminal Justice System," in *The Administration and Management of Criminal Justice Organizations*, eds. Stan Stojkovic, John Klofas, and David Kalinich (Long Grove, IL: Waveland Press, 2010), 39–50.

[13] Daniel P. Mears, "Towards Rational and Evidence-Based Crime Policy," *Journal of Criminal Justice* 35, no. 6 (2007): 667–682.

[14] David M. Kennedy, "Pulling Levers: Chronic Offenders, High-Crime Settings, and a Theory of Prevention," *Valparaiso University Law Review* 3, no. 2 (1997): 449–484.
[15] David M. Kennedy, "Old Wine in New Bottles: Policing and the Lessons of Pulling Levers," in *Police Innovation: Contrasting Perspectives*, eds. David Weisburd and Anthony A. Braga (New York: Cambridge University Press, 2006), 155–170.
[16] David M. Kennedy, Anne M. Piehl, and Anthony A. Braga, "Youth Violence in Boston: Gun Markets, Serious Youth Offenders, and Use-Reduction Strategy," *Law and Contemporary Problems* 59, no. 1 (1996): 147–196.
[17] Anthony A. Braga and David L. Weisburd, "The Effects of Focused Deterrence Strategies on Crime: A Systematic Review and Meta-Analysis of the Empirical Evidence," *Journal of Research in Crime & Delinquency* 49, no. 3 (2012): 323–358.
[18] Jens Ludwig, "Better Gun Enforcement, Less Crime," *Criminology & Public Policy* 4, no. 4 (2005): 677–716.
[19] Anthony A. Braga, David M. Hureau, and Andrew V. Papachristos, "Deterring Gang-Involved Gun Violence: Measuring the Impact of Boston's Operation Ceasefire on Street Gang Behavior," *Journal of Quantitative Criminology* 30, no. 1 (2014): 113–139.
[20] Kennedy et al., "Youth Violence in Boston."
[21] Ludwig, "Better Gun Enforcement, Less Crime."
[22] Kennedy et al., "Youth Violence in Boston."
[23] Kennedy, "Pulling Levers."
[24] Braga et al., "The Effects of Focused Deterrence Strategies on Crime."
[25] Anthony A. Braga, David Weisburd, and Brandon Turchan, "Focused Deterrence Strategies and Crime Control: An Updated Systematic Review and Meta-Analysis of the Empirical Evidence," *Criminology and Public Policy* 17, no. 1 (2018): 205–250.
[26] Office of Justice Programs, "Focused Deterrence Strategies," accessed November 18, 2019, https://crimesolutions.gov/PracticeDetails.aspx?ID=11
[27] Rachel B. Santos, "The Effectiveness of Crime Analysis for Crime Reduction: Cure or Diagnosis?" *Journal of Contemporary Criminal Justice* 30, no. 2 (2014): 147–168.
[28] Marie S. Tillyer, Robin S. Engel, and Brian Lovins, "Beyond Boston: Applying Theory to Understand and Address Sustainability Issues in Focused Deterrence Initiatives for Violence Reduction," *Crime & Delinquency* 58, no. 6 (2012): 973–997.
[29] Edmund F. McGarrell, "Strategic Problem Solving, Project Safe Neighborhoods, and the New Criminal Justice," in *The New Criminal Justice*, eds. John Klofas, Natalie Hipple, and Edmund McGarrell (New York: Routledge, 2010), 28–36; Edmund F. McGarrell and Timothy S. Bynum, "Strategic Problem-Solving Gun Crime Reduction," *The New Criminal Justice*, eds. John Klofas, Natalie Hipple, and Edmund McGarrell (New York: Routledge, 2010).
[30] Michael S. Scott, *Focused Deterrence of High-Risk Individuals* (Washington, DC: Bureau of Justice Assistance, 2017); Tillyer et al., "Beyond Boston."
[31] McGarrell, "Strategic Problem Solving, Project Safe Neighborhoods, and the New Criminal Justice."
[32] Andrew V. Papachristos, Tracey L. Meares, and Jeffrey Fagan, "Attention Felons: Evaluating Project Safe Neighborhoods in Chicago," *Journal of Empirical Legal Studies* 4, no. 2 (2005): 223–272.
[33] Scott H. Decker, Beth M. Huebner, Adam Watkins, and Lindsey Green, *Project Safe Neighborhoods: Strategic Interventions, Eastern District of Missouri: Case Study* 7 (Washington, DC: U.S. Department of Justice, 2007),; Edmund F. McGarrell, Nicholas Corsaro, Natalie K. Hipple, and Timothy S. Bynum, "Project Safe Neighborhoods and Violent Crime Trends in US Cities: Assessing Violent Crime Impact," *Journal of Quantitative Criminology* 26, no. 2 (2010): 165–190.
[34] Danielle Wallace, Andrew V. Papachristos, Tracey Meares, and Jeffrey Fagan, "Desistance and Legitimacy: The Impact of Offender Notification Meetings on Recidivism among High Risk Offenders," *Justice Quarterly* 33, no. 7 (2016): 1237–1264.
[35] McGarrell et al., "Project Safe Neighborhoods and Violent Crime Trends in US Cities."
[36] Office of Justice Programs, *Program Profile: Project Safe Neighborhoods (National Evaluation)*, accessed November 15, 2019, https://crimesolutions.gov/ProgramDetails.aspx?ID=448.

[37] Papachristos et al., "Attention Felons."
[38] Wallace et al., "Desistance and Legitimacy."
[39] Decker et al., *Project Safe Neighborhoods.*
[40] Papachristos et al., "Attention Felons."
[41] Edmund McGarrell, Natalie Hipple, Nicholas Corsaro, Timothy Bynum, Heather Perez, Carol A. Zimmermann, and Melissa Garmo, *Project Safe Neighborhoods—A National Program to Reduce Gun Crime* (Washington, DC: National Institute of Justice, 2009).
[42] J. C. Barnes, Megan C. Kurlychek, Holly V. Miller, J. Mitchell Miller, and Robert J. Kaminski, "A Partial Assessment of South Carolina's Project Safe Neighborhoods Strategy: Evidence from a Sample of Supervised Offenders," *Journal of Criminal Justice* 38, no. 4 (2010): 383–389.
[43] Decker et al., *Project Safe Neighborhoods.*
[44] McGarrell et al., *Project Safe Neighborhoods.*
[45] Decker et al., *Project Safe Neighborhoods.*
[46] James J. Fyfe, John S. Goldkamp, and Michael D. White, *Strategies for Reducing Homicide: The Comprehensive Homicide Initiative in Richmond, California* (Washington, DC: Bureau of Justice Assistance, Office of Justice Programs, U.S. Department of Justice, 1997).
[47] Michael D. White, James J. Fyfe, Suzanne P. Campbell, and John S. Goldkamp, "The Police Role in Preventing Homicide: Considering the Impact of Problem-Oriented Policing on the Prevalence of Murder," *Journal of Research in Crime and Delinquency* 40, no. 2 (2003): 194–225.
[48] Fyfe et al., *Strategies for Reducing Homicide.*
[49] Ibid.
[50] White et al., "The Police Role in Preventing Homicide."
[51] Office of Justice Programs, *Program Profile: Richmond (CA) Comprehensive Homicide Initiative*, accessed November 19, 2019, https://crimesolutions.gov/ProgramDetails.aspx?ID=244.
[52] Michael D. White, James J. Fyfe, Suzanne P. Campbell, and John S. Goldkamp, "The School-Police Partnership: Identifying At-Risk Youth through a Truant Recovery Program," *Evaluation Review* 25, no. 5 (2001): 507–532.
[53] Fyfe et al., *Strategies for Reducing Homicide.*

2

Response Essay

Chief Art Acevedo
Houston Police Department

Police executives face inordinate challenges. Resources grow inevitably more constrained as rising health care costs, pensions, and—in some cases—tax revenue caps, force arbitrary budget cuts despite community growth. A shrinking labor force and a new generation of cadets less inclined to spend their entire career with one agency further complicate the once straightforward task of recruitment. Yet, in many ways, law enforcement also has more tools at its disposal than ever before. Technology continues to evolve at record speed. Patrol vehicles are smarter and more connected. Patrol officers are better equipped. Investigators and analysts have a wealth of new tools to help them identify and locate suspects. Where limited budgets have pushed agencies toward creative and collaborative solutions, technology has facilitated them. Regional intelligence sharing and response operations that engage city, county, state, and federal partners are now the norm, and strategic crime-control initiatives have become the way to tackle complex problems.

It may be counterintuitive that during a time of dwindling resources, strategic crime control would emerge as successful framework, particularly given the extensive investment of time and effort needed to realize this model's success. Yet, it is perhaps because it is fundamentally an evolution of past best practices that strategic crime control is such a powerful methodology. One specific application, the Comprehensive Gang Model (CGM), provides an opportunity to reiterate the core components of strategic crime control while also emphasizing how each is an application of well-known policing practices.

Originally developed through the work of Irving Spergel at the University of Chicago, the CGM prescribes five strategies for addressing youth gang crime: community mobilization, opportunity provision, social intervention, suppression, and organizational change and development. While these five strategies are deployed as the interventions, it is the broader model that demonstrates the elements of strategic crime control to the letter.

Strategic crime-control initiatives are generally undertaken by collaborative partnerships. Communities implementing the CGM initially engage a steering committee composed of decision-makers from organizations with the responsibility for addressing the gang crime problem and the authority to deploy resources. Most critically, these partners must each acknowledge that there is, in fact, a gang crime problem. The steering committee is supported by staff or research partners that undertake an assessment (described below); through the assessment, new stakeholders are invariably identified that will engage in strategic planning and implementation. This group becomes a multidisciplinary intervention team that is the collaborative vehicle for service delivery.

Strategic crime control requires a community-wide problem analysis, and the CGM delivers this through a comprehensive assessment of the youth gang problem. The Office of Juvenile Justice and Delinquency Prevention and the National Youth Gang Center developed *A Guide to Assessing Your Community's Youth Gang Problem* to help communities undertake this work. It calls for data collection and analysis across a wide number of domains that include community demographics, law enforcement data on gang crime, student and school data, perceptions from diverse community stakeholders including the gang members themselves, and a gap analysis on available community resources.

The targeted, evidence-based responses prescribed by strategic crime control are, in the CGM, the five strategies themselves: community mobilization, opportunity provision, social intervention, suppression, and organizational change and development. These five strategies provide an evidence-based framework for addressing the problems identified in the assessment phase. As the model has been tested in large and small communities across the country, so too have various communities' responses within each of the five strategies, and this body of knowledge is available online to serve as a reference for any agency. It is not unlike a cafeteria: the collective wisdom of the field is available for each of the five strategies, served up for law enforcement agencies implementing the model to help themselves to the right combination to address their specific challenges.

This pairing of the right component interventions to the community's unique youth gang problems is accomplished through strategic planning, exactly as strategic crime-control efforts dictate. Following the CGM comprehensive assessment, the steering committee must work to identify key findings and develop an implementation plan that identifies the target community and populations for prevention, intervention, and suppression activities. Problems are identified and prioritized, goals and objectives are developed, and activities are planned within each of the five core strategy areas.

Accountability, the fifth principle of strategic crime control, is an equally central component of the CGM that is realized in several ways. Initially, organizations on the steering committee are accountable to one another for the work being undertaken. With researchers, the assessment uncovers the realities of the gang crime problem and the community's responses to it. As strategic planning is undertaken, all participating organizations effectively tie themselves to a common plan. Most critically, all agree to the ongoing evaluation of the effort's effectiveness, with regular meetings to brief the steering committee on the progress, and some level of tracking to measure the success of the specific tactics undertaken through each of the five strategies. Rigorous evaluations help feed the body of knowledge about the CGM and provide critical intelligence for other agencies that would seek to replicate the model.

Strategic crime control offers an evolution in policing that borrows from and integrates the prior great ideas of proactive policing. The CGM aligns perfectly with strategic crime control, and like a good cross-section of a hillside, it provides a clear view of the layers of other effective strategies on which it is based. The engagement of a steering committee, incorporation of community voices and opinions through the assessment, and use of a multidisciplinary intervention team are influenced by community policing and community problem-solving, recognizing that policing is best done in partnership with community. The assessment itself pulls together details on the nature and extent of the youth gang problem in a way that will satisfy those who subscribe to an intelligence-led policing philosophy. The use of proven, evidence-based methods and a commitment to evaluating results and refining methods based on what is and isn't working is consistent with evidence-based policing committed to scientific methods and replication of past successes. Finally, focusing on a specific challenge—youth gang crime in a particular community—will feel somewhat familiar for those who are used to problem-oriented policing, and some communities may choose to deploy suppression approaches that are place-based, if such efforts have worked before.

For some, the comprehensive nature of the CGM will be a radical shift in methodology, and surely all strategic crime-control initiatives do not necessitate an assessment that can take as much as a full year to complete. This is a process that takes a department and community on a journey that begins with an acknowledgment of a problem followed by a rigorous evaluation of that problem. This time devoted to working together allows relationships to develop and trust to grow between the community and the police. Relational policing embraces every interaction between law enforcement and community, and it is an opportunity to forge relationships. Strategic crime-control efforts take relational policing to another level, as they are not about hearing a complaint and promising to investigate. Rather, law enforcement gets to walk hand in hand with the community, acknowledging a problem, investigating the extent of that problem, designing solutions, and seeing those solutions in action. Most critical is the feedback—returning to the stakeholders to inform them of the effort's success—because, through this direct accountability, agencies can demonstrate legitimacy. Beyond the crime reductions realized through strategic crime control, the relationships established and the trust that grows through this process make it well worth the investment.

3

Institutionalize Procedural Justice

Michael D. Reisig
Arizona State University

Background

Over the course of my career, I have had the privilege to work with many different police departments. One such experience that I still think about to this day involved a local police department in a Midwestern city that was working to improve public satisfaction with how their officers handled traffic stops, car crashes, victimization incidents, and the like. On the second night of the visit, after spending a long day in meetings with the Chief and the command staff, I was able to venture out into the city on a ride-along. The patrol officer I was teamed with was very well educated but relatively inexperienced, with just under two years on the force. We spent most of that evening listening to the local hair metal radio station and "hunting"—the term she used for traffic patrol. Much later that evening, we received a call. An officer was requesting backup at a nearby trailer court.

In short time we arrived at a relatively well-kept mobile home park. Most of the trailers exhibited a pride of ownership, but a few had seen better days. The officer on the scene was a veteran patrol sergeant (we will refer to him as "Sgt. Gene" hereafter), who was set to retire later that month. Sgt. Gene greeted me with a smile and a firm handshake. He said a park resident (let's call him "Jesse"), whom he knew well, was reportedly high on drugs ("Probably meth," said the sergeant) and threatening a neighbor, a woman who lived across the parking lot. Sgt. Gene had already interviewed the woman. As we began walking, the sergeant turned to me and said, "Professor, I'll tell you what, the best way to handle these situations is to treat people the same way I would want them to treat my mother—with respect. Smiling, he pointed at the patrol officer I was riding with and said, "These youngsters think it's about writing tickets, chasing bad guys, and making arrests. But being a good cop depends a lot on how you treat people."

Critics have often charged that too many police officers in the United States treat people unfairly—they boss people around unnecessarily; they are too quick to get physical; and on occasion, they shoot unarmed suspects. And video evidence of the police taking things too far is available for all to see via the Internet. Some observers even claim that the police are in the throes of a "legitimacy crisis," and only by adopting proven reforms can the police win back the public's trust. Whether the police are uniformly suffering a crisis of legitimacy is debatable, and the list of failed policing reforms that once promised reductions in crime and increased community tranquility is quite long. Nevertheless, the current turmoil has certainly helped open the eyes and ears of local officials. And these people are probably more open to change at this time than they were just ten years ago. This chapter argues for police departments—large and small, urban and rural—to institutionalize practices consistent with the principle of procedural justice.[1] The amount of research that supports such implementation is substantial and growing. What's more, such a reform is consistent with the historical roots of American policing and will improve the image of the police in the eyes of the public. There is also reason to believe that doing so will improve police effectiveness as well.

What Is Procedural Justice?

Over the past three decades, procedural justice has been described in different ways and applied to various contexts. For our purposes, procedural justice is defined as the fair application of authority by social control agents (e.g., police officers, prison officers, and probation officers). In terms of context, this chapter focuses on the application of procedural justice principles during police-citizen encounters (sometimes referred to as "external procedural justice"). Police practices consistent with the concept of procedural justice are said to consist of the following four elements.

Participation opportunity. Police officers satisfy this aspect of procedural justice when they allow people to tell their side of the story—this may be especially crucial in highly charged, emotional situations. Police officers who do not provide an opportunity for individuals to voice their concerns or who shut them down in the middle of them doing so risk being judged as unfair. Such behavior on the part of the police may actually make encounters more difficult to resolve. Importantly, police officers should provide a genuine offer of participation, and they should avoid patronizing citizens. For example, when conducting a traffic stop, patrol officers who lead with the question, "Do you know why I pulled you over?", begin such encounters on the wrong foot in terms of procedural justice. Condescending and rhetorical questions should be avoided at all costs. Just like police officers, citizens do not appreciate such questions.

Decision neutrality. When police officers effectively demonstrate to the people they come into contact with that they do their best to make fair decisions based on the facts—not on their personal opinions—they satisfy a second aspect of procedural justice. This requires that the police explain their decisions to all affected parties. Overall, when making decisions on how best to resolve a situation, police officers need to remain levelheaded and communicate a rational decision based on the available information. In some cases, the information necessary to do so may not be forthcoming, which may require officers to seek additional information, such as finding additional people to interview.

Respectful treatment. High-quality interpersonal treatment is a third dimension of procedural justice. Satisfying this aspect involves adherence to politeness norms. For example, officers should extend basic courtesies like referring to adult males as "sir" or, when appropriate, saying "please," "thank you," and "you're welcome"—all of which helps set the tone for how encounters with the public will unfold. Such courtesy is more likely to be reciprocated by citizens who are treated accordingly by the police. Never should police officers use pejorative terms—such as racial slurs and other terms of disparagement—or profanity that can be interpreted as disrespectful. Such behavioral indicators of procedural *injustice* will ultimately prove detrimental when it comes to successfully resolving police-public interactions and those involving the same people in the future.

Trustworthy motives. Police officers' abilities to convey to the people they come into contact with that their actions are motivated by shared values—such as the well-being of all citizens and the welfare of the larger community—are a key aspect of procedural justice.[2] Effectively doing so means that suspects are not left wondering whether the police stopped and talked to them for some extralegal reason, such as their race, how they were dressed, or because of the color of the car they were driving. Motives based on bias and prejudice are clear indicators of injustice and are associated with things that the police do not find helpful, such as resistance and defiance.

When it comes to institutionalizing procedural justice in police departments, more of it is better than less of it. In short, implementation should focus on all four elements that make up procedural justice. Successfully institutionalizing procedural justice will not only satisfy the normative claim that the police in a free and democratic society should behave in this way, but it will also enhance police legitimacy and improve community engagement in crime prevention—benefits that are intangible but critically important to the police and the communities they serve.

The Process-Based Model

Expecting good things to result when applying the concept of procedural justice rests on a solid theoretical foundation. More specifically, the process-based model holds that police practices consistent with the principles of procedural justice will yield two types of outcomes—perceptual and behavioral—that are beneficial to the police and community at large.[3] Procedural justice is thought to directly influence levels of general compliance. Examples of general compliance include upholding criminal statutes, obeying local ordinances and regulations, and adhering to traffic laws. Also included under this heading are cooperative behaviors that help the police fight crime—calling the police to report suspicious behavior or to report a crime. In sum, the process-based model holds that individuals who believe the police behave in a manner that is procedurally just—either because of direct or secondhand experience—are also more likely to obey the law and call the police when crime is afoot.

It is also important to point out that, according to the process-based model, police action that follows procedural justice principles can promote general compliance indirectly through the development of beliefs, attitudes, and perceptions that are supportive of the law and legal institutions, such as the police. Perhaps the most commonly used example is police legitimacy. Much like procedural justice, scholars sometimes disagree on the proper definition of police legitimacy. For purposes of this essay, police legitimacy is defined as the belief that the police possess the necessary authority to make decisions that influence people's lives and that such decisions (or directives) should be obeyed by those with whom the police come into contact.[4] High levels of police legitimacy, it is said, create a reservoir of support for and good will towards the police that they can rely on to help get the job done. The more favorably the public perceives police behavior to conform to procedural justice standards, the more likely they are to believe that the police have the authority to act, which in turn increases the likelihood that they will obey the law and take the initiative to mobilize the police.[5]

Procedural justice in action. It is one thing to talk about the influence of "variables" in "theoretical models," but it is quite another to ask whether things actually work in the real world as theories predict. For purposes of illustration, let's return to the police encounter involving Sgt. Gene that was discussed in the opening of this chapter. We will not concern ourselves with the entire 20 minutes or so over which the incident took place. Rather, we'll focus on some key exchanges—those that typify the application of procedural justice principles by Sgt. Gene. To do so, we'll break the encounter down into four parts: initiation, framing the issue, resolution, and completion.

Initiation. Sgt. Gene knocked on the door, which was answered by a woman who appeared to be in her mid-60s. She seemed distressed, perhaps from the events of the evening. "Hello Mrs. Dunham," said Sgt. Gene, "Is Jesse home?" The woman said he was in his bedroom, she'd get him, and invited us to come in. The sergeant thanked her and deliberately and thoroughly wiped his feet on the welcome mat. After doing so, he turned to us and asked that we do the same. Upon entering the home, we were quickly engulfed by a thick blue haze of cigarette smoke. Jesse appeared from the kitchen/dining area. A short white male in his mid-30s, blonde hair, wearing a soiled T-shirt and cutoff jean shorts, tattoos on his forearms and hands, and dirty bare feet. He sat on the couch, smoking and fidgety. I could see his dilated pupils. "Hi Jesse, I'm here because your neighbor said you were causing some trouble a little earlier," said Sgt. Gene. At that point Jesse nearly jumped off the couch, raising his voice stating that the neighbor was a liar and that she was harassing him. But before he could finish his tirade, Sgt. Gene held out the palm of his hand (signaling Jesse to stop) and said, "Jesse, I have plenty of time to hear your side of the story. Right now, I'm just letting you know why I am here. Okay?" Jesse nodded his head in agreement, sat back on the couch, took a drag from his smoke, and gazed off into the distance. Sgt. Gene continued to frame the situation as he currently understood it.

Framing. "Your neighbor told me that you were outside earlier, making a bunch of noise, and when she asked you to keep it down or she'd call the police, you threatened to kill her dog," Sgt. Gene calmly explained. Jesse stayed seated, struggling to stay quiet. He continued, "I know you've had issues with your neighbor before, because I've been out here a few times. Can you tell me what happened tonight?" Jesse responded, "I was working on my car, listening to the radio, minding my own business, and that bitch came out and told me to turn it off or she'd have me fuckin' arrested again."

"Did you threaten to kill her dog?," asked Sgt. Gene. "No!," said Jesse. "What did you say about the dog?," Sgt. Gene asked. "When she opened the door to yell at me, that stupid little mutt ran out and was barking at me. I told her that he better not shit in my yard again or I'd boot his ass," Jesse replied in a self-righteous tone. For the next several minutes, the two men engaged in conversation ranging from their mutual love of dogs and other animals, to treating neighbors like we want them to treat us, and how well Jesse gets along with some of the other neighbors. This conversation was interrupted periodically by laughter, questions directed toward Jesse's parents, and other things unrelated to the neighbor's complaint. "Okay Jesse,"

Sgt. Gene said, "The way that I see it, the neighbor and you don't really care for one another. She doesn't like your loud music and you don't like her dog doing his business in your yard. Is that fair?" "Ya," Jesse replied.

Resolution. "So, what I think should happen from now on," Sgt. Gene continued, "is for you to keep your music at a reasonable level when you are outside and she needs to control where Fido poops." Laughing under his breath, Jesse responded, "That works." "If I go over and talk to her and she agrees, will you promise to keep your music down next time?," asked Sgt. Gene. He continued, "You know, if it bothers her, it probably bothers your other neighbors, and you don't have any issues with them." "Ya, I can do it," Jesse said while nodding his head in agreement. "Well, that makes me happy," replied Sgt. Gene. Taking two steps toward Jesse and extending his hand, Sgt. Gene said, "Let's shake on it." Jesse somewhat reluctantly shook hands. Holding Jesse's hand, Sgt. Gene looked Jesse in the eyes and said, "Now I have your word, as a man, that this kind of thing won't happen again, especially not tonight. Am I right?" "Ya, you have my word," replied Jesse.

Completion. Jesse stood up from the couch, told his parent he was going to watch television in his room, and left the room quietly. Upon exiting the trailer, Sgt. Gene wished Jesse's parents a good night and said he was going back to talk to the neighbor. Sgt. Gene knocked on the neighbor's door. He said he talked to Jesse and that there shouldn't be any more trouble for the rest of the night, but that if there was to please call the police and they'll come out again. As he was walking away, Sgt. Gene turned around and said, "One more thing, could you please make sure your dog doesn't do his business in their grass?" "Sure thing," replied the neighbor.

Back at the parked squad cars, I asked Sgt. Gene if he always took as much time when dealing with such situations. "Not always," he responded smiling, "but it's Friday night and it's about to get busy. I really don't want to come out here again and arrest Jesse. My time is better spent out on the road handling calls." On that note, we shook hands and went our separate ways into the night.

Synopsis of encounter. This section highlights some of the ways Sgt. Gene worked elements of procedural justice into this particular call. In terms of participation opportunity, Sgt. Gene was interrupted by Jesse, who was eager to tell his side of the story. Adhering to the elements of procedural justice doesn't mean that officers let people walk all over them verbally—rather, they provide opportunity to speak when appropriate as encounters unfold. After gently cutting Jesse off, Sgt. Gene explained that he wanted to hear Jesse's side, but he first wanted to explain the reason for his visit that evening. Though agitated, this explanation seemed to satisfy Jesse. And, later in the encounter, Jesse got his opportunity to tell his version of what happened.

Sgt. Gene successfully demonstrated quality decision making by telling Jesse the information he had. And, after collecting Jesse's side of the story, he clearly communicated his understanding of the problem and what he believed was the appropriate course of action. Though reluctant, Jesse agreed with the sergeant. In this particular encounter, Sgt. Gene explained his motives as he communicated his decision—that is, the resolution was in the best interest of the entire trailer court, especially those residents who did not have problems with Jesse. The resolution was not simply an exercise in placating the neighbor at Jesse's expense but rather a solution that was in everybody's interest. The neighbor lady no longer had to listen to Jesse's music; her dog now defecates somewhere more appropriate; and the rest of the trailer park inhabitants benefit from no more rumpus.

The element of respect was probably the most obvious characteristic of the encounter between the sergeant and Jesse. Sgt. Gene was very respectful to the Dunham family and their home. For example, he made a point of wiping his feet and insisting we do likewise. He thanked Mrs. Dunham on several occasions, such as after she invited us in and on our way out. When making requests, Sgt. Gene made a habit of using what many refer as "the good word" (i.e., "please"). Importantly, the sergeant avoided condescending, patronizing, or disrespectful behavior. Overall, Sgt. Gene hit all four elements of procedural justice. According to the process-based model, the odds were pretty good that Jesse would follow the sergeant's directive and call it a night.

■ Research Evidence

Anecdotes like the one involving Sgt. Gene and Jesse are helpful to convey how theoretical concepts can be applied in practice. And for many observers, they can serve as powerful lessons. However, social scientists generally view anecdotal evidence as weak. In place of anecdotes, social scientists interested in criminal justice policy and practice use systematic research to guide their recommendations. What follows is a cross section of research that tests the key hypotheses from the process-based model. Care was taken to select studies using different methodologies because no one approach is perfect. In other words, all methodologies have strengths *and* weaknesses. But if we observe the same thing across studies using different research designs, then confidence in the findings increases.

The Classic Chicago Study

Much of the interest in the application of procedural justice to policing has developed over a thirty year period, but the exact origins of this widespread interest are rarely discussed. One early and influential source was Tom Tyler's Chicago study that was featured in his 1990 book, *Why People Obey the Law.*[6] It was this book that outlined the major components of the process-based model, discussed the application of the model to the criminal justice setting, and provided an early test of the hypotheses of interest. To do so, Tyler used data from telephone interviews that were conducted with adults living in Chicago. The results confirmed Tyler's expectations. Simply put, participants who reported more favorable procedural justice judgments toward criminal justice authorities (the police and courts) perceived such authorities as more legitimate. Importantly, Tyler also found that individuals who viewed legal authorities more positively in terms of legitimacy were more likely to obey the law. Needless to say, Tyler's seminal work spurred a lot of research activity on the influence of procedural justice and legitimacy.[7] Much of it was geared toward improving upon Tyler's early effort.

Though highly influential, Tyler's research was not beyond criticism. For some, the use of a random, general population sample that included individuals with and without recent contact with legal authorities was a cause for concern. If people had not had contact with the courts and the police, then what were they basing their procedural justice judgments on? Another concern was lumping together the evaluations of the courts and the police. Those critical of this methodological maneuver pointed out that these two legal institutions are very different and may be judged accordingly. Lumping information for both together into a single measure may mask important differences. Others expressed concern with Tyler's compliance measure, noting that some of the legal violations he used—traffic violations, parking violations, littering, and shoplifting—were minor offenses. What about more serious offenses, like assault and grand larceny? Finally, it is also the case that many of Tyler's results were generated using cross-sectional data—information collected at a single time period. While such data are often used to test correlational relationships (i.e., that two things might be related to one another), they are not well-suited for testing causal hypotheses (i.e., that one thing actually causes another). Therefore, it is impossible to determine from much of Tyler's work whether people who committed less crime simply viewed the police more favorably and not the other way around.

Evidence from Experimental Vignettes

Another approach to studying the influence procedural justice has on how people view and act toward legal authorities involves the use of experimental vignettes. This methodology involves the use of hypothetical scenarios that are presented to study participants to elicit judgments about the situations. Importantly, key theoretical elements of these scenarios are systematically manipulated. These experimental conditions are then assessed to see whether they impact the variable being tested.[8]

The number of vignette-based studies evaluating the influence of procedurally-just applications of authority is growing.[9] One recent study, conducted by a team of researchers at the School of Criminology and Criminal Justice (SCCJ) at Arizona State University (ASU), used experimental vignettes to determine whether procedural injustice in a policing context influenced whether students would cooperate with the police.[10] The study of 594 students looked at two different hypothetical scenarios—noise complaint and traffic encounter—that students could relate to. Researchers manipulated two conditions. The first was how the police officer on the scene behaved. For half of the sample, the police officer was condescending, very judgmental, asked rhetorical questions, and used profanity (the "procedural injustice" stimulus). The other half received scenarios where the police officer was very professional, polite, and service oriented (the control condition). The second condition focused on the outcome of the encounter. It has been argued that procedurally-just treatment is more important when it comes to cooperating with the police in the future than the actual outcome of the police-citizen encounter—such as whether the police issue a citation.[11] So, the second experimental condition involved the police officer issuing the student a citation (no citation was the control condition). The results from the study were clear: students who received the procedural injustice stimulus were not only far more negative in their evaluative judgments of the police officer's behavior, but they were also more likely to report that they would not follow the officer's directives or accept the officer's decision. As expected, the impact of the procedural injustice stimuli was often stronger than whether a ticket was issued.

Although experimental vignette research certainly has strengths relative to other social science methodologies, it has limitations too. One of the criticisms that is frequently advanced is that such research, like all experimental research, is artificial. The situations presented to study participants are contrived and may not be realistic or easy to imagine. Another concern is that many of these studies use university-based samples. So, while we may feel confident that college students react negatively to perceived police mistreatment, whether similar effects would be observed in other populations remains an open question. Finally, and importantly, experimental vignettes capture "behavioral intentions"—participants report what they think they would do if they found themselves in a particular situation. Some people feel that, although such intentions and actual behavior are related, they are not the same thing. Accordingly, the results from experimental vignettes, while suggestive, do not provide conclusive evidence.

Longitudinal Research with Serious Offenders

It is certainly the case that much of the research investigating the utility of procedural justice has used samples drawn from the general public and college students. Naysayers and cynics point out that of course the process-based model would appear to hold true for these largely law-abiding groups. But does procedural justice produce positive results among those who come into contact with the police—those individuals who are criminally active? This is a fair question. Another recent study conducted at the SCCJ at ASU sheds light on this matter. Researchers tested the process-based model using data from the Pathways to Desistance study, which has conducted over 20,000 interviews with 1,354 "serious adolescent offenders" in Phoenix, Arizona and Philadelphia, Pennsylvania.[12] Such interviews were conducted over 11 different time periods to investigate how participants transitioned out of crime.[13] This very important study included procedural justice items for both the police and the courts. So, the structure of the data allowed for an assessment of procedural justice judgments of the police on legitimacy and self-reported offending over time. Indeed, using these data allowed researchers to investigate whether procedural justice judgments, measured at various time periods, influence legitimacy perceptions and criminal activity among individuals who are involved in the criminal justice system.

Using very powerful multivariate, longitudinal statistical modeling techniques, researchers found that procedural justice judgments were susceptible to change over time. In other words, among the serious offenders who made up the sample, procedural justice judgments fluctuated—improving for some, getting worse for others. But what was more interesting was that these judgments also influenced legitimacy. Individuals who judged their recent interactions with legal authorities more favorably in terms of procedural justice were also more likely to view such authorities as legitimate. Interestingly, secondhand judgments of legal authorities, such as stories of the police told to participants by friends, also influenced legitimacy perceptions. Such perceptions, the authors found, were inversely related to criminal offending. In other words, as legitimacy perceptions of legal authorities improve, involvement in crime decreased. These findings support the process-based model.

This longitudinal study was able to address many of the perceived shortcomings that characterized previous procedural justice studies. First, the study was longitudinal, so many of the unattractive qualities of cross-sectional designs were avoided. So, we are able to say with more certainty that procedural justice judgments result in positive outcomes that are of interest to legal authorities. In addition, the Pathways to Desistance study contains adolescents who were adjudicated mostly for felonies. This is a crowd that tends to be cynical about the law and legal institutions and about the motivations of legal authorities. One might expect these individuals to be immune to the effects of procedurally-just treatment. The good news for police and court officials is that this does not appear to be the case. Finally, the types of criminal offending included in this study are far more serious than those used by others.[14] For example, among the 24 different types of legal violations included in the Pathway to Desistance study, some reflect relatively minor offenses (e.g., shoplifting and vandalism), but more serious crimes are also included too (e.g., carjacking, gun violence, and sexual assault). Arguably, this measure of criminal activity provides a more complete assessment. Despite these improvements, this study also has limitations. There is no such thing as a perfect (or flawless) study. For example, the study focused on adolescents and young adults. Accordingly, it fails to shed light on the influence of procedural justice at other stages of the life course, such as childhood and late adulthood. At the end of the day, to best understand the value of procedural justice when it comes to policing, we must weigh the existing evidence—a task to which we now turn.

Weighing the Evidence

When considering the weight of the research evidence in support of policing consistent with the concept of procedural justice, it is helpful to consider the nature of the existing studies. For example, not only has research been conducted using national samples and from local jurisdictions throughout the United States but studies have also been conducted around the world, often in very interesting cultural settings. The extent to which the research supports the process-based model would indicate that the relationships hold across different settings. What does the research show? Research testing the impact of procedural justice in a policing context and confirming a positive impact has been conducted in Australia,[15] China,[16] England,[17] Jamaica,[18] Slovenia,[19] Sweden,[20] Trinidad and Tobago,[21] and elsewhere. To be clear, the relationship between police legitimacy and general compliance in these studies is not always as hypothesized—that part of the process-based model seems to be more culturally variable. However, when it comes to procedural justice, it is clear that fair treatment pays dividends to the police worldwide.

Yet another way to gauge the merit of any particular theory is to look at the different populations that have been used to test the theory. Much like the different cultural settings, the influence of procedural justice judgements on preferred outcomes has been demonstrated using a variety of samples, including school children[22], college students[23], general population[24], community corrections[25], and incarcerated samples.[26] Clearly other groups, such as the elderly, immigrants, and members of the LGBTQ+ community, should also be sampled and included in procedural justice studies to better determine the generality of the positive effect. Nevertheless, the available evidence is encouraging in that procedurally-just treatment by the police has a favorable influence across different groups.

When weighing the empirical evidence, it is also important to consider research generated from systematic social observation (SSO). This approach involves the collection of detailed accounts of how transactions between police officers and individuals unfold, as recorded by trained observers following a predetermined protocol.[27] Arguably, this methodological approach better captures objective accounts of police behavior than do survey-based studies. SSO studies provide support for the process-based model. Early research focused on the different elements of procedural justice. For example, researchers have found that citizens who encountered police officers who acted disrespectfully toward them (e.g., made a derogatory remark) were less likely to comply with police directives (e.g., cease illegal behavior).[28] More recently, social scientists have begun creating procedural justice scales that capture different important elements. One such study reports that higher levels of observed procedural justice during police encounters was significantly related to behavioral expression of satisfaction with the police by individuals involved in the encounters.[29] Research in this area has also started to investigate the situations under which police officers are less likely to use procedural justice in their daily encounters.[30] But what is interesting is that this line of research is consistent with the pioneering observational studies conducted by Albert J. Reiss. In his now classic book, *The Police and the Public,* Reiss found that police officers whose demeanor was outwardly polite were much more likely to be treated in kind by citizens.[31] Interestingly, Reiss's research was conducted nearly two decades prior to Tyler's introduction of the procedural justice concept to the field of policing.[32]

The weight of the evidence is becoming increasingly clear: citizens' procedural justice judgments regarding legal authorities (including the police) are associated with many outcomes—perceptions of police legitimacy, calling the police to report a crime, and obeying the law—that help police officers fulfill their mission. This is not to say that knowledge gaps do not exist. Research that identifies the situational factors that nullify or elevate the power of procedural justice should be examined carefully. Nevertheless, the evidence in support of exercising police authority in a manner consistent with procedural justice principles is sizable, derived from a variety of research methodologies, and continually growing. Put differently, if the focus of this chapter was on the evidence supporting an experimental drug and whether the science indicated it was successful at helping the sick, nearly everyone familiar with the evidence would enthusiastically advocate for approval from the Food and Drug Administration.

■ Solutions

Many social scientists are uncomfortable using the term "solution" because it implies that a single factor can solve a problem. Rarely are problems that simple and straightforward, especially when dealing with social phenomenon. Police reform clearly falls into this category. Municipal police departments are complex organizations with multiple goals, turbulent and changing environments, bureaucratic red tape, a division of labor, a chain of command, specialization, and the like. Therefore, any so-called solution will at best focus on one aspect of police reform and should be viewed as one piece of a much larger puzzle. With that said, institutionalizing procedural justice so that police encounters with the public involve the application of procedural justice principles is currently the most promising way to enhance the legitimacy of police in the eyes of the community and to promote general compliance. Despite its promise, however, the successful institutionalization of procedural justice in police departments will inevitably involve many challenges—four of which include finding effective procedural justice training curricula, the selection of personnel who will faithfully apply the principles, convincing police officers that procedurally just tactics do not jeopardize officer safety, and motivating command staff to practice procedural justice inside the police bureaucracy.

The Challenge of Training and Evaluation

Police academy and in-service training curricula that is predicated upon the utility and application of procedural justice principles in everyday police encounters with the public is currently being developed and evaluated. One evaluation study that focused on a training program to improve police-community relations in Chicago found that officers who received training on procedural justice in the academy and later participated in workshops were far more supportive of applying procedural justice principles (e.g., demonstrating neutrality and treating citizens with respect) than officers who did not receive such training.[33] Although such studies are in short supply, the available evidence is encouraging.

The Challenge of Personnel Screening

While pitching the use of procedural justice to some officers will be like preaching to the choir, others may express resistance. Although convincing such officers of the usefulness of procedural justice may take time, it is worth the effort. Importantly, moving forward, police departments should consider screening candidates for their receptiveness to using procedural justice. For example, it is well-known that certain personality traits are likely not conducive to the regular practice of procedural justice, especially under stressful conditions. One such trait—low self-control—has been shown to be related with a host of behaviors that are inconsistent with procedural justice, such as quick-temperedness, public use of profanity, and violence.[34] The problem lies in the fact that self-control is fairly stable. Put simply, individuals who are deficient in their ability to control their behavior and emotions in adulthood are not likely to improve very much as they age. Accordingly, these individuals should be identified during the recruitment stage using scientifically-validated instruments and carefully evaluated for their ability to practice procedural justice on the streets.[35]

But even among the most disciplined individuals, depletion in self-control can happen under the right conditions. Some researchers think that self-control is a lot like a muscle.[36] That is, high levels of self-control are maintained with practice and doing what is required to ensure that it is available when needed. Put another way, the muscle model holds that for police officers to exercise self-control in stressful situations, they must train to do so regularly. This would entail periodic in-service training focusing on such demands. Second, the muscle model holds that factors such as getting enough sleep, regular exercise, following a healthy diet, and not consuming too much alcohol are vital if police officers are going to be able to successfully exercise high levels of self-control shift after shift, year after year, and so on.[37] To sum up, one important factor to ensure police officers are equipped to practice procedural justice is to take the necessary steps to also make certain their levels of self-control are not depleted.

The Challenge of Culture

Yet another potential challenge to institutionalizing procedural justice in police departments are attitudes, beliefs, and norms among officers that help make up the occupational culture of police. In contemporary police departments, it is unlikely that a monolithic police culture exists. However, aspects of cultural systems certainly can be identified in various occupations, such as physicians, professional athletes, academics, chefs, and the police. One cultural element that persists to this day in police departments is the belief that "officer safety" is priority number one. Put differently, police officers widely believe that the most important thing is to protect themselves and each other while on duty. Few observers immediately outside the police world would argue that this concern is not valid. Indeed, most citizens feel the same as the police. However, similar to academics at institutions of higher learning who employ encroachment on their "academic freedom" to resist organizational change, so too do the police use officer safety in attempts to discredit proposed reforms. Convincing skeptical police officers will entail knocking down strawman arguments regarding the use of procedural justice and directing them toward the evidence demonstrating its merits. While such a task will sometimes prove vexing, it's worth it over the long term.

The Challenge of Police Management

Organizational justice (see Trinkner and Tyler's chapter in this volume) complicates the issue. Police officers working in departments headed by leaders who recklessly exercise their authority, make arbitrary and capricious decisions, and are widely viewed as unfair will ultimately fail at institutionalizing procedural justice among the line staff. Indeed, a recent study conducted in Chicago found that police officers' judgements regarding how fairly they were treated by their supervisors (termed "internal procedural justice") was positively correlated with their views on the utility of procedural justice (termed "external procedural justice").[38] In short, police leaders working to institutionalize procedural justice need also commit to doing so in their managerial practice.

■ Next Steps

The time has come for police departments throughout the United States—north and south, east and west—to formally adopt and institutionalize everyday police practices consistent with the principles of procedural justice. Doing so is consistent with recent high-profile calls for reform. For example, The President's Task Force on 21st Century Policing concluded:

> Agencies should adopt procedural justice as the guiding principle for internal and external policies and practices to guide their interactions with rank and file officers and with the citizens they serve.[39]

Such calls are not only steeped in mountains of supportive scientific evidence but are also consistent with the roots of American policing. Sir Robert Peel, who was responsible for the establishment of the London Metropolitan Police Service in 1829 upon which early American forces were modeled, did not tolerate "rude answers to citizens' questions," "verbal abuse," and other "minor irritants" that could breed public contempt for the police. Police officers were expected to be "models of restraint and politeness" because doing so, he believed, would "win respect" of citizens.[40] So, as can be seen, the idea of fair, just, and evenhanded treatment has stood the test of time. Now is the time to institutionalize procedural justice, enhance police legitimacy, and promote general compliance.

A Postscript about Sgt. Gene

I ran into the sergeant the day following our encounter at the trailer court. I asked him if he saw Jesse again. "No, thankfully," he said, "we got busy last night. And as far as I know the trailer court had a peaceful evening." Before we parted ways, the sergeant said that the problem probably won't go away until Jesse got some help for his drug problem. With a firm handshake and a smile, Sgt. Gene said, "Good luck, professor." Looking at his watch with anticipation, he reminded me, "This time next month I'll be fishing." On that note, we parted ways. Though Sgt. Gene retired, his approach to handling encounters serves as a powerful example of procedural justice in action.

NOTES

[1] The term institutionalize refers to the process through which any particular practice becomes expected behavior in an organization.

[2] Tal Jonathan-Zamir, Stephen D. Mastrofski, and Shomron Moyal, "Measuring Procedural Justice in Police-Citizen Encounters," *Justice Quarterly* 32, no. 5 (2015): 845–871.

[3] Tom Tyler, "Procedural Justice, Legitimacy, and the Effective Rule of Law," *Crime and Justice: A Review of Research* 30 (2003): 283–357.

[4] See Tom R. Tyler, Phillip Atiba Goff, and Robert J. MacCoun, "The Impact of Psychological Science on Policing in the United States: Procedural Justice, Legitimacy, and Effective Law Enforcement, *Psychological Science in the Public Interest* 16, no. 3 (2015): 75–109.

[5] Tyler, "Procedural Justice, Legitimacy, and the Effective Rule of Law."

[6] Tom Tyler, *Why People Obey the Law* (New Haven, CT: Yale University Press, 1990).

[7] See Justice Tankebe, "Police Legitimacy," in *The Oxford Handbook on Police and Policing,* eds. Michael D. Reisig and Robert J. Kane (New York: Oxford University Press, 2014), 238–259.

[8] See Herman Aguinis and Kyle J. Bradley, "Best Practice Recommendations for Designing and Implementing Experimental Vignette Methodology Studies, *Organizational Research Methods* 17, no. 4 (2014): 351–371.

[9] See, for example, Edward R. Maguire, Belén B. Lowrey, and Devon Johnson, "Evaluating the Relative Impact of Positive and Negative Encounters with Police: A Randomized Experiment," *Journal of Experimental Criminology* 13, no. 3 (2016): 367–391.

[10] Michael Reisig, Ryan D. Mays, and Cody W. Telep, "The Effects of Procedural Injustice During Police–Citizen Encounters: A Factorial Vignette Study," *Journal of Experimental Criminology* 14, no. 1 (2018): 49–58.

[11] Tom R. Tyler and Yuen J. Huo, *Trust in the Law: Encouraging Public Cooperation with the Police and Courts* (New York: Russell Sage Foundation, 2002).

[12] Kimberly Kaiser and Michael Reisig, "Legal Socialization and Self-Reported Criminal Offending: The Role of Procedural Justice and Legal Orientations," *Journal of Quantitative Criminology* 35, no. 1 (2019): 135–154.

[13] For more detail about the study, visit www.pathwaysstudy.pitt.edu.

[14] See, for example, Tyler, *Why People Obey the Law.*

[15] Kristina Murphy, Ben Bradford, and Jonathan Jackson, "Motivating Compliance Behavior Among Offenders: Procedural Justice or Deterrence?" *Criminal Justice and Behavior* 43, no. 1 (2016): 102–118.

[16] Ivan Y. Sun, Yuning Wu, Rong Hu, and Ashley K. Farmer, "Procedural Justice, Legitimacy, and Public Cooperation with Police: Does Western Wisdom Hold in China?" *Journal of Research in Crime and Delinquency* 54, no. 4 (2017): 454–478.

[17] Jonathan Jackson, Ben Bradford, Mike Hough, Andy Myhill, Paul Quinton, Tom Tyler, "Why Do People Comply with the Law? Legitimacy and the Influence of Legal Institutions," *British Journal of Criminology* 52, no. 6 (2012): 1051–1071.

[18] Michael D. Reisig and Camille Lloyd, "Procedural Justice, Police Legitimacy, and Helping the Police Fight Crime: Results from a Survey of Jamaican Adolescents," *Police Quarterly* 12, no. 1 (2008): 42–62.

[19] Michael Reisig, Justice Tankebe, and Gorazd Meško, "Compliance with the Law in Slovenia: The Role of Procedural Justice and Police Legitimacy," *European Journal on Criminal Policy and Research* 20, no. 2 (2014): 250–276.

[20] Anjuli van damme, Lieven J. R. Pauwels, and Robert Svensson, "Why Do Swedes Cooperate with the Police? A SEM Analysis of Tyler's Procedural Justice Model," *European Journal on Criminal Policy and Research* 21, no. 1 (2015): 15–33.

[21] Tammy R. Kochel, Roger Parks, and Stephen D. Mastrofski, "Examining Police Effectiveness as a Precursor to Legitimacy and Cooperation with Police," *Justice Quarterly* 30, no. 5 (2013): 895–925.

[22] Jeffrey Fagan and Tom R. Tyler, "Legal Socialization of Children and Adolescents," *Social Justice Research* 18, no. 3 (2005): 217–242.

[23] Jacinta M. Gau, "The Convergent and Discriminant Validity of Procedural Justice and Police Legitimacy: An Empirical Test of Core Theoretical Propositions, *Journal of Criminal Justice* 39, no. 6 (2011): 489–498.

[24] Michael D. Reisig, Jason Bratton, and Marc G. Gertz, "The Construct Validity and Refinement of Process-Based Policing Measures," *Criminal Justice and Behavior* 34, no. 7 (2007), 1005–1028.

25 Brandy L. Blasko and Faye S. Taxman, "Are Supervision Practices Procedurally Fair? Development and Predictive Utility of a Procedural Justice Measure for Use in Community Corrections Settings," *Criminal Justice and Behavior* 45, no. 3 (2018): 402–420.

26 Karin A. Beijersbergen, Anja J. E. Dirkzwager, Veroni I. Eichelsheim, Peter H. Van der Laan, and Paul Nieuwbeerta, "Procedural Justice, Anger, and Prisoners' Misconduct: A Longitudinal Study," *Criminal Justice and Behavior* 42, no. 2 (2015): 196–218.

27 Robert E. Worden and Sarah J. McLean, "Systematic Social Observation of the Police," in *The Oxford Handbook on Police and Policing,* eds. Michael D. Reisig and Robert J. Kane (New York: Oxford University Press, 2014), 471–496.

28 Stephen D. Mastrofski, Jeffrey B. Snipes, and Anne E. Supina, "Compliance on Demand: The Public's Response to Specific Police Requests," *Journal of Research in Crime and Delinquency* 33, no. 3 (1996): 269–305.

29 Jonathan-Zamir, Mastrofski, and Moyal, "Measuring Procedural Justice in Police-Citizen Encounters."

30 See Stephen D. Mastrofski, Tal Jonathan-Zamir, Shomron Moyal, and James J. Willis, "Predicting Procedural Justice in Police-Citizen Encounters," *Criminal Justice and Behavior* 43, no. 1 (2016): 119–139.

31 Albert J. Reiss, *The Police and the Public* (New Haven, CT: Yale University Press, 1973).

32 Tyler, *Why People Obey the Law.*

33 Wesley G. Skogan, Maarten Van Craen, and Cari Hennessy, "Training Police for Procedural Justice," *Journal of Experimental Criminology* 11, no. 3 (2015): 319–334.

34 See, e.g., Denise De Ridder, Gerty Lensvelt-Mulders, Catrin Finkenauer, Marijn Stok, and Roy Baumeister, "Taking Stock of Self-Control: A Meta-Analysis of How Trait Self-Control Relates to a Wide Range of Behaviors," *Personality and Social Psychology Review* 16, no. 1 (2012): 76–99.

35 See June P. Tangney, Roy Baumeister, and Angie Luzio Boone, "High Self-Control Predicts Good Adjustment, Less Pathology, Better Grades, and Interpersonal Success," *Journal of Personality* 72, no. 2 (2004): 271–324.

36 Mark Muraven and Roy F. Baumeister, "Self-Regulation and Depletion of Limited Resources: Does Self-Control Resemble a Muscle?" *Psychological Bulletin* 126, no. 2 (2000): 247–259.

37 Matthew T. Gailliot, Roy F. Baumeister, C. Nathan DeWall, Jon K. Maner, E. Ashby Plant, Dianne M. Tice, Lauren E. Brewer, and Brandon J. Schmeichel, "Self-Control Relies on Glucose as a Limited Energy Source: Willpower is More than a Metaphor," *Journal of Personality and Social Psychology* 92, no. 2 (2007): 325–336.

38 Maarten Van Craen and Wesley G. Skogan, "Achieving Fairness in Policing: The Link between Internal and External Procedural Justice," *Police Quarterly* 20, no. 1 (2017): 3–23.

39 President's Task Force on 21st Century Policing, *Final Report of the President's Task Force on 21st Century Policing* (Washington, DC: Office of Community Oriented Policing Services, 2015), 1.

40 Wilbur R. Miller, *Cops and Bobbies: Police Authority in New York and London, 1830–1890* (Chicago: University of Chicago Press, 1977), 38.

3

Response Essay

Chief Theron Bowman (Ret.)
Arlington, Texas Police Department

Michael D. Reisig presents an interesting take on the complexities of procedural justice in action. His insights into the elements of procedural justice and their application in today's world are much needed, and this chapter achieves the worthy tasks of not only appropriately defining procedural justice and applying it in the practical world of policing but also providing some interesting solutions for policing organizations to consider. Although this response outlines some additional considerations, the chapter clearly delineates the complexity and challenges of procedural justice. Reisig's empathy for the real-world implications of the application of procedural justice is underscored by the way he begins his chapter, with a retelling of his personal experience in a Midwestern police department—a sharp way to set the stage. This gives the reader a vivid example of an everyday law enforcement activity, the call for service, in which procedural justice principles and practices can be applied. This response outlines some additional considerations.

Endorse the Standard of Transparency

The chapter's background section clearly and concisely lays out what procedural justice is, and Reisig's outline of the four elements of the working definition is well thought out and well articulated. However, he only implicitly addresses the concept of "transparency" in the second element, "decision neutrality." He points to the role of transparency when he notes that the police should "explain their decisions to all affected parties" and "communicate a rational decision based on the available information" to those parties. Rather than just announcing their decisions, however, the police should strive to convey the bases for those decisions so that affected parties can clearly see how the police reached their conclusions.

Transparency is an important component of procedural justice. When considering police-citizen interactions, people who view the police as legitimate are more likely to defer to police decisions. The public confers legitimacy only on those whom they believe are acting in procedurally just ways, as manifested through transparency in police-citizen interactions. People generally believe that when officers transparently explain their decisions, such as telling someone why they were stopped or what department policy states and why, they are acting in a neutral and unbiased way and are sincerely trying to be responsive. When this occurs, people typically exhibit lower levels of anger, and the risk of escalation is reduced. Thus, acceptance of police decisions by the public becomes more voluntary over time, improving both citizens' attitudes toward the police and officer safety.

But there's more to transparency than these immediate police-citizen interactions. As recommended in the Final Report of the President's Task Force on 21st Century Policing, police agencies should "embrace a culture of transparency" and "make all department policies available for public review." They should also "regularly post on the department's website information about stops, summonses, arrests, reported crime, and other law enforcement data aggregated by demographics." Allowing the public viewing access to department policies and aggregate data will encourage a perception of legitimacy and fairness, supporting officers' efforts at transparency as they explain to the public what their department's policies state and the rationale for their decisions during police-citizen interactions. Ultimately, people see fairness and transparency as evidence of trustworthiness and integrity.

■ Consider Both Internal and External Procedural Justice

Though the chapter focuses on external procedural justice, its "Solutions" section does mention some internal procedural justice remedies. Readers should keep in mind that internal procedural justice is as important as external procedural justice, and the two are complexly intertwined. As you might expect, it is not very effective to expect officers to treat people fairly on the street if they do not experience this same fair treatment within their own departments. Giving officers a voice in their departments, explaining department policies and decisions, treating other officers with respect, and having department leadership clearly display integrity and trustworthiness, as shown by their responsiveness to officer concerns, are all important components of internal procedural justice. For a fuller discussion of these issues, see chapter 10.

■ Incorporate Accountability, Oversight, Policies, and Procedures into Procedural Justice Standards

The "Solutions" section of the chapter provides a variety of interesting offerings. The emphasis on training is correct and relevant to today's concerns in policing organizations. Including the issues of accountability, oversight, policies, and procedures that incorporate the tenets of procedural justice would be a valuable addition to this set of solutions. As just discussed, policies, procedures, and decision-making processes inside the department must be perceived as fair and equitable. When officers feel they are being treated fairly—when they benefit from internal procedural justice—they are more likely to treat the public fairly. In procedurally just agencies, both sworn officers and professional staff members participate in transparent planning and policy-making efforts.

Regarding issues of accountability and oversight in department policies and procedures, transparency in a formal disciplinary process is a core component of procedural justice. This ensures that sanctions are applied fairly and consistently and that clear parameters are defined for the application of discipline. These parameters may consist of a disciplinary matrix or guidelines so that department members are aware of exactly what behaviors result in what disciplinary sanctions. This discipline should be progressive and directed more toward improving behavior than punishing misdeeds. Using a disciplinary matrix or guidelines also ensures consistency and fairness in applying disciplinary sanctions and enhances adherence to internal procedural justice practices. Finally, a disciplinary policy should describe the overall program (including the roles and responsibilities for each rank), should be appropriately disseminated, and should be accompanied by training for all department members (including those supervisors and managers responsible for compliance with disciplinary procedures).

Departments should also consider supporting procedural justice by adopting an early intervention system or process to hold officers and the department accountable. An early intervention system is a supervisory risk management tool that identifies at-risk officers for intervention based on thresholds of officer activities and can also be used as a professional development and mentoring tool. Addressing issues early—before they develop into more serious incidents—is a key component of this process. In addition, early intervention systems can assist supervisors in ensuring officer safety and wellness through monitoring and improving individual officers' behavior and health. Rather than feeding into a disciplinary pipeline, these early intervention systems can assist departments in developing procedurally just solutions, such as revising policies when appropriate, providing additional training to at-risk officers, improving the overall training curriculum, increasing officer health and wellness, and allowing officers a voice in their own career progress. Early intervention can be a valuable tool to increase agency accountability and transparency and can help employees meet the agency's values and mission statement, including the tenets of procedural justice.

Another option for increasing accountability and oversight of policies and procedures is implementing a regular audit or review process that assesses departmental compliance with policies and procedures. This process results in reports that can be disseminated across the entire department, complete with findings and recommendations that provide opportunities to improve deficient areas. In accordance with the tenets of procedural justice, having such transparency and accountability in this audit process and allowing officers the opportunity for improvement bolster the department's interest in integrity and trustworthiness.

■ Pay Attention to the Role of Diversity in Promoting Procedural Justice

With respect to the challenges of training, the chapter skips an initial step that should occur prior to implementing any training or evaluation process: a focus on diversity recruitment. The racial and gender makeup of a department may not directly dictate its relationship with a community, but the modern era of policing requires that departments take proactive measures to mirror the community they serve. To effectively navigate complex societal issues such as domestic violence, poverty, mental illness, political alienation, and general distrust of the government and police, especially by various minorities and ethnic groups, police must engage the entire community. This effort should include opening employment pipelines into those communities that will eventually create informal ambassadors who can serve as liaisons between the community and the police.

■ Clarify the Pathways for Modifying Attitudes, Beliefs, and Norms to Promote Procedural Justice

The chapter's discussion of the attitudes, beliefs, and norms among officers is well placed, as these are important factors in procedural justice. The discussion of officer safety is particularly relevant in the national policing conversation. As stated, "convincing police officers . . . will entail knocking down strawman arguments regarding the use of procedural justice," but it would be useful to have more specific details about how this could be accomplished. For example, we need to change officers' mind-sets from asking "Can I do this?" to "Should I do this?" This shift might be accomplished through education about the virtuous cycle whereby a perception that officers are treating members of the public fairly and equitably increases police legitimacy, which itself leads to increased public compliance and cooperation, which, over time, gradually reduces both complaints and crime. In this way, procedural justice encourages and strengthens community policing. With respect to officer safety, health and wellness, and appropriate conduct, further suggestions include encouraging departments to adopt officer safety and wellness programs as well as early intervention systems, both of which can assist in the promotion of tenets of internal and external procedural justice regarding managing officer safety, at-risk behavior, and well-being.

■ Dive Deeper into Peel's Principles

The inclusion of Peelian principles, which urge that "rude answers to questions," "verbal abuse," or other "minor irritants" should never be permitted, reminds us that procedural justice is actually well established in American history. Sir Robert Peel, through his principles, pointed the way toward general compliance—but a few additional core principles would add value. First, the ability of the police to perform their duties depends upon public approval of police existence, actions, and behaviors. In that same vein, the ability of the police to secure the willing cooperation of the public in voluntary compliance with the law depends upon their ability to secure and maintain public respect. Finally, the ability of the police to serve and preserve public favor depends upon constantly demonstrating their absolutely impartial service to the law. These additional principles also support officer safety and wellness, as Peel correctly noted that the degree of public cooperation that can be secured reduces, in proportion, the necessity for the use of physical force and compulsion in achieving police objectives. Lastly, Peel's belief that "the absence of crime and disorder, not the visible evidence of police action in dealing with them, was the measure of police efficiency" supports Reisig's argument regarding trustworthy motives leading to "enhanced police legitimacy and community engagement in crime prevention."

Overall, the chapter on institutionalizing procedural justice, enhancing police legitimacy, and promoting general compliance is well thought out, articulated clearly, and supported by both research and practical definitions, theoretical framework, and application. This topic is very relevant in today's national conversation on police legitimacy, and the need for procedural justice could not be any timelier. The chapter covers many of the components of procedural justice in the definitions and research as well as varied solutions that are both much needed and suitably challenging. Reisig should be commended for his work and the scholarly research that clearly established foundational support for this worthy contemporary chapter.

4

Reduce Use of Force

William Terrill
Arizona State University

Background

The 2014 Michael Brown shooting in Ferguson, Missouri, began a series of police use-of-force incidents across the United States, resulting in civil unrest not witnessed since the civil rights protests of the 1960s.[1] These events demonstrate how police use-of-force incidents can spark outcry among groups and communities that believe officers are using overly coercive tactics. While one could debate the relative level of discourse and harm done in the two time periods, it is clear that police-community relations are at the forefront once again—bolstered by the role that technology (e.g., smartphones and body-worn cameras) plays in capturing use-of-force interactions. In fact, the force encounter is perhaps the most important type of police-citizen interaction when it comes to assessing the legitimacy of the police role.

Nonetheless, while public concern over perceived police mistreatment of citizens is well founded in some cases, such events are not representative of day-to-day interactions. The vast majority of encounters between the police and the public do not involve the overt use of physical or deadly force.[2] Moreover, when officers do use coercion, they often rely on less severe forms of force than what law and organizational policy would permit based on the circumstances of the encounter.[3] Thus, we should be cautious not to overestimate media depictions of force incidents.

Much of the content in this chapter has already been covered in previous writings (i.e., published in various articles, chapters, and books), but the present format offers the opportunity to bring many of relevant aspects of this prior work together into one digestible summary. Within this context, the chapter begins with a review of the literature and research evidence on police use of force, starting with difficult definitional challenges and assessing how often the police resort to forceful tactics. The chapter is then divided into four subsections intended to help police practitioners think through the issues from an operational perspective. Those subsections focus on (1) recruitment strategies, (2) organizational policy and training, (3) assignment practices, and (4) tracking and assessing force and cultural patterns. The chapter concludes with a snapshot of seven specific recommendations drawn from these areas of focus.

■ Research Evidence

Definitional Challenges

It is not easy to define the level of force that is appropriate in a situation, a topic that has been discussed for years.[4] Many have struggled with a variety of terms, including "excessive use of force," "use of excessive force," "brutality," "unauthorized force," "wrongful force," "unjustified force," "misuse of force," and "unnecessary force." While these words and phrases are interchangeable to some, others have noted important distinctions. For example, the use of excessive force can be defined as the use of more force than needed to gain compliance in any given incident, while excessive use of force may be defined as resorting to force across too many incidents.[5] Fyfe distinguishes between "brutality" (a willful and knowingly wrongful use of force) and "unnecessary force" (force used by well-meaning officers who are ill-equipped to handle certain incidents).[6] Worden also distinguishes between different types of force: he defines "excessive force" as force that is more than required to subdue a citizen and "unnecessary force" as that which precedes a citizen's resistance or continues after the cessation of that resistance.[7]

Others believe that emphasizing inappropriate force in a traditional sense is an inadequate approach to the issue in general. Klockars argued that most police agencies gauge officer use of force using minimum standards.[8] That is, use of force is legitimate when it does not present a criminal violation, a civil liability, or an embarrassment to the department. These standards are necessary, but are they sufficient? Klockars observed, "We would not find the behavior of a physician, lawyer, engineer, teacher, or any other professional acceptable merely because it was not criminal, civilly liable, or scandalous, and it is preposterous that we continue to do so for police."[9] He called for broadening the focus of excessive force to include "the use of more force than a highly skilled police officer would find necessary to use in [a] particular situation."[10] Although requiring that all officers be "highly skilled" would be a tall order—there are, after all, average employees in every occupation—his general point is well taken. Furthermore, in relation to police use of force, there has been an awareness dating back to Bittner that "the skill of policing consists in finding ways to *avoid its use*."[11]

Frequency of Force

So how often do police officers rely on forceful tactics as part of their everyday duties? Although media reports could easily lead one to believe that the police routinely use force in their interactions with the public, the available evidence generally indicates that the frequency of force is relatively low, with the caveat that this conclusion depends on how force is defined and what research methodology is used. Many police agencies only document force that involves hands-on physical tactics in excess of simple restraint or the use of a weapon (e.g., OC spray, TASER, baton, or firearm).[12] Hence, cases where officers only physically restrain citizens (e.g., by using a firm grip or handcuffing) are not counted as involving force. Using the definition applied by most police agencies, then, prior research has found that while the exact percentage varies from city to city, officers generally use force in less than 5 percent of all police-citizen encounters[13] and less than 20 percent of arrests.[14]

Despite studies indicating that officers do not often rely on force, citizens often report more negative views.[15] A study conducted by the U.S. Bureau of Justice Statistics revealed that about 3 percent of the public experienced nonfatal threat or use of force during the most recent contact with police; about 48% felt that it was excessive. Of the less than 1 percent of citizens who experienced threatened force, 84 percent believed that the force used was excessive in some manner.[16] Nor are these negative perceptions restricted to citizens with personal experience involving police force. The media, through overexposure of isolated forceful incidents or failure to show the entire sequence of events from start to finish, can also negatively affect public confidence in the police, albeit indirectly.[17] Such depictions can lead citizens to conclude that the police are not behaving appropriately in exercising their coercive authority, even when the officer may have been operating within all appropriate legal and organizational parameters. Nonetheless, citizen views regarding police use of force are important for at least two reasons. First, the general citizenry determines the overall legitimacy of the police occupation as a whole. Second, citizens serve as jurors that often sit in judgment of the police, assessing the appropriate legal threshold for their use of force.

Moving Forward Within the Context of Prior Research

The remainder of the chapter focuses on practices and policies that police organizations should consider in helping to reduce the use of excessive or inappropriate force, in the context of what is known (or not) from an empirical standpoint. As highlighted above, while the police do not necessarily rely on forceful means in most encounters, when they do, citizens often believe it to be improper—and it certainly is at times. In my view, however, such force most often falls more in line with Fyfe's description of "unnecessary force"—force used by well-meaning officers ill-equipped to handle various incidents.[18] Fortunately, there are strategies that organizational leaders can draw on to better equip their officers and thus decrease their use of unnecessary force.

1. Recruitment strategies. Given the incredibly broad mandate of the police and the wide range of situations they encounter, it can be difficult to identify particular attributes that characterize good policing.[19] Thus, the default position often focuses on the law enforcement role (via arrest) as the primary aspect of the job. Yet, for over fifty years, research has consistently shown that police work is much more about social work and maintaining order than anything else.[20] The belief that policing primarily involves enforcement of laws is simply a myth. For example, Whitaker's analysis of the Police Services Study data, collected across 24 jurisdictions in the 1970s, revealed that among the thousands of encounters that police had with the public, only 38 percent were related to crime.[21] Going back even further, Reiss examined data collected in Boston, Chicago, and Washington, D.C., during the 1960s for the President's Commission on Law Enforcement and Administration of Justice and noted that the typical tour of duty failed to involve a single arrest.[22] Studies throughout the 1990s and 2000s in numerous cities, including Cincinnati, Flint, Indianapolis, and St. Petersburg, confirm that officers are more apt to spend time on non-law enforcement activities than on traditional law enforcement.[23] Finally, research shows that even when officers are dealing with clear-cut crimes where there is probable cause to make an arrest, non-arrest is often the outcome.[24]

Unfortunately, the media (entertainment and news), the general public, and police institutions themselves often highlight the crime-fighting aspects of policing. Students who aspire to become police officers often mistakenly buy into the crime-fighting myth, whereby the early formation of police culture begins to take root. Police culture comprises the attitudes, values, and norms that are transmitted and shared among groups of law enforcement professionals in an effort to collectively cope with their occupational (i.e., street-level interactions with citizens) and organizational (i.e., departmental interactions with supervisors) work environments.[25] In policing, the seeds of this culture are primarily found in views toward danger and coercive authority, which are deemed to be best handled by being suspicious and distrustful[26] and remaining one up on (or in control of) citizens at all times.[27] This approach has fostered the growing characterization that the police have come to see themselves more as "warriors" than as "guardians."[28]

One way to begin chipping away at this unfortunate state of affairs is for police organizations to begin dispelling the crime-fighting myth during the recruitment process. First, organizations can forthrightly explain to candidates that the exciting crime-fighting style of policing most often seen on television is more the exception than the norm. Second, agencies can work with local media outlets to properly establish the context of everyday policing, encouraging news stories that go beyond standard crime fighting. Third, recruitment practices should center on seeking to identify officers and trainees who wish to be part of an occupation where the majority of the work does not involve chasing and catching the "bad guy." Agencies should solicit applicants who embrace the "softer" (and frankly less glamorous) aspects of policing.[29] Here, the emphasis is on providing "service" to citizens, which goes beyond the commonly understood law enforcement function.

Finally, while there is as yet little hard empirical evidence demonstrating a connection with reduced use of force,[30] organizations should actively recruit for diversity of race, ethnicity, gender, age, and educational level. This recommendation dates all the way back to the 1967 President's Commission report (restated in the 2015 President's Task Force report) that stated diversity would invariably bring a variety of backgrounds, viewpoints, and experiences to the occupation.[31]

2. Organizational policy and training. The Supreme Court set the legal standard for determining the appropriateness of police use of force in *Graham v. Connor*,[32] holding that force must be judged under an "objectively reasonable" standard.[33] Among other specifications, the Court noted that force should be judged "from the perspective of a reasonable officer on the scene, rather than with the 20/20 vision of hindsight" and "in light of the facts and circumstances confronting [the police], without regard to their underlying intent or motivation."[34] Yet there is still no magic formula as to what may, and what may not, constitute objectively reasonable force. Hence, from an organizational perspective, police departments must rely heavily on policy directives and training to establish parameters for the application of force and to offer more explicit direction to officers about what may be considered appropriate force.

There is perhaps no greater example of the influence that organizational policy can have on police behavior than that of the use of lethal force in the 1970s.[35] Fyfe's early work demonstrated the effect that restrictive lethal force policies can have,[36] which helped stimulate a national shift in policy and legal development, culminating in the Supreme Court case of *Tennessee v. Garner*.[37] *Garner*, just a few years prior to *Graham v. Connor*, established a defense of life standard for the use of lethal force. Along with Fyfe, scholars such as Geller and Scott,[38] Walker,[39] and White[40] offered further support for the impact that administrative policy can have on use of lethal force. Much of this work illustrated that policies more severely restricting the use of lethal force are related to a reduction in the overall number of police shootings and deaths as well as in the racial disparity of those incidents while neither increasing the danger of death for officers nor increasing the overall crime rate. Thus, restrictive deadly force policies are often referred to within scholarly circles as the epitome of policy success.

Research on less lethal force policies has taken a somewhat different direction in general, focusing instead on describing the disparate approaches that police agencies use.[41] Specifically, studies have illuminated the various structural features of force policies, such as the existence of written directives, the designation of permissible tactics, the creation of thresholds of reporting, and the training and review processes.[42] They have also examined how agencies regulate conducted energy devices within organizational policies,[43] examined the extent to which a use-of-force continuum is used,[44] assessed the different types of use-of-force continuum designs,[45] and ranked various forms of hand- and weapon-based force tactics relative to citizen resistance along a continuum.[46]

Yet one of the ongoing challenges for police administrators attempting to chart a less lethal policy course is that there is no commonly accepted approach. In a national study examining use-of-force policies, Terrill and Paoline found that the policy approach most frequently used by agencies was used by just 20 percent of departments, with the second and third most frequent approaches used by just 10 percent of agencies.[47] Moreover, since policies vary from one department to another in terms of restrictiveness, force that would be appropriate in one department can be viewed as completely inappropriate in another department (e.g., use of a TASER on a verbally resistant suspect may comply with the policy in one agency but not in another). Thus, the field of policing as a whole views the appropriateness of a given level of force differently depending on the agency and department involved. In addition, organizations do not always emphasize the importance of establishing good police practice but rather focus on avoiding lawsuits. In this sense, appropriate force is the level of force that does not result in a financial payout, or, in the case of frontline supervisors, the level of force that does not bring undue attention to the involved officers or their supervisors.

Moreover, unlike the research on deadly force policies, the effect of less lethal force policies on officer use-of-force behavior has received little empirical attention, thus providing police executives with little guidance as to which type of policy they should implement. In fact, only one study to date has examined such a potential connection, considering a full range of forceful tactics from hands-on to weapons-based force. Terrill and Paoline used data collected from three cities (Albuquerque, Charlotte-Mecklenburg, and Colorado Springs), each with a different level of policy direction and restrictiveness.[48] Their work consistently found that officers in Charlotte-Mecklenburg, which relied on a more restrictive policy framework, used force less readily than officers in Colorado Springs or Albuquerque, which both operated within less restrictive policy environments. Interestingly, Charlotte-Mecklenburg was the largest of the three study sites in terms of both the number of sworn officers and the citizen population and had the highest crime rate, yet its officers used less force. Moreover, the results showed that officers in Colorado Springs, the agency with the least restrictive or loosely coupled policy, were most likely to resort to force. In a related study, Terrill and Paoline also found that officers working in Colorado Springs were significantly less likely to believe that their agency policy offered them adequate guidance in terms of when force could, and could not, be used.[49] Thus, given the available evidence to date, it appears there is merit to incorporating an administrative policy that directs officers in how to use a linear and specific progression of less lethal force.

Of course, policy directives do not stand alone; they must be reinforced through training, starting in the academy and continuing with in-service training as well as through first-line supervision. Unfortunately, however, virtually nothing is known about the relationship between training and use of force, as credible scientific evidence on the subject is nearly nonexistent. That is, we know little to nothing about "what works" when it comes to training and use of force. Much of the training industry is based on non-tested—and thus non-verified—experiential modules used by police trainers as well as the offerings of an industry of private vendors hawking their alleged "successful" training models, which are subject to little or no external objective testing to establish their effectiveness.

Nonetheless, there are two important elements to consider from a training perspective. First, *Graham v. Connor* established no legal requirement that officers use the *least* amount of force.[50] In this respect, appropriateness from a lawful perspective (i.e., within the realm of being objectively reasonable) and the use of "good force" do not always equate.[51] There are certainly uses of force that are essentially "lawfully awful" (e.g., an officer verbally provokes a suspect, who in turn physically resists, which then permits the officer to legally respond to that resistance with physical coercion). Thus, while requiring via policy that officers use the least amount of force may not be realistic in all instances for any number of reasons, a least force approach is something that agencies can still encourage from a training standpoint when feasible. As Sir Robert Peel noted in 1829, the police should "use physical force to the extent necessary to secure observance of the law or to restore order only when the exercise of persuasion, advice, and warning is found to be insufficient."[52]

Second, police administrators and trainers should continually seek to balance the amount of time spent on traditional law enforcement aspects (e.g., strategic operations, firing range proficiency, felony traffic stops, and so on) and the amount of time spent on other important skills for effective policing (e.g., garnering good police-community relations, establishing trust and legitimacy, enhancing officers' ability to resolve conflict using noncoercive tactics, and so on).

3. Assignment practices. Similar to the gaps in the literature on training, we have little empirical knowledge about assignment practices and what works to reduce the inappropriate use of force. However, it seems rather safe to note that most police agencies tend to assign the least experienced officers to the most difficult assignments in terms of both time (i.e., night shift) and place (i.e., high-crime areas). Within this context, three related areas of research can inform a discussion on how assignment practices contribute to coercive policing tactics.

First, prior research indicates that officer experience plays a role in minimizing the use of force.[53] Scholars argue that policing is a "craft" best learned on the street over time.[54] The idea is that experience provides the benefit of repetitive exposure to the various situational contingencies of policing. Several studies support this notion. For instance, Bayley and Garofalo, in a study of New York City patrol officers, found that more experienced officers were identified by their peers as being the most skilled at dealing with conflict in encounters with citizens.[55] Later, Paoline and Terrill,[56] as well as Rydberg and Terrill,[57] drew on data collected as part of the Project on Policing Neighborhoods (POPN) observational study and controlled for a host of situational factors. These researchers found that more experienced officers do indeed rely on less coercive tactics in police-suspect encounters. The obvious policy implication is that police agencies should take this research into account by assigning experienced officers during times and in areas where violence and crime are expected to be higher and giving less experienced officers less demanding assignments.

Second, and in a similar vein, the existing research also shows that officers who are more educated bring many benefits to the field.[58] For example, college-educated officers have been found to have higher citizen satisfaction ratings as well as fewer citizen complaints compared to their less educated peers.[59] Moreover, college-educated officers have also been found to have higher ratings from their superiors,[60] as well as fewer injuries, preventable accidents, and sick days.[61] With respect to their approaches in the field, college-educated officers have been noted to be less authoritarian,[62] place a higher value on ethical behavior,[63] have more open belief systems that are less dogmatic,[64] and be better at verbal communication.[65] The results of these studies suggest that there are measurable differences, and potentially positive policing attributes, associated with college education. Moreover, and directly related to the topic at hand, both the Paoline and Terrill[66] as well as the Rydberg and Terrill[67] analyses showed that officers with a four-year college degree were significantly less likely to rely on forceful means to resolve conflicts with suspects. Hiring more officers with college educations may thus benefit agencies and the communities they serve.

Third, several pieces of research on police culture are relevant to assignment practices. Terrill et al., using data from the aforementioned Project on Policing Neighborhoods (POPN) study, found that officers who bought into traditional facets of police culture, such as distrust of citizens and an aggressive approach to patrol, were more likely to use higher levels of force.[68] Paoline and Terrill, using these same data, found that traditionally police-culture-oriented officers were two and a half times more likely to conduct searches compared to their culturally divergent counterparts.[69] A third and more recent study by Ingram et al., using data from the Assessing Police Use-of-Force Policy and Outcomes study, found that officers working within the same group (e.g., squads) tended to share cultural attitudes.[70] Hence, each of these studies indicate that officer views or attitudes toward traditional depictions of police culture matter. As a result, administrators should be aware of these attitudes and should consider how officers are assigned so that they do not cluster similarly thinking pro-culture carriers together on the same squad. Unfortunately, I know of no police department that assesses the culture of its members in any systematic way, despite the survey tools available to do so.

4. Tracking and assessing force and cultural patterns. Many police organizations now use some form of risk management system to track potentially problematic officers.[71] Alternatively referred to as early warning systems, early intervention systems, and performance measurement information systems, these systems generally operate quite similarly in that they seek to take into account a number of indicators. For example, risk management systems typically track the number of times an officer uses force, the number of complaints received regarding that officer, the number of civil litigation cases levied against the officer, the number of police vehicle accidents involving the officer, the number of sick leave days the officer has used, and the number of times that officer has been late for work.

The underlying reason for using a risk management system is grounded in prior research indicating that a small number of officers tend to be involved in a disproportionate number of use-of-force incidents, complaints, and the like.[72] Along similar lines, Terrill et al. developed a management tool that enables departments to use agency data on use-of-force incidents to assess and track force by individual officer, assignment, experience level, ethnicity, gender, unit, or any number of variables.[73] Further, the expansive use of body-worn cameras should provide yet another opportunity to examine how officers in the field use force. These approaches can provide police managers with important information about the behavior of officers in the field, the need for training, or the need to modify policy.

The goal of these various types of approaches is to identify potentially problematic officers early, before their behavior blossoms into a major problem. Ideally, agencies would then offer retraining for officers who have been "flagged," although such systems can also result in escalated punishment. While empirical evidence is lacking as to how effective such systems are at actually identifying problematic officers,[74] at a minimum they provide organizational leaders with data on who is, and who is not, regularly using force. Of course, managers must also recognize that there will be variation in force usage due to officer assignments.[75] Further, another critical component to understanding the use of force is the role of supervisors, especially frontline supervisors (e.g., sergeants), who are closest to officers in the field. Immediate supervisors will often know—well before more distant supervisors—the manner in which their officers go about policing the public, which means they play an important role in uncovering potentially problematic officer behavior.

Another strand of research that helps to inform this area is once again the research that explicitly deals with police culture. Culture is crucial for understanding socialization, accountability, and the success (or failure) of policing reform efforts.[76] Of critical importance, however, is the extent to which culture affects officer behaviors. Cultural prescriptions provide accepted guidelines for officer behaviors.[77] The President's Task Force on 21st Century Policing emphasized the role that culture plays in influencing officer discretion and authority, even going so far as to state that "behavior is more likely to conform to culture than to rules."[78] As highlighted above, a number of studies to date have demonstrated an empirical link between how officers view police culture (their attitudes) and the extent to which they use force (their behavior).[79] Collectively, these studies demonstrate that police administrators should be aware of how officers within their departments view culture, as this can play a predictive role in how often, and how heavily, they will rely on coercive means.

■ Next Steps

While prior research on police use of force is not always fully consistent and has taken a number of diverging directions, it is nonetheless quite informative if we step back and look at this body of work as a collective whole. The available research offers tangible mechanisms that police leaders can implement in an effort to reduce inappropriate use of force (albeit taking into account the varying ways in which force may be defined, as outlined at the beginning of the chapter). What follows is a snapshot of recommendations. Applying these recommendations as a comprehensive and inclusive set of strategies, from recruitment onward, will likely lead to better use-of-force tactics. If full adoption cannot be achieved, there is merit to implementing at least some of these approaches.

1. Police Organizations Should Actively Seek to Dispel the Crime-Fighting Perception

Police administrators should ensure that their promotional and recruitment efforts do not focus primarily on the law-enforcement role of the police but rather on the social welfare role. Officials should also work with local media outlets to properly establish the context of everyday policing, encouraging news stories that go beyond traditional crime fighting. The crime-fighting aspect of the occupation, as most frequently depicted in the media, is but a narrow slice of what the policing job entails, as scores of prior research studies demonstrate.

2. Police Organizations Should Actively Recruit Guardians

Tightly tied to the initial recommendation is that organizations should seek to develop means whereby they can identify officers who are interested in what is described above as the "softer" aspects of police work, where the emphasis is on providing "service" to citizens beyond the traditional law-enforcement function. These efforts may involve lessening the focus on outcomes such as testing candidates on memorization of names, places, and faces; observational skills of crime scenes and evidence collection; or physical attributes and firing range capabilities. While these things are still important and need some focus, broadening the search to include candidates who are well-versed in human nature and who display empathy, analytical skills, and problem-solving capabilities would better reflect the day-to-day reality of what police officers do. Further, such active recruitment should carefully consider how promoting diversity of race, ethnicity, gender, age, and educational level might help to develop a more well-rounded workforce that more accurately reflects the community it serves.

3. Police Organizations Should Incorporate a Linear-Based Force Continuum Policy

Police executives should adopt an administrative use-of-force policy that directs officers in the use of a linear and specific progression of force in relation to suspect resistance. As demonstrated in a series of articles using data collected from the Assessing Police Use-of-Force Policy and Outcomes study, not only do officers feel that such an approach helps them make better decisions about the use of force but it also leads to less actual usage of force.[80] These findings are particularly interesting given prior discussions within the literature concerning the potential negatives of force and resistance continua in general and linear designs in particular.[81] Hence, this is a great example of the importance of relying on carefully constructed and methodologically rigorous studies published in peer-reviewed journals rather than on articles from police magazine outlets.

4. Police Organizations Should Emphasize the Least Amount of Force Within Training Protocols

As outlined earlier in the chapter, the legal standard established in *Graham v. Connor* does not require officers to use the least amount of force in any given incident but rather to use a level of force that is objectively reasonable.[82] Police departments, however, can still encourage and train their officers to use the least amount of force possible. This parallels the development of deadly force policies prior to *Tennessee v. Garner*, when many police agencies voluntarily chose to ban their officers from shooting at fleeing felons before the Court made that policy the law. In effect, many police agencies implemented a deadly force policy that was more restrictive than what the law required. The same type of approach should be used now in relation to preparing officers to use the least amount of force possible. This policy orientation will help prevent cases of "lawfully awful" force.

5. Police Organizations Should Increase Analytical and Problem-Solving Training

In line with the first and second recommendations, both academy and in-service training should focus a larger percentage—and a higher quality—of training on the non-law enforcement, community relations aspects of the job. As prior research has consistently demonstrated, much of what police officers do on a daily basis is oriented more toward social work and problem solving than crime fighting. Training should reflect this reality.

6. Police Organizations Should Incorporate Officer Experience, Education, and Cultural Orientation into Assignment Practices

Current officer street assignments primarily center on officer seniority. The result is that the least experienced officers are often given the most challenging assignments (i.e., the night shift in high-crime areas). Yet, as prior research demonstrates, less experienced officers more readily rely on forceful means. Similarly, the existing research shows that noncollege-educated officers and those who buy into traditional views of police culture (such as negative views of citizens and a preference for aggressive patrol tactics) more readily rely on force. Thus, administrators should take experience, educational level, and cultural views into account when assigning officers. Police leaders can easily track both the number of years on the job and the highest level of education attained for their officers, and a well-grounded survey tool exists that could easily be used to tap into officers' cultural views.[83] Admittedly, this recommendation would be a rather drastic departure from past custom and practice in many agencies, but barring collectively bargained union agreements, this approach is doable and could pay great dividends (e.g., less force, complaints, and injuries, along with greater legitimacy and trust) for communities, police departments, and officers themselves.

7. Police Organizations Should Routinely Track and Assess Use of Force

It is important for agencies to know how, and how often, their officers use force. As detailed above, a number of tools are available for police administrators to track this information. Whether it is an early warning system approach,[84] a use-of-force management tool,[85] or a method that draws on body-worn camera footage, agencies should ensure that they are in some way routinely and systematically examining their officers' use of force. Too often, agencies are primarily reactive, only discovering problem officers after a critical incident or questionable application of force, rather than being proactive and helping officers before a harmful incident unfolds.

■ Concluding Note

Finally, and within the context of all seven recommendations, police executives should reassess the reward structure within their organizations regarding a key aspect of the occupation: the importance placed on arrests. Many within the field still view arrest as the ultimate outcome of successful policing. The result is that officers who are good crime fighters and who make many arrests are often regarded within policing circles as the best cops and are rewarded as such. In many ways, this is understandable, as keeping the public safe is clearly *the* top priority. Yet, the overwhelming importance that practitioners place on arrest is misplaced to at least some degree. This is clear given the countless studies showing that much of what officers do on a daily basis has little to do with law enforcement, the research showing that—even when probable cause exists—officers are much more likely not to arrest than to arrest, the broad-based community policing movement that now dates back forty years, and the civil unrest witnessed in communities across the United States over the last few years. Perhaps most importantly, though, is this fact: if a crime has already occurred, such that an arrest is required, to a large degree the police have already failed in their duty. To again quote Sir Robert Peel, "The test of police efficiency is the absence of crime and disorder, not the visible evidence of police action in dealing with them."[86]

NOTES

1 William Terrill and Jason R. Ingram, "Citizen Complaints against the Police: An Eight-City Examination," *Police Quarterly* 19, no. 2 (2006): 150–179.

2 William Terrill, "Police Use of Force and Suspect Resistance: The Micro-Process of the Police-Suspect Encounter," *Police Quarterly* 6, no. 1 (2003): 51–83; Michael D. White, "Controlling Police Decisions to Use Deadly Force: Reexamining the Importance of Administrative Policy," *Crime & Delinquency* 47, no. 1 (2001): 131–151.

3 William Terrill, *Police Coercion: Application of the Force Continuum* (New York: LFB Scholarly Publishing, 2001); Terrill, "Police Use of Force and Suspect Resistance"; William Terrill, "Police Use of Force: A Transactional Approach," *Justice Quarterly* 22, no. 1 (2005): 107–138.

4 Terrill, "Police Use of Force and Suspect Resistance"; William Terrill and Stephen D. Mastrofski, "Situational and Officer Based Determinants of Police Coercion," *Justice Quarterly* 19, no. 2 (2002): 215–248.

5 Kenneth Adams, "Measuring the Prevalence of Police Abuse of Force," in *And Justice for All: Understanding and Controlling Police Abuse of Force*, eds. William A. Geller and Hans Toch (Washington, DC: Police Executive Research Forum, 1995), 61–97.

[6] James J. Fyfe, "The Split-Second Syndrome and Other Determinants of Police Violence," in *Critical Issues in Policing,* eds. Roger C. Dunham and Geoffrey P. Alpert (Long Grove, IL: Waveland Press, 2015), 517–531.

[7] Robert E. Worden, "The 'Causes' of Police Brutality: Theory and Evidence on Police Use of Force," in *And Justice for All: Understanding and Controlling Police Abuse of Force*, eds. William A. Geller and Hans Toch (Washington, DC: Police Executive Research Forum, 1995), 31–60.

[8] Carl B. Klockars, "A Theory of Excessive Force and Its Control," in *And Justice for All: Understanding and Controlling Police Abuse of Force*, eds. William A. Geller and Hans Toch (Washington, DC: Police Executive Research Forum, 1995), 11–29.

[9] Ibid., 17.

[10] Ibid., 18.

[11] Egon Bittner, "Florence Nightingale in Pursuit of Willie Sutton: A Theory of the Police," in *Thinking about Police: Contemporary Readings*, eds. Carl B. Klockars and Stephen D. Mastrofski (New York: McGraw-Hill, 1974), 35–51, 40 (emphasis added).

[12] For a discussion as to a broader view of what constitutes coercion or force, see Terrill, *Police Coercion: Application of the Force Continuum*, and Terrill, "Police Use of Force and Suspect Resistance."

[13] Terrill, "Police Use of Force and Suspect Resistance."

[14] William Terrill, Eugene A. Paoline, and Jason Ingram, Final Technical Report Draft: Assessing Police Use of Force Policy and Outcomes, 2012.

[15] William Terrill, "The Elusive Nature of Reasonableness," *Criminology and Public Policy* 8, no. 1 (2009): 163–172.

[16] Elizabeth Davis, Anthony Whyde, and Lynn Langton published in October 2018, *Contacts between the Police and the Public, 2015* (Washington, DC: Bureau of Justice Statistics, 2018).

[17] Renee G. Kasinsky, "Patrolling the Facts: Media, Cops, and Crime," in *Media, Process, and the Social Construction of Crime*, ed. Gregg Barak (New York: Garland Publishing, Inc., 1995), 203–234.

[18] Fyfe, "The Split-Second Syndrome and Other Determinants of Police Violence."

[19] James J. Fyfe, "Good Policing," in *The Administration and Management of Criminal Justice Organizations*, eds. Stan Stojkovic, John Klofas, and David Kalinich (Long Grove, IL: Waveland, 2010), 133–152; Peter K. Manning, *Police Work: The Social Organization of Policing* (Cambridge, MA: M.I.T. Press, 1997).

[20] Roger B. Parks, Stephen D. Mastrofski, Christina DeJong, and M. Kevin Gray, "How Officers Spend Their Time with the Community," *Justice Quarterly* 16, no. 3 (1999): 483–518; Reiss, *The Police and the Public*; Gordon P. Whitaker, "What Is Patrol Work?" *Police Studies* 4, no. 4, 13–22 (1982).

[21] Whitaker, "What Is Patrol Work?"

[22] Reiss, The Police and the Public.

[23] Parks, Mastrofski, DeJong, and Gray, "How Officers Spend Their Time with the Community"; William Terrill, Michael T. Rossler, and Eugene A. Paoline, "Police Service Delivery and Responsiveness in a Period of Economic Instability," *Police Practice and Research: An International Journal* 15, no. 6 (2014): 490–504, doi: 10.1080/15614263.2013.829606.

[24] William Terrill and Eugene A. Paoline, "Non-Arrest Decision Making in Police-Citizen Encounters," *Police Quarterly* 10, no. 3 (2007): 308–331.

[25] Eugene A. Paoline and William Terrill, *Police Culture: Adapting to the Strains of the Job* (Durham, NC: Carolina Academic Press, 2014).

[26] Jerome H. Skolnick, *Justice Without Trial: Law Enforcement in Democratic Society* (New York: John Wiley & Sons, 1966); William A. Westley, *Violence and the Police* (Cambridge, MA: MIT Press, 1970).

[27] John Van Maanen, "Working the Street: A Developmental View of Police Behavior," in *The Potential for Reform of Criminal Justice*, ed. H. Jacob (Beverly Hills, CA: Sage, 1974), 83–103.

[28] COPS Office, *The President's Task Force on 21st Century Policing* (Washington, DC: Office of Community Oriented Policing Services, 2015).

[29] Stephen D. Mastrofski, *Policing for People: Ideas in American Policing* (Washington, DC: Police Foundation, 1999).

[30] For a recent study on race and use of force, see Eugene A. Paoline, III, Jacinta M. Gau, and William Terrill, "Race and the Police Use of Force Encounter in the United States," *British Journal of Criminology* 58, no. 1 (2018), doi:10.1093/bjc/azw089.

[31] President's Commission on Law Enforcement and Administration of Justice, *Challenge of Crime in a Free Society* (Washington, DC: U.S. Government Printing Office, 1967).

[32] *Graham v. Connor*, 490 U.S. 386 (1989).

[33] Terrill, "The Elusive Nature of Reasonableness."

[34] *Graham v. Connor*, 490 U.S. 386 (1989).

[35] William Terrill and Eugene A. Paoline, "Police Use of Less-Lethal Force: Does Administrative Policy Matter?" *Justice Quarterly* 34, no. 2 (2017), 193–216.

[36] James J. Fyfe, "Shots Fired: An Analysis of New York City Police Firearms Discharges" (PhD diss. State University of New York at Albany, 1978), Ann Arbor, MI: University Microfilms.

[37] *Tennessee v. Garner*, 471 U.S. 1 (1985).

[38] William A. Geller and Michael S. Scott, *Deadly Force: What We Know* (Washington D.C., Police Executive Research Forum, 1992).

[39] Samuel Walker, Taming the System: The Control of Discretion in Criminal Justice, 1950–1990 (New York: Oxford University Press, 1993).

[40] White, "Controlling Police Decisions to Use Deadly Force."

[41] Terrill and Paoline, "Police Use of Less-Lethal Force."

[42] Antony M. Pate and Lorie A. Fridell, "Toward the Uniform Reporting of Police Use of Force: Results from a National Study," *Criminal Justice Review* 20, no. 2 (1995): 123–145.

[43] Kyle J. Thomas, Peter A. Collins, and Nicholas P. Lovrich, "An Analysis of Written Conducted Energy Device Policies: Are Municipal Policing Agencies Meeting PERF Recommendations?" *Criminal Justice Policy Review* 23, no. 4 (2012): 399–426.

[44] William Terrill and Eugene A. Paoline, "Examining Less-Lethal Force Policy and the Force Continuum: Results from a National Use of Force Study," *Police Quarterly* 16, no. 1 (2013): 38–65.

[45] Ibid.

[46] Ibid.

[47] Ibid.

[48] Terrill and Paoline, "Police Use of Less-Lethal Force."

[49] William Terrill and Eugene A. Paoline, III, "Less-Lethal Force Policy and Police Officer Perceptions: A Multisite Examination," *Criminal Justice and Behavior* 40, no. 10 (2013): 1109–1130.

[50] *Graham v. Connor*, 490 U.S. 386 (1989).

[51] William Terrill, "The Elusive Nature of Reasonableness."

[52] Keith L. Williams, "Peel's Principles and Their Acceptance by American Police: Ending 175 Years of Reinvention," *Police Journal* 76, no. 2 (2003): 97–120, 100.

[53] William Terrill and Eugene A. Paoline, "Non-Arrest Decision Making in Police-Citizen Encounters."

[54] David H. Bayley and Egon Bittner, "Learning the Skills of Policing," in *Critical Issues in Policing: Contemporary Readings*, eds. Roger G. Dunham and Geoffrey P. Alpert (Long Grove, IL: Waveland, 1997): 114–137.

[55] David H. Bayley and James Garofalo, "The Management of Violence by Police Patrol Officers," *Criminology* 27, no. 1 (1989): 1–27.

[56] Eugene A. Paoline and William Terrill, "Police Education, Experience, and the Use of Force," *Criminal Justice and Behavior* 34, no. 2 (2007): 179–196.

[57] Jason Rydberg and William Terrill, "The Effect of Higher Education on Police Behavior," *Police Quarterly* 13, no. 1 (2010): 92–120.

[58] Paoline and Terrill, "Police Education, Experience, and the Use of Force."

[59] Wayne F. Cascio, "Formal Education and Police Officer Performance," *Journal of Police Science and Administration* 5, no. 1 (1977): 89–96; Victor E. Kappeler, Allen D. Sapp, and

David L. Carter, "Police Officer Higher Education, Citizen Complaints and Departmental Rule Violations," *American Journal of Police* 11, no. 2 (1992): 37–54.

[60] David L. Carter, Allen D. Sapp, and Darrel W. Stephens, *The State of Police Education: Policy Direction for the 21st Century* (Washington, DC: Police Executive Research Forum, 1989).

[61] Cascio, "Formal Education and Police Officer Performance"; Cohen and Chaiken, *Police Background Characteristics and Performance.*

[62] Alexander B. Smith, Bernard Locke, and Abe Fenster, "Authoritarianism in Policemen Who Are College Graduates and Noncollege Police," *Journal of Criminal Law, Criminology, and Police Science* 61, no. 2 (1970): 313–315.

[63] Stanley K. Shernock, "The Effects of College Education on Professional Attitudes among Police," *Journal of Criminal Justice Education* 3, no. 1 (1992): 71–92.

[64] Roy R. Roberg, "An Analysis of the Relationships among Higher Education, Belief Systems, and Job Performance of Patrol Officers," *Journal of Police Science and Administration* 6, no. 3 (1978): 336–344.

[65] Robert E. Worden, "A Badge and a Baccalaureate: Policies, Hypotheses, and Further Evidence," *Justice Quarterly* 7, no. 3 (1990): 565–592.

[66] Terrill and Paoline, "Non-Arrest Decision Making in Police-Citizen Encounters."

[67] Rydberg and Terrill, "The Effect of Higher Education on Police Behavior."

[68] William Terrill, Eugene A. Paoline, III, and Peter K. Manning, "Police Culture and Coercion," *Criminology* 41, no. 4 (2003): 1003–1034.

[69] Eugene A. Paoline, III and William Terrill, "The Impact of Police Culture on Traffic Stop Searches: An Analysis of Attitudes and Behavior," *Policing: An International Journal of Police Strategies and Management* 28, no. 3 (2005): 455–472.

[70] Jason R. Ingram, Eugene A. Paoline, III, and William Terrill, "A Multilevel Framework for Understanding Police Culture: The Role of the Workgroup. *Criminology* 51, no. 2 (2013): 365–397.

[71] Robert E. Worden, Christopher Harris, and Sarah J. McLean, "Risk Assessment and Risk Management in Policing," *Policing: An International Journal of Police Strategies & Management* 37, no. 2 (2014): 239–258; Walker, *Taming the System.*

[72] Terrill, *Police Coercion*; Terrill and Ingram, "Citizen Complaints against the Police"; William Terrill and John D. McCluskey, "Citizen Complaints and Problem Officers: Examining Officer Behavior," *Journal of Criminal Justice* 30, no. 2 (2002): 143–155.

[73] William Terrill, Geoffrey A. Alpert, Roger D. Dunham, and Michael R. Smith, "A Management Tool for Evaluating Police Use of Force: An Application of the Force Factor," *Police Quarterly* 6, no. 2 (2003): 150–171.

[74] Worden, Harris, and McLean, "Risk Assessment and Risk Management in Policing."

[75] For guidance on differentiating problem officers from productive officers, see Terrill and McCluskey, "Citizen Complaints and Problem Officers."

[76] Eugene A. Paoline, III, "Taking Stock: Toward a Richer Understanding of Police Culture," *Journal of Criminal Justice* 31, no. 3 (2003): 199–214.

[77] Stephen D. Mastrofski, "Controlling Street-Level Police Discretion," *The Annals of the American Academy of Political and Social Science* 593, no. 1 (2004):100–18; William Terrill, Eugene A. Paoline, III, and Peter K. Manning, "Police Culture and Coercion," *Criminology* 41, no. 4 (2003): 1003–1034.

[78] COPS Office, The President's Task Force on 21st Century Policing, 12.

[79] William Terrill, Eugene A. Paoline, III, and Peter K. Manning, "Police Culture and Coercion," *Criminology* 41, no. 4 (2003): 1003–1034; Paoline and Terrill, "The Impact of Police Culture on Traffic Stop Searches"; John D. McCluskey, William Terrill, and Eugene A. Paoline, III, "Peer Group Aggressiveness and the Use of Coercion in Police-Suspect Encounters," *Police Practice and Research: An International Journal* 6, no. 1 (2005): 19–37.

[80] Terrill and Paoline, "Examining Less-Lethal Force Policy and the Force Continuum"; Terrill and Paoline, "Police Use of Less-Lethal Force."

[81] John G. Peters and Michael A. Brave, "Force Continuums: Are They Still Needed?" *Police and Security News* 22, no. 1 (2006): 1–5; George T. Williams, "Force Continuums: A Liability to Law Enforcement?" *The FBI Law Enforcement Bulletin* 71, no. 6 (2002): 14–19.

[82] *Graham v. Connor*, 490 U.S. 386 (1989).

[83] Ingram, Paoline, and Terrill, "A Multilevel Framework for Understanding Police Culture"; Paoline and Terrill, *Police Culture*; William Terrill, Eugene A. Paoline, III, and Peter K. Manning, "Police Culture and Coercion," *Criminology* 41, no. 4 (2003): 1003–1034.

[84] Worden, Harris, and McLean, "Risk Assessment and Risk Management in Policing."

[85] William Terrill, Geoffrey A. Alpert, Roger D. Dunham, and Michael R. Smith, "A Management Tool for Evaluating Police Use of Force: An Application of the Force Factor," *Police Quarterly* 6, no. 2 (2003): 150–171.

[86] Williams, "Peel's Principles and Their Acceptance by American Police: Ending 175 Years of Reinvention," 100.

4

Response Essay

Chief Michael L. Brown, PhD
Alexandria (Virginia) Police Department

The chapter on police use of force is a comprehensive overview of the research and law related to this very important aspect of policing. The chapter's coverage of the importance of use of force in community relations and how the use of force is defined is outlined exceptionally well. Equally important in the discussion is the importance of context in assessing the level of force that should be used. I thought the treatment of the different possible interpretations of police force was very objective. The discussion also highlights the importance of the issue and its relationship to police legitimacy. It appropriately calls for police agencies to pay attention to the issues involving police use of force.

The chapter also provides keen insight into the importance of how departments recruit and train officers and assign them to specific policing activities. It weaves in findings from prior research to clearly lay out the relevance of recruiting potential officers who are likely to better fit the professional dimensions required of today's police officer. The chapter also notes the gaps that exist in research related to effective use-of-force training. Despite those gaps, it provides some clear suggestions that police departments can follow in their efforts to enhance their officers' training.

The chapter further suggests that law enforcement agencies pay attention to the manner in which they assign personnel. The recommendation to minimize the assignment of new officers to those times and locations where there may be a greater possibility of encountering a situation requiring force is something few agencies consider. The chapter fairly notes the implementation limitations of that suggestion, such as labor-related issues. However, the discussion presents a credible argument that agencies should consider their assignment protocols.

The references throughout the chapter to the limitations and gaps in prior research on police use of force are of particular note. This is especially true in the area of police training in the use of force. These are important considerations for academics and police leaders alike. The use of force is such a compelling and important issue that additional research in these areas would greatly inform the profession.

Use of force is an issue that all law enforcement agencies address on a regular basis. An agency's review of an officer's use of force is more than a function of compliance with departmental policy and legal requirements; it also must be conducted through the prism of community perspectives and local expectations. In my experience, use-of-force incidents that are not handled with a comprehensive sensitivity to these various perspectives can affect an agency's relationship with their community and overall effectiveness within that community. The material covered in this chapter offers perspectives from experts in this subject that should be considered in the development and implementation of departmental policy, training, and incident review protocols relating to the use of force by police officers.

This chapter is a very instructive and objective overview of police use of force. I found the seven recommendations at the conclusion of the chapter to be objective and helpful. There are most likely numerous police departments that have already incorporated one or more of these suggestions into their operations. However, the discussion of each recommendation should give police leadership everywhere pause to consider whether their departments are doing enough to deal professionally with the use-of-force issue. It will be valuable for police leaders both new and seasoned.

5

Reduce Racial Inequality in Police Practices

Danielle Wallace
Carlena Orosco
Brooks Louton
Arizona State University

Background

Over the past fifty years, the United States has experienced a number of events that have showcased the tenuous relationship between minorities and the police. In 1968, Lyndon B. Johnson established the National Advisory Commission on Civil Disorders, often known as the Kerner Commission, to investigate the race riots of 1967, which initially started after a police raid. The infamous beating of Rodney King by the Los Angeles Police Department in 1991 was one of the first violent police interactions caught on tape. In the summer of 2014, riots broke out following the deaths of black men at the hands of the police. There were riots in Ferguson, Missouri, over the death of Michael Brown and protests in New York City, Oakland, Chicago, Baltimore, Atlanta, and Minneapolis over the death of Eric Garner. In 2015, the death of Freddie Gray, Jr., from injuries sustained while being transported by the police in Baltimore sparked more protests regarding police mistreatment and killing of black men across multiple cities.[1]

While these incidents point to an ongoing historical problem between minority communities and the police, empirically demonstrating the occurrence and severity of racially biased policing is difficult. Extreme events display the fragile relationship between minorities and the police, but these events do little to expose the everyday realities of both police officers and minorities when they interact. Scholars have shown that both blacks and Latinos fear undeserved treatment at the hands of the police;[2] these perceptions likely affect interactions between the police and minorities. Moreover, scholars have consistently shown that minorities, particularly blacks, are more likely to be cited for crimes,[3] arrested,[4] and searched[5] than are whites. Given the considerable amount of research, we will not detail these disparities here.

Of course, racially biased policing is not measured *just* by police killings or even arrests or searches but also by incidents that leave the minority populace feeling that they are being treated unfairly. Unfortunately, scholars of racially biased policing have a good sense that racial disparities exist in stop outcomes, but they have an incomplete understanding of precisely how officers racially discriminate—either intentionally or unintentionally—within those stops.

In this chapter, we introduce a taxonomy of racially biased policing. We label the different ways that racially biased policing manifests as either related to stop procedures (procedure based) or the interaction between social and cultural norms of the individuals involved in the stop (sociocultural). Procedure-based racially biased policing involves bias that is tied to formal aspects of a stop, whether street or traffic, and includes the commonly studied outcomes of arrest, search, and citation, as well as less researched forms of bias, such as the decision to initially contact a citizen,[6] an officer's determinations of why a citizen or vehicle is suspicious, physical restraints such as handcuffing, or the time involved in the stop. Conversely, sociocultural racially biased policing focuses on aspects of the police-citizen interaction that are tied to social norms about authority, politeness, respect, body language, and differences in cultural norms that guide how both the officer and the citizen perceive they should interact. This taxonomy will assist both scholars and policing executives in thinking about constructive ways to remediate racially biased policing, given that, until now, scholars have been focused more on identification and less on manifestation of racially biased policing.

This chapter begins by walking readers through our taxonomy of procedure-based and sociocultural racially biased policing, providing some examples of each and discussing the implications of both for police departments. Next, we discuss potential solutions to racially biased policing in the form of recommendations for proactive means of reducing racially biased policing among law enforcement agency leadership and field-level sworn and professional staff. We conclude with a final takeaway regarding the importance of understanding and addressing racially biased policing.

Research Evidence

Procedure-Based Racially Biased Policing

As noted above, *procedure-based racially biased policing* refers to racially biased policing actions that are tied to formal aspects of a stop, whether that stop is street- or traffic-based. We begin this review of evidence by discussing pretextual stops, which enables a larger discussion about how officers establish suspicion. The decision to stop an individual is predicated on how suspicious the officer deems the individual to be. If the method the officer uses to determine suspicion has racial undertones, this decision itself becomes a form of procedure-based racially biased policing.

In pretextual traffic stops, minorities may feel that they are stopped unjustly, that there is no legitimate reason for the stop, or that the police officer is using an insignificant violation to justify extensive or invasive contact with those in the vehicle. Pretextual stops are particularly subject to discretion and potential bias given that they occur when traffic or other law violations "serve as a pretext for police motivated by other concerns" to stop the vehicle.[7] Put simply, the driver is getting pulled over not because of the stated reason, such as a lane change or an equipment violation, but because the officer is suspicious of drug use or some other, more serious illegal behavior.[8] The primary issue with pretextual stops is less the stop itself and more the manner in which the officer forms that suspicion of the driver.

When determining whether an individual is suspicious, "police officers are taught to look for nonverbal indicators of deception,"[9] even though many of these indicators, which are commonly taught throughout criminal justice textbooks and training materials, are not valid indicators of deception.[10] Moreover, officers' schemas regarding suspicion and deception are also built by their lived experiences.[11] In American culture, being black is synonymous with being a criminal;[12] these stereotypes about black males are consistently put forth by the media, film, and television industries and are replicated in social media. Thus, police officers are simultaneously exposed to both the stereotypical portrayal of black Americans by the media and arts industries and through their lived experience as police officers. What defines suspicious behavior, then, is an amalgam of cognitive schemas influenced by culture and stereotypes and the direct and indirect realities of the job.[13] For instance, Alpert and colleagues report that their findings are "consistent with psychological theory of cognitive schema in suggesting that blacks are more likely to be suspiciously viewed by the police for reasons that appear innocuous."[14] Stereotype activation is automatic and unconscious (i.e., it reflects implicit bias); thus, even if police officers are aware of their implicit biases, those biases will be active when they confront minority citizens and will have the potential to influence their judgment, perceptions, and actions.[15]

Place can influence suspicion as well. The environmental context of a stop provides police officers with both information regarding who belongs in that environment[16] and whether that person is committing a crime.[17] Werthman and Piliavan show the local context (neighborhood racial and ethnic characteristics) helps police officers define who they think is suspicious.[18] This process was defined as ecological contamination, where all individuals in the neighborhood assume the moral liability of the neighborhood.[19] More specifically, citizens encountered in crime-ridden neighborhoods must, by nature of ecological contamination, be criminals themselves. This attachment of suspicion to a person based on the neighborhood in which the police encounter them may be "independent of the suspect's personal characteristics or behavioral manifestations."[20] This may not be purposefully done by the police, but ecological contamination leans upon racial stereotypes of neighborhoods[21] as well as the consistent interactions that police officers have in high-crime minority neighborhoods.[22] The daily work of police officer officers, in short, reinforces American stereotypes regarding minorities and criminality, both for police officers and the public.

Suspicion can also be formed by an incongruence between a place and a person. Known as out-of-place policing or the offense of "driving while black,"[23] police officers tend to be more suspicious of individuals in neighborhoods where the predominant race of residents is inconsistent with the individual's race.[24] Meehan and Ponder show that blacks are subject to more surveillance and more frequent stops by the police when they are in predominantly white neighborhoods. Furthermore, Meehan and Ponder also find that racial profiling "increases as African Americans move farther from stereotypically 'black' communities into wealthier, whiter areas."[25] Ultimately, when an officer's suspicion of wrongdoing is tied to someone's race or ethnicity, that officer may be engaging in racially biased policing without knowing it.[26]

Scholars researching pretextual stops have shown that minorities—particularly blacks—are more likely to be stopped, even when taking into account a multitude of characteristics of the actors (i.e., citizens, bystanders, and officers) involved in the stop and the environment and characteristics of the stop itself.[27] Pretextual stops are not limited to traffic stops: this is an issue for street stops, or pedestrian stops, as well. In New York City, scholars have found that black males were more likely to be stopped and searched than nonblack males.[28] Other scholars show a disparity between searches and hit rates, where minorities were searched more frequently, yet the police discovered a weapon in less than 1 percent of those cases.[29] In essence, race and ethnicity are tied up in how officers determine suspicion.

Procedure-based racially biased policing—when racial disparities in outcomes arise from the procedural aspects of a stop—can also manifest as increased use of force. An excellent example of this is handcuffing. Handcuffing is used when police officers feel the need to detain the suspect or believe the suspect is dangerous.[30] In general, handcuffing is a type of use of force that involves restraint, though a relatively mild one.[31] The act of being handcuffed may convey to subjects that the officer believes they are dangerous in general, that they are an immediate threat, or that they are guilty of the crime for which they are a subject. As such, handcuffing leads to negative attitudes toward the police.[32] A recent study in Oakland, California, shows differences in handcuffing rates by race: of all the officers who made at least one stop in the 13-month study window, "only 26 percent [of officers] handcuffed a white person, while 72 percent handcuffed an African American person (excluding arrests)."[33] Other studies confirm the Oakland findings.[34] While many would condone an officer's use of handcuffs when needed, handcuffing is nonetheless a type of force[35] that deprives citizens, at least temporarily, of their freedom. If, when released from handcuffs, the suspect is neither cited nor arrested, this conveys a message to minorities about their race and how their race influences the law.[36]

Sociocultural Racially Biased Policing

Sociocultural racially biased policing focuses on aspects of the police-citizen interaction that are tied up in social and cultural norms about authority, politeness, and body language that guide how both the officer and the citizen should interact.[37] Here, we suggest that racially biased policing can occur not only in officer decisions about how to handle a citizen encounter procedurally (choosing who to stop, when to search, and so on) but also in the ways that officers communicate with citizens.

The majority of what a police officer does is communicate with the public,[38] and communication provides important moments for shaping public attitudes about the police.[39] Communication is thought of as the most important tool police officers have during police-citizen interactions,[40] yet how communication is undertaken by a police officer can undermine citizens' perceptions of procedural justice and police legitimacy.[41] Both procedural justice (the perception that the way the police treat citizens and make decisions during citizen encounters is fair) and legitimacy (the belief that the police have the right to be the legal authority)[42] are associated with individuals' willingness to obey the law.[43] That makes these two concepts vital to understanding and producing quality policing strategies.

Two forms of sociocultural racially biased policing are disrespect and communication style. Recently, a team of social psychologists and linguists found that police officers are objectively more disrespectful to black citizens.[44] These disrespectful communications came in the form of commonly using informal titles to refer to black citizens and asking black citizens to place their hands on the steering wheel in the officers' line of sight. Voigt and colleagues use the following example to show both informal communication and the officer's automatic distrust of a black citizen: "All right, my man. *Do me a favor.* Just keep your hands on the steering wheel real quick."[45] Another study showed the opposite, though the scholars involved defined disrespect more severely. Mastrofski and colleagues found that minorities experienced lower levels of disrespect from police officers during stops, where disrespect was measured as "name calling, derogatory statements about the citizen or the citizen's family, belittling remarks, slurs, cursing, ignoring the citizen's questions (except in an emergency), using a loud voice or interrupting the citizen (except in an emergency), obscene gestures, or spitting."[46] Given the findings from these studies, it appears that minorities may be more likely to receive disrespect through communication style and less likely to receive the more extreme forms of disrespect.

Next, communication style may express sociocultural racially biased policing to the recipient citizen. Using body-worn camera footage from the Cincinnati Police Department, communication and linguistics researchers show that interactions with black citizens, regardless of the officer's race, are on the whole more negative.[47] More specifically, Dixon and colleagues found that black citizens were more likely to be involved in stops where officers communicated indifference, were dismissive, or showed an air of superiority.

Conversely, a separate body of work shows that when the police engage in accommodative communication, citizens are more trustful and have higher rates of satisfaction with the police.[48] Accommodative communication occurs when individuals adjust their communication style to match the style of the individual with whom they are conversing.[49] For instance, an accommodative interaction is one where "conversational partners listen to one another, take the other's views into account, and explain things in ways that 'sit right' with their [conversational] partner."[50] A police-citizen interaction that is accommodative may be pleasant (with the officers introducing themselves) and use questions to ask for identification (e.g., "May I see your ID?") rather than demands.[51] This style of communication in police-citizen interactions reinforces citizens' perceptions of procedural justice, trust, and satisfaction with the police.[52]

Note, though, that the underlying racial animus between whites and blacks, for example, may lead blacks to interpret excessive accommodating communication by the police as disrespectful. This is known as overaccommodation, which occurs when the accommodation of an individual's communication style is "taken past the point where it is considered socially appropriate by the conversational participant."[53] Overaccommodation in a police setting may occur through the use of slang that the officer sees as specific to the group or culture of the stopped citizen. Citizens may also see overaccommodation as overly informal, which subsequently affects their perceptions of police authority or professionalism. While one study demarked disrespect as speech that was more casual (e.g., not using formal titles), it is possible that the officers personally saw this as an attempt to accommodate the black citizen (e.g., using means of communicating that are popularly associated with black American culture).[54] In turn, this perceived disrespect influences citizen compliance with the officer and the law.[55] As Lowrey and colleagues note, "When it comes to accommodation, perhaps a little goes a long way."[56]

■ Solutions

Defining forms of racially biased policing can help police organizations recognize these moments when they occur. However, this studied reflection is a far cry from the on-the-ground realities of everyday policing. In this section, we detail some potential internal policy responses to racially biased policing that are both practical and proactive. We want to provide options to combat racially biased policing for police departments beyond training on implicit bias and cultural sensitivity. Although these trainings are appearing more frequently,[57] their material is often delivered in a single session that may only lead to short-term, unsustainable effects.[58] Ultimately, it takes courage and commitment for law enforcement agencies to examine themselves to determine if some of their policies and practices are harmful to their community. In this section, we discuss a number of ways that agencies can be forward-thinking in furtherance of equitable policing.

Collect Race Data on Citizen Contacts

One core component of addressing racially biased policing is collecting the right information. The President's Task Force on 21st Century Policing issued a general call for departments to collect better data on their activities to begin evidence-based practices.[59] Many agencies do not currently collect race information during citizen contacts, and some states, like Arizona, do not include race or ethnicity information on identification documents. This lack of data enables departments to avoid confronting any issues of racial bias by claiming, truthfully, that there is no data available to study racial bias. While there are issues with collecting data on race and ethnicity (e.g., changes to forms and procedures, added documentation, and the need for data management), this is an area where data collection can assist law enforcement agencies in considering the extent of any potential problems they have and showing their positive changes over time. In much the same way that targeted approaches such as crime mapping and Compstat can help to identify high-crime locations and allow appropriate interventions, comprehensive data on race[60] can assist departments in revealing any racial bias issues as well as in determining the nature and prevalence of those issues. Moreover, agencies may want to consider collecting other valuable pieces of information, such as rates of handcuffing, suspect resistance, and demeanor, along with information about the presence of third parties, all of which may affect racial disparities in stop outcomes. Remember that procedure-based racially biased policing occurs when the procedural aspects of stops are applied differently across different citizen races or ethnicities. To understand these relationships, agencies need to collect pertinent data about their stops.

Analyze Video Footage for Quality of Interactions

Body-worn camera (BWC) technology stands out as a valuable tool through which departments can gain insight into their officers' behavior. Recent estimates find that 50 percent of police departments have implemented body-worn cameras in police-citizen interactions.[61] Policies vary as far as when camera use is required, and not all departments issue cameras to all officers. That said, many departments are willing to use the videos they have as training tools and checks on the use of force and as a means of documenting activation compliance.[62]

We suggest that agencies also look at BWC videos to review officer demeanor and language as a part of their existing BWC footage review policies. This is a particularly easy and fruitful means of proactively fighting racially biased policing, given that most departments already regularly audit BWC footage for a variety of reasons. Communication style and demeanor are core elements of a police stop[63] that influence citizen perceptions of police legitimacy and procedural justice,[64] and therefore they should be regularly evaluated. Police supervisors should engage in frequent, *nonpunitive* conversations about their officers' communication and demeanor with citizens, with an eye toward reinforcing positive and equitable behavior and using coaching to improve less-desirable behavior. For example, upon review of BWC footage, supervisors may see that some officers overaccommodate in their communication style when interacting with minority citizens, which has the potential to be seen as disrespectful. Other elements of communication style (e.g., exchanging pleasantries or introducing oneself) can easily be addressed with officers. Using trained supervisors who have a demonstrated adherence to these practices and an understanding of the less obvious nuances of communication to coach other officers in their communication styles may go a long way toward changing citizens' perceptions of procedural justice and police legitimacy as well as their experiences of racial bias.

This is not to say that egregious or overt racially biased behavior should be tolerated. Instead, review and coaching that target positive communication styles should become more entrenched in day-to-day police-citizen interactions and in the organizational environment as a means of preventing racially biased policing. This will likely require a shift in organizational and training culture, as officers value their independence and have expressed documented concerns about the possibility that BWCs will reduce officer discretion.[65] Acceptance of cameras has typically been encouraged through promoting them as tools for officer safety, evidence collection, and protection against unwarranted citizen complaints.[66] Use of BWC video footage outside of these areas may make some officers uncomfortable; however, using videos to examine the quality of interactions between officers and citizens in a regular, low-stakes manner can increase citizens' perceptions of procedural justice and police legitimacy while avoiding any attempts by officers to game the system.[67]

Leverage Crime Analysts and Research Partners

Agencies should also use partnerships with local researchers and, at the same time, take statistical analysis into their own hands. The majority of law enforcement agencies employ crime analysts who are uniquely positioned to determine what measures and data will be meaningful for their agencies. Having these crime analysts at the table can help prevent the deployment of misguided policing strategies or tactics that are driven by incomplete interpretations of data (e.g., raw data instead of incident rates) or interpretations that lack an evidentiary base and are instead based on anecdotal accounts of success or historical familiarity. For example, internal crime analysts are well-positioned to conduct thorough internal evaluations of racially biased policing. To do so, however, they may need to overcome some obstacles. Research on officers' receptivity to empirical research has found that officers prefer less rigorous methods to thorough evaluations[68] and that analysts themselves may not feel well supported by the officers in their departments.[69] Taylor and colleagues raised the concern that lack of integration may result in underutilization of crime analysts. These issues will need to be carefully considered for departments to get the most value from this existing resource.

Next, external researchers may also lend depth to analyses, provide additional resources for data collection, and help agencies develop insights that can drive their responses to issues of racially biased policing. Departments may form research-practitioner partnerships to closely examine departmental metrics that may be driving racial bias.[70] Local colleges and universities regularly welcome relationships with organizations in their local community, such as police departments, and are often willing to investigate particular problems facing the department in exchange for the ability to publish the resulting data or have students use it for their theses and dissertations. Moreover, external researchers, especially those nested within academia, have institutional access to peer-reviewed articles and recent research findings. Through these partnerships, law enforcement agencies can access the newest and best research developments on racially biased policing.

Pay Attention to Dispatchers

When developing policies and protocols to proactively address racial bias, departments may benefit from including police dispatchers alongside sworn personnel in conversations and training about racially biased policing. Although the importance of educating sworn personnel cannot be overstated, the first point of contact for citizens seeking police assistance is often the emergency communications department (i.e., call-takers and dispatchers). As gatekeepers of the police agency, they are an integral component of the department, yet they are often neglected when training decisions are made. Little attention is given to dispatchers as decision-makers,[71] despite the influence that their actions may have on community perceptions.[72] In addition, previous studies have shown that the characteristics of a neighborhood may strongly influence police decision pathways[73] and levels of perceived deservedness for response services.[74] Dispatchers in a given jurisdiction typically develop familiarity with the communities they serve through their interactions with citizens and officers; this familiarity may inadvertently lead to both positive and negative perceptions about residents. Although prioritization guidelines should dictate how much attention a call receives (e.g. number of assigned officers, code response), dispatchers possess immense discretion that they will ultimately use to classify incidents based on perceived risk to person and property. The discretionary, stressful nature of this position,[75] coupled with ambiguity in call protocols and the pressure to resolve incidents quickly, may culminate in racially disparate responses.

Should citizens feel that they were mistreated or were not considered a priority during a police encounter, beginning with the initial call for emergency services, they may lose their sense of trust and belief in the legitimacy of the entire department. Training for police dispatchers should emphasize the importance of their role in fostering positive community-police relations in addition to adherence to prioritization guidelines and protocols. Department policy makers should consider reformulating dispatcher manuals to reflect and account for deviations in the guidelines based on other variables (e.g., past threats of violence or presence of a weapon) to minimize the available room for discretionary interpretation.

Similarly, including emergency dispatchers in training on recognizing racial bias, crisis intervention and stress resilience,[76] and empathy may be beneficial given their interactions with community members who are often concerned, agitated, or fearful. Similar to using BWC footage to examine communication styles of officers, dispatch administrators should implement a series of quality-control checks, including a comprehensive review of randomly selected 911 calls for each dispatcher. These reviews provide an opportunity to determine whether call-takers are using the appropriate tone and language and to identify areas of improvement for individual employees and overall training programs. The tactics used by call-takers and dispatchers may pay huge dividends for police departments in the form of de-escalating callers before responding officers arrive, improving both officer and citizen safety as well as decreasing repeat calls for service and/or false reporting to elicit a desired police response.

Encourage Community Activism

Members of community activist groups should have a seat at the table with law enforcement organizations and oversight bodies to enable productive discourse regarding the impact of policing strategies and to make race salient to police officers.[77] Community members and police departments often struggle to find common ground, resulting in a divide that erodes police-community relations. Departments should move beyond symbolic gestures of community involvement, such as community meetings or events that are often only attended by a small, self-selected group of residents and that serve only the interests of those in attendance rather than those of the community at large. Departments should instead seek to engage with community sectors that may otherwise be unwilling or unable to attend police-hosted events due to negative perceptions of the police or feelings of marginalization by the police. Police leaders and politicians must be visible champions of reform,[78] elevating concerns raised by accountability groups to other stakeholders who are influential in shaping policies.[79] It is imperative that police departments make a concerted effort to understand the experience and perspective of community members across all parts of a given jurisdiction—even those members who reside in areas that are deemed problematic from an enforcement lens.

Opportunities for gaining insight may come in the form of extended exposure to a community before patrol certification or racial bias training that focuses on building trust and legitimacy[80] moves beyond the structure of information sessions[81] and has been rigorously evaluated. Task forces that consist of sworn personnel, community members, union leadership, and civil rights groups should convene and collaborate on implementation strategies to reduce racial bias and metrics to assess progress toward that goal.[82]

Overall, engaging and aligning with community activist groups can spark important conversations about the deleterious impacts of certain police-citizen interactions while allowing police departments and residents to find common ground and shared objectives for the community's safety and well-being.

■ Next Steps

In this chapter, we have made a case for a more robust understanding of racially biased policing, one that allows us—scholars, police executives, researchers, and law enforcement agencies—to better prevent its occurrence. Goff and colleagues discussed a number of reasons why scholars have encountered serious impediments to fully understanding racially biased policing.[83] They note that law enforcement culture, academic culture, a lack of access to data, and insufficient methodological rigor inhibit scholars from gaining a deeper understanding of racially biased policing in the United States. We add that both scholars and police agencies have insufficient means of defending against allegations of racially biased policing because, as a discipline, we have focused more on identifying when racially biased policing occurs and determining how to measure it and less on categorizing and theorizing about its causes and solutions. By introducing the ideas of procedure-based and sociocultural racially biased policing, we hope to suggest fruitful, proactive ways that law enforcement agencies can detect and combat racially biased policing.

Remediating racially biased policing should be a part of every law enforcement agency's work toward increasing procedural justice and police legitimacy. Whether a traffic stop is pretextual (procedure based) or a police officer is not respectful (sociocultural), any form of racially biased policing can damage the relationship that a law enforcement agency has with its larger community. Indeed, this is much of what the President's Task Force on 21st Century Policing was about: minority communities did not feel safe or treated equally under the law.[84] Scholars pointed to the issues of procedural justice and legitimacy, while minority communities across the United States felt unfairly treated by the police, with the death of black men at the hands of the police as the ultimate examples. Scholars have dubbed this a "crisis of legitimacy" within U.S. policing.[85] By contrast, organizations experience a number of benefits when their communities see them as legitimate: citizens are more likely to comply with the law, accept police decisions, and cooperate with the police.[86] This is why it is vitally important to understand how racially biased policing manifests and how it has a detrimental impact on people, communities, officers, and law enforcement agencies.

We conclude with two notes of caution. First, the examples we detail above are not the sole ways in which procedure-based and sociocultural racially biased policing occur. For instance, extended detention could be a form of procedure-based racially biased policing, while different forms of body language may be sociocultural racially biased policing. We propose this taxonomy of racially biased policing to motivate scholars, analysts, and policing executives to think critically not just about *when* racially biased policing appears but also *how* it appears.

Finally, when tackling the difficult problem of racially biased policing, we must be cognizant that the various parties (i.e., citizens, police officers, dispatchers, the community, and the agency) each bring to the encounter their own culture, which influences the police-citizen interaction. Race, place, and immigration status all come with their own histories of dealing with law enforcement.[87] Black males, in particular, have accumulated a number of adverse experiences with the police.[88] These histories likely impact citizens' behavior toward the police and weigh heavily on each interaction. The literature on racially biased policing, procedural and distributive justice, and legitimacy is often divorced from the cultural perspective of the involved citizen[89] relative to the police. It is unfortunate that today's police officers and departments have to deal with the scars that the police from decades before inflicted on the citizenry they serve. That said, when departments can acknowledge the historical hurt that the police have brought to the citizenry, they lay a path forward toward a working relationship between the police and the people and communities they serve.

NOTES

[1] For a timeline of events surrounding police killings, see Willie F. Tolliver, Bernadette R. Hadden, Fabienne Snowden, and Robyn Brown-Manning, "Police Killings of Unarmed Black People: Centering Race and Racism in Human Behavior and the Social Environment Content," *Journal of Human Behavior in the Social Environment* 26, no. 3 (2016): 279–286.

[2] Tom R. Tyler and Yuen Huo, *Trust in the Law: Encouraging Public Cooperation with the Police and Courts* (New York: Russell Sage Foundation, 2002); Samuel E. Walker and Carol A. Archbold, *The New World of Police Accountability,* 3rd ed. (Los Angeles, CA: Sage Publications, 2020); Ronald Weitzer and Steven A. Tuch, "Race, Class, and Perceptions of Discrimination by the Police," *Crime & Delinquency* 45, no. 4 (1999): 494–507.

[3] Rob Tillyer and Robin S. Engel, "The Impact of Drivers' Race, Gender, and Age During Traffic Stops: Assessing Interaction Terms and the Social Conditioning Model," *Crime & Delinquency* 59, no. 3 (2013): 369–395.

[4] For a meta-analysis on arrests, see Tammy Rinehart Kochel, David B. Wilson, and Stephen D. Mastrofski, "Effect of Suspect Race on Officers' Arrest Decisions," *Criminology* 49, no. 2 (2011): 473–512.

[5] Jeff Dominitz and John Knowles, "Crime Minimisation and Racial Bias: What Can We Learn from Police Search Data?" *The Economic Journal* 116, no. 515 (2006): F368–F382; Nicola Persico and Petra E. Todd, "The Hit Rates Test for Racial Bias in Motor-Vehicle Searches," *Justice Quarterly* 25, no. 1 (2008): 37–53; Jeff Rojek, Richard Rosenfeld, and Scott Decker, "Policing Race: The Racial Stratification of Searches in Police Traffic Stops," *Criminology* 50, no. 4 (2012); Richard Rosenfeld, Jeff Rojek, and Scott Decker, "Age Matters: Race Differences in Police Searches of Young and Older Male Drivers," *Journal of Research in Crime and Delinquency* 49, no. 1 (2011): 31–55.

[6] Observing an officer's decision to stop is methodologically difficult. Moreover, understanding whether an officer's decision to stop certain citizens means that minorities are more likely to be stopped than whites taps into problems surrounding external benchmarking (Samuel Walker, "Searching for the Denominator: Problems with Police Traffic Stop Data and an Early Warning System Solution," *Justice Research and Policy* 3, no. 1 (2001)). Both of these issues make studying the decision to stop tremendously difficult.

[7] Richard J. Lundman and Robert L. Kaufman, "Driving While Black: Effects of Race, Ethnicity, and Gender on Citizen Self-Reports of Traffic Stops and Police Actions," *Criminology* 41, no. 1 (2003): 195–220, 197.

[8] Lorie Fridell, Robert Lunney, Drew Diamond, and Bruce Kubu, *Racially Biased Policing: A Principled Response* (Washington, DC: Police Executive Research Forum, 2001); David A. Harris, *Profiles in Injustice: Why Racial Profiling Cannot Work* (New York: The New Press, 2002); Ronald Weitzer and Steven A. Tuch, "Perceptions of Racial Profiling: Race, Class, and Personal Experience," *Criminology* 40, no. 2 (2002): 435–456.

[9] Geoffrey P. Alpert, John M. MacDonald, and Roger G. Dunham, "Police Suspicion and Discretionary Decision Making During Citizen Stops," *Criminology* 43, no. 2 (2005): 407–434, 414.

[10] William R. King and Thomas M. Dunn, "Detecting Deception in Field Settings: A Review and Critique of the Criminal Justice and Psychological Literatures," *Policing: An International Journal of Police Strategies & Management* 33, no. 2 (2010): 305–320.

[11] Alpert, MacDonald, and Dunham, "Police Suspicion and Discretionary Decision Making During Citizen Stops."

[12] Glenn C. Loury, *The Anatomy of Racial Inequality* (Cambridge, MA: Harvard University Press, 2002).

[13] Leo Carroll and M. Lilliana Gonzalez, "Out of Place: Racial Stereotypes and the Ecology of Frisks and Searches Following Traffic Stops," *Journal of Research in Crime and Delinquency* 51, no. 515 (March 2014): 559–584.

[14] Alpert, MacDonald, and Dunham, "Police Suspicion and Discretionary Decision Making During Citizen Stops," 426.

[15] Patricia G. Devine, "Stereotypes and Prejudice: Their Automatic and Controlled Components," *Journal of Personality and Social Psychology* 56, no. 1 (1989): 5–18; Lincoln Quillian, "New Approaches to Understanding Racial Prejudice and Discrimination," *Annual Review of Sociology* 32 (2006): 299–328.

[16] Kenneth J. Novak and Mitchell B. Chamlin, "Racial Threat, Suspicion, and Police Behavior: The Impact of Race and Place in Traffic Enforcement," *Crime & Delinquency* 58, no. 2 (2008): 275–300.

[17] Terrill, William, and Michael Reisig, "Neighborhood Context and Police Use of Force," *Journal of Research in Crime and Delinquency* 40, no. 3 (2003): 291–321; Carl Werthman and Irving Piliavin, "Gang Members and the Police," in *The Police: Six Sociological Essays*, ed. David Bordua (New York: Wiley, 1967), 55–98.

[18] Werthman and Piliavan, "Gang Members and the Police." For a discussion of the ways that place affects officers' understandings of crime and deviance, see David A. Klinger, "Negotiating Order in Patrol Work: An Ecological Theory of Police Response to Deviance," *Criminology* 35, no. 2 (1997): 277–306.

[19] Werthman and Piliavan, "Gang Members and the Police."

[20] Terrill and Reisig, "Neighborhood Context and Police Use of Force," 295.

[21] Elijah Anderson, "The Iconic Ghetto," The Annals of the American Academy of Political and Social Science 642, no. 1 (2012): 8–24.

[22] Alpert, MacDonald, and Dunham, "Police Suspicion and Discretionary Decision Making During Citizen Stops"; Robert J. Kane, "Social Control in the Metropolis: A Community-Level Examination of the Minority Group-Threat Hypothesis," *Justice Quarterly* 20, no. 2 (2003): 265–295.

[23] David A. Harris, "Driving While Black and All Other Traffic Offenses: The Supreme Court and Pretextual Traffic Stops," *Journal of Criminal Law and Criminology* 87, no. 2 (1997); Harris, *Profiles in Injustice*; Albert J. Meehan and Michael C. Ponder, "Race and Place: The Ecology of Racial Profiling African American Motorists," *Justice Quarterly* 19, no. 3 (2002): 399–430.

[24] Albert J. Meehan and Michael C. Ponder, "Race and Place: The Ecology of Racial Profiling African American Motorists," *Justice Quarterly* 19, no. 3 (2002): 399–430.

[25] Ibid., 401.

[26] Using race or ethnicity as an indicator of suspicion may not be racially biased (see Harris, *Profiles in Injustice*, for a discussion of driving while black and the U.S. Supreme Court case of *Whren v. the United States*, 506 U.S. 806 (1996), which allowed race to be a factor in suspicion).

[27] Rick Trinkner and Phillip Atiba Goff, "The Color of Safety: The Psychology of Race and Policing," in *The Sage Handbook of Global Policing* (London, England: Sage Publications Ltd., 2016), 61–81.

[28] Jeffery Fagan and Garth Davies, "Street Stops and Broken Windows: *Terry*, Race, and Disorder in New York City," *Fordham Urban Law Journal* 28, no. 2 (2000); Andrew Gelman, Jeffery Fagan, and Alex Kiss, "An Analysis of the New York City Police Department's 'Stop-and-Frisk' Policy in the Context of Claims of Racial Bias," *Journal of the American Statistical Association* 102, no. 479 (2007): 813–823, https://doi.org/10.1198/016214506000001040.

[29] Sharad Goel, Justin M. Rao, and Ravi Shroff, "Precinct or Prejudice? Understanding Racial Disparities in New York City's Stop-and-Frisk Policy," *The Annals of Applied Statistics* 10, no. 1 (2016): 365–394.

[30] Joscha Legewie, "Racial Profiling and Use of Force in Police Stops: How Local Events Trigger Periods of Increased Discrimination," *American Journal of Sociology* 122, no. 2 (2016): 379–424.

[31] William Terrill, "Police Use of Force and Suspect Resistance: The Micro Process of the Police-Suspect Encounter," *Police Quarterly* 6, no. 1 (2003): 51–83; William Terrill, "Police Use of Force: A Transactional Approach," *Justice Quarterly* 22, no. 1 (2005): 107–138; William Terrill, Geoffrey A. Alpert, Roger G. Dunham, and Michael R. Smith, "A Management Tool for Evaluating Police Use of Force: An Application of the Force Factor," *Police Quarterly* 6, no. 2 (2003): 150–171.

[32] Yasmeen I. Krameddine and Peter H. Silverstone, "Police Use of Handcuffs in the Homeless Population Leads to Long-Term Negative Attitudes within This Group," *International Journal of Law and Psychiatry* 44 (2016): 81–90, https://doi.org/10.1016/J.IJLP.2015.08.034

[33] Rebecca C. Hetey, Benoit Monin, Amrita Maitreyi, and Jennifer L. Eberhardt, *Data for Change: A Statistical Analysis of Police Stops, Searches, Handcuffings, and Arrests in Oakland, California, 2013–2014* (Stanford, CA: Stanford University, 2016), 10.

[34] Tim Bates and David Fasenfest, "Enforcement Mechanisms Discouraging Black-American Presence in Suburban Detroit," *International Journal of Urban and Regional Research* 29, no. 4 (2005): 960–971.

[35] Terrill, "Police Use of Force and Suspect Resistance"; Terrill, "Police Use of Force"; Terrill et al., "A Management Tool for Evaluating Police Use of Force."

[36] For a discussion, see Rob Voigt, Nicholas P. Camp, Vinodkumar Prabhakaran, William L. Hamilton, Rebecca C. Hetey, Camila M. Griffiths, David Jurgens, Dan Jurafsky, and Jennifer L. Eberhardt, "Language from Police Body Camera Footage Shows Racial Disparities in Officer Respect," *Proceedings of the National Academy of Sciences of the United States of America* 114, no. 25 (2017): 6521–6526.

[37] By social norms, we mean "shared understandings about actions that are obligatory, permitted or forbidden" (Elinor Ostrom, "Collective Action and the Evolution of Social Norms," *Journal of Economic Perspectives* 14, no. 3 (2000): 137–158, 144). See also Sue E. S. Crawford and Elinor Ostrom, "A Grammar of Institutions," *American Political Science Review* 89, no. 3 (1995): 582–600. By cultural norms, we mean the rules about behavior in specific situations that are determined by a person's specific group membership, such as being Latinx, an immigrant, or a woman. See Jack P. Gibbs, "Norms: The Problem of Definition and Classification," *American Journal of Sociology* 70, no. 5 (1965): 586–594; Robin M. Williams, *American Society: A Sociological Interpretation* (New York: Knopf).

[38] Howard Giles, Jennifer Fortman, Rene M. Dailey, Valerie Barker, Christopher Hajek, Michelle C. Anderson, and Nicholas O. Rule, "Communication Accommodation: Law Enforcement and the Public," in *Applied Interpersonal Communication Matters: Family, Health, and Community Relations*, eds. René M. Dailey and Beth A. Le Poire (New York: Peter Lang, 2006), 241–269.

[39] Patrick A. Langan, Lawrence A. Greenfeld, Steven K. Smith, Matthew R. Durose, and David J. Levin, *Contacts between Police and the Public: Findings from the 1999 National Survey* (Washington, DC: Bureau of Justice Statistics, U.S. Department of Justice, 2001).

[40] Morris M. Womack and Hayden H. Finley, *Communication—A Unique Significance for Law Enforcement* (Springfield, IL: Charles C. Thomas, 1986).

[41] Trinkner and Goff, "The Color of Safety"; Tom R. Tyler, *Why People Obey the Law* (Princeton, NJ: Princeton University Press, 2006); Tyler and Huo, *Trust in the Law*; Voigt et al., "Language from Police Body Camera Footage Shows Racial Disparities in Officer Respect."

[42] Tom R. Tyler and Steven L. Blader, "The Group Engagement Model: Procedural Justice, Social Identity, and Cooperative Behavior," *Personality and Social Psychology Review* 7, no. 4 (2003): 349–361.

[43] Andrew V. Papachristos, Tracey L. Meares, and Jeffrey Fagan, "Why Do Criminals Obey the Law? The Influence of Legitimacy and Social Networks on Active Gun Offenders," *Journal of Criminal Law and Criminology* 102, no. 2 (2012): 397–440; Michael D. Reisig, Scott E. Wolfe, and Kristy Holtfreter, "Legal Cynicism, Legitimacy, and Criminal Offending," *Crimi-*

nal Justice and Behavior 38, no. 12 (2011): 1265–1279; Danielle Wallace, Andrew V. Papachristos, Tracey Meares, and Jeffrey Fagan, “Desistance and Legitimacy: The Impact of Offender Notification Meetings on Recidivism among High Risk Offenders,” *Justice Quarterly* 33, no. 7 (2016): 1237–1264.

[44] Voigt et al., “Language from Police Body Camera Footage Shows Racial Disparities in Officer Respect.”

[45] Ibid., 6523.

[46] Stephen D. Mastrofski, Michael D. Reisig, and John D. Mccluskey, “Police Disrespect Towards the Public: An Encounter-Based Analysis,” *Criminology* 40, no. 3 (2002): 518–552, 529–530.

[47] Travis L. Dixon, Terry L. Schell, Howard Giles, and Kristin L. Drogos, “The Influence of Race in Police-Civilian Interactions: A Content Analysis of Videotaped Interactions Taken During Cincinnati Police Traffic Stops,” *Journal of Communication* 58, no. 3 (2008): 530–549.

[48] Belen V. Lowrey, Edward R. Maguire, and Richard R. Bennett, “Testing the Effects of Procedural Justice and Overaccommodation in Traffic Stops: A Randomized Experiment,” *Criminal Justice and Behavior* 43, no. 10 (2016): 1430–1449. See also Giles et al., “Communication Accommodation”; Howard Giles, Christopher Hajek, Valerie Barker, Mei-Chen Li, Yan B. Zhang, Mary L. Hummert, and Michelle C. Anderson, “Accommodation and Institutional Talk: Communicative Dimensions of Police—Civilian Interactions,” in *Language, Discourse and Social Psychology*, eds. Ann Weatherall, Bernadette Watson, and Cindy Gallois (London: Palgrave Macmillan UK, 2007), 131–159.

[49] Lowrey et al., “Testing the Effects of Procedural Justice and Overaccommodation in Traffic Stops.”

[50] Howard Giles, Daniel Linz, Doug Bonilla, and Michelle L. Gomez, “Police Stops of and Interactions with Latino and White (Non-Latino) Drivers: Extensive Policing and Communication Accommodation,” *Communication Monographs* 79 no. 4 (2012): 407–427, 409.

[51] For examples, see the experimental methods used in Lowrey et al., “Testing the Effects of Procedural Justice and Overaccommodation in Traffic Stops.”

[52] Giles et al., “Communication Accommodation”; Giles et al., “Accommodation and Institutional Talk.”

[53] Lowrey et al., “Testing the Effects of Procedural Justice and Overaccommodation in Traffic Stops,” 1434.

[54] For a discussion, see Dixon et al., “The Influence of Race in Police-Civilian Interactions.”

[55] Giles et al., “Communication Accommodation”; Giles et al., “Accommodation and Institutional Talk”; Lowrey et al., “Testing the Effects of Procedural Justice and Overaccommodation in Traffic Stops.”

[56] Lowrey et al., “Testing the Effects of Procedural Justice and Overaccommodation in Traffic Stops,” 1442.

[57] Robert J. Smith, “Reducing Racially Disparate Policing Outcomes: Is Implicit Bias Training the Answer? *University of Hawai'i Law Review* 37, no. (2015): 295–312.

[58] Patricia G. Devine, Patrick S. Forscher, Anthony J. Austin, and William T. L. Cox, “Long-Term Reduction in Implicit Race Bias: A Prejudice Habit-Breaking Intervention,” *Journal of Experimental Social Psychology* 48, no. 6 (2012): 1267–1278; Calvin K. Lai, Maddalena Marini, Steven A. Lehr, Carlo Cerruti, Jiyun-Elizabeth L. Shin, Jennifer A. Joy-Gaba, Arnold K. Ho, Bethany A. Teachman, Sean P. Wojcik, Spassena P. Koleva, Rebecca S. Frazier, Larisa Heiphetz, Eva A. Chen, Rhiannon N. Turner, Jonathan Haidt, Selin Kesebir, Carlee Beth Hawkins, Hillary Schaefer, Sandro Rubichi, Giuseppe Sartori, Christopher M. Dial, N. Sriram, Mahzarin R. Banaji, and Brian A. Nosek, “Reducing Implicit Racial Preferences: A Comparative Investigation of 17 Interventions,” *Journal of Experimental Psychology* 143, no. 4 (2014): 1765–1785.

[59] Task Force on 21st Century Policing, *Final Report of the President's Task Force on 21st Century Policing* (Washington, DC: Office of Community Oriented Policing Services, 2015).

[60] David A. Harris, “The New Data: Over-Representation of Minorities in the Criminal Justice System,” *Law and Contemporary Problems* 66, no. 3 (2003): 71–98.

[61] Police Executive Research Forum, *Cost and Benefits of Body-Worn Camera Deployments: Final Report* (Washington, DC: Police Executive Research Forum, 2018).

[62] E. C. Hedberg, Charles M. Katz, and David E. Choate, "Body-Worn Cameras and Citizen Interactions with Police Officers: Estimating Plausible Effects Given Varying Compliance Levels," *Justice Quarterly* 34, no. 4 (2016): 1–25; Charles M. Katz, David E. Choate, Justin R. Ready, and Lidia Nuno, *Evaluating the Impact of Officer Worn Body Cameras in the Phoenix Police Department* (Phoenix: Center for Violence Prevention & Community Safety, Arizona State University, 2014).

[63] Lowrey et al., "Testing the Effects of Procedural Justice and Overaccommodation in Traffic Stops"; Mastrofski, Reisig, and Mccluskey, "Police Disrespect Towards the Public: An Encounter-Based Analysis."

[64] Christina L. Patton, Michael Asken, William J. Fremouw, and Robert Bemis, "The Influence of Police Profanity on Public Perception of Excessive Force," *Journal of Policing and Criminal Psychology* 32, no. 4 (2017): 340–357; Tyler, *Why People Obey the Law*; Tyler and Huo, *Trust in the Law.*

[65] Katz et al., *Evaluating the Impact of Officer Worn Body Cameras in the Phoenix Police Department.*

[66] Ibid.; John O. Smykla, Matthew S. Crow, Vaughn J. Crichlow, and Jamie A. Snyder, "Police Body-Worn Cameras: Perceptions of Law Enforcement Leadership," *American Journal of Criminal Justice* 41, no. 3 (2016): 424–443.

[67] Jerry Z. Muller, *The Tyranny of Metrics* (Princeton, NJ: Princeton University Press, 2017).

[68] Cody W. Telep and Cynthia Lum, "The Receptivity of Officers to Empirical Research and Evidence-Based Policing: An Examination of Survey Data from Three Agencies," *Police Quarterly* 17, no. 4 (2014): 359–385.

[69] Bruce Taylor, Apollo Kowalyk, and Rachel Boba, "The Integration of Crime Analysis into Law Enforcement Agencies: An Exploratory Study into the Perceptions of Crime Analysts," *Police Quarterly* 10, no. 2 (2007): 154–169.

[70] Kimberly Kahn, and Karin D. Martin, "Policing and Race: Disparate Treatment, Perceptions, and Policy Responses," *Social Issues and Policy Review* 10, no. 1 (2016): 82–121.

[71] George Antunes and Eric J. Scott, "Calling the Cops: Police Telephone Operators and Citizen Calls for Service," *Journal of Criminal Justice* 9, no. 2 (1981): 165–180; James D. Sewell and Linda Crew, "The Forgotten Victim: Stress and the Police Dispatcher," *FBI Law Enforcement Bulletin* 53, no. 3 (1984): 7–11.

[72] Raymond Parnas, "Police Discretion and Diversion of Incidents of Intra-Family Violence," *Law and Contemporary Problems* 36, no. 4 (1971): 539–565; Sean P. Varano, Joseph A. Schafer, Jeffery M. Cancino, and Marc L. Swatt, "Constructing Crime: Neighborhood Characteristics and Police Recording Behavior," *Journal of Criminal Justice* 37, no. 6 (2009), 553–563.

[73] Cynthia Lum, "The Influence of Places on Police Decision Pathways: From Call for Service to Arrest," *Justice Quarterly* 28, no. 4 (2011): 631–665; H. Richard Uviller, "The Unworthy Victim: Police Discretion in the Credibility Call," *Law and Contemporary Problems* 47, no. 4 (1984): 15–33; Varano et al., "Constructing Crime."

[74] David A. Klinger, "Negotiating Order in Patrol Work: An Ecological Theory of Police Response to Deviance," *Criminology* 35, no. 2 (1997): 277–306.

[75] Tod W. Burke, "Dispatcher Stress," *FBI Law Enforcement Bulletin* 64, no. 10 (1995): 1–6; William G. Doerner, "Police Dispatcher Stress," *Journal of Police Science & Administration* 15, no. 4 (1987): 257–261.

[76] Gershon Weltman, Jonathan Lamon, Elan Freedy, and Donald Chartrand, "Police Department Personnel Stress Resilience Training: An Institutional Case Study," *Global Advances in Health and Medicine* 3, no. 2 (2014): 72–79.

[77] David A. Harris, "The Importance of Research on Race and Policing: Making Race Salient to Individuals and Institutions within Criminal Justice," *Criminology & Public Policy* 6, no. 1 (2007): 5–23.

[78] Sandra Bass, "Negotiating Change: Community Organizations and the Politics of Policing," *Urban Affairs Review* 36, no. 2 (2000): 148–177.

[79] James E. Hawdon, John Ryan, and Sean P. Griffin, "Policing Tactics and Perceptions of Police Legitimacy," *Police Quarterly* 6, no. 4 (2003): 469–491.

[80] Kahn and Martin, "Policing and Race."

[81] Jillian K. Swencionis and Phillip A. Goff, "The Psychological Science of Racial Bias and Policing," *Psychology, Public Policy, and Law* 23, no. 4 (2017): 398–409.

[82] Harris, "The Importance of Research on Race and Policing."

[83] Phillip A. Goff and Kimberly B. Kahn, "Racial Bias in Policing: Why We Know Less Than We Should," *Social Issues and Policy Review* 6, no. 1 (2012): 177–210.

[84] Task Force on 21st Century Policing, *Final Report of the President's Task Force on 21st Century Policing*.

[85] Michael D. White and Henry F. Fradella, *Stop and Frisk: The Use and Abuse of a Controversial Policing Tactic* (New York: New York University Press, 2016).

[86] Kristina Murphy, Lyn Hinds, and Jenny Fleming, "Encouraging Public Cooperation and Support for Police," *Policing and Society* 18, no. 2 (2008): 136–155; Michael D. Reisig, Jason Bratton, and Marc G. Gertz, "The Construct Validity and Refinement of Process-Based Policing Measures," *Criminal Justice and Behavior* 34, no. 8 (2007): 1005–1028; Tyler and Huo, *Trust in the Law*; Tom R. Tyler, *Why People Obey the Law* (New Haven, CT: Yale University Press, 2000); Scott E. Wolfe, Justin Nix, Robert Kaminski, and Jeff Rojek, "Is the Effect of Procedural Justice on Police Legitimacy Invariant? Testing the Generality of Procedural Justice and Competing Antecedents of Legitimacy," *Journal of Quantitative Criminology* 32, no. 2 (2016): 253–282.

[87] Goff and Kahn, "Racial Bias in Policing."

[88] Rod K. Brunson, "'Police Don't Like Black People': African-American Young Men's Accumulated Police Experiences," *Criminology & Public Policy* 6, no. 1 (2007): 71–101.

[89] That is, with the exception of literature surrounding urban black men. For examples, see Mark T. Berg, Eric A. Stewart, Jonathan Intravia, Patricia Y. Warren, and Ronald L. Simons, "Cynical Streets: Neighborhood Social Processes and Perceptions of Criminal Injustice," *Criminology* 54, no. 3 (2016): 520–547; Rod K. Brunson and Ronald Weitzer, "Police Relations with Black and White Youths in Different Urban Neighborhoods," *Urban Affairs Review* 44, no. 6 (2008): 858–885; Stewart et al. "Neighborhood Racial Context and Perceptions of Police-Based Racial Discrimination Among Black Youth."

5

Response Essay

Chief Calvin Williams
Cleveland Division of Police

Upon reading the chapter "Reduce Racial Inequalities in Police Practices," I was struck by its last two sentences. These words give me hope and let me know that citizens and members of law enforcement are so much closer on their messaging than common knowledge would have us believe. We have the same hopes for continued growth and, although we may not yet be on the same page, I believe we are one simple turn of the page apart.

The chapter ends:

> It is unfortunate that today's police officers and departments have to deal with the scars that the police from decades before inflicted on the citizenry they serve. That said, when departments can acknowledge the historical hurt that the police have brought to the citizenry, they lay a path forward toward a working relationship between the police and the people and communities they serve.

I have been in law enforcement for over 30 years. I grew up in the inner city, raised by a single mother, and I faced many of the issues that still face those in the inner city today. I became a police officer during a much different time in our history, and I have seen, from the inside, the growth and progress that the law enforcement community has made. I will admit that this can be—and it has been—a slow process. As a profession, we are still striving to build the trust of the community, become more inclusive, and be as transparent as possible.

It is no secret that law enforcement, as a profession, needs to evolve with the times. Racially biased policing is unethical and immoral. Our agency is working to address this issue through developing new policies reflecting best practices, training our officers on those practices, and using a discipline matrix to address issues regarding police conduct as they arise.

The Cleveland Division of Police has entered into a settlement agreement with the U.S. Department of Justice to rectify our past wrongs. The settlement agreement outlines many procedural changes and, as a division, we have made great strides toward compliance with the agreement in most areas. Most notably, our division has been trained on best practices in handling situations regarding crisis intervention, de-escalation techniques, and bias-free policing and procedural justice.

As part of our effort to improve, the division has instituted tracking system software that traces each officer's incident history, including incidents involving the use of force. From the data collected, we can determine which officers may need to be updated on our policies or retrained on our practices. This officer-specific data allows the division to compare and analyze incidents overall and consider areas where special attention may be needed.

The Cleveland Division of Police was one of the first big-city police departments to adopt a city-wide body-worn camera policy. Our administration uses the resulting video to analyze officer interactions, ensure the best possible citizen-to-officer experience, and guide our officers as they strive to communicate professionally and appropriately. Body-worn camera video has been and will continue to be considered in cases of officer discipline and as a training aid. Since Cleveland implemented its body-worn camera policy, citizen complaints against officers have dropped dramatically.

Our recruitment efforts have also changed dramatically over the last few years. The city has instituted a Public Safety Recruitment Team that is actively engaged in the community, allowing us to identify and recruit people for our safety forces across all disciplines and levels of education. We target many minority communities and participate in traditional job-seeking venues like job fairs and college campus hiring events. In addition, the division is committed to promoting a diverse leadership—one that includes minorities and women in significant roles.

In some ways, our officers do bear witness to the scars caused by those who came before us. To grow as a profession, we need to learn what we can from the past and use that knowledge to shape our future. Growth comes from knowing where we were as a profession, where we are now, and where we are going—and having the vision to reach that destination. If we continue to engage with the community and listen to one another, I am confident that the Cleveland Division of Police will continue to grow to be the best police agency in our nation.

6

Options for Increasing Civilian Oversight of the Police

Scott H. Decker
Arizona State University
John A. Shjarback
Rowan University

Background

In 1967, the National Advisory Commission on Civil Disorders, known familiarly as the Kerner Commission, issued its report on the causes of civil disorder and urban riots in the 1960s. The Commission concluded that the United States was evolving into two societies, "separate and unequal . . . one Black, one White."[1] At the core of the racial unrest was a fundamental lack of trust among black Americans in the institutions of government, particularly the police. This was not the first such commission to investigate relationships between citizens and the police, nor would it be the last. Indeed, the most recent iteration of such a commission was the Obama-appointed President's Task Force on 21st Century Policing—created in response to highly publicized instances where the police used deadly force against unarmed black citizens (e.g., Michael Brown and Eric Garner). The conclusions reached by that 2015 Commission bear a striking resemblance both to those of the 1967 Kerner Commission as well as the 1929 National Commission on Law Observance and Enforcement, known as the Wickersham Commission. Each concluded that better police-community relationships should be built by enhancing trust between them. Over the years, researchers have proposed a variety of steps to achieve this goal, such as increasing diversity in police hiring as well as changing the philosophy of policing from "warrior" to "guardian" or from "enforcer" to "problem-solver."

The 2015 President's Task Force on 21st Century Policing also included recommendations for improving police-community relations and restoring public faith in law enforcement through civilian oversight. In fact, the Task Force titled the second pillar of its final report "Policy and Oversight," explaining that "to ensure policies are maintained and current, law enforcement agencies are encouraged to . . . establish civilian oversight mechanisms with their communities."[2] Similarly, "Campaign Zero," a community-based platform launched in August 2015, includes the element of civilian oversight as one of its ten policy solutions aiming to reform the police.[3]

The rationale behind civilian oversight is simple: when the police are left to investigate officer misconduct or to review critical incidents themselves, the community perceives a lack of accountability. Under such circumstances, only the most major infractions receive attention.[4] Indeed, much of the unrest following the deaths of Michael Brown in Ferguson, Eric Garner in Staten Island, and Laquan McDonald in Chicago, among others, arose from the failure of public officials to take action against the police officers in those cases. This chapter provides an overview of civilian oversight in American policing, including its evolution as an accountability mechanism, the different models of police review, the existing empirical research on the topic, and potential solutions to increase the practice's effectiveness moving forward.

Sometimes referred to as "citizen oversight," "civilian review," "external review," or "citizen review boards,"[5] civilian oversight generally includes the use of non-police actors working in groups to provide input into police department operations, often with a focus on the citizen complaint and review process. Models of civilian oversight groups vary widely in structure, purpose, composition, and jurisdiction. For instance, some groups have paid positions, whereas others have elected or volunteer positions; some have independent investigatory powers, while others simply monitor complaint investigations conducted by internal affairs units. Some oversight agencies have a narrow focus, exclusively reviewing complaints that citizens have lodged against officers, whereas others also handle officer complaints initiated by supervisors in addition to reviewing select critical incidents (e.g., use of force or officer-involved shootings). There are also oversight agencies that play a more pivotal role in reviewing, analyzing, and monitoring aggregate organizational policies, practices, training, and systemic conduct.

Put differently, there is no "one size fits all" civilian oversight model.[6] The diversity in jurisdiction, membership, purpose, and structure illustrates a fundamental challenge in assessing the impact of such groups. Because there is no standard oversight model, evaluations of one model (which are rare to begin with) may not apply to another model. In the end, civilian oversight is a concept that has not yet been systematically evaluated, leading the Major Cities Chiefs Association (MCCA) to urge refinement of the oversight model and careful assessment of its impact.[7]

■ History and Growth over Time

Policing scholars have provided detailed accounts of civilian oversight and how the practice has grown and evolved over time.[8] Most types of civilian oversight have emerged after periods of tension and conflict between police and minority communities.[9] This follows a broader pattern of crisis-led policing reform in response to negative events.[10] For example, De Angelis and colleagues found that just 11 percent of the 97 oversight agencies that they reviewed were created "proactively" without a damaging incident(s) to provide the impetus.[11] Unfortunately, oversight boards created in the face of a crisis have certain liabilities: for example, a sense of urgency may color the process, creating adversarial relationships between law enforcement and the civilian body from the start. Like so many aspects of civilian oversight of the police, little is known about whether groups formed in response to a crisis are ultimately more or less successful in restoring public trust in the police and arriving at just decisions.

The precursor to oversight as we know it today took the form of police commissions during the early years of the Reform Era of policing (1890s to 1920s).[12] Those commissions were designed to remove political influence from local police departments and root out large-scale corruption. Usually composed of judges, attorneys, and reformers, early police commissions represented a general practice of oversight that excluded community members.

Modern types of civilian oversight—such as review boards—initially began in several large U.S. cities, including New York City and Philadelphia, in the mid-twentieth century. They either received citizen complaints directly or reviewed completed internal affairs investigations of alleged police misconduct. These review boards were short-lived; nearly all were eliminated due to a lack of funding or resources as well as resistance from police unions.[13] More contemporary models of civilian oversight were created in the wake of the civil unrest and urban riots of the 1960s. In 1967, the Kerner Commission identified police action (e.g., brutalization and harassment of black Americans and other abuses of power) as being a contributing factor to those civil conflicts.[14] This next wave of oversight introduced bodies that had greater investigatory power to conduct independent reviews, better resources and funding, and expanded authority over police agencies.[15]

Similarly, the 1990s saw another tremendous increase in oversight agencies following the high-profile videotaped beating of Rodney King by officers of the Los Angeles Police Department. The number of review boards grew from just a few in the early 1990s to more than 100 by 2001.[16] According to the National Association for Civilian Oversight of Law Enforcement (NACOLE), a leading advocate for police accountability and transparency through external review, more than 200 civilian oversight bodies are now operating at the local government level; 46 of those jurisdictions are members of the MCCA.[17] Still, this represents only a small fraction—just 1 percent—of the 12,000 local and municipal police departments across the United States.[18] This illustrates how the practice of civilian oversight has not yet been institutionalized in the American law enforcement community. Moreover, law enforcement groups, primarily among rank-and-file and union groups, have vigorously opposed such oversight.

■ Overview of Different Civilian Oversight Models

There have been multiple attempts to create schemas to classify civilian oversight programs over the years. De Angelis and colleagues, in a report on behalf of NACOLE, grouped policing oversight bodies into three categories based on two criteria:

1. the measures and data that each oversight agency received and
2. an evaluation of each agency's mission statement and its foundational legal authority.[19]

De Angelis named these categories based on their primary focus: investigation, review, and auditor/monitor.

Investigation-Focused

This common model of civilian oversight operates as a separate entity from the police or sheriff's department, conducting its own independent investigations into allegations of police misconduct.[20] In this model, the oversight agency either completely replaces the law enforcement organization's internal affairs unit, or it conducts investigations that parallel the work of internal affairs, such as interviewing officers, complainants, and witnesses.[21] Although the structure and authority of investigation-focused oversight agencies vary across jurisdictions, compared to other types of oversight agencies, they usually have more resources and a larger, better-trained staff who tend to be full-time employees as opposed to volunteers. De Angelis categorized the Office of Police Complaints in Washington, D.C.; the Office of Citizen Complaints in San Francisco, California; and the Citizens' Law Enforcement Review Board in San Diego County, California, as examples of investigation-focused models.

Review-Focused

Rather than conducting independent investigations, this type of civilian oversight model simply evaluates the quality of investigations already completed by internal affairs units. Many review-focused agencies consist of volunteer review boards or commissions; they are usually created with the purpose of bringing community input into the existing internal affairs process.[22] As such, these oversight groups are typically less expensive to create and operate, which particularly benefits smaller jurisdictions. Review-focused agencies, however, tend to have limited authority and fewer organizational resources compared to other forms of oversight. For example, these agencies do not typically have the power to subpoena witnesses or records; they are less likely to review complaints made by supervisors or those that involve critical incidents (e.g., officer-involved shootings); and volunteer members may have less expertise and training in police issues. De Angelis counted the Citizens' Police Review Board in Albany (New York), the Citizens' Police Complaint Board in Indianapolis (Indiana), and the Citizen Police Review Committee in St. Petersburg (Florida) as examples of review-focused models.

Auditor-/Monitor-Focused

This is the newest form of civilian oversight. Agencies falling under the auditor-/monitor-focused model seek to achieve large-scale, systemic reform of police departments. Unlike investigation- and review-focused forms of oversight, agencies following this model conduct evaluations of department training, policies, and practices using more rigorous research methods. For accountability purposes, they also critically assess broad patterns of both citizen- and internally generated complaints as well as critical incidents through the use of robust data collection systems.[23] Auditors/monitors tend to have better access to departmental records and databases, including individual officer measures (e.g., use-of-force incidents), larger budgets with more resources (e.g., trained policing experts), and are usually in a better position to track whether departments implement their recommendations and make suggested organizational changes. The Independent Police Auditor in San Jose (California), the Office of the Independent Monitor in Denver (Colorado), and the Independent Police Monitor in New Orleans (Louisiana) operate under this model.

Oversight agencies vary widely in their jurisdiction, structure, and roles. Indeed, there is considerable variation even among agencies within the same broad category. Such variation may be beneficial, as different models fit different needs. In developing an oversight body, mayors and city councils can try to match the organizational characteristics of a model to the needs and resources of their particular jurisdiction.[24] However, this variation creates difficulties in making appropriate "apples-to-apples" comparisons across jurisdictions.

■ Research Evidence

Although much has been written about the history and methodology of civilian oversight, there is limited empirical research on the general practice's effectiveness. Most of the evaluations that have been conducted are case studies of individual oversight agencies. While these are important for examining the performance of specific agencies, the case-study approach limits our ability to make meaningful comparisons across agency types. In short, there is a severe lack of systematic research backing up this anecdotal evidence, due to two primary challenges: data limitations and the difficulty of measuring law enforcement performance.

Data Shortcomings

Police department data are not usually accessible to researchers who seek to evaluate the effectiveness of civilian oversight agencies. While few agencies provide adequate information about the complaints they handle (e.g., investigation-focused models), the majority either do not make that information available for public consumption or do not update complaints in a timely fashion. One example of an agency that does supply timely complaint information is the Office of Police Complaints (OPC) for the Metropolitan Police Department in Washington, D.C. The OPC publishes yearly databases that catalogue each complaint, complete with a summary of specific allegations (e.g., harassment, excessive force, and language/conduct) and findings of fact, as well as the examiner's decisions regarding whether complaints were sustained or unfounded. Researchers may be able to use this type of data to examine the correlates of complaints that are sustained versus those that are unfounded. In this vein, previous studies[25] have reviewed publicly available reports and documents from agencies to evaluate oversight performance. Still, data availability remains limited.

Measuring Law Enforcement Performance

Even when departmental and complaint data is available, the lack of consistent reporting and measurement standards across jurisdictions make it difficult to assess law enforcement performance. Although a number of studies have set out to assess different performance measures,[26] there is still no consensus on how to best measure organizational performance. One data source, the Law Enforcement Management and Administrative Statistics (LEMAS) survey, provides the ability to calculate department-level measures of complaint rates (i.e., complaints per officer or citizen) and the percentage of those complaints that are ultimately "sustained." However, scholars have long argued that such measures should not be used for comparative purposes for a variety of reasons.[27] For example, departments and their civilian oversight agencies differ in their complaint intake process; the ease with which formal complaints can be made varies considerably. Some agencies allow complaints to be submitted online, while others require an in-person visit to department headquarters. The reception of citizens seeking to make a complaint can vary as well. In some cases, citizens are greeted with respect and courtesy, whereas in others, they are met with intimidation, threats, and hostility.[28] In fact, there is documentation that some departments have a history of threatening complainants with prosecution for making false statements should their allegation of misconduct not be substantiated.[29] The review and adjudication processes are complex as well, and they also vary across agencies.

Case Studies

The available research evidence regarding case studies of individual oversight agencies is mixed. The literature provides a few examples of successful oversight endeavors, most of which are based on independent evaluation, and describes their development in depth.[30] However, other evaluations have been more critical, such as the report from the Chicago Police Accountability Task Force. Created in the wake of the city's unrest after the shooting death of Laquan McDonald, the Police Accountability Task Force released a scathing report of the Chicago Police Department's civilian oversight agency, the Independent Police Review Authority. It concluded, "Chicago's police accountability system does not work. The system should identify and investigate police misconduct and then impose appropriate punishment. But at every step, there are enormous barriers."[31]

A review prompted by a series of controversial officer-involved shootings made a similar determination of ineffectiveness about the Albuquerque Police Department's oversight agency.[32] It is not clear, however, what has changed as a result of these two reviews and their criticism of local police oversight in their jurisdictions. That said, the Chicago Police Department now faces a consent decree that may lead to changes in the role and jurisdiction of police accountability.

Information on another civilian oversight body highlights some of the previously raised concerns. The City of St. Louis's Civilian Oversight Board (COB)[33] consists of seven members of the public appointed by the mayor. Established in 2015, the board is tasked with addressing "police accountability and professional conduct" of the Metropolitan Police Department of the City of St. Louis. The COB's jurisdiction includes the following acts of misconduct by law enforcement officers:

- excessive use of force,
- abuse of authority,
- sexual harassment and assault,
- discourtesy,
- racial profiling, or
- use of offensive language, including, but not limited to, slurs relating to race, ethnicity, religion, gender, sexual orientation, gender identity, immigration status, and disability.[34]

The COB forwards complaints to the Internal Affairs Division of the Metropolitan Police Department for investigation; it does not conduct its own independent investigation. Following the Internal Affairs investigation, cases are then returned to the COB, which may recommend mediation but has no formal power to sanction. In 2018, the COB heard 39 complaints and did not differ with the Internal Affairs Division in the disposition of any. In the 42 cases heard in 2017, the COB disagreed in only one case involving the beating of a suspect.[35] This low rate of disagreement may demonstrate a lack of true oversight.

Comparative Research and Organizational Characteristics

De Angelis and colleagues performed what is arguably the most rigorous categorization and evaluation of the organizational characteristics of oversight agencies and their respective impacts on effectiveness. They collected organizational and attitudinal data on 97 civilian oversight bodies, including measures of legal authority or powers granted to the agency, budget and staffing, perceived support from stakeholders, and data collection and analysis practices.[36] This research found that 34 agencies (35 percent) could be classified as "investigation-focused," with another 39 (40 percent) classified as "review-focused" and 24 (25 percent) classified as "auditor-/monitor-focused." Based on previous literature and the original data collected, they identified 12 core elements of successful oversight agencies, at least to the extent we can draw such conclusions:

- independence,
- adequate jurisdictional authority,
- unfettered access to records,
- full cooperation,
- access to law enforcement executives and internal affairs staff,
- support of process stakeholders,
- adequate resources,
- public reporting/transparency,
- use of statistical pattern analysis,
- community outreach,
- community involvement, and
- respect for confidentiality.

It also appears that oversight personnel themselves have disparate perceptions of success. Those working for auditor-/monitor-focused agencies were most likely to report that their police or sheriff's department frequently or very frequently implemented their recommendations (72 percent), compared to personnel working for investigation-focused (42 percent) or review-focused (34 percent) oversight agencies.[37]

Impact on Public Perception and Trust

In principle, civilian oversight should improve public perception and trust in law enforcement as well as increase citizen participation and engagement in the process. If nothing else, it should provide citizens with the comfort that an external entity is "policing the police" or at least "watching the police," thereby increasing accountability and transparency in the complaint and review process. Yet not much is known about the impact that civilian oversight has on citizens' perceptions, which broadly mirrors the trend of research on the topic. One function of most civilian oversight agencies is providing residents with an opportunity to address issues of concern in their communities through public community meetings. A recent study examined more than seven years of transcripts from monthly community meetings facilitated by the civilian oversight body of the Chicago Police Department (CPD).[38] It found that only 230 unique citizens spoke and that CPD representatives (e.g., the superintendent or his deputy) replied to only 26 percent of those speakers, meaning that police department representatives remained silent in the face of 74 percent of civilian complaints. This anecdote shows the profound lack of both community participation and police department engagement. Overall, little research has focused on civilian oversight. As a result, the field has a relatively limited knowledge base on the organizational factors that influence effectiveness.[39]

■ Next Steps

Based on the lack of systematic and comparative research, our choice of solutions is limited in comparison with some of the other recommendations in this volume, such as enhancing procedural justice, that are supported by more extensive evidence. Therefore, we start with the belief that police executives and scholars, as well as community groups, should temper their expectations for civilian oversight. It appears that simply having a civilian oversight body is not sufficient to ensure either its effectiveness or any ultimate police reform. Some oversight bodies have been affirmatively shown to be merely symbolic, with no real power or independent authority. The results of the Chicago and St. Louis models, respectively, may be instructive in these matters.

Instead, effectiveness and reform, in the form of increased accountability and transparency as well as citizen satisfaction, are likely to be affected by the organizations in which those agencies operate—contingent upon a host of both department- and oversight-level factors. These factors include the police department's level of organizational commitment and the funding and resources afforded to the oversight agency. As previously discussed, a high degree of variation exists across civilian oversight bodies, which might be beneficial for law enforcement agencies, as it provides a number of potential options rather than a "one-size-fits-all" approach.

Building on the observation that there is considerable variation in "civilian oversight," our first primary recommendation is that those communities interested in implementing or amending their civilian oversight capabilities should engage in a rigorous and extensive planning phase that includes citizen input. This planning should be conducted proactively with an adequate timeline leading up to implementation as opposed to waiting for a negative event or a breakdown in citizen trust and police legitimacy. In fact, some evidence suggests that oversight groups formed in the wake of a negative event are more likely to end in failure. Egregious use-of-force incidents and patterns of misconduct—with the political climate that follows—do not create ideal conditions in which to begin the citizen oversight process. Under such circumstances, oversight agency members may feel substantial pressure to seek measures that police and police unions would view as too punitive. Likewise, law enforcement may be more defensive and apprehensive about the development of civilian oversight. By instead forming oversight groups under more normalized and less politicized circumstances, the negotiation process between the municipality, the police department and its union(s), and community organizations can unfold in a more orderly and productive fashion. This allows all interested parties more time and opportunity both to communicate the features they would like to see incorporated in an oversight agency and to voice potential concerns.

Planning in a proactive manner allows a department to explore its options, as different models of oversight fit different needs. Access to information is paramount: interested parties (e.g., mayors, city councils, and police leadership) must be apprised of the different forms of civilian oversight—investigation-focused, review-focused, and auditor-/monitor-focused—as well as their strengths and weaknesses. The organizational characteristics of the oversight model must be matched to the needs and resources of a particular jurisdiction. Furthermore, oversight development must include as many factors that have been shown to increase the likelihood of success as possible, particularly in the areas of independence and authority. For example, more effective oversight agencies have been found to have adequate resources, subpoena power, and better access to records and executives or internal affairs staff.[40] Perceptions from civilian oversight personnel suggest that they view auditor-/monitor-focused models as being the most effective, followed by investigation-focused models, with review-focused models as the least effective. While acknowledging that more empirical evaluation research is needed, we recommend that communities give adequate consideration to all of this information during the planning phase.

While a number of researchers have contributed to what we currently know about civilian oversight of the police, the gaps in the literature are still quite large. As a result, our final recommendation is to increase the amount of evidence-based research on the practice of civilian oversight of the police. Only then can we draw firmer conclusions about what is effective and what is not in terms of organizational characteristics and which broad oversight models work best. To this end, we suggest increasing the incentives for researchers to conduct systemic, empirical evaluations of civilian oversight agencies. Increased funding is an important part of that effort. Brian Buchner, the former President of NACOLE, encourages federal and state agencies as well as private organizations and corporations that support applied research in law enforcement to consider developing new and sustained funding streams for research into civilian oversight of police.[41] Professional police organizations should prioritize evaluation research, as recently conducted in a roundtable discussion by the MCCA in conjunction with the U.S. Department of Justice Office of Community Oriented Policing Services.[42] Peer-reviewed journals can follow suit with special editions dedicated to creating an evidence base for civilian oversight efforts. For example, *Criminal Justice Policy Review* recently released a special issue featuring manuscripts presented at the NACOLE Academic Symposium at John Jay College of Criminal Justice.[43]

Police accountability has grown in importance over the last decade. Accountability within the community is understood as a necessary condition for effective and constitutional policing. Such accountability is usually built over the course of years, perhaps decades, and rarely emerges in the immediate aftermath of a highly publicized negative interaction between citizens and police. Working collaboratively, though, law enforcement and the citizens they serve can search for common ground and begin to develop trust, perhaps by way of small steps that increase police accountability through meaningful oversight.

Notes

[1] National Advisory Commission on Civil Disorders, *Report of the National Advisory Commission on Civil Disorders* (Washington, DC: U.S. Government Printing Office, 1968), 1.

[2] COPS Office, *The President's Task Force on 21st Century Policing* (Washington, DC: Office of Community Oriented Policing Services, 2015), p. 2.

[3] More information about Campaign Zero can be accessed online at https://www.joincampaignzero.org/#vision.

[4] Jeff Rojek, Scott H. Decker, and Allen E. Wagner, "Addressing Police Misconduct: The Role of Citizen Complaints," in *Critical Issues in Policing: Contemporary Readings*, eds. Roger G. Dunham and Geoffrey P. Alpert (Long Grove, IL: Waveland Press, Inc. 2015), 162–182.

[5] Geoffrey P. Alpert, Tyler Cawthray, Jeff Rojek, and Frank V. Ferdik, "Citizen Oversight in the United States and Canada: Applying Outcome Measures and Evidence-Based Concepts," in *Civilian Oversight of Police: Advancing Accountability in Law Enforcement*, eds. Tim Prenzler and Garth den Heyer (New York: CRC Press, 2016), 179–204; Samuel Walker and Carol A. Archbold, *The New World of Police Accountability,* 3rd ed. (Los Angeles, CA: Sage, 2020).).

[6] Joseph De Angelis, Richard Rosenthal, and Brian Buchner, *Civilian Oversight of Law Enforcement: Assessing the Evidence* (Washington, DC: Office of Justice Programs Diagnostic Center, 2016). This report presents a number of benefits as well as limitations that will be discussed throughout the chapter.

[7] Darrel W. Stephens, Ellen Scrivner, and Josie F. Cambareri, *Civilian Oversight of the Police in Major Cities* (Washington, DC: Office of Community Oriented Policing Services, 2018), https://cops.usdoj.gov/RIC/Publications/cops-w0861-pub.pdf.

[8] Alpert, Cawthray, Rojek, and Ferdik, "Citizen Oversight in the United States and Canada"; Merrick Bobb, "Civilian Oversight of the Police in the United States," *Saint Louis University Public Law Review* 22, no. 1 (2003): 151–156; Walker and Archbold, *The New World of Police Accountability*; Samuel Walker, "The History of the Citizen Oversight," in *Citizen Oversight of Law Enforcement*, ed. Justina C. Perino (Chicago: American Bar Association, 2006), 1–10.

[9] Walker and Archbold, *The New World of Police Accountability.*

[10] Michael D. White, "Transactional Encounters, Crisis-Driven Reform, and the Potential for a National Police Deadly Force Database," *Criminology & Public Policy* 15, no. 1 (2016): 223–235.

[11] De Angelis, Rosenthal, and Buchner, *Civilian Oversight of Law Enforcement.*

[12] George L. Kelling and Mark H. Moore, "The Evolving Strategy of Policing," *Perspectives on Policing*, no. 4 (Nov. 1988).

[13] Andrew J. Goldsmith, "Complaints against the Police: The Trend to External Review," *Contemporary Sociology* 22, no. 1 (1993); Walker, "The History of the Citizen Oversight"; Walker and Archbold, *The New World of Police Accountability.*

[14] National Advisory Commission on Civil Disorders, Report of the National Advisory Commission on Civil Disorders.

[15] De Angelis, Rosenthal, and Buchner, *Civilian Oversight of Law Enforcement.*

[16] Walker and Archbold, *The New World of Police Accountability.*

[17] National Association for Civilian Oversight of Law Enforcement (NACOLE) provides a list of civilian oversight bodies on its website, which can be accessed at https://www.nacole.org/police_oversight_by_jurisdiction_usa. Yet, the organization specifies that it "does not officially endorse, certify, or recommend any of the agencies listed above. Further, inclusion on this list does not indicate membership in NACOLE. This list, which is for informational purposes only, represents agencies that came to the attention of NACOLE over time and also have websites. This IS NOT an exhaustive or complete list of oversight entities in the U.S. NACOLE continually adds to and revises the list." See also De Angelis, Rosenthal, and Buchner, *Civilian Oversight of Law Enforcement*, and Stephens, Scrivner, and Cambareri, *Civilian Oversight of the Police in Major Cities.*

[18] Shelley S. Hyland and Elizabeth Davis, Local Police Departments, 2016: Personnel (Washington, DC: Bureau of Justice Statistics, 2019); De Angelis, Rosenthal, and Buchner, *Civilian Oversight of Law Enforcement*; Tim Prenzler and Carol Ronken, "Models of Police Oversight: A Critique," *Policing and Society: An International Journal* 11, no. 2 (2001): 151–180; Walker and Archbold, *The New World of Police Accountability.*

[19] De Angelis, Rosenthal, and Buchner, *Civilian Oversight of Law Enforcement.*

[20] Barbara Attard and Kathryn Olson, *Overview of Civilian Oversight of Law Enforcement in the United States*, 2013, http://accountabilityassociates.org/wp-content/uploads/Oversight-in-the-US-%E2%80%A6FINAL.pdf; Peter Finn, *Citizen Review of Police: Approaches and Implementation* (Washington, DC: National Institute of Justice, 2001), https://www.ncjrs.gov/pdffiles1/nij/184430.pdf; Police Assessment Resource Center, *Review of National Police Oversight Models for the Eugene Police Commission* (Los Angeles: Author, 2005).

[21] Police Assessment Resource Center, *Review of National Police Oversight Models.*

[22] Walker and Archbold, *The New World of Police Accountability.*

[23] De Angelis, Rosenthal, and Buchner, *Civilian Oversight of Law Enforcement.*

[24] Frank V. Ferdik, Jeff Rojek, and Geoffrey P. Alpert, "Citizen Oversight in the United States and Canada: An Overview," *Police Practice and Research* 14, no. 2 (2013): 104–116; Tim Prenzler and Colleen Lewis, "Performance Indicators for Police Oversight Agencies," *Australian Journal of Public Administration* 64, no. 2 (2005): 77–83.

[25] David Brereton, "Evaluating the Performance of External Oversight Bodies," in *Civilian Oversight of Policing: Governance, Democracy and Human Rights*, eds. Andrew Goldsmith

and Colleen Lewis (Portland, OR: Hart Publishing, 2000): 105–124; Beth A. Mohr, *The Use of Performance Measurement in Civilian Oversight in the United States*, Thesis (University of New Mexico, 2007).

[26] Rojek, Decker, and Wagner, "Addressing Police Misconduct"; Walker and Archbold, *The New World of Police Accountability.*

[27] Rojek, Decker, and Wagner, "Addressing Police Misconduct."

[28] Gerald Caiden, G. and Harlan Hahn, "Public Complaints against the Police," in *Evaluating Alternative Law-Enforcement Policies*, eds. Ralph Baker and Fred A. Meyer, Jr. (Lexington, ME: Lexington Books, 1979): 169–176.

[29] Kathryn Olson and Barbara Attard, "Analysis of Police Oversight Models for the City of Pasadena" (Pasadena, CA: 2016); Police Assessment Resource Center, *Review of National Police Oversight Models.*

[30] Police Accountability Task Force, *Recommendations for Reform: Restoring Trust between the Chicago Police and the Communities They Serve* (Chicago, IL: City of Chicago, 2016).

[31] Ibid., p. 63.

[32] Ad Hoc Police Oversight Task Force, *Report on the Activities of the Ad Hoc Police Oversight Task Force* (Albuquerque: City Council, 2014).

[33] City of St. Louis, Missouri, "About the Civilian Oversight Board," https://www.stlouis-mo.gov/government/departments/public-safety/civilian-oversight-board/about.cfm.

[34] City of St. Louis, Missouri, "How to File a Complaint against a St. Louis Metropolitan Police Officer," https://www.stlouis-mo.gov/government/departments/public-safety/civilian-oversight-board/complaint-process.cfm.

[35] City of St. Louis, Missouri, Civilian Oversight Board, "Annual Report 2018," May 21, 2019, https://www.stlouis-mo.gov/government/departments/public-safety/civilian-oversight-board/documents/upload/Annual-Report-2018-PDF-Final-Document.pdf

[36] De Angelis, Rosenthal, and Buchner, *Civilian Oversight of Law Enforcement.*

[37] See the following two sources for exceptions: Tim Prenzler, "Democratic Policing, Public Opinion and External Oversight," in *Civilian Oversight of Police: Advancing Accountability in Law Enforcement*, eds. Tim Prenzler and Garth den Heyer (Boca Raton: FL: CRC Press, 2016): 51–72; Robert E. Worden and Sarah J. McLean, *Citizen Oversight of the Albany Police, 2010* (Albany, NY: John F. Finn Institute for Public Safety, Inc.).

[38] Tony Cheng, "Input without Influence: The Silence and Scripts of Police and Community Relations," *Social Problems* spz049, (2019): 1–19.

[39] De Angelis, Rosenthal, and Buchner, *Civilian Oversight of Law Enforcement.*

[40] Ibid.

[41] Brian Buchner, *NACOLE President Brian Buchner's Oral Testimony for the President's Task Force on 21st Century Policing, Policy and Oversight Listening Session* (Cincinnati, OH: National Association for Civilian Oversight of Law Enforcement, 2015).

[42] Stephens, Scrivner, and Cambareri, *Civilian Oversight of the Police in Major Cities.*

[43] Daniel L. Stageman, Nicole M. Napolitano, and Brian Buchner, "New Approaches to Data-Driven Civilian Oversight of Law Enforcement: An Introduction to the Second NACOLE/CJPR Special Issue," *Criminal Justice Policy Review* 29, no. 2 (2016): 1–17.

6

Response Essay

Sheriff Margo L. Frasier
Travis County, Texas (ret.)
Police Monitor, Austin, Texas (ret.)

Recently, there has been a lot of talk about increasing the role of civilian oversight of law enforcement. The reality is that civilian oversight of law enforcement has always existed. In every community, the public assesses the effectiveness, efficiency, and appropriateness of the actions of its law enforcement agency. Nowhere is that more obvious than when the community demands change in its law enforcement agency by protesting, confronting city hall, or, in the case of an elected sheriff's office, expressing its satisfaction or dissatisfaction through the ballot box.

The establishment of an agency to formally perform the function of civilian oversight of a community's law enforcement agency has the potential to provide a mechanism for the community to voice its concerns contemporaneously through a complaint process that does not require the citizen to complain to the very agency that employs the subject of the complaint. It also may allow for individuals independent of the internal affairs unit of the law enforcement agency to be a part of the investigative process. The level of the civilian oversight agency's involvement in the investigative process can vary from reviewing and commenting on the final report produced by the internal affairs unit after the fact, joining with the internal affairs unit to conduct the investigation, and/or initiating and conducting its own separate investigation. The civilian oversight agency may also examine data, analyze the extent to which a law enforcement agency is complying with policies and training requirements, and point out issues of a systemic nature, such as racial profiling and use of force.

In chapter 6, the authors do a good job of outlining the functions of the three main models of civilian oversight agencies: investigation, review, and auditor/monitor. However, civilian oversight agencies are often a hybrid of the three models, and the chapter does not explore how a community decides what its civilian oversight should look like. As a community seeks to establish a civilian oversight agency or evaluate an existing civilian oversight agency, what is most important is that it adjust the model of civilian oversight to match what is sustainable in that community and what will meet its specific needs. Complicating the issue is the fact that the decision is seldom made in a vacuum. Often, advocates demand increased power for civilian oversight and law enforcement unions or associations call for limiting the power of civilian oversight. As result, the formation of a civilian oversight agency is frequently the result of negotiation as opposed to collaboration. This can result in a civilian oversight agency that is considered both lacking by the advocates for civilian oversight and overreaching by the law enforcement unions or associations.

To view civilian oversight as simply a response to public mistrust of the police and their ability to police themselves when there has been a major critical incident is to sell civilian oversight's role in improving the overall quality of law enforcement short. Many more important outcomes are gained through civilian oversight. One that warrants highlighting is the development of policies, along with the evaluation of the extent to which law enforcement adheres to those policies and the training required to implement them.

A good example is a policy on the use of body cameras. What a law enforcement agency believes is a proper policy as to when interactions should be recorded and who should have access to the video may very well not meet the expectations of the community. Such a situation arose in Austin, Texas, when the police department developed its body camera policy without obtaining input from the public or the civilian oversight agency. Eventually, the city council, responding to concerns expressed by the civilian oversight agency executive and advocates, required the police department to collaborate with the agency and advocates. While the police department and the police union were initially reluctant to accept outside input, after the collaborative process was completed, the police department, the police union, advocates, and the civilian oversight agency all agreed that the resulting policy addressed the interests of law enforcement while reflecting the values and concerns of the community.

In chapter 6, the authors take the position that the concept of civilian oversight has yet to be systemically evaluated. They bolster that position by noting that the Major Cities Chiefs Association (MCCA) has urged refinement of the oversight model and careful assessment of its impact. I participated in the MCCA's roundtable discussion as the designated representative of the National Association for Civilian Oversight of Law Enforcement (NACOLE). While I agree that assessment is appropriate, there are issues to be addressed before undertaking an assessment. When assessing the impact of civilian oversight, the first issue to address is what that assessment should look like. What is the correct measurement of success? If the goal of civilian oversight is increasing public trust in a law enforcement agency, as the authors of the chapter suggest, and research reveals that trust has not increased through civilian oversight, does the fault lie at the doorstep of the civilian oversight agency or the law enforcement agency?

Complicating the matter of assessing the effectiveness of a civilian oversight agency are the impediments placed in the way of the civilian oversight agency performing its functions or revealing to the public its efforts to influence the way in which a law enforcement agency handled a particular case of alleged misconduct or a systematic issue. If the public's goals for a civilian oversight agency are not correlated with the structure of the civilian oversight agency, the agency will seldom be able to demonstrate its attainment of the goals. For instance, if one of the agency's goals is to review the investigations of the internal affairs unit to determine whether a policy violation occurred and recommend suitable sanctions, the public must be notified of those findings. However, often recommendations on particular cases or policy issues in general are prohibited from being released to the public by the terms of the agreement under which the civilian oversight agency operates. This leaves the public unaware of the work being performed on its behalf.

One example of this occurred with an officer who was involved in a use-of-force case that gained national attention. The public questioned why this officer's propensity for violence had not been addressed beforehand. In reality, there had been numerous complaints about the officer to the civilian oversight agency. Those complaints had resulted in recommendations that the officer be found guilty of violation of the use-of-force policy and be disciplined and retrained, but to no avail; the law enforcement agency had declined to follow the oversight agency's recommendations. None of the prior recommendations on complaints regarding this officer were allowed to be made public under the terms of state law and the agreement through which the civilian oversight agency existed. This left the public unaware of the considerable efforts that the civilian oversight agency had made—and questioning its effectiveness.

In addition to the research pointed out by the authors of chapter 6, NACOLE, in collaboration with the U.S. Department of Justice Office of Community Oriented Policing Services (COPS), is finalizing a publication entitled "Civilian Oversight of Law Enforcement: Report on the State of the Field and Effective Oversight Practices." This publication will act as a guide to communities considering the development of a civilian oversight agency, as it not only includes a comprehensive overview of the current state of the field, but also provides a decision-making guide for the formation of a civilian oversight agency and an interactive online toolkit.

7

Implement a Body-Worn Camera Program

Michael D. White
Arizona State University
Janne E. Gaub
East Carolina University
Natalie Todak
University of Alabama at Birmingham

Background

Police in the United States have come under significant scrutiny for their use of force in recent years, particularly in cases involving unarmed African American men. The deaths of Michael Brown, Eric Garner, Freddie Gray, and Walter Scott, among others, have highlighted a crisis in American policing and led to widespread calls for police reform. In response to the public demand for reform, the White House created the President's Task Force on 21st Century Policing in late 2014. Former President Obama "charged the task force with identifying best practices and offering recommendations" to build community trust and enhance police accountability.[1] Its final report, published in May 2015, included dozens of recommendations for change and highlighted police body-worn cameras (BWCs) as a tool that may enhance citizen trust in police and improve police accountability.[2]

Although policing as an institution is typically resistant to change,[3] BWCs have diffused rapidly in law enforcement in the United States and abroad. There are several potential explanations for the widespread adoption of BWCs. First, the technology is supported across a diverse range of sectors, including police leadership organizations,[4] civil rights groups (including the ACLU),[5] and citizens.[6] Second, since 2015, the U.S. Department of Justice (DOJ) has awarded nearly $70 million in grants to more than 330 law enforcement agencies, resulting in the deployment of more than 70,000 BWCs across the country.[7] Third, findings from a handful of early research studies that suggest cameras can produce a range of positive outcomes have also driven the rapid spread of BWCs. These outcomes include reductions in use of force and citizen complaints,[8] enhanced prosecution outcomes,[9] and increased perceptions of procedural justice among citizens.[10]

However, more recent research demonstrates that BWCs do not guarantee positive outcomes. Several studies have documented no impact on the use of force and citizen complaints.[11] Ariel and colleagues reported an association between BWCs and increased rates of assaults on officers.[12] There has also been strong resistance to BWCs in some jurisdictions. In August 2016, the Boston police union sought a federal court injunction to stop the department's leadership from creating a BWC program.[13] Moreover, critics have raised a number of concerns about BWCs, including potential violations of officer and citizen privacy, policy questions, and cost and resource requirements. In fact, some critics view BWCs as part of a larger technological movement to publicly scrutinize the police, leading officers to engage in de-policing.[14]

One explanation for these inconsistent research findings, as well as the resistance to the technology in some jurisdictions, involves the manner in which a BWC program is implemented.[15] There is a long history of implementation failure in the criminal justice system,[16] with sometimes negative side effects.[17] Given the speed at which law enforcement agencies are adopting BWCs, the consequences of poor BWC program implementation could be significant, from resistance among line officers to low or no usage by downstream criminal justice actors (e.g., prosecutors) and backlash from citizens. In short, poor planning and implementation failure can quickly erode the potential benefits of BWCs.

The DOJ is acutely aware of the challenges associated with successful implementation of a BWC program. In May 2015, the Bureau of Justice Assistance (BJA), part of the DOJ, rolled out a National Body-Worn Camera Toolkit.[18] This toolkit is designed to provide police agencies with a wide range of resources about BWCs, including the latest research, guidance on policy and training, and information on stakeholder engagement. The toolkit also includes a Law Enforcement Implementation Checklist, which serves as a best practices guide for successful planning and implementation of a BWC program.[19] The checklist, which is grounded in the evidence base on effective program implementation,[20] provides over two dozen steps for an agency to follow when implementing a BWC program. The checklist centers on six core principles: learn the fundamentals and develop a plan, form a working group, develop policy, define the technology solution (procurement), communicate with and educate stakeholders, and execute phased rollout and implementation. We believe adherence to these best practices will optimize the likelihood of successful BWC implementation, which will, in turn, increase the potential for positive program outcomes.

The remainder of this chapter accomplishes two objectives. First, we review the primary claims that both advocates and critics make about BWCs and summarize the body of research on each of those claims. Our discussion of the research centers on questions about transparency and accountability, citizen perceptions (e.g., acceptance and impact on perceptions of procedural justice and police legitimacy), officer perceptions (e.g., acceptance), evidentiary value, officer training, cost, and the impact on officer activity, use of force, and citizen complaints against officers. With this comprehensive review as a backdrop, we then turn to the BJA checklist to outline the principles for effective planning, implementation, and management of a BWC program.

■ Research Evidence: What We Know About Body-Worn Cameras

While BWC programs did not proliferate in the United States until around 2014, some American agencies implemented them as early as 2009, and Canadian and European agencies began testing them in the early 2000s.[21] According to a Bureau of Justice Statistics survey of police agencies in the United States, roughly one-third of agencies had some form of BWC deployment as of 2013, though most were limited programs or pilot studies.[22] More recently, data from the 2016 Law Enforcement Management and Administrative Statistics survey's BWC supplement show that nearly 50 percent of all police departments and sheriff's offices had BWCs,[23] including 80 percent of large agencies (those with 500 or more sworn personnel).

Table 1 Benefits and Concerns of BWCs

Benefits	Concerns
• Transparency and accountability	• Privacy concerns
• Citizen and officer perceptions	• Management of public expectations
• Reductions in use of force and citizen complaints	• Retaining officer buy-in
• Evidentiary benefits	• Impact on officer activity
• Training capacities	• Financial and resource commitment

Benefits of BWCs

Transparency and accountability. BWCs have been promoted as tools that can help police officers, supervisors, and citizens alike. Perhaps the most fervent interest in BWCs stems from their potential to reduce police misconduct, ensure fair police treatment of citizens, and improve citizen trust in police.[24] Proponents have argued that recording the police will hold them accountable to internal and external scrutiny because the presence of the camera will either deter misbehavior or uncover it when it occurs and ensure officers are disciplined.[25] Ariel and colleagues note that the effects of BWCs on officer behavior are determined by a delicate balance between officer discretion and deterrence.[26] BWCs have a deterrent effect on officer misuse of force in that the technology provides surveillance, which increases the likelihood of sanctions. Optimal deterrence can be achieved when there are strong controls on discretion, proscribed and enforced in administrative policy. Highlighting its strong support for BWCs, the American Civil Liberties Union (ACLU) concluded:

> Although we at the ACLU generally take a dim view of the proliferation of surveillance cameras in American life, police on-body cameras are different because of their potential to serve as a check against the abuse of power by police officers.[27]

Dunn and Lieberman of the ACLU also highlighted the value of BWCs for shedding light on high-profile, controversial in-custody deaths, noting the deaths of Eric Garner, Walter Scott and others would have never drawn national attention if not for the video.[28]

Accountability and transparency are often two of the primary reasons that police agencies implement a BWC program.[29] A survey of leaders at small law enforcement agencies indicated that 97 percent of respondents listed accountability and transparency as driving motivations for their BWC programs.[30] Those outside of the department recognize these important goals as well, leading municipal leaders, criminal justice actors, and other external stakeholders to support adopting the technology.[31]

Citizen and officer perceptions. Studies have similarly shown that citizen support for BWCs is high, both among the general population[32] and among citizens who have had BWC-recorded encounters with police.[33] For example, we interviewed 279 citizens who had recent encounters with police officers in Tempe, Arizona.[34] More than 90 percent of those citizens agreed or strongly agreed that all Tempe officers should wear BWCs. Nearly 80 percent agreed or strongly agreed that BWCs will make officers behave more professionally and citizens act more respectfully. And 84 percent agreed or strongly agreed that the benefits of BWCs outweigh the costs. We reported similarly positive results in Spokane, Washington, where we also found a connection between citizen awareness of BWCs and increased citizen perceptions of procedural justice.[35]

A number of studies have explored officer perceptions of BWCs.[36] Jennings and colleagues noted that more than 60 percent of Orlando officers believed that their agency should adopt BWCs for all officers, and 77 percent agreed that they would feel comfortable wearing the cameras.[37] We conducted six waves of surveys with officers in the Tempe Police Department.[38] The officers reported high levels of pre-deployment support and we found that officer attitudes either remained positive or became increasingly positive over time. For example, in wave 1, 88 percent of officers agreed or strongly agreed that BWCs improve the quality of evidence. By wave 6, 95 percent of officers agreed or strongly agreed with this statement. A study of command staff also found strong support for BWCs.[39] Gaub and colleagues examined officer attitudes toward BWCs pre- and post-deployment in three agencies and concluded:

> There is significant variation across departments' pre-deployment. Comparatively, Phoenix officers have negative perceptions of BWCs, Tempe officers have largely positive perceptions, and Spokane officers' perceptions generally lie somewhere in between. This trend continues post-deployment . . . Tempe and Spokane officers, overall, increasingly recognized the positive effects of BWCs, whereas Phoenix did not see this trend.[40]

Two notable exceptions exist to the positive trends in officer perceptions. The first involves the impact of BWCs on citizen behavior. For example, in Tempe, officers became increasingly skeptical that citizens would improve their behavior as a result of BWCs. Agreement with the statement "citizens will become more cooperative" declined from 65.7 percent to 47.5 percent.[41] Similar results have been reported in Spokane and Phoenix.[42] Second, officers did not believe BWCs would affect their use of force. For example, in Orlando, only 3.3 percent of officers believed that BWCs would reduce their own use of force, and 20 percent felt that BWCs would reduce force agency wide.[43] Officers in Hallandale Beach, Florida, had increasingly negative views about the ability of BWCs to reduce either use of force or complaints.[44] A similarly low percentage (20.9 percent) of command staff respondents believed that BWCs would affect officer behavior.[45]

Reductions in use of force and citizen complaints. More broadly, it has been suggested that BWCs have a civilizing effect on both citizens and officers, thereby reducing use of force, citizen resistance, injuries, and fatalities.[46] This claim is grounded in evidence that people are more likely to behave in socially desirable ways if they know they are being observed.[47] Early research on use of force and complaints showed dramatic declines in both outcomes associated with the use of BWCs. A study of the Rialto (California) Police Department—the first-ever randomized controlled trial (RCT) of BWCs—showed that use-of-force rates for officers on shifts with BWCs were 60 percent lower than force rates on shifts without them.[48] Moreover, the lower rates of force persisted for several years after the introduction of BWCs.[49]

Other departments experienced notable, though less dramatic, declines as well. Rates of force among officers wearing BWCs were consistently lower than those of their non-BWC counterparts in Las Vegas[50] and Orlando.[51] In many jurisdictions, rates of force declined for officers wearing BWCs during the period of the RCT, ranging from 8 percent in the Tampa (Florida) Police Department to 53 percent in the Orlando Police Department.[52] Similar declines were seen once previously non-BWC officers received their cameras at the end of the RCT period.[53] While thus far no researchers have found overall increases in use of force, several recent studies observed no statistically or substantively significant changes in use of force.[54] In sum, by spring 2019, nineteen published studies or reports have examined the impact of BWCs on use of force, and eleven of those have documented notable or statistically significant declines following camera deployment.[55]

In addition to reductions in the use of force, purported reductions in citizen complaints—and decreased time required to investigate those complaints—convinced many agencies to deploy BWCs. The Rialto study showed an unprecedented 92 percent reduction in citizen complaints.[56] While no other department has had such a dramatic decline, most agencies have experienced notable decreases in rates of complaints after implementing BWCs. Reductions between non-BWC and BWC groups in RCT or similarly designed studies range from 12 percent in Phoenix to 53 percent in Orlando.[57] In sum, by spring 2019, twenty-six published studies or reports have examined the impact of BWCs on citizen complaints against officers, and 20 of those have documented notable or statistically significant declines.[58] These findings led Malm to conclude: "If an agency wants to reduce complaints against officers, it should consider a BWC program."[59]

The mixed results on both use of force and complaints indicate that the effect of BWCs is heavily influenced by both local context and implementation. In terms of local context, one of the key factors involves a given department's starting point. What was the state of the department prior to BWC deployment? Had the department recently experienced a scandal or controversial event? Was the department already under federal oversight through a consent decree? Did the department have the necessary accountability mechanisms in place to ensure professionalism among its officers? This starting point varies substantially among departments and is likely critically important for interpreting the impact of BWCs. In simple terms, police departments that are already highly professional will be less likely to see such declines.

These inconsistent results may be further explained by the considerable difficulties associated with BWC program implementation. BWCs require a tremendous investment of internal resources. BWCs affect every aspect of police operations as well as numerous stakeholders outside of the police department. BWCs touch upon a number of sensitive issues such as citizen privacy, public records laws, and recording of vulnerable populations.[60] Additionally, in many jurisdictions, BWCs have been adopted in a contentious political environment following a controversial incident. These difficulties are compounded by the consequences of poor BWC program implementation, from resistance among line officers and unions and low BWC activation rates due to problems with technology integration, data storage, and unintended costs, financial and otherwise.[61] We will address BWC implementation in the final part of this chapter.

Evidentiary benefits. BWCs have also been promoted as an evidentiary tool. For example, it is believed that BWCs will influence the number of citizen complaints and internal affairs investigations filed against officers. On one hand, the existence of video evidence may reduce the number of cases filed against police because the participants in the encounter will know that there is evidence to conclusively contradict unfounded claims.[62] On the other hand, citizens and supervisors may be more likely to file valid cases against officers if they know the case will be supported with BWC evidence. In either case, BWC evidence may reduce the time it takes to investigate and close cases. Braga and colleagues, in their cost-benefit analysis of the Las Vegas Metropolitan Police Department, reported cost savings of nearly $4 million per year, with the vast majority of that savings resulting from reduced investigative time devoted to citizen complaints.[63] Additionally, Katz and colleagues reported that officers wearing body cameras in Phoenix who received a citizen complaint were significantly more likely (than officers with no BWC) to have that complaint unsubstantiated upon investigation (i.e., the BWC footage led to their exoneration).[64]

BWC evidence could similarly improve downstream court case processing for several reasons. Though direct evidence of such effects is still sparse, attitudinal studies are consistent in terms of documenting these perceived effects. Officer surveys in England and Scotland found that most officers believed that BWCs produce increased evidence quality and lead to an increased likelihood of conviction.[65] Similarly, between 78 and 80 percent of Phoenix, Spokane, and Tempe police officers agreed that BWCs will produce more accurate accounts of incidents, especially when they can "paint a picture" of the encounter.[66] These same sentiments are echoed by criminal justice professionals in Spokane and Tempe. As one prosecutor described:

> [BWC footage] can be very beneficial when dealing with DUI suspects because it provides . . . the visual evidence of what the officer's trying to describe when it comes to their physical impairment . . . our very first [video] request was for DUI and it was fairly stunning to see what the officer saw.[67]

Additionally, BWC footage can reduce the time spent on investigations, and, in turn, reduce the time prosecutors need to devote to a case throughout the judicial process. This is especially true in situations where victims recant, as is common for crimes like domestic violence. Between 66 and 87 percent of officers in Phoenix, Spokane, and Tempe believed that BWCs improve evidence quality, and 47 to 64 percent viewed BWCs as advantageous in the prosecution of domestic violence cases specifically, especially when the victim proves unwilling to testify (49 percent to 70 percent).[68] Criminal justice stakeholders such as judges and prosecutors also see the utility in these circumstances; one judge observed:

> What I'd like to see more of [BWC footage] is on . . . a domestic violence case, because every Monday I have motions to recall a no-contact order that we put in place and I have a room full of victims who tell me, you know, when the prosecutor reads the police report, they say "I didn't say that, I never said that" . . . and it would just be nice to have a body camera that said, you did say this.[69]

When prosecutors are able to provide video evidence that clearly demonstrates what happened in an encounter, this can lead to better criminal justice outcomes through improved charging and plea agreements. In Essex, England, Owens and colleagues found that domestic violence incidents handled by officers wearing BWCs were significantly more likely to result in a criminal charge.[70] Beyond charging, researchers in Scotland found that BWC cases resulted in a guilty plea more often than non-BWC cases, and those pleas were entered at earlier stages in the process.[71] In cases of intimate partner violence in Phoenix, Morrow and colleagues found that BWCs had a statistically significant positive effect at all stages of the process, from arrest to guilty pleas and verdicts.[72]

The presence of footage can both expedite removal of cases that are unsupported by the evidence (e.g., charges are not filed or cases are dismissed) and push cases toward early disposition (e.g., a guilty plea is entered at an earlier stage in the process). The implementation of cameras in Phoenix led to statistically significant declines in the time to disposition overall and specifically the time to dismissal and time to guilty plea.[73] Tempe saw similar declines (an 8 percent decline in time to disposition and a 6 percent increase in guilty outcomes), though these levels did not reach statistical significance.[74] In a separate analysis of misdemeanor drug and alcohol cases in Tempe, White and colleagues found that BWCs were associated with no change in the likelihood of a guilty outcome but statistically significant declines in time to disposition—leading them to conclude BWCs may sometimes benefit the police and other times may benefit the defendant (BWCs may both implicate and exonerate, depending on the evidence captured).[75] Either way, BWCs allow criminal cases to be adjudicated more quickly.

Training capacities. Finally, BWCs can be a valuable training tool for new recruits in the academy, field training officers assigned to rookie officers, and in-service sessions and specialty units.[76] Many agencies use

BWCs as both formal and informal training tools to provide tailored feedback, either in staged training scenarios or through a form of nonpunitive sentinel-events review.[77] The use of BWC footage is especially common in specialized units that can use recordings compiled over time for scenario-based training in their specific domain. The Tempe bike squad explained:

> We're able to take incidents that happen on the street, good or bad, and then use them when we're teaching our bike schools to show our bike students good examples of what we're trying to teach, and then examples of even us as bike cops having messed up, and to learn from that. [. . .] We probably have twenty videos now that we can rotate through for bike school.[78]

Video footage recorded from the officer's perspective has the unique potential to provide full insight into what transpired during interactions between officers and citizens, uncover deficits in police training, and show real-life situations with skilled police behaviors that can be taught to other officers in training.[79] Locally recorded footage can further illuminate issues specific to the community that may not be evident in official reports or published research from other areas. To this point, the former chief of the Linden (New Jersey) Police Department argued that:

> Instead of trying to reduce demeanor complaints, which manufacturers tout as the devices' main selling point, law enforcement agencies should be using the cameras as a tool to monitor and improve the efficacy and safety of officers and the people they interact with.[80]

Concerns with BWCs

Privacy concerns. It has become quickly apparent that BWCs have significant implications for citizen and officer privacy. The potential for BWCs to violate individuals' privacy, especially in vulnerable, traumatic, or sensitive moments of their lives, was swiftly critiqued.[81] As White observed, BWCs capture victims of crimes or traumatic accidents, grieving families, and other individuals in their worst moments, including those who are intoxicated, mentally ill and in crisis, or being arrested or detained.[82] If a video of one these moments is publicly shared and preserved online, this could exacerbate the negative effects of a trauma for those involved. These concerns were echoed by stakeholders in Tempe and Spokane, including victim advocates, mental health advocates, judges, prosecutors, and defense attorneys.[83]

Considering the widespread diffusion of BWCs across U.S. police agencies, the full impact the technology could have on citizen privacy is not well understood.[84] With this in mind, the ACLU's official stance on BWCs holds that the challenge "is the tension between their potential to invade privacy and their strong benefit in promoting police accountability."[85] Both individual agencies and professional organizations have taken steps to address privacy-related concerns. For example, the International Association of Chiefs of Police held a National Forum on Body-Worn Cameras and Violence Against Women and issued a report with recommendations for agency practice and policy for recording female assault victims.[86]

Public expectations. One of the most difficult aspects of implementing BWCs is managing public expectations. A key concern in this area is the fear that BWCs will suffer from a new version of the "CSI effect." This is a term used by criminal justice practitioners to describe two seemingly contradictory reactions by jurors in response to forensic evidence. Criminal defense attorneys claimed that trial jurors were overly impressed by, and uncritical of, fingerprint or DNA test results, whereas prosecutors complained that jurors would not convict unless forensic evidence was presented at trial, even for cases in which such evidence was unrelated to the issue at hand.[87] Some legal experts are concerned that BWC footage will become so normalized that jurors will be unwilling to convict someone without it. Many officers have expressed similar concerns, specifically the fear that people will view BWC footage as a necessary piece of evidence and any lack thereof as evidence of some deeper, nefarious cover-up of police misbehavior.[88]

Similarly, officers and legal scholars alike have expressed concerns that the general public may not fully understand the limitations of BWCs. The reality is that BWCs do not provide perfect quality picture or audio, particularly when the officer is in close quarters with others (such as in a crowd), is involved in a physical altercation, or is in a low-light situation.[89] There are also numerous concerns regarding how the impact of BWCs can be short-circuited, from citizens' lack of awareness of the BWC to officers' memory distortion following the review of footage.[90] Moreover, the devices are typically attached by a magnet or clip, and many officers have reported them falling off.[91] The perspective from which they are recorded (either on the officer's chest, temple, or lapel) can also distort what actually happened, leading to perspective bias.[92] Technological features during playback, such as slow motion or repeated review of footage, can create a situation wherein courtroom actors, jurors, the media, or the public second-guess actions made by officers in the moment, akin to "Monday morning quarterbacking."[93]

Finally, there is concern regarding the public's expectations of release of footage. Nearly all police departments have some mechanism for public request and release of BWC footage, but how that release plays out in reality varies widely. In the state of Washington, where public records laws are unusually open, the Seattle Police Department responded to a wave of public records requests by redacting all footage and uploading it to a public YouTube channel.[94] On the opposite end of the spectrum, many state laws give agencies discretion to withhold footage in certain situations, such as during active investigations, and available data indicates that all but twelve states have passed legislation to restrict public access to BWC footage in some way.[95] In 2016, for example, the North Carolina General Assembly passed House Bill 972, which classified BWC and dashboard camera footage as part of officers' personnel records, which require a court order for public release.[96] The most common officer concern related to public release of BWC footage is that most people cannot fully understand the types of situations that police routinely handle. Encounters—especially those involving force—are viewed out of the context of police purpose and procedure. As a canine handler explained,

> If we get sued and they have a jury trial, and they show this video of a dog attacking somebody that we directed him to attack [. . .] we can put an expert witness up there that's done dog stuff for 30 years, say that's exactly what it should look like, and the jury is still going to look at that and say, "Nobody should have to go through that."[97]

Officer buy-in. As the primary users of BWCs, it is logical that officers would have concerns about the technology's impact on their daily work. They can be hesitant for a host of reasons, including wariness about recording vulnerable or recently victimized citizens or private locations such as houses or hospitals, concerns regarding supervisor review and resulting "fishing expeditions" for minor policy violations, the potential negative impacts on officer discretion, and worries stemming from compromised officer safety.[98]

As first responders in difficult situations, officers are keenly aware of the potential for a video camera to exacerbate a crisis. Often a collaborative planning process and clear department policy on camera use can alleviate these concerns.[99] Moreover, many policies also allow for officer discretion in terms of BWC activation, particularly in encounters with vulnerable populations (e.g., victims) where use of the BWC may inhibit the officer's ability to do the job.

One of the most prevalent concerns among officers concerns organizational misuse of footage, especially in retaliation against officers who cause problems, such as whistleblowers or union representatives.[100] This concern can often be addressed by including line officers and their union representatives in the BWC policy development process. Moreover, nearly all agencies allow for supervisor review of BWC footage as a matter of course in administrative investigations of use-of-force incidents or citizen complaints.[101] Over time, allowing supervisor review for compliance with BWC policy has also become more commonplace. Developing a policy in conjunction with both line officers and supervisors can ensure that the needs of both are balanced.

Perhaps the biggest concern for police officers today regarding BWCs is their potential to compromise officer safety. For example, officers may fear that the presence of the BWC, combined with the increased public scrutiny of police behaviors in recent years, could cause some police officers to hesitate to act in potentially dangerous situations. This may be especially true for younger or less experienced officers who are not as sure of their decisions in crisis situations. Others have voiced a concern about whether the presence of the BWC, or the act of videotaping citizens, may aggravate some individuals and cause them to lash out against officers. This concern is supported by a recent study by Ariel and colleagues that found that officers wearing BWCs actually suffered more attacks than non-BWC officers.[102] However, other research has found no effect of BWCs on officer assaults and injuries.[103]

Impact on officer discretion and activity. Critics of BWCs have argued that the technology will reduce officer discretion, a core component of the job.[104] Surveys of officers have found variation in this concern. For example, over 85 percent of Phoenix officers believe that BWCs will limit their discretion, while just over 50 percent of Tempe and Spokane officers agreed with that sentiment.[105] The limits on officer discretion may play out in terms of changes in officer activity levels, particularly with regard to stops, citations, and arrests. For example, Katz and colleagues found that BWC-assigned officers increased their arrest activity by more than 40 percent following camera deployment.[106] Braga and colleagues also reported increases in arrests and citations among BWC officers but no change in officer-initiated activity.[107] Alternatively, Grossmith and colleagues found no impact on "the number or type of stop and searches," self-reported activity, or arrest decisions.[108] Young and Ready did find BWC officers made fewer arrests and issued more citations, which the authors attributed to officers' concerns about supervisory review of their decisions.[109] Wallace and colleagues examined the impact of BWCs on Spokane officers' arrests, self-initiated stops, response time, and time on scene.[110] They found no evidence of reduced activity or de-policing. In fact, officer self-initiated activity actually *increased* after officers were assigned BWCs.

Financial and resource commitment. Finally, agencies must consider the enormous costs—financial and otherwise—associated with developing, implementing, and sustaining a new BWC program. Direct costs like equipment purchase and officer training, while an important consideration, are dwarfed by the immense ongoing costs of data storage and redaction.[111] For example, the Denver Police Department negotiated a contract for 800 cameras and associated data storage at a cost of $6.1 million.[112] Each camera costs between $400 and $600, accounting for less than 10 percent of the cost of the Denver BWC program. As part of their cost-benefit analysis of the Las Vegas Metropolitan Police Department's BWC program, Braga and colleagues estimated the program cost at $1,097 per user, for a total annual cost of $891,390.[113]

Following the purchase of cameras, agencies must dedicate human resources to reviewing and redacting BWC footage for public records and court requests, providing hardware and software technical assistance to officers and other users, and other system maintenance. An unexpected expense is the technical and human resource cost to prosecutor's offices, which can be left out of the budget negotiations between police departments and municipal governments.[114]

There can be long-term financial savings, however, to agencies that implement a BWC program. Fewer use-of-force incidents and citizen complaints can translate to cost savings in terms of the time, resources, and money devoted to investigating those claims.[115] An independent evaluation of the Las Vegas BWC program included the first cost-benefit analysis of BWCs.[116] This analysis documented the estimated monetary benefits driven by cost savings from reduced complaints (at a savings of $4,006 per user per year), costs related to purchase and maintenance of the technology (at an overall cost of $828 per user per year), costs for initial and refresher training (at an average cost of $1,097 per user per year), and estimated costs associated with fulfilling public records requests (at a cost of $40 per user per year), for a net benefit of $2,041 per user per year. Taken together, Braga and colleagues concluded that the BWC program generated over $4 million in cost savings per year. The extent to which the savings measured in Las Vegas might extend to other jurisdictions remains unknown.

■ Solutions: Planning and Implementing a BWC Program

The discussion above highlights a central theme of this chapter: BWCs have tremendous promise in terms of delivering important benefits to police and their communities. However, those positive benefits are by no means guaranteed, and significant concerns are associated with deployment of the technology. We believe the mixed research findings on BWC impacts, as outlined in this chapter, are explained at least in part by the difficulties surrounding BWC implementation. The BJA, which manages the DOJ's BWC funding program called the Policy and Implementation Program (PIP), has developed several resources to facilitate BWC program planning, implementation, and management. The most notable of these resources is its Law Enforcement Implementation Checklist. The final objective of this chapter is to provide a review of the principles outlined in the checklist.

BJA Law Enforcement Implementation Checklist

1. Learn the fundamentals and develop a plan
2. Form a working group
3. Define policies and key protocols
4. Define the technology solution (procurement)
5. Communicate with and educate stakeholders
6. Execute phased rollout and implementation

The BJA Law Enforcement Implementation Checklist is grounded in principles drawn from the larger evidence base on successful program implementation in the criminal justice system,[117] including policing,[118] courts,[119] and corrections.[120] This section describes the core principles of the BJA-recommended process.

Learn the Fundamentals and Develop a Plan

The BJA checklist emphasizes that an effective BWC program starts with careful planning.[121] First and foremost, agency leaders should identify the goal(s) they want to achieve through their BWC program. The goal of a BWC program can significantly affect its design and operation. Moreover, agency leaders should "do their homework" to guarantee that they have a clear understanding of the benefits and limitations of BWCs (as outlined above) as well as the costs and resources required to manage a BWC program.

Form a Working Group

The BJA checklist recommends that an agency create a BWC working group with internal stakeholders who will assume responsibility for the planning and implementation process.[122] This working group should meet regularly to assess progress, discuss emerging challenges and identify solutions, and, more generally, keep the planning and implementation process on track. All relevant units within the law enforcement agency should have representation in this group to gather insights, ask questions, and raise concerns. At a minimum, this should include agency leadership, command and first-line supervisors, patrol officers, union representatives, investigators, and records management, information technology, legal, and training staff.[123] Specialized units should also be represented if the agency plans to deploy BWCs beyond patrol. Comprehensive participation will help overcome initial internal resistance to the technology and will allow the working group to troubleshoot problems as they arise.

Define Policies and Key Protocols

A thorough and uniformly enforced administrative policy is the centerpiece of a successful BWC program. More than four decades of research have highlighted the importance of administrative policy as an effective method for guiding and controlling police officer decision-making across a range of field behaviors, including use of deadly force,[124] use of less lethal force,[125] high-speed pursuits,[126] use of police dogs,[127] foot pursuits,[128] and responses to domestic violence incidents.[129] This robust body of research on the importance of administrative policy applies equally well to a BWC program.

The policy development process should be deliberate and inclusive.[130] The BWC working group should begin with a review of relevant local and state laws as well as policies from peer and neighboring agencies. The BJA's

National Body-Worn Camera Toolkit includes dozens of sample administrative policies and provides links to model policies from the International Association of Chiefs of Police and the United Kingdom Home Office. The BJA checklist highlights six core policy areas: video capture, video viewing, video use, video release to the public, video storage, and process/data audits and controls such as compliance monitoring. Both line officers and their union representative should play an important role in discussing key elements of the policy, such as camera activation, officer discretion in deactivation, and supervisory review of BWC footage. Moreover, the BWC policy should be a "living document"—that is, reviewed and updated regularly based on changes in the law, available best practices, and local needs.

Define the Technology Solution (Procurement)

Law enforcement agencies are typically required to follow a formal city procurement process when they purchase equipment such as BWCs. The procurement process should become a primary responsibility of the BWC working group. The working group should initiate the procurement process with an evaluation of the agency's hardware and software needs and limitations (e.g., desired camera resolution), financial and resource parameters, and consideration of data storage options (e.g., local servers or third-party cloud storage[131]). These issues are typically delineated in a request for proposals (RFP) that is released to BWC vendors. Those vendors—of which there are more than sixty in the market as of spring 2019—will submit bids in response to the agency's RFP. The BWC working group should then develop a bid review and scoring process that can guide vendor selection.

Communicate With and Educate Stakeholders

The agency should develop an effective communication plan to publicize, both internally and externally, the BWC program.[132] An internally focused marketing campaign can facilitate BWC deployment by describing the relevant aspects of the BWC planning and implementation process, from program goals, policy decisions, and vendor selection to training and deployment schedules. Internal transparency is an excellent way to short-circuit resistance to the BWC program. A similar campaign with external stakeholders can reduce concerns and questions among citizens, advocacy groups, and other downstream criminal justice actors. The local media may also be useful in terms of publicizing the BWC program.

Execute Phased Rollout and Implementation

The BJA checklist highlights several key developments during the implementation of a BWC program, including the training of officers, continued communication with stakeholders, and regular program monitoring.[133] Training for officers should focus on operation of the technology, including activation, battery life, buffering, tagging of videos, and downloading. But policy should also be a centerpiece of this training, as should scenario or role-play training to expose officers to "real-world" applications and build their experience with the camera. The PIP TTA team has developed a guide to facilitate effective BWC training.[134]

The checklist also recommends a phased deployment rather than a one-time, agency-wide rollout. The deployment of BWCs is complex, even for an agency that has adhered to these principles. The phased rollout is more measured and provides additional flexibility to adjust the BWC program as needed. The phased rollout can also allow researchers to apply rigorous research designs, such as RCTs or quasi-experimental matched designs. Last, the checklist highlights post-implementation assessments of BWC operations and outcomes as well as periodic reviews of policy and training. Conventional wisdom and best practices with BWCs are constantly changing given the rapid, widespread diffusion of the technology. BWC programs should not be static; agencies should modify their policies and programs as our knowledge about BWCs improves.

■ Next Steps

Police BWCs have spread rapidly in law enforcement over the last few years. Our chapter is grounded in two realities associated with this development. First, we believe BWCs will continue to diffuse throughout law enforcement until a saturation point is achieved, much like what has occurred with the TASER device.[135] Support for BWCs has been nearly universal across a wide range of constituencies that are traditionally at odds with each other, such as advocacy groups, police unions, police leadership organizations, researchers, and the federal government.[136] This "perfect storm" of support is a recipe for continued integration of BWC technology into the daily routines of law enforcement officers throughout the country.

Second, the body of research on the impact and consequences of BWCs will continue to expand, and the findings will likely grow increasingly mixed. Some agencies will experience significant declines in key outcomes such as use of force and citizen complaints. Others will not. Acceptance and integration of BWCs by officers and external stakeholders will be seamless in some jurisdictions. In other jurisdictions, officers may resist the deployment of BWCs. Citizens, prosecutors, and other external stakeholders may do the same. The mixed findings across studies and agencies will be driven by several important factors, most notably the "state" of an agency and its community prior to BWC deployment and the nature of the BWC planning and implementation process (i.e., did the agency follow the principles outlined in this chapter?). In plain terms, an agency that adopts BWCs in the wake of a misconduct scandal has a very different starting point than an agency that adopts BWCs as part of its continued professionalization effort. Troubled agencies that adopt BWCs may see the Rialto-like declines in use of force and citizen complaints because there is so much room for improvement. Highly professional agencies with robust employee selection, training, policy, supervision, and accountability processes will probably not experience those same large declines because there is less room for improvement in an agency that is already high functioning.

While the challenges associated with starting a BWC program can be overwhelming, the BJA checklist is designed to optimize successful planning and implementation of a BWC program—in effect, it is designed to produce a positive BWC story. The checklist takes an agency from "point A" to "point Z," ensuring that the BWC program is developed in accordance with well-established principles of criminal justice program planning. BWCs represent an enormous undertaking in terms of resources, both financial and otherwise. A number of complex issues represent barriers to successful implementation, from technology infrastructure requirements and immediate and continuing costs to concerns over citizen and officer privacy. Moreover, interest in a BWC program may come from outside the police department (through a local politician or an advocacy group, for example), and there may be significant pressure to implement the program quickly (often in the wake of a controversial incident). However, not only will poor BWC deployment fail to achieve the stated program goals but it may also *create* additional harms for officers, citizens, and other stakeholders. For example, a failure on the part of a police officer to activate the BWC during a controversial incident could exacerbate the community's mistrust of the police department. Comprehensive, collaborative planning is essential to prevent further deterioration of the police-community relationship.

It is in this context that the value of the BJA checklist becomes evident. The checklist gives an agency concrete, clear guidance to facilitate its BWC planning and implementation. Moreover, we recently observed one police department that carefully followed the BJA checklist, concluding:

> Close adherence to those principles may produce high levels of integration and acceptance of BWCs among a diverse group of important stakeholders. Police departments considering a BWC program would be well-advised to pay close attention to the BJA implementation resources.[137]

The checklist also represents a "line of defense" for an agency should critics question the manner in which the BWC program is implemented, as the agency can point to empirically supported best practices developed by the DOJ as the foundation for its BWC program.

NOTES

[1] President's Task Force on 21st Century Policing, *Final Report of the President's Task Force on 21st Century Policing* (Washington, DC: Office of Community Oriented Policing Services (2015), 1.

[2] Ibid., 32.

[3] Dorothy Guyot, "Bending Granite: Attempts to Change the Rank Structure of American Police Departments," *Journal of Police Science and Administration* 7, no. 3 (1979): 253–284.

[4] International Association of Chiefs of Police, "Body-Worn Cameras Model Policy," accessed June 15, 2019, https://www.theiacp.org/resources/policy-center-resource/body-worn-cameras.

[5] Jay Stanley, *Police Body-Mounted Cameras: With Right Policies In Place, A Win for All* (New York: American Civil Liberties Union, 2015), accessed June 15, 2019.

[6] William H. Sousa, Terance D. Miethe, and Mari Sakiyama, "Inconsistencies in Public Opinion of Body-Worn Cameras on Police: Transparency, Trust, and Improved Police-Citizen Relationships," *Policing: A Journal of Policy and Practice* 12, no. 1 (2018): 100–108; Michael D. White, Natalie Todak, and Janne E. Gaub, "Assessing Citizen Perceptions of Body-Worn Cameras after Encounters with Police," *Policing: An International Journal of Police Strategies & Management* 40, no. 4 (2017): 689–703.

[7] "Training and Technical Assistance," Bureau of Justice Assistance, accessed June 15, 2019, http://www.bwctta.com/training-and-technical-assistance.

[8] Barak Ariel, William Farrar, and Alex Sutherland, "The Effect of Police Body-Worn Cameras on Use of Force and Citizens' Complaints against the Police: A Randomized Controlled Trial," *Journal of Quantitative Criminology* 33, no. 3 (2015): 509-535; Charles M. Katz, and David E. Choate, "Body-Worn Cameras and Citizen Interactions with Police Officers: Estimating Plausible Effects Given Varying Compliance Levels," *Justice Quarterly* 34, no. 4 (2017): 627–651.

[9] Weston J. Morrow, Charles M. Katz, and David E. Choate, "Assessing the Impact of Police Body-Worn Cameras on Arresting, Prosecuting, and Convicting Suspects of Intimate Partner Violence," *Police Quarterly* 19, no. 3 (2016): 303–325; Catherine Owens, David Mann, and Rory Mckenna, *The Essex Body Worn Video Trial: The Impact of Body Worn Video on Criminal Justice Outcomes of Domestic Abuse Incidents* (London, England: College of Policing, 2014).

[10] White, Todak, and Gaub, "Assessing Citizen Perceptions of Body-Worn Cameras after Encounters with Police."

[11] Edmonton Police Service, *Body Worn Video: Considering the Evidence (Final Report of the Edmonton Police Service Body Worn Video Pilot Project)* (Edmonton, Alberta: Edmonton Police Service, 2015); Lynne Grossmith, Catherine Owens, Will Finn, David Mann, Tom Davies, and Laura Baika, *Police, Camera, Evidence: London's Cluster Randomised Controlled Trial of Body Worn Video* (London, England: College of Policing and Mayor's Office for Policing and Crime, 2015); David Yokum, Anita Ravishankar, and Alexander Coppock, *Evaluating the Effects of Police Body-Worn Cameras: A Randomized Controlled Trial* (Washington, DC: The Lab @ DC, Office of the City Administrator, Executive Office of the Mayor, 2017.

[12] Barak Ariel, Alex Sutherland, Darren Henstock, Josh Young, Paul Drover, Jayne Sykes, Simon Megicks, and Ryan Henderson, "Wearing Body Cameras Increases Assaults against Officers and Does Not Reduce Police Use of Force: Results from a Global Multi-Site Experiment," *European Journal of Criminology* 13, no. 6 (2016): 744–755.

[13] Michael Levenson and Evan Allen, "Boston Police Union Challenges Body Camera Program," *Boston Globe*, Aug. 26, 2016.

[14] Danielle Wallace, Michael D. White, Janne Gaub, and Natalie Todak, "Body-Worn Cameras as a Potential Source of De-Policing: Testing for Camera-Induced Passivity," *Criminology* 56, no. 3 (2018): 481–509.

[15] Michael D. White, Natalie Todak, and Janne Gaub, "Examining Body-Worn Camera Integration and Acceptance among Police Officers, Citizens, and External Stakeholders," *Criminology & Public Policy* 17, no. 3 (2018): 649–677.

[16] Mark W. Lipsey, John L. Adams, Denise C. Gottfredson, John V. Pepper, and David L. Weisburd, *Improving Evaluation of Anticrime Programs* (Washington, DC: National Academies Press, 2005); Daniel P. Mears, *American Criminal Justice Policy: An Evaluation Approach to Increasing Accountability and Effectiveness* (New York: Cambridge University Press, 2010);

Charlotte Price, *Cognitive Behavioral Interventions: Process Evaluation Report* (Raleigh: North Carolina Department of Correction, Office of Research and Planning, 2004); Suzanne Pullen, *Evaluation of the Reasons and Rehabilitation Cognitive Skills Development Program as Implemented in Juvenile ISP in Colorado* (Lakewood: Colorado Division of Criminal Justice, 1996), accessed June 15, 2019; Edward E. Rhine, Tina L. Mawhorr, and Evalyn C. Parks, "Implementation: The Bane of Effective Correctional Programs," *Criminology & Public Policy* 5, no. 2 (2006): 347–358.

[17] Brandon C. Welsh and Michael Rocque, "When Crime Prevention Harms: A Review of Systematic Reviews," *Journal of Experimental Criminology* 10, no. 3 (2014): 245–266.

[18] Bureau of Justice Assistance, *Body-Worn Camera Toolkit*, accessed June 15, 2019, https://www.bja.gov/bwc/.

[19] Bureau of Justice Assistance, *Law Enforcement Implementation Checklist* (Washington, DC: Author, 2015), accessed June 15, 2019, https://www.bja.gov/bwc/pdfs/BWCImplementationChecklist.pdf; Lindsay Miller, Jessica Toliver, and Police Executive Research Forum, *Implementing a Body-Worn Camera Program: Recommendations and Lessons Learned* (Washington, DC: Office of Community Oriented Policing Services, 2014). One of the authors served as a consultant to the DOJ and participated in the development of the National Body-Worn Camera Toolkit and Law Enforcement Implementation Checklist.

[20] J. Mitchell Miller and Holly V. Miller, "Rethinking Program Fidelity for Criminal Justice," *Criminology & Public Policy* 14, no. 2 (2015): 339–349; Pew Charitable Trusts, *Implementation Oversight for Evidence-Based Programs: A Policymaker's Guide to Effective Program Delivery* (Philadelphia: Author, 2016); Michael D. White, "Restraint and Technology: Exploring Police Use of the TASER through the Diffusion of Innovation Framework," in *The Oxford Handbook of Police and Policing*, eds. Michael D. Reisig and Robert J. Kane (Oxford, England: Oxford University Press, 2014), 280–301.

[21] Ariel, Farrar, and Sutherland, "The Effect of Police Body-Worn Cameras on Use of Force and Citizens' Complaints against the Police"; Edmonton Police Service, *Body Worn Video*; Tony Farrar and Barak Ariel, *Self-Awareness to Being Watched and Socially-Desirable Behavior: A Field Experiment on the Effect of Body-Worn Cameras on Police Use-of-Force* (Washington, DC: Police Foundation, 2003); Martin Goodall, *Guidance for the Police Use of Body-Worn Video Devices* (London, England: Home Office, 2007); Darren Laur, Brendon LeBlanc, Trevor Stephen, Peter Lane, and Debra Taylor, *Proof of Concept Study: Body Worn Video and In-Vehicle Video* (Victoria, British Columbia: Victoria Police Service, 2010).

[22] Brian A. Reaves, *Local Police Departments, 2013: Equipment and Technology* (Washington, DC: Bureau of Justice Statistics, 2015).

[23] Shelley S. Hyland, *Body-Worn Cameras in Law Enforcement Agencies, 2016* (Washington, DC: Bureau of Justice Statistics, 2018).

[24] David Hudson, "Building Trust between Communities and Local Police," *The White House Blog*, December 1, 2014; President's Task Force on 21st Century Policing, 2015, 32; Michael D. White, *Police Officer Body-Worn Cameras: Assessing the Evidence* (Washington, DC: Office of Community Oriented Policing Services, 2014).

[25] White, *Police Officer Body-Worn Cameras*.

[26] Barak Ariel, Alex Sutherland, Darren Henstock, Josh Young, and Gabriela Sosinski, "The Deterrence Spectrum: Explaining Why Police Body-Worn Cameras 'Work' or 'Backfire' in Aggressive Police–Public Encounters," *Policing: A Journal of Policy and Practice* 12, no. 1 (2018): 6–26.

[27] Stanley, *Police Body-Mounted Cameras*, 2.

[28] Chris Dunn and Donna C. Lieberman, "Body Cameras Are Key for Police Accountability. We Can't Let Them Erode Our Rights," *The Washington Post*, June 1, 2017.

[29] Miller et al., *Implementing a Body-Worn Camera Program*; White, *Police Officer Body-Worn Cameras*.

[30] Janne E. Gaub, Michael D. White, Kathleen E. Padilla, and Charles M. Katz, *Implementing a Police Body-Worn Camera Program in a Small Agency* (Phoenix: Arizona State University Center for Violence Prevention and Community Safety, 2017).

[31] Natalie Todak, Janne Gaub, and Michael D. White, "The Importance of External Stakeholders for Police Body-Worn Camera Diffusion," *Policing: An International Journal* 41, no. 4 (2018): 448–464.

[32] Matthew S. Crow, Jamie A. Snyder, Vaughn J. Crichlow, and John O. Smykla, "Community Perceptions of Police Body-Worn Cameras: The Impact of Views on Fairness, Fear, Performance, and Privacy," *Criminal Justice and Behavior* 44, no. 4 (2017): 589–610; Sousa, Miethe, and Sakiyama, "Inconsistencies in Public Opinion of Body-Worn Cameras on Police."

[33] White, Todak, and Gaub, "Assessing Citizen Perceptions of Body-Worn Cameras after Encounters with Police."

[34] White, Todak, and Gaub, "Examining Body-Worn Camera Integration and Acceptance among Police Officers, Citizens, and External Stakeholders."

[35] White, Todak, and Gaub, "Assessing Citizen Perceptions of Body-Worn Cameras after Encounters with Police."

[36] Mesa Police Department, *On-Officer Body Camera System: Program Evaluation and Recommendations* (Mesa, AZ: Mesa Police Department, 2013); William V. Pelfrey, Jr. and Steven Keener, "Police Body Worn Cameras: A Mixed Method Approach Assessing Perceptions of Efficacy," *Policing: An International Journal of Police Strategies & Management* 39, no. 3 (2016): 491–506; Justin T. N. Young and Jacob Ready, "Diffusion of Policing Technology: The Role of Networks in Influencing the Endorsement and Use of On-Officer Cameras," *Journal of Contemporary Criminal Justice* 31, no. 3 (2015): 243–261.

[37] Wesley G. Jennings, Lorie Fridell, and Mathew D. Lynch, "Cops and Cameras: Officer Perceptions of the Use of Body-Worn Cameras in Law Enforcement," *Journal of Criminal Justice* 42, no. 6 (2014): 549–556.

[38] White, Todak, and Gaub, "Examining Body-Worn Camera Integration and Acceptance among Police Officers, Citizens, and External Stakeholders."

[39] John O. Smykla, Matthew S. Crow, Vaughn J. Crichlow, and Jamie A. Snyder, "Police Body-Worn Cameras: Perceptions of Law Enforcement Leadership," *American Journal of Criminal Justice* 41, no. 3 (2016): 424–443.

[40] Janne E. Gaub, David E. Choate, Natalie Todak, Charles M. Katz, and Michael D. White, "Officer Perceptions of Body-Worn Cameras before and after Deployment: A Study of Three Departments," *Police Quarterly* 19, no. 3 (2016): 275–302, 292.

[41] White, Todak, and Gaub, "Examining Body-Worn Camera Integration and Acceptance among Police Officers, Citizens, and External Stakeholders." 661.

[42] Gaub et al., "Officer Perceptions of Body-Worn Cameras before and after Deployment."

[43] Jennings, Fridell, and Lynch, "Cops and Cameras."

[44] Andrea M. Headley, Rob T. Guerette, and Auzeen Shariati, "A Field Experiment of the Impact of Body-Worn Cameras (BWCs) on Police Officer Behavior and Perceptions," *Journal of Criminal Justice* 53(C) (2017): 102–109.

[45] Smykla, Crow, Crichlow, and Snyder, "Police Body-Worn Cameras."

[46] White, *Police Officer Body-Worn Cameras*.

[47] Farrar and Ariel, *Self-Awareness to Being Watched and Socially-Desirable Behavior*; Kristen Munger and Shelby J. Harris, "Effects of an Observer on Hand Washing in a Public Restroom," *Perceptual and Motor Skills* 69, no. 3 (1989), 733–734; Thomas J. L. van Rompay, Dorette J. Vonk, Marieke L. Fransen, "The Eye of the Camera: Effects of Security Cameras on Prosocial Behavior," *Environment and Behavior* 41, no. 1 (2009): 60–74; Georgia M. Wahl, Tareq Islam, Bridget Gardner, Alan B. Marr, John P. Hunt, Norman E. McSwain, Christopher C. Baker, and Juan Duchesne, "Red Light Cameras: Do They Change Driver Behavior and Reduce Accidents?" *Journal of Trauma and Acute Care Surgery* 68, no. 3 (2010): 515–518.

[48] Ariel, Farrar, and Sutherland, "The Effect of Police Body-Worn Cameras on Use of Force and Citizens' Complaints against the Police."

[49] Alex Sutherland, Barak Ariel, William Farrar, and Randy De Anda, "Post-Experimental Follow-Ups—Fade-Out versus Persistence Effects: The Rialto Police Body-Worn Camera Experiment Four Years On," *Journal of Criminal Justice* 53(C) (2017): 110–116.

[50] Anthony A. Braga, James R. Coldren, William Sousa, Denise Rodriguez, and Omer Alper, *The Benefits of Body-Worn Cameras: New Findings from a Randomized Controlled Trial at the Las Vegas Metropolitan Police Department* (Final Report to the National Institute of Justice) (CNA Analysis & Solutions, 2017).

[51] Jennings, Fridell, and Lynch, "Cops and Cameras."

[52] Braga et al., *The Benefits of Body-Worn Cameras*; Darren Henstock and Barak Ariel, "Testing the Effects of Police Body-Worn Cameras on Use of Force during Arrests: A Randomised Controlled Trial in a Large British Police Force," *European Journal of Criminology* 14, no. 6 (2017), 720–750; Wesley G. Jennings, Lorie A. Fridell, Mathew Lynch, Katelyn Jetelina, and Jennifer M. Reingle Gonzalez, "A Quasi-Experimental Evaluation of the Effects of Police Body-Worn Cameras (BWCs) on Response-to-Resistance in a Large Metropolitan Police Department," *Deviant Behavior* 38, no. 11 (2017): 1332–1339; Jennings, Fridell, and Lynch, "Cops and Cameras"; Michael D. White, Janne E. Gaub, and Natalie Todak, "Exploring the Potential for Body-Worn Cameras to Reduce Violence in Police-Citizen Encounters," *Policing: A Journal of Policy and Practice* 12, no. 1 (2018): 66–76.

[53] For exceptions, see Braga et al., *The Benefits of Body-Worn Cameras*; Jennings, Fridell, Lynch, Jetelina, and Reingle Gonzalez, "A Quasi-Experimental Evaluation of the Effects of Police Body-Worn Cameras (BWCs) on Response-to-Resistance in a Large Metropolitan Police Department."

[54] Barak Ariel, "Police Body Cameras in Large Police Departments," *Journal of Criminal Law and Criminology* 106, no. 4 (2016); 729–768; Barak Ariel, Alex Sutherland, Darren Henstock, Josh Young, Paul Drover, Jayne Sykes, Simon Megicks, and Ryan Henderson, "Report: Increases in Police Use of Force in the Presence of Body-Worn Cameras Are Driven by Officer Discretion: A Protocol-Based Subgroup Analysis of Ten Randomized Experiments," *Journal of Experimental Criminology* 12, no. 3 (2016): 453–463; Anthony A. Braga, William H. Sousa, James R. Coldren, Jr., and Denise Rodriguez, "The Effects of Body Worn Cameras on Police Activity and Police-Citizen Encounters: A Randomized Controlled Trial," *Journal of Criminal Law and Criminology* 108, no. 3 (2018): 511–538; Edmonton Police Service, *Body Worn Video*; Headley et al., "A Field Experiment of the Impact of Body-Worn Cameras (BWCs) on Police Officer Behavior and Perceptions"; Yokum, Ravishankar, and Coppock, *Evaluating the Effects of Police Body-Worn Cameras.*

[55] Michael D. White, Janne E. Gaub, and Kathleen E. Padilla, *Impacts of BWCs on Use of Force: Directory of Outcomes*, accessed June 15, 2019, http://www.bwctta.com/resources/bwc-resources/impacts-bwcs-use-force-directory-outcomes.

[56] Ariel, Farrar, and Sutherland, "The Effect of Police Body-Worn Cameras on Use of Force and Citizens' Complaints against the Police"; Sutherland et al., "Post-Experimental Follow-Ups—Fade-Out versus Persistence Effects."

[57] Wesley G. Jennings, Mathew D. Lynch, and Lorie Fridell, "Evaluating the Impact of Police Officer Body-Worn Cameras (BWCs) on Response-to-Resistance and Serious External Complaints: Evidence from the Orlando Police Department (OPD) Experience Utilizing a Randomized Controlled Experiment," *Journal of Criminal Justice* 43, no. 6 (2015): 480–486; Charles M. Katz, David E. Choate, Justin T. Ready, and Lidia Nuño, *Evaluating the Impact of Officer Worn Body Cameras in the Phoenix Police Department* (Phoenix: Arizona State University Center for Violence Prevention and Community Safety, 2014). See also Braga et al., *The Benefits of Body-Worn Cameras*; Grossmith et al., *Police, Camera, Evidence*; Hedberg et al., "Body-Worn Cameras and Citizen Interactions with Police Officers"; Mesa Police Department, *On-Officer Body Camera System.* For an exception, see Ariel, "Police Body Cameras in Large Police Departments."

[58] White, Gaub, and Padilla, *Impacts of BWCs on Use of Force: Directory of Outcomes.*

[59] Malm, Aili. "The Promise of Police Body-Worn Cameras," *Criminology and Public Policy* 18, no. 1 (2019): 119–131, 121.

[60] Natalie Todak, "Using Body-Worn Cameras to Create an Evidence-Based De-Escalation Training Program," in *Evidence Based Policing: An Introduction to Key Ideas*, eds. Renée J. Mitchell and Laura Huey (Bristol, UK: Policy Press, 2018); White, *Police Officer Body-Worn Cameras.*

[61] Janne E. Gaub, Natalie Todak, and Michael D. White, "One Size Doesn't Fit All: The Deployment of Police Body-Worn Cameras to Specialty Units," *International Criminal Justice Review* (2018): doi:10.1177/1057567718789237; White, Todak, and Gaub, "Examining Body-Worn Camera Integration and Acceptance among Police Officers, Citizens, and External Stakeholders."

[62] Stanley, *Police Body-Mounted Cameras.*

[63] Braga et al., *The Benefits of Body-Worn Cameras.*

[64] Katz et al., *Evaluating the Impact of Officer Worn Body Cameras in the Phoenix Police Department.*

[65] Tom Ellis, Craig Jenkins, and Paul Smith, *Evaluation of the Introduction of Personal Issue Body Worn Video Cameras (Operation Hyperion) on the Isle of Wight: Final Report to Hampshire Constabulary* (Portsmouth, Hampshire: University of Portsmouth, 2015); Goodall, *Guidance for the Police Use of Body-Worn Video Devices*; ODS Consulting, *Body Worn Video Projects in Paisley and Aberdeen, Self Evaluation* (Glasgow: ODS Consulting, 2011); Owens, Mann, and Mckenna, *The Essex Body Worn Video Trial.*

[66] Gaub et al., "Officer Perceptions of Body-Worn Cameras before and after Deployment."

[67] Todak, Gaub, and White, "The Importance of External Stakeholders for Police Body-Worn Camera Diffusion." 454.

[68] Gaub et al., "Officer Perceptions of Body-Worn Cameras before and after Deployment."

[69] Todak, Gaub, and White, "The Importance of External Stakeholders for Police Body-Worn Camera Diffusion." 454.

[70] Owens, Mann, and Mckenna, *The Essex Body Worn Video Trial.*

[71] ODS Consulting, *Body Worn Video Projects in Paisley and Aberdeen.*

[72] Morrow, Katz, and Choate, "Assessing the Impact of Police Body-Worn Cameras on Arresting, Prosecuting, and Convicting Suspects of Intimate Partner Violence."

[73] Ibid.

[74] White, Todak, and Gaub, "Examining Body-Worn Camera Integration and Acceptance among Police Officers, Citizens, and External Stakeholders."

[75] Michael D. White, Janne E. Gaub, Aili Malm, and Kathleen E. Padilla, "Implicate or Exonerate? The Impact of Police Body-Worn Cameras on the Adjudication of Drug and Alcohol Cases," *Policing: A Journal of Policy and Practice*, 2019, doi:10.1093/police/paz043.

[76] Gaub, Todak, and White, "One Size Doesn't Fit All: The Deployment of Police Body-Worn Cameras to Specialty Units"; Nancy Perry, *How Body Camera Footage Can Enhance Officer Training*, last modified September 21, 2017, www.policeone.com; Pamela Richards, Deborah Roberts, Mark Britton, and Nathan Roberts, "The Exploration of Body-Worn Video to Accelerate the Decision-Making Skills of Police Officers within an Experiential Learning Environment," *Policing: A Journal of Policy and Practice* 12, no. 1 (2018): 43–49; Todak, "Using Body-Worn Cameras to Create an Evidence-Based De-Escalation Training Program"; Colin Wood, "Police Could Be Doing So Much More with Body Cameras, Says Former Chief," *State Scoop*, Jan. 22, 2018.

[77] Gaub et al., *Implementing a Police Body-Worn Camera Program in a Small Agency.*

[78] Janne E. Gaub, Natalie Todak, and Michael D. White, *Beyond Patrol: Exploring the Perceptions of Body-Worn Cameras among Officers in Specialized Units* (Phoenix: Arizona State University Center for Violence Prevention and Community Safety, 2017), 5.

[79] Todak, "Using Body-Worn Cameras to Create an Evidence-Based De-Escalation Training Program."

[80] Wood, "Police Could Be Doing So Much More with Body Cameras," 1.

[81] Stanley, *Police Body-Mounted Cameras.*

[82] White, *Police Officer Body-Worn Cameras.*

[83] Todak, "Using Body-Worn Cameras to Create an Evidence-Based De-Escalation Training Program."

[84] White, *Police Officer Body-Worn Cameras.*

[85] Stanley, *Police Body-Mounted Cameras*, 2.

[86] International Association of Chiefs of Police, *Deliberations from the IACP National Forum on Body-Worn Cameras and Violence Against Women*, January 27, 2017.
[87] Paula Hannaford-Agor, "Are Body-Worn Cameras the New CSI Effect?" *The Court Manager* 30, no. 3 (2015): 72–73.
[88] Gaub, Todak, and White, *Beyond Patrol.*
[89] Michael D. White and J. R. C. Coldren, "Body-Worn Police Cameras: Separating Fact from Fiction," *PM Magazine* (March 2017): 6–9.
[90] Michael D. White and Henry F. Fradella, "The Intersection of Law, Policy, and Police Body-Worn Cameras: An Exploration of Critical Issues," *North Carolina Law Review* 96, no. 5 (2018): 1579–1638.
[91] See, e.g., Gaub, Todak, and White, *Beyond Patrol.*
[92] Rémi Boivin, Annie Gendron, Camille Faubert, and Bruno Poulin, "The Body-Worn Camera Perspective Bias," *Journal of Experimental Criminology* 13, no. 1 (2017): 125–142; Scott W. Phillips, "Eyes Are Not Cameras: The Importance of Integrating Perceptual Distortions, Misinformation, and False Memories into the Police Body Camera Debate," *Policing: A Journal of Policy and Practice* 12, no. 1 (2018): 91–99.
[93] Gaub, Todak, and White, *Beyond Patrol*; Todak, "Using Body-Worn Cameras to Create an Evidence-Based De-Escalation Training Program."
[94] Kate Knibbs, "Seattle Police Put Redacted Body Cam Footage on YouTube," *Gizmodo*, March 4, 2015.
[95] Urban Institute, Police Body-Worn Camera Legislation Tracker (Washington, DC: Author, last updated October 29, 2018), http://apps.urban.org/features/body-camera-update/
[96] Mark Binker, "New NC Body Camera Law Will Mean Court Order Required for Police Video Release," Sept. 22, 2016.
[97] Gaub, Todak, and White, *Beyond Patrol.* 7.
[98] Miller et al., *Implementing a Body-Worn Camera Program*; White, *Police Officer Body-Worn Cameras.*
[99] White, Todak, and Gaub, "Examining Body-Worn Camera Integration and Acceptance among Police Officers, Citizens, and External Stakeholders."
[100] Stanley, *Police Body-Mounted Cameras.*
[101] Michael D. White, Michaela Flippin, and Charles M. Katz, *Key Trends in Body-Worn Camera Policy and Practice: A Policy Analysis of US Department of Justice-Funded Law Enforcement Agencies* (Phoenix: Arizona State University Center for Violence Prevention and Community Safety, 2018).
[102] Ariel et al., "Wearing Body Cameras Increases Assaults against Officers and Does Not Reduce Police Use of Force."
[103] White, Gaub, and Todak, "Exploring the Potential for Body-Worn Cameras to Reduce Violence in Police-Citizen Encounters."
[104] Ariel et al., "The Deterrence Spectrum."
[105] Gaub et al., "Officer Perceptions of Body-Worn Cameras before and after Deployment."
[106] Charles M. Katz, Mike Kurtenbach, David E. Choate, and Michael D. White, *Smart Policing Initiative: Evaluating the Impact of Police Officer Body-Worn Cameras* (Smart Policing Initiative Spotlight Report) (Washington, DC: CNA, 2015).
[107] Braga et al., *The Benefits of Body-Worn Cameras.*
[108] Grossmith et al., *Police, Camera, Evidence*, 1.
[109] Josh T. N. Young and Jacob T. Ready, "A Longitudinal Analysis of the Relationship between Administrative Policy, Technological Preferences, and Body-Worn Camera Activation among Police Officers," *Policing: A Journal of Policy and Practice* 12, no. 1 (2018), 27–42.
[110] Wallace et al., "Body-Worn Cameras as a Potential Source of De-Policing."
[111] White, "Restraint and Technology."
[112] Noelle Phillips, "Body Cameras for Denver Police to Cost $6.1 Million over Five Years," *The Denver Post*, July 7, 2015.
[113] Braga et al., *The Benefits of Body-Worn Cameras.*

[114] Todak, "Using Body-Worn Cameras to Create an Evidence-Based De-Escalation Training Program."

[115] Braga et al., *The Benefits of Body-Worn Cameras*; White, *Police Officer Body-Worn Cameras*.

[116] Braga et al., *The Benefits of Body-Worn Cameras*.

[117] Amanda Cissner, Donald J. Farole, Jr. and Center for Court Innovation, *Avoiding Failures of Implementation: Lessons from Process Evaluations* (Washington, DC: Bureau of Justice Assistance, June 2009); Miller and Miller, "Rethinking Program Fidelity for Criminal Justice"; Pew Charitable Trusts, *Implementation Oversight for Evidence-Based Programs*.

[118] Melissa Reuland, *A Guide to Implementing Police-Based Diversion Programs for People with Mental Illness* (Delmar, NY: Police Executive Research Forum, 2004); Susan Sadd and Randolph M. Grinc, *Implementation Challenges in Community Policing: Innovative Neighborhood-Oriented Policing in Eight Cities* (Washington, DC: U.S. Department of Justice, Office of Justice Programs, National Institute of Justice, 1996.

[119] Lisa S. Nored, Philip E. Carlan, and Doug Goodman, "Incentives and Obstacles to Drug Court Implementation: Observations of Drug Court Judges and Administrators," *Justice Policy Journal* 6, no. 1 (2009).; Pretrial Justice Institute, *Pretrial Services Program Implementation: A Starter Kit* (Rockville, MD: Pretrial Justice Institute, 2010)

[120] Janet Reno, Raymond C. Fisher, Laurie Robinson, and Nancy E. Gist, *Critical Elements in the Planning, Development, and Implementation of Successful Correctional Options* (Washington, DC: U.S. Department of Justice, Office of Justice Programs, 1998).

[121] Bureau of Justice Assistance, *Law Enforcement Implementation Checklist*.

[122] Ibid.

[123] Smaller agencies may not have all the aforementioned units.

[124] James J. Fyfe, "Police Use of Deadly Force: Research and Reform," *Justice Quarterly* 5, no. 2 (1988): 165–205; Michael D. White, "Controlling Police Decisions to Use Deadly Force: Reexamining the Importance of Administrative Policy," *Crime & Delinquency* 47, no. 1 (2001), 131–151.

[125] William Terrill and Eugene A. Paoline, "Police Use of Less Lethal Force: Does Administrative Policy Matter?" *Justice Quarterly* 34, no. 2 (2017): 193–216.

[126] Geoffrey P. Alpert, Dennis J. Kenney, and Roger Dunham, "Police Pursuits and the Use of Force: Recognizing and Managing 'The Pucker Factor'—A Research Note," *Justice Quarterly* 14, no. 2 (1997): 371–385.

[127] Merrick J. Bobb, *13th Semiannual Report* (Los Angeles, CA: Police Assessment Resource Center, 2000), http://www.parc.info/s/13th-Semiannual-Report.pdf.

[128] Samuel Walker and Carol A. Archbold, *The New World of Police Accountability* (Thousand Oaks, CA: Sage Publications, 2014).

[129] Michael D. White, *Current Issues and Controversies in Policing* (Boston, MA: Allyn & Bacon/Pearson, 2007).

[130] Bureau of Justice Assistance, *Law Enforcement Implementation Checklist*.

[131] Bureau of Justice Assistance, *Law Enforcement Implementation Checklist*.

[132] Bureau of Justice Assistance, *Law Enforcement Implementation Checklist*.

[133] Ibid.

[134] Charles Katz, Michael White, and Jessica Herbert, *Body-Worn Camera Training Guide* (Washington, DC: Bureau of Justice Assistance, 2018), https://www.bwctta.com/sites/default/files/BWC%20facilitator%20training%20guide%2012_5_2018.pdf.

[135] Axon, *How Safe Are TASER Weapons?*, accessed June 15, 2019, https://www.axon.com/how-safe-are-taser-weapons; White, *Police Officer Body-Worn Cameras*.

[136] We do acknowledge that these constituencies often have very different ideas about the "ground-level" use of BWCs. We are referring to support in principle for the technology.

[137] White, Todak, and Gaub, "Examining Body-Worn Camera Integration and Acceptance among Police Officers, Citizens, and External Stakeholders," 672.

7

Response Essay

Chief Edward A. Flynn (Ret.)
Milwaukee Police Department

The Milwaukee Police Department (MPD) began to implement a body-worn camera (BWC) program with a pilot project in 2013. The program began for the same reasons that many similarly situated departments have undertaken this initiative: increasing accountability and transparency, aiding in the investigations of violent crime, and fulfilling community expectations that police departments embrace BWC programs.

Milwaukee is, in many ways, a jurisdiction that benefits from a BWC program. It is a "majority minority" city of nearly 600,000 with the fourth-highest poverty rate of any major American city. That poverty is highly concentrated in neighborhoods suffering from a wide variety of social disadvantages, among them stubbornly high rates of violent crime. The 1,800 officers of the MPD seize roughly 3,000 firearms a year in the course of their anti-crime work, resulting in a gun seizure rate per 100,000 thousand residents higher than that of even New York, Chicago, Los Angeles, or Philadelphia.

Although police use-of-force data and citizen complaint data have indicated consistent declines in both metrics over the past ten years (as evaluated by the University of Wisconsin–Milwaukee under an agreement with the Fire and Police Commission), tensions remain among some residents and the police department, exacerbated by periodic critical incidents in the city and extensive news coverage of critical incidents involving police departments in other cities. In response to both of these realities, BWCs have the potential, in combination with adjustments in training, policy and community outreach, to enhance community trust through increased transparency and accountability.

■ The Implementation of BWCs in the MPD

The program began as a small pilot: one of the city's seven policing districts used just five cameras from four vendors. However, a critical incident in 2014 involving a controversial use of deadly force by a department member provided the impetus (and the funding) to rapidly expand the program to include 1,200 uniformed officers by the end of 2016. Given that the RFP process did not result in the award of a contract until June 2015, the implementation schedule was one of the most aggressive in the nation. Nonetheless, by the use of an iterative process—similar to the one chapter 7 recommended—the implementation succeeded in distributing the devices, providing appropriate training, soliciting user feedback during the process, using feedback to improve training as well as equipment, and securing the widespread support of the officers themselves. Finally, the Bureau of Justice Assistance (BJA) awarded MPD a Smart Policing Initiative Grant to partner with the Urban Institute to, among other things, conduct a randomized controlled trial (RCT) to evaluate the impact of BWCs on police use of force and citizen complaints. The findings of this RCT were consistent with the findings of chapter 7.

The Milwaukee BWC program had four major implementation phases. In October 2015, the first 179 cameras were assigned to three police districts. This had been preceded by extensive "train the trainer" classes that had been conducted for officers from all the affected work locations. They would provide local training and troubleshooting at the job sites. Supervisors, Internal Affairs personnel, and Open Records employees had also been previously trained. For the first three months, the three districts were the only ones with the cameras. In January 2016, seven feedback sessions were held where 38 of the 179 officers with cameras were interviewed. Overwhelmingly, those officers believed the cameras were an excellent tool, that video evidence would result in better prosecutions and court outcomes, and that the cameras would protect them from false allegations. The support emanating from that first group had a significant impact on the receptiveness of personnel who were scheduled to receive cameras in the ensuing months.

In March, June, and November, the MPD started the second, third, and fourth phases, respectively. Each phase lasted about three months, giving ample time for training and constant adjustments. For example, it became apparent that no one mount for the camera would suit all eligible assignments: mounting units appropriate for the uniform shirts didn't work well with the ballistic vests that went over the uniform shirts. Ultimately, mounts for shirts, vests, sunglasses, and head were all approved and assigned.

The BWC program has also posed several challenges for the MPD. After implementation, "muscle memory" became an issue. The requirement to activate the camera was well understood, but the habit took time to ingrain in officers, particularly given the fact that cameras are frequently activated in stressful encounters. Even some years later, officers were receiving significant discipline when audits discovered that they were not routinely using their BWCs.

Although not entirely unanticipated, the volume of "open records" requests for BWC footage has been nearly overwhelming. Media requests, combined with requests from defense attorneys, prosecutors, and local activists, have greatly diminished the ability of the Open Records Section to respond promptly, even with the addition of personnel. Furthermore, as many critical incidents involve numerous officers with BWCs, it can take hundreds of hours to properly "tag" and redact these videos.

Another problem has resulted from prosecuting attorneys' heavy reliance on the recordings before making a charging decision. Because the district attorney's office suffers from outdated technology, the police department must burn a DVD of each relevant recording to send to the prosecutors, delaying the charging process and burdening police personnel.

Finally, the storage issue for the purposes of complying with Open Records laws has become significant. In the first fourteen months of operation, the BWC program required the storage of 799,000 videos covering 152,000 hours using 117.7 terabytes of storage capacity.

■ The Urban Institute RCT

As part of the BJA Smart Policing Initiative grant previously mentioned, the Urban Institute conducted an RCT involving over 500 MPD officers. The findings indicated that BWCs had no overall impact on the use of force. There was no difference between officers who didn't have cameras and those who did in the numbers of injuries to officers or suspects. Nor was there any difference in the race or ethnicity of suspects who were the subject of the use of force.

During the RCT, officers with cameras received fewer citizen complaints than officers without them. However, agency wide, citizen complaints continued to decline—a downward trend that had begun several years earlier. There was also a measurable decrease in the amount of proactive officer activity that was identified in the RCT among those assigned cameras, some of which was associated with the additional time those with BWCs had to spend downloading and tagging their videos.

Overall, the findings are consistent with those of chapter 7, which indicates that departments already experiencing declines in uses of force and citizen complaints before the implementation of a BWCs initiative are not going to experience the dramatic declines in both that are experienced by police agencies at a different stage of organizational development.

■ The Future of BWCs

BWCs continue to hold great promise for the police profession, as identified in the chapter. There are, and will continue to be, implementation and technological issues that can only be overcome by trial, error, and a commitment to learning from the experience of others. But BWCs, despite their promise, will never be the panacea that some proponents suggest. Hopes that BWCs will improve police legitimacy and community trust by increasing "transparency and accountability" may well be undercut by the power of the visual image itself. Ironically, a single dramatic image, replayed hundreds of times on local or national television, can create a narrative absolutely at variance with the actual practices or experiences of the affected police department. Regardless of whether uses of force or complaints are at multiyear lows, an agency can suffer a significant crisis of confidence among citizens and elected officials because of a single negative or ambiguous incident. This problem can be exacerbated by the inevitable pressure to "release the video now" after such an event. Responsible officials in such cases face the dilemma of not seeming "transparent" or "having something to hide" balanced against the likely use of the videos as a critical piece of evidence in a criminal trial. Those most strident in demands to see such videos immediately might do well to remember that in the Rodney King trial, the video of LAPD officers beating him had been played so many times that it lost its power over the jury, which acquitted the officers at their first trial.

Enormous improvements have been made in the technology of BWCs and in training on their use. Policies of police departments and district attorneys are continuing to evolve. But much work remains to be done, including devising ways to integrate even controversial videos into the broader context of actual police practice as undramatically recorded in hundreds of thousands of video records. Unless improvements are made in that regard, BWCs may not fulfill the hopes of the profession to improve relations with their communities.

8

Improve Prevention of Police-Involved Harm through Sentinel Event Reviews

Michael S. Scott
Arizona State University

Background

Policing is among the occupations in which either the practitioners or their clients are at a statistically higher-than-average risk of being injured or killed in the course of the performance of occupational tasks.[1] Athletes, construction workers, fire fighters, and loggers, among workers in other occupations, face similar risks. Doctors do as well, although the field of medicine is also high risk, but less so for the practitioners than for the patients, of whom about a quarter of a million die each year in the United States from medical-care errors.[2]

Of these higher-risk occupations, policing is distinct in that both practitioners and "clients"[3] are at high risk of injury or death from occupational tasks. Police are also distinct in that a high percentage of injuries and deaths are due to intentional acts.

In policing, injuries and fatalities to police officers and their clients commonly occur in the types of situations listed in table 8.1.[4]

Table 8.1 Common Causes of Injury, Fatality, and Harm to Police and Police Clients

Common causes of injury, fatality, and harm of police officers	Common causes of injury, fatality, and harm of clients
Ambush assaults	Using or threatening force against police or others
Custodial arrests by resisting suspects (or victims in domestic disputes)	Resisting custodial arrests
Vehicle crashes (police pursuits, other vehicles hitting an officer on the roadway)	Fleeing police (innocent motorists are also at risk during police vehicle pursuits)
Investigating suspicious persons	Wrongful arrest
Exposure to toxic materials (e.g., smoke, chemicals, drugs, infectious bodily fluids) and dangerous implements (e.g., hypodermic needles, knives, razors, explosives)	Violations of civil liberties (e.g., unlawful intrusions of privacy and personal dignity; denial of freedoms to speak, assemble, or protest; denial of access to legal counsel; physical or psychological coercion to compel testimony)
Psychological stress from exposure to traumatic incidents	Unequal treatment (e.g., unlawful discrimination on the basis of race, ethnicity, gender, sexual orientation, religion, etc.)

All occupations have a strong interest in reducing the occupational risks of injury and death to both practitioners and clients, but how each occupation goes about doing so varies considerably. Some occupations go about this routinely, rigorously, and systemically, while others do so sporadically, casually, and in a limited fashion.[5] The central argument here is that policing needs to move further away from the latter approach toward the former.

Reviews of the sort contemplated here—those that seek to learn systematically from failures—are referred to by various terms across professions, including: organizational learning,[6] root cause analysis,[7] systems-crash prevention,[8] system improvement,[9] risk management,[10] controlling harm,[11] injury control strategies,[12] human factors evaluation,[13] and sentinel event reviews.[14] This last term is commonly used in the medical profession and has most recently been used in the context of policing, so, for lack of a better one, I will use it for present purposes.

To be sure, the police profession does put considerable effort into investigating injurious and fatal incidents involving its members. When police officers or civilians are harmed in the course of policing, police administrators typically launch investigations to discover precisely what caused the harm and who is responsible for it. Two types of police-led investigations predominate: criminal and administrative. In some cases, a private civil lawsuit is also filed which also entails considerable investigation of the incident. Journalists sometimes exercise their unofficial government-oversight function by conducting their own investigation of the incident. Government law enforcement agencies, such as the U.S. Department of Justice or state departments of justice, sometimes step in to investigate the actions of subordinate police agencies where they have such jurisdiction. And in some instances, an outside entity is retained by the government to conduct yet another investigation, or a review of the original investigation, as a second opinion about the facts of the incident, sometimes accompanied by recommendations for future action. With all this investigating going on, what could possibly be overlooked?

Each of these types of investigations serves valuable, although not the same, purposes. But each also leaves something to be desired when it comes to identifying systemic failures and formulating improvements. Criminal investigations serve the important purpose of gathering facts related to the harmful incident. Criminal investigators have substantial powers that other investigators might not possess to compel the collection of evidence from those reluctant to provide it. But the principal purpose of a criminal investigation, while important, is a rather narrow one: to determine whether any criminal acts were committed in the incident and, if so, who committed them. Ordinarily, this leaves criminal investigators focused on the statutory elements of any criminal act, with some attention also paid to the criminal offender's motives for committing the crime. (Notwithstanding that motive usually is not an element of a crime, jurors tend to want to understand it.) In incidents in which a police officer causes physical harm to a civilian, the criminal investigation and the subsequent decision whether to prosecute the officer for a crime tend to occur rather quickly and decisively. In the vast majority of such incidents, the police officer clearly lacks the requisite criminal intent to cause the harm; rather, the harm emanates from the officer's carrying out of official duties, which might be negligent or reckless, but are seldom either intentional or legally unjustified.

Police administrative investigations can be as broad as the police chief executive desires them to be, but as a matter of practice, they too tend to be relatively narrow in focus: determining whether any department rules or regulations were violated during the incident. And so, while police rules and regulations can and often do set higher standards for officers than does the criminal law, the investigation is concerned principally with the police officer's actions and not the full panoply of factors contributing to a harmful incident.

If a private civil lawsuit is filed, whether by a police officer or a civilian harmed in the incident, the scope of the investigation can be somewhat broader than a criminal investigation, but it, like a criminal investigation, must be carried out within the constraints of civil procedure and the legal remedies available to the plaintiff. In most private civil suits, the plaintiff is an individual who is primarily interested in obtaining recompense for the harm caused to him or her, and less to preventing future harm to unknown other people. So most such cases with merit are resolved—either in or out of court—with financial payment to the plaintiff, but with little direct remediation of the various causes and conditions that contributed to the harm. Of course, the government body that ultimately pays these civil judgments or settlements might be motivated to take remedial measures to reduce their future risk of similar liability, but here too, the government is less interested in remedial measures for which it bears little or no liability. And all too often, government bodies aren't sufficiently motivated by financial liability payouts to make substantial changes to policies, practices or conditions, treating the payouts as an unavoidable cost of doing government business.[15]

As to the contribution that investigative journalism can make as part of society's response to harmful policing incidents, it has potential to spur officials to action by mobilizing public demand for it, but it is ultimately limited by the journalist's expertise to ask the right questions, secure answers to them, and write a persuasive account that impels those in power to effect changes designed to prevent future similar harm.

Government law enforcement agencies such as the U.S. Department of Justice and state justice departments can invoke various types of statutory authority—criminal, civil rights, professional regulation—to conduct separate investigations into incidents involving subordinate police agencies. The best known of these is the so-called "pattern-and-practice" lawsuits that can be filed by the U.S. Department of Justice.[16] Some state attorneys general occasionally investigate serious incidents involving local police.[17] While these sorts of investigations can be extraordinarily impactful, they too are conducted only episodically and typically only in cases of repeated or especially egregious police misconduct, and then within the constraints established by state laws.

This leaves for consideration those outside investigations that are commissioned by government officials, occasionally in lieu of internal police administrative investigations but more often as secondary reviews of the primary investigation. At least in theory, these types of investigations have the greatest latitude to explore any and all causes and conditions that might have contributed to the harmful incident. Being externally conducted, they can actually be, and be perceived as being, less biased in favor of the police. Neither are they constrained by criminal or civil procedure in their scope or methods. Of all the investigation types, well-designed and well-executed independent investigations of this sort can come closest to serving the purpose of preventing future similar harm. The police are generally accustomed to after-action reports of critical incidents—including those involving police use of force,[18] police actions in crowd control,[19] or police responses to mass shootings[20]—some of which are conducted within the police profession and some external to it. Similarly, police have become accustomed to occasional wider investigations and public reports of systemic policing practices, including police corruption and brutality.[21]

Sometimes these investigations and reports prompt meaningful changes in police policies and practices, and sometimes they do not.[22] Their limitations are several. First, they are only episodically conducted. That they are conducted at all is optional and at the discretion of a governing body with authority over the involved police agency, and governing bodies are not always interested in having their policing business so examined. Second, it can be costly to fund these sorts of investigations, and less affluent jurisdictions, in which harmful policing might be more likely to occur, will be least able to afford them. Third, their value depends heavily on the professional expertise and competence of the retained investigators; ascertaining and finding that expertise and competence can be difficult for the funding authorities. Fourth, as nongovernmental investigations, investigators usually lack access to the compulsory legal process sometimes needed to gather information that those possessing it might be reluctant to provide. Fifth, typically, the investigative findings and recommendations are provided only to the commissioning authority, which might be under no obligation to disseminate them outside the jurisdiction. And sixth, perhaps inescapably, political considerations tend to influence the commission, conduct, and findings of the investigations. Political considerations are not inherently improper, but they are highly variable.

■ Solutions

The sort of investigation most needed to prevent recurrences of harms caused in the course of policing falls between the gaps of these other types of investigations. What is needed for prevention purposes is an investigation that is all of the following: (1) routinely conducted after specified types of harmful events occur, (2) oriented to preventing future harm rather than to assigning retrospective blame, (3) oriented to a broad examination of any and all relevant causes of and contributing factors to the harmful incident, (4) independently conducted by investigators not too closely affiliated with the principal actors in the harmful incident, (5) competently conducted by investigators with expertise requisite for the particular circumstances of the harmful incident, (6) reviewed and approved by people with sufficient expertise and credibility to comprehend, and either endorse or refute, the findings and recommendations of the investigators, and (7) routinely and systematically disseminated to the public and to all people and institutions likely to experience risks of similar harmful incidents (especially all other police agencies). These essential characteristics are explained below.

Routinize the Investigation of Harmful, "Near Miss," and Other Qualifying Events

Most critically, a sentinel event review should be conducted after any police-involved fatality, whether of an officer or of a civilian at the hands of an officer. Reviews of "near misses"—incidents in which a fatality was narrowly avoided—would also be important, both because they are more numerous and therefore more likely to yield generalizable findings and because they also offer positive insights about why a fatality did not occur. Sentinel event reviews might also profitably be conducted after major crowd events that resulted in injuries or substantial damage to property, wrongful arrests of innocent suspects, and major acts of police corruption or brutality.

Focus on the Prevention of Future Harm, Not Assignment of Blame

Investigations of any sort need not have only one aim, but most investigations carry a primary orientation that prioritizes one aim over others. As noted above, a criminal investigation's primary aim is to determine whether a crime was committed and, if so, by whom. A police administrative investigation's primary aim is to determine if a department rule or policy was violated. A sentinel event review's primary aim is to prevent recurrences of similar harms occurring in future incidents. This distinction in aim is critically important for several reasons. First, as will be discussed in the point below, it invites examination of any and all factors that might have contributed to the harm. Second, it minimizes the obstacles to truth-finding that typically arise when people are preoccupied by the prospect of punishment. When people are not concerned that revealing the truth will get them or others punished, they tend to be more forthcoming with information.

Examine Any and All Relevant Causes of and Contributing Factors

Because criminal law, police administrative regulations, and civil tort liability all tend to be intricately bound to varying notions of culpability (i.e., blame), they tend to seek out the principal cause of the harm—in legal terms, the "proximate cause." However, in many critical policing incidents, harm occurs due to a confluence of actions, conditions, and other factors that combine to increase the risk of the resultant harm. They often include actions of the police officer, the subject of the police action, and third parties; environmental conditions (weather, lighting, noise, surface and object characteristics); rules, policies, and orders governing actions; sensory inputs and psychological and physiological reactions to them; availability and feasibility of alternative actions; and so forth. Anything that might be said to have contributed to the harm is thereby open to consideration in efforts to prevent or reduce risks of similar future harms. Importantly, as the number of contributing factors increases, so too does the possibility that people other than just the principal actors involved in the harmful incident (e.g., a police officer and the person who is the object of police action) might bear some capacity and responsibility for preventing future harm. By way of illustration, consider the following hypothetical situation.

> A police officer attempts to conduct a *Terry* stop of a young man who appears suspicious to the officer in part because he is present in an area known to be an active illegal drug market and in part because the young man is repetitively and furtively looking around. The man suddenly starts running away from the officer, and the officer pursues him on foot. The officer shouts at the fleeing man, "Stop, or I'll shoot!" Suddenly, the man stops and abruptly turns around toward the officer. The officer observes the man's arms swinging away from his body as he turns, leading the officer to think he might be drawing and aiming a gun. The officer shoots the man. After paramedics arrive and transport the man to the hospital, he eventually bleeds out and dies. The man turns out not to have had a gun, although he did have a record of several prior arrests for selling drugs. The criminal investigation concludes that the officer committed no crime. The police administrative investigation concludes that the officer violated no department policies. A civil lawsuit filed by the man's family results in an out-of-court settlement payment to the family, with the police agency admitting no fault.

This not implausible and not uncommon scenario might well end here. But, assuming a desire to prevent the ultimate harm that occurred in this hypothetical—the death of the man—and to likewise prevent police officers from being shot by fleeing criminal suspects, a sentinel event review of this critical incident could, in addition to considering what the law and the department's use-of-deadly-force policy permitted or prohibited the officer from doing, examine the following factors that might have contributed in some measure to the harms:

- the validity of the officer's initial suspicion precipitating the attempt to make a *Terry* stop of the man;
- the tactical approach in executing the stop, including the decision to try to make the stop without a backup officer and the words the officer used in his initial contact with the man;
- the officer's decision to chase the man on foot;
- the communication the officer made, if any, to dispatchers, both prior to attempting the stop and while in pursuit;
- the officer's visual acuity (i.e., whether the officer should have been able to discern, under the lighting and time conditions, whether there was an object in the man's hands and, if so, whether it was a gun);
- the department's written policies and procedures governing the conduct of *Terry* stops and use of deadly force;
- the training the officer received from the department in the tactics used by the officer and in the relevant policies and procedures;

- the availability of alternative weapons to the officer (and whether use of them would have been justified or feasible under the circumstances);
- the information known or available to the officer about this drug-market problem;
- the information known or available to the officer about this particular suspect;
- the actions (or inactions) of third parties related to conditions that either facilitated or deterred the continuing operation of an illegal drug market in the area;
- the departmental strategy (either explicitly designed or informal) in effect for dealing with the drug market (e.g., whether an intensive stop-and-frisk or drug-enforcement strategy was to be employed or some alternative strategy that focused on disrupting the drug market through the actions of third-party place managers);
- the quality of the emergency medical response to the gunshot wounds of the man (by the police officer who shot him, other responding police officers, emergency medical crews, and hospital trauma-care staff).

Many of these, and perhaps other, factors that might have contributed to the critical incident would most likely be of little or no concern in a criminal or administrative investigation, and some likely would not be raised even in a civil liability lawsuit.

Ensure that Event Reviews are Conducted by Independent Investigators

Because people tend to be biased in favor of others with whom they share a close affiliation[23] and because outside observers tend to believe this to be true (whether or not it is in fact), it is critical that sentinel event investigators not be—or be perceived to be—closely affiliated with any of the principal actors involved in the incident being investigated. In policing, there are varying levels of affiliation that must be considered. The most obvious ones to avoid are those in which the investigator and the investigated are family members or friends. Moreover, they probably should not work for the same police organization. While it might be argued that all police officers are favorably biased toward all other police officers, even if true, a prohibition against police investigators in these types of reviews is untenable for reasons next explained.

Ensure that Events are Investigated by Qualified Experts

A sentinel event review of critical policing incidents calls for investigators with expertise of various sorts—not just police expertise. Nonetheless, some expertise that is distinctive to policing will almost invariably be required. Few other professional fields combine expertise in law, criminal investigative procedure, police policy, police tactics, and police weapons and equipment, to name but a few of the areas of expertise likely to be relevant. As a consequence, if sentinel event reviews are to be competently conducted, the investigative team must include skilled police investigators. This means that even if there might be some affiliation bias by police investigators, that consideration is at least partially offset by the necessity of their expertise. However, a sentinel event review that extends beyond the parameters of a criminal or conventional administrative investigation might well call for expertise from other fields, possibly to include academia, engineering, medicine, chemistry, metallurgy, and psychology. Accordingly, a fully functional sentinel event review system in policing must incorporate ready access to experts from a variety of fields.

Ensure that Report Findings Are Reviewed by Qualified, Credible Authorities

Criminal investigation reports are the province of the jurisdiction's prosecutor to review. Police administrative investigation reports are principally the province of the police chief executive to review.[24] Because preventive reviews are intended to be more encompassing, extending beyond the application of the criminal law and administrative rules, they ought to be submitted to a body of reviewers not restricted to, though not excluding, the police chief executive and chief prosecutor. Some of the jurisdiction's elected officials, magistrates, police scholars, police union officials, government liability insurance officials, civilian police overseers, and lay experts might be considered as members of an official reviewing body. A credible and broad-based body that reviews preventive-review findings and recommendations has potential to carry great weight in both explaining the report to the public and urging that preventive actions be taken by those in a position to do so.

Disseminate Report Findings Routinely and Systematically to the Public and to Organizations Likely to Benefit

Lastly, the larger return on the investment made in conducting and reviewing preventive-review investigations is to be realized by more widely disseminating the report to the public, the press, and, perhaps most importantly, to the police profession. There are tens of thousands of police agencies in the United States, all of which stand to benefit from reviewing the critical-incident experiences of other police officers and agencies. But without a system to make these reports accessible to police across the country—or, at a minimum, to those across the state in which the incident occurred—whatever benefits are derived from a thorough preventive review will be confined to a relatively few sets of eyes in the jurisdiction in which the incident occurred.

There remains, of course, an important role for police researchers to play in carrying out meta-analyses of policing critical incidents, looking for trends and patterns in the causes and contributing factors of the various types of incidents (use of force, crowd control, wrongful arrest, etc.) across incidents within a jurisdiction and across different jurisdictions and recommending profession-wide improvements aimed at reducing risks of harmful outcomes.[25] But if the investigations of the critical incidents themselves are more broadly aimed at understanding the full panoply of contributing factors to the harms caused, that will only enhance the value of scholarly meta-analyses.

Challenges

Moving from the current state of affairs in which critical incidents in policing are reviewed principally in the limited contexts of criminal law and administrative policy to a future state of affairs in which they are also routinely reviewed in a broader, prevention-oriented fashion will encounter some formidable, but not insurmountable, challenges.

Persuading Key Stakeholders

The first challenge is in making the case to all essential stakeholders that this new type of review is necessary. Essential stakeholders include police executives, rank-and-file police officers and their union representatives, government executives and elected representatives, government-liability insurers, and prosecutors. As noted previously, with all the investigating that already routinely ensues a critical policing incident, the argument that more investigation is needed will surely try some people's patience.

Safeguarding the Integrity of Other Investigations

The second challenge is in ensuring that a sentinel event review will not compromise the other investigations that must, of necessity, be conducted, namely the criminal and administrative investigations but also potential investigations into civil rights violations or tort liability. Prosecutors and police executives, for good reason, jealously guard their own prerogatives and professional obligations to carry out their investigatory duties in these matters and to take what they deem to be appropriate remedial actions.

Ensuring Requisite Confidentiality

The third challenge is in ensuring requisite confidentiality of investigative findings to guarantee that witnesses will not be subject to greater legal jeopardy by cooperating than they would be for refusing to cooperate in sentinel event investigations.[26]

Creating a Sentinel Event Review Infrastructure

The fourth challenge is to create the legal and administrative infrastructure, including the requisite funding, to ensure that sentinel event reviews can and will be conducted as a matter of course and in a fair and competent manner. To expect that reviews of this type can happen within existing frameworks is not realistic.

Taking Preventive Action

The fifth challenge will be the biggest: Even if the other challenges can be met, and sentinel event reviews of critical police incidents become the norm, their ultimate value is realized only if they actually result in systemic improvements that in fact reduce risks of future harmful events. But changing systems, while not necessarily technically difficult to do, is often politically difficult to do. It is usually harder to do than prosecuting or disciplining one or a few police officers or civilians. Effecting systemic changes requires the cooperation of people in positions of high power and influence, many of whom might prefer to resist the change than to acknowledge the possibility that their prior policies and practices contributed to the harms caused. Were this easy, sentinel event review systems likely would have been in place long ago.

■ Next Steps

To date, no such routinized external sentinel event system for policing exists in the United States.[27] The furthest progress toward creating one is occurring in the State of Wisconsin.[28] Wisconsin's legislature and governor took an initial step several years ago in mandating by state law that police-involved fatalities be investigated by an outside agency. In 2017, an exploratory meeting was held among state legislators, legal scholars, police executives, police union officials, municipal liability insurers, local government executives, and experts from other fields (aviation, aerospace, and medicine) to discuss the issues and challenges associated with sentinel event reviews and to map out a plan for creating a statewide system.[29] At the national level, the Bureau of Justice Assistance and the National Institute of Justice, in partnership with the Quattrone Center for the Fair Administration of Justice at the University of Pennsylvania Law School, launched in 2017 a Sentinel Events Initiative[30] to provide technical assistance to jurisdictions interested in developing a sentinel event system that can serve as demonstration models.

Although the feasibility and effectiveness of sentinel event review systems in policing has not yet been tested rigorously, the merit of parallel systems in other occupations has been more firmly established. The need for such reviews remains pressing in American policing, and the political and professional support for them appears to be building. Once the first true external sentinel event review system for policing is established and in operation, the painstaking work of assessing, modifying, replicating, and institutionalizing such systems across the nation and the police profession can begin.

Notes

[1] Henry Reeve, Shane Stephens, and Stephen Pegala, and Ryan Farrell, "25 years of Worker Injury, Illness, and Fatality Case Data," Washington, DC: Bureau of Labor Statistics, 2019, p. 5.

[2] Martin A. Makary and Michael Daniel, "Medical Error—the Third Leading Cause of Death in the U.S.," *BMJ: British Medical Journal (Online)* i2139, no. 353 (2016).

[3] Police "clients" encompass a wide range of types, including complainants, crime and accidents victims, witnesses, bystanders, information seekers, civil-law violators, and criminal offenders; some of whom receive police service beneficially and some adversely. Those at highest risk of suffering death or physical harm at the hands of police are offenders, although risks are incurred by others as well. Truck driving is likewise risky for both drivers and other drivers sharing the road. The risks of death and injury in taxi driving and retail cashiering also arise mainly from intentional acts such as robbery-related homicides which are relatively common occupational hazards.

[4] Steven G. Brandl and Meghan S. Stroshine, "Toward an Understanding of the Physical Hazards of Police Work," in *Critical Issues in Policing: Contemporary Readings*, 7th ed., eds. Roger G. Dunham and Geoffrey P. Alpert, (Long Grove, IL: Waveland Press, Inc, 2015), 385–400; Federal Bureau of Investigation, Law Enforcement Officers Killed and Assaulted, https://ucr.fbi.gov/leoka/2018; National Law Enforcement Officers Memorial Fund, Facts & Figures: Causes of Law Enforcement Deaths (Washington, DC: Author, 2019).

[5] Mohammed Shu'aibu Abubakar, Desa Ahmad, and Fatai Bukola Akande, "A Review of Farm Tractor Overturning Accidents and Safety," *Pertanika Journal of Science & Technology* 18, no. 2 (2010): 377–85; Risto Rautiainen, Marika M. Lehtola, Lesley Margaret Day, Eva Schonstein, Juha Suutarinen, Simo Salminen, and Jos H. Verbeek, "Interventions for Preventing Injuries in the Agricultural Industry," *Cochrane Database of Systematic Reviews* 1, no. CD006398 (2008); Herbert W. Heinrich, *Industrial Accident Prevention. A Scientific Approach* (New York and London: McGraw-Hill, 1941); Paul Barach and Stephen D. Small, "Reporting and Preventing Medical Mishaps: Lessons from Non-Medical Near Miss Reporting Systems," *British Medical Journal* 320, no. 7237 (2000): 759–63; James M. Doyle, "What Medicine Could Teach Our Flawed Justice System," *The Crime Report,* April 11, 2017; Phillip J. Kolczynski, "NTSB Accident Investigations: What You Need to Know," *AV Web,* September 8, 1997.

[6] Michael D. Cohen and Lee S. Sproull, *Organizational Learning* (Thousand Oaks, CA: Sage Publications, 1996).

[7] Paul F. Wilson, Larry D. Dell, and Gaylord F. Anderson, *Root Cause Analysis: A Tool for Total Quality* Management (Milwaukee, WI: American Society for Quality, 1993); John Holloway, Calvin Lee, and Sean Smoot, "Root Cause Analysis: A Tool to Promote Officer Safety and Reduce Officer Involved Shootings Over Time," *Villanova Law Review* 62, no. 5 (2017): 883–924.

[8] Lawrence W. Sherman, "Reducing Fatal Police Shootings as System Crashes: Research, Theory, and Practice," *Annual Review of Criminology* 1, no. 19 (2018): 1–19, 29.

[9] Anita L. Tucker, "An Empirical Study of System Improvement by Frontline Employees in Hospital Units," *Manufacturing & Service Operations Management* 9, no. 4 (2007): 492–505.

[10] Jens Rasmussen, "Risk Management in a Dynamic Society: A Modeling Problem," *Safety Science* 27, no. 2/3 (1997): 183–213.

[11] Malcolm K. Sparrow, *The Character of Harms: Operational Challenges in Control* (Cambridge, UK: Cambridge University Press, 2008).

[12] Scott E. Geller, Thomas D. Berry, Timothy D. Ludwig, Robert E. Evans, Michael R. Gilmore, and Steven W. Clarke "A Conceptual Framework for Developing and Evaluating Behavior Change Interventions for Injury Control," *Health Education Research: Theory and Practice* 5, no. 2 (1990): 125–137.

[13] Robert T. Nullmeyer, D. Stella, G. Montijo, and Stephen W. Harden, "Human Factors in Air Force Mishaps: Implications for Change," *Proceedings of the Interservice/Industry Training Systems and Education Conference,* Orlando, Florida, 2005.

[14] James M. Doyle, "Learning from Error in the Criminal Justice System: Sentinel Event Reviews," in *Mending Justice: Sentinel Event Reviews*, National Institute of Justice (Washington, DC: National Institute of Justice, 2014), 3–18; For an excellent, accessible review of systematic learning from failure across occupations, see Matthew Syed, *Black Box Thinking: Marginal Gains and the Secrets of High Performance* (London: John Murray Publishers, 2015).

[15] Joanna Schwartz, "Myths and Mechanics of Deterrence: The Role of Lawsuits in Law Enforcement Decisionmaking," *UCLA Law Review* 57, (2010): 1023–1094.

[16] This authority is found in 42 U.S.C. §14141, established under the Violent Crime Control and Law Enforcement Act of 1994. As of early 2017, the U.S. Department of Justice had initiated 69 such investigations, leading to 40 police-reform agreements. See U.S. Department of Justice, Civil Rights Division, *The Civil Rights Division's Pattern and Practice Police Reform Work: 1994–Present* (Washington, DC: U.S. Department of Justice, 2017).

[17] The New York State Attorney General's Office recently established a Special Investigations and Prosecutions Unit within its Criminal Division to investigate some police-involved fatalities. See, Eric T. Schneiderman, *Biennial Report of the Office of the Attorney General's Special Investigations and Prosecutions Unit* (Albany, NY: Office of the Attorney General, 2017), https://ag.ny.gov/sites/default/files/sip_biennial_report_2017_0.pdf

[18] The post-incident review of police use of deadly force in Baltimore in 2011 is an example. See Independent Review Board, *The Baltimore Police Department Police-Involved Shooting of January 9, 2011: A Report by the Independent Review Board,* October 17, 2011.

[19] See, for instance, the post-incident reviews of police responses to political protests and other crowd-disorder incidents in Los Angeles's MacArthur Park in 2007 (Los Angeles Police Department, *Report to the Board of Police Commissioners: An Examination of May Day 2007,* October 9, 2007); at University of California campuses in 2011 (Christopher F. Edley, Jr., and Charles F. Robinson, *Response to Protests on UC Campuses: A Report to University of California President Mark G. Yudof,* September 13, 2012), in Baltimore in 2015 (see Police Executive Research Forum, *Lessons Learned from the 2015 Civil Unrest in* Baltimore, (Washington, DC: Police Executive Research Forum, 2015), and in Charlottesville, Virginia in 2017 (see Hunton & Williams, LLP, *Independent Review of the 2017 Protest Events in Charlottesville, Virginia. Final Report*, 2017).

[20] The post-incident investigations of the police response to mass shootings at the Sandy Hook Elementary School in Newtown, Connecticut, in 2012, the Pulse Nightclub in Orlando, Florida in 2016, and in Las Vegas in 2017 are examples. (See Connecticut Police Chiefs Association *Newtown Police Response to the Sandy Hook Elementary School Shooting* (Rocky Hill, CT: Connecticut Police Chiefs Association, 2013); Frank Straub, Jack Cambria, Jane Castor, Ben Gorban, Brett Meade, David Waltemeyer, and Jennifer Zeunik, *Rescue, Response and Resilience: A Critical Incident Review of the Orlando Public Safety Response to the Attack on the Pulse Nightclub* (Washington, DC: U.S. Office of Community Oriented Policing Services and the Police Foundation, 2017). The Sandy Hook incident was also reviewed by bodies external to the police profession, though with police input (See Sandy Hook Advisory Commission, *Final Report of the Sandy Hook Advisory Commission*, March 6, 2015 and Office of the Child Advocate, *Shooting at Sandy Hook Elementary School: Report of the Office of the Child Advocate* (Hartford, CT: State of Connecticut Office of the Child Advocate, November 21, 2014).

[21] The external investigations and reports of systemic policing problems in Los Angeles (Independent Commission on the Los Angeles Police Department, *Report of the Independent Commission on the Los Angeles Police Department*, 1991; Rampart Independent Review Panel, *Report of the Rampart Independent Review Panel: A Report to the Los Angeles Board of Police Commissioners Concerning the Operations, Policies and Procedures of the Los Angeles Police Department in the Wake of the Rampart Scandal. Executive Summary,* November 16, 2000); New York City (Milton Mollen, *Commission to Investigate Allegations of Police Corruption and the Anti-Corruption Procedures of the Police Department: Commission Report*, 1994); and Ferguson, Missouri (Ferguson Commission, *Forward Through Ferguson: A Path Toward Racial Equity,* 2015) are but a few examples.

[22] Samuel Walker, "Setting the Standards: The Efforts and Impact of Blue-Ribbon Commissions on the Police," in *Police Leadership in America: Crisis and Opportunity,* ed. William A. Geller (Chicago: American Bar Foundation and Praeger Publishers, 1985); Michael S. Scott, "Progress in Policing? Reviewing the National Reviews," *Law & Social Inquiry* 34, no. 1 (2008): 171–185.

[23] Werner Guth, Matteo Ploner, and Tobias Regner, "Determinants of In-Group Bias: Is Affilia-tion Mediated by Guilt-aversion?" *Journal of Economic Psychology* 30, no. 5 (2009): 814–827.

[24] In some jurisdictions, various civilian oversight bodies might also have authority to review police administrative investigation reports, either in the first instance or upon appeal of actions taken as a result of them.

[25] William A. Geller and Michael S. Scott, *Deadly Force: What We Know. A Practitioner's Desk Reference on Police-Involved Shootings* (Washington, DC: Police Executive Research Forum, 1992); William A. Geller and Hans Toch, *And Justice for All: Understanding and Controlling Police Abuse of* Force (Washington, DC: Police Executive Research Forum, 1995); Lawrence W. Sherman, "Reducing Fatal Police Shootings as System Crashes: Research, Theory, and Practice," *Annual Review of Criminology* 1, no. 19 (2018): 1–19, 29.

[26] Bryan A. Liang, "Risks of Reporting Sentinel Events," *Health Affairs* 19, no. 5 (2000): 112–120.

[27] The Tucson, Arizona, Police Department is among a number of police agencies that have established internal critical incident review boards, and it explicitly invokes the terminology of sentinel event reviews. However, although some non-police city officials and community representatives serve as voting board members, this local review board is predominated by internal police personnel (Tucson Police Department, *Critical Incident Review Board Operations Pamphlet,* February 15, 2018, https://www.tucsonaz.gov/files/police/CIRB/CIRB_OPS_Pamphlet_021518.pdf); The National Police Foundation, a private police think tank, has created an online reporting system for capturing and sharing details of police incidents in which fatalities or serious injuries were only just avoided—so-called "near misses." While a positive development, this system falls short of a true sentinel event review system. (National Police Foundation, *LEO Near Miss* (Arlington, VA: Author, 2019). https://www.leonearmiss.org/

[28] In 2014, the State of Wisconsin enacted a law requiring that officer-involved deaths be investigated by investigators not from the same agency as the officer(s) involved in the fatal incident. (See Yamiche Alcindor, "Wis. Bill Mandates Rules for Officer-involved Deaths," *USA Today,* April 26, 2014). This law is believed to be the first, or among the first, of its kind in the United States.

[29] University of Wisconsin Law School and The Johnson Foundation at Wingspread, *Best Practices for Review and Prevention of Deadly Incidents in High-Hazard Professions: Lessons for Police. Summary of Conference Proceedings, May 9–11, 2017.* On file with author. Note that the author was one of the planners and the moderator of this meeting.

[30] See the National Institute of Justice's Sentinel Events Initiative website for further details: https://www.nij.gov/topics/justice-system/Pages/sentinel-events.aspx.

8

Response Essay

Chief David W. McGill (Ret.)
Sedona Police Department

One of the many observations I have witnessed in over 30 years in the law enforcement profession is that, by and large, true professional leaders make it a habit to continuously assess and learn from past mistakes. They are committed to making their profession and their organization better by striving to obtain the utmost quality of work through continuous improvement of their policies and practices. I have also figured out, albeit a little more slowly, that our profession cannot attain any level of perfection or near perfection alone, and Scott and academic colleagues like him are helping law enforcement get better through thoughtful and relevant research, investigation, and collaboration. Chapter 8 hits the mark by encouraging us to broaden our examination of critical events so that we learn from them, while taking certain actions to improve our practices so that we continuously improve ourselves and our profession. More importantly, the suggestion that reviews of critical events be completed by entities outside the agency involved has theoretical merit. It lends itself well to the practice of transparency for which all agencies strive and is worthy of debate, but actual practice will involve tremendous effort, political finesse, and collective push from those involved to become a reality.

One of the tidbits in this article I find very astonishing, and a little disheartening, is the statistic of the number of deaths attributed to medical malpractice or mistakes in the United States: in the neighborhood of 250,000 each and every year. By comparison, about 1,000 deaths are attributed to law enforcement officers each year on average. Although every death at the hands of another should be cause for concern and empathy, the media attention focused on police contacts resulting in a death is grossly imbalanced when taking into consideration deaths attributed to other professions. However, as we have come to know quite well, the law enforcement profession is unlike any other profession, for many reasons. This is our reality, and it will probably not change anytime soon. So, we must continue to work hard to reduce the number of contacts that result in police-involved harms, and we readily look to Scott and others to help us do just that.

I agree with the suggestion that conducting thorough sentinel event reviews will have a positive effect on involved agencies and will help to improve their practices with the goal of preventing similar events. Although I am not inclined to believe that conducting these reviews will prevent *all* police-involved harms, I am confident that they will certainly help to reduce future police-involved harmful events if done correctly and as suggested in the chapter.

In my experience, focused primarily in the western United States, many law enforcement agencies already conduct after-action reviews of critical events, particularly in larger, metropolitan police organizations that tend to be the focus of most of the media attention. As the chapter correctly points out, the depth and scope of these reviews can vary greatly, depending on a host of external and internal influences. Scott makes a compelling argument to standardize these reviews throughout our profession to bring consistency and effectiveness to our work, especially when such standardized reviews are conducted regionally or via a statewide entity yet to be determined.

When I was working for the Los Angeles Police Department (1987–2012), we instituted a practice of evaluating critical incidents with a lens as wide as we could imagine. This practice was refined as we moved through major incidents including the Rampart scandal, the Rodney King incident, the L.A. Riots, the MacArthur Park melee, and others. Field supervisors also started conducting more frequent "hot washes" or debriefs after most incidents that resulted in more than the usual policing responses. More and more large police agencies seem to be adopting these practices as time moves forward.

During this time, we also formed a more robust officer-involved shooting section that rolled out after every deadly force incident or other activities resulting in major media attention, or a death or serious injury caused by an officer. Particularly enlightening were our critical examinations of the seconds, hours, and even days prior to the event, so that we understood as many factors as possible that contributed to the incident from the perspective of the involved officers, the suspect, and the community. Some of us who moved to other police departments took this training and experience to our new cities and towns, and we have refined our versions of sentinel event reviews to fit our new culture.

The more we examine these incidents, the more we realize or reaffirm that our workforce and the "clients" we come in contact with are human beings, with all the frailties and idiosyncrasies that each of us possesses—and the more we realize that policing is generally similar throughout the United States, albeit with subtle differences due to the many cultural anomalies found in different parts of the country. Police work is similar in all parts of the country because we all deal with the same phenomena—human beings employed as police officers trying to deal with other human beings, usually at their worst moments. Scott's point about standardizing these critical reviews of sentinel events, and conducting them in a nonpunitive manner, is not lost on those who have worked so long in this field. We have found repeatedly that the more we work together on solving problems, in a way that elicits the facts of what occurred without bias or ego, the more successful we will be. If all policing leaders adopt the suggestions in this chapter, or versions as similar as possible, we will be better off, and we will move toward that seemingly unachievable goal of being the best we can be.

The chapter proposes the need for a yet-to-be-formed team of specially trained investigators from an outside entity to respond to significant events on a regular basis. However, entities like the Police Foundation and others already make themselves available to do exactly this, and their products of reviewed events of national interest to date have yielded interesting information from which others have learned. The difference between what the Police Foundation and others do, and what Scott is proposing, is that past reviews by the Police Foundation and others have been completed *at the request of the agency involved.* These invitations come with a critical and required aspect—access to agency data, reports, and information, so that a proper review can be conducted. Without this critical access, similar reviews cannot occur with any degree of clarity, and the final work product will not have credibility.

Forming a dedicated team to critically and honestly review sentinel events is the easy part. Gaining the political will, the commitment from the heads of the agencies in the region or state where they reside, and obtaining the trust of the communities most impacted will be more difficult. A good place to start is an audience of like-minded professionals who understand the importance of standardized and unbiased reviews of sentinel events and how such reviews can help their respective agencies and their profession form even more trust and respect from the communities they serve. Getting a room full of chiefs and sheriffs to agree on what that looks like is another challenge indeed.

9

Build Police-Researcher Partnerships to Advance Policing

Vincent J. Webb
Charles M. Katz
Michaela R. Flippin
Arizona State University

This chapter calls for the institutionalization of police-university collaborations, hereafter referred to as "police-researcher partnerships," to advance knowledge of what works in policing and to aid in the production of use-inspired research to improve community safety. Although police-researcher partnerships have existed for decades, the development of reciprocal research partnerships as a form of collaboration is more recent, and their expansion has been nearly geometric in recent years.[1]

In the United States, the expansion of police-researcher partnerships can be attributed to at least three major sources. First has been the rapid development of criminology and criminal justice programs in higher education beginning in the late 1960s and the role of the federal government in fostering the development of those programs. The growth in these academic programs, as well as in the fields of criminology and criminal justice more generally, created a supply of university-based police researchers eagerly seeking opportunities to engage in police-related research. The expansion of criminal justice education programs also produced a generation of police leaders exposed to research used to identify and solve crime-related problems.[2]

The second major source in the expansion of police-researcher partnerships has been the federal funding requirements imposed on the police when they apply for and are awarded grant funds by federal agencies, such as the Department of Justice's Bureau of Justice Assistance. Requiring local law enforcement agencies to have a research partner as a condition of receiving grant funding has become a routine part of the grant award and implementation process.[3]

The third source in the expansion of these partnerships has been the increased recognition by the police of the need for evidence-based approaches to policing, which necessarily requires systematic research for planning and evaluation. The availability of local university-based researchers has become a natural source for supplying police agencies with the affordable research capacity required to implement contemporary evidence-based approaches to policing.

In addition to examining the development and workings of police-researcher partnerships, this chapter considers the challenges that both the police and the university—institutions with very different and sometimes incompatible cultures—face in building and maintaining productive collaborations. The chapter then explores the features of and prerequisites for successful police-researcher partnerships as well as strategies for building and sustaining such collaborations.

■ Background

The evolution of police-researcher partnerships has been fueled by several sources, including calls for police professionalism,[4] the tremendous growth in criminal justice and criminology education programs, and the development of models of policing and crime control that rely on systematic research and evaluation.[5] The growth curve in the development of such collaborations and research partnerships over the past century is probably best described as geometric rather than linear. As early as 1917, August Vollmer promoted using higher education and scientific knowledge to advance police professionalism.[6] However, most police scholars attribute the rapid growth of police-researcher partnerships to developments that took place in the late 1960s, namely the 1967 President's Commission on Law Enforcement and Administration of Justice and the 1968 Omnibus Crime Control and Safe Streets Act. Spin-offs from this Act included the development of the Law Enforcement Education Program (LEEP) and what is now known as the National Institute of Justice (NIJ), the major federal funding agency supporting police-related research.[7] Both the Commission and the Act greatly influenced the supply and demand for police-related research, thus promoting the establishment of police-researcher collaborations and partnerships.[8]

LEEP

LEEP was a major stimulus for the development of criminal justice agency programs.[9] In the early 1960s, only a small handful of criminal justice education programs existed. However, by the late 1970s, there were more than a thousand programs. This growth included two-year, baccalaureate, and graduate programs. LEEP provided both pre-service and in-service students with funding to study in these programs; as a result, large numbers of aspiring and in-service police officers were exposed to scholarly research on crime and the criminal justice system, including research on policing. At the same time, growth in criminal justice and criminology graduate education, especially at the doctoral level, resulted in an increase in trained researchers, many of whom specialized in police-related research and sought opportunities to conduct this research, though much of the research they produced was research *on the police* and not *for* or *with the police*, the latter being characteristic of police-researcher partnerships.[10] Nevertheless, this doctoral-level interest greatly expanded the body of police-related research.

Pilot Cities

As noted above, the Omnibus Crime Control and Safe Streets Act led to the establishment of the Law Enforcement Assistance Administration (LEAA). Within that organization, a research branch then known as the National Institute of Law Enforcement and Criminal Justice, now known as the NIJ, was developed. This organization serves as the research and evaluation arm of the U.S. Department of Justice. In 1969, LEAA, through its research arm, proposed an innovative concept that would lead to the establishment of some of the earliest police-researcher partnerships. Murray and Krug described this concept as follows: "This is a proposal to establish a correctional laboratory at the local government level. The goal is to create, in a generally representative urban area, a laboratory in which the introduction of correctional and related law enforcement and social innovations will lead to optimization of the criminal justice system and where these innovations can be systematically introduced and studied."[11] This concept was operationalized as the Pilot Cities Program, and it included all components of the criminal justice system (i.e., police, courts, and corrections).

The Pilot Cities Program, very much a predecessor of today's police-researcher partnerships, possesses several aspects that are especially noteworthy when tracing the evolution and development of police-researcher partnerships. First, the program, which was implemented in eight cities across the United States, called for a team approach. Each team was composed of four associate directors (one for each of the three major components of the criminal justice system and one for "systems analysis") and a small supporting staff. Second, the Pilot Cities' teams were to operate independently from local and state agencies. Third, one of the criteria for site selection was the "availability of a university or private nonprofit organization with a law enforcement or criminal justice research capacity as a possible applicant for the actual Pilot City grant."[12] Of the eight Pilot Cities, six involved universities, and the remaining two involved nonprofit research organizations. Fourth, one of the recommendations that came out of the national evaluation of the Pilot Cities Program was that a member with expertise in social science research should be represented on the team.

Funding for six of the eight Pilot Cities was administered by a local university "partner," with $400,000 being awarded annually for team operations and another $500,000 awarded to criminal justice agencies through the local Pilot Cities team. The Pilot Cities Program was subjected to a national evaluation, which provided several lessons learned (to be discussed below) that informed the development of future collaborations and research partnerships.

Recent Drivers of Police-Researcher Partnerships

Interestingly, much of the literature on research collaborations and partnerships has overlooked Pilot Cities as one of the early formal attempts by the NIJ (its predecessor) to establish police-researcher partnerships. Although scholars trace the origins of funding for police-researcher partnerships to the 1968 Omnibus Crime Control and Safe Streets Act, they also point to a variety of other federally funded programs to highlight such collaborations. These include the Drug Market Analysis Program, the Locally Initiated Research Partnerships Program, Operation Ceasefire, and the Strategic Approaches to Community Safety Initiative.[13] Additionally, the establishment of the Office of Community Oriented Policing Services further promoted programs aimed at creating partnerships among the police and universities or researchers. More recently, the Bureau of Justice Assistance (BJA) funded programs such as the SMART Policing Initiative and the Crime Gun Intelligence Center (CGIC) program, which require grant recipients to have a research partner. Although this requirement does not call for research partners from universities exclusively, other research organizations can and do collaborate. However, for the purposes of this chapter, we will solely focus on police-researcher partnerships.

Innovations in policing and crime control strategies have played an important role in the proliferation of police-researcher partnerships. The emphasis on evidence-based policy and practice in the public sector has contributed greatly to the need for more research and evaluation to answer the question, "What works?"[14] More specifically, in policing, a rising emphasis on the use of research evidence to direct strategy and practice has increased the demand for research and research partnerships. Recent approaches such as evidence-based policing and strategic crime control all require access to rigorous research evidence.[15] As pointed out by the International Association of Chiefs of Police (IACP), police-researcher partnerships are one way to generate the research evidence that informs agency decision-making within the specific agency hosting the partnership while expanding the broader base of evidence on what works in policing. Trained academic researchers are required to disseminate knowledge through publications.

Police-researcher partnerships can be a cost-effective way of building research capacity within the police agency—a capacity that is used to inform strategic planning and policy formation and evaluation.[16] The importance of establishing and maintaining police-researcher partnerships is reflected in the IACP call for all police agencies to participate in such partnerships.[17]

■ Contemporary Police-Researcher Partnerships

Today, there are at least four major reasons why police practitioners enter into research partnerships. First, they recognize and value the unique perspectives and skills that research can provide. In addition to possessing substantive knowledge about the topic(s) to be researched, researchers also have the methodological and technical skills required to design research and to analyze and interpret research findings. Second, researchers from outside the agency provide "third-party credibility," which enhances the legitimacy of research findings and their interpretation. Third, research partnerships are an efficient, cost-effective way to increase the agency's research capacity. Finally, agencies are committed to improving public safety and recognize that participating in research partnerships will help them achieve this goal.[18]

While research partnerships provide important benefits to agencies involved in such partnerships, the benefits flow both ways: not just to agencies but also to researchers. These benefits include providing researchers with access to crime data and police personnel, further enabling them to engage in publishable research. Additionally, partnerships enable researchers to apply their experience working with police agencies to their teaching. Working in a collaborative manner with police agencies also gives local researchers direct opportunities to serve their community by working jointly with the local police to improve public safety.[19]

Successful research partnerships often exhibit similar characteristics in terms of the reasons for their formation. First, successful partnerships develop out of necessity, since it is increasingly common for funding agencies to require that funded projects include a research partner. This is primarily done for both process and outcomes evaluations but also to assist in the in-depth analysis of the problem the agency is addressing through grant funding. Second, successful partnerships are based on the recognition that combining practitioner expertise and research adds value to the practitioner's capacity to make data-driven decisions that result in more effective and efficient policies and practices.[20]

The Prevalence of Police-Researcher Partnerships

Police-researcher partnerships have been classified in three different ways: cooperation, coordination, and collaboration.[21] Cooperation partnerships are those that are informal and generally short-term with a focus on a single project. Coordination partnerships are more formal with a focus on a specific project. Last, collaboration partnerships are formal, long-term partnerships that encompass multiple projects, often involving a formal agreement or memorandum of understanding. Police-researcher partnerships can consist of a police agency working with individual researchers, a university academic research center, a department or school, or researchers from different academic institutions partnering together. Of course, not all police-researcher partnerships involve universities as a partner, since private research organizations can also serve this same purpose.

Today, about 32 percent of law enforcement agencies report participating in a research partnership. Of those that do participate in research partnerships, about 66 percent report participating in cooperation partnerships, 57 percent report participating in coordination partnerships, and 30 percent report participating in collaboration partnerships. Larger agencies and agencies that use research in their decision-making are more likely to report having a research partner.[22]

Characteristics of Police-Researcher Partnerships

A substantial body of research and proscriptive scholarship exists that provides insight into the development and sustainability of police-researcher partnerships.[23] We know, for instance, that police-researcher partnerships are related to the structural characteristics (e.g., lack of financial support, geographic proximity of partners, permanence of key participants) and organizational demands placed on both participating police departments and researchers. For example, many police departments require university researchers to go through criminal background checks and polygraphs to access confidential police records data. Further, many universities have policies relating to confidentiality and Institutional Review Board requirements related to the protection of human subjects when partaking in external partnerships.

In addition to the structural and organizational characteristics bearing on the success of the partnership, so too do the "value orientations" and "interpersonal relationships" of the participants. Greene notes that a major barrier to successful police-researcher partnerships is the "receptivity" of practitioners to evaluation by "outsiders" and the belief of academics that the police do not use research evidence to guide practice and policy.[24] Cordner and White point out the need to avoid two common stereotypes that can have an adverse impact on police-researcher partnerships.

The police, who deal on a regular basis with disorder, conflict, and danger, often maintain a surprising degree of optimism and idealism. Amazingly, this optimism even extends to universities and researchers—many police actually seem to think that professors have something useful to offer! Don't count on it though—in the research world, scientific skepticism easily slides into cynicism, the null hypothesis of no effects is the most common finding, and a 'nothing works' mentality is pervasive.[25]

Successful partnerships tend to exist when law enforcement professionals appreciate the value of research as well as the opportunity to work with researchers.

Likewise, researchers who value working with agencies and who are optimistic about the possibility of producing evidence-based research that inspires positive change are an important ingredient in successful partnerships. The value orientation of many researchers, however, does not necessarily reward partnerships with police organizations. Faculty employed by research universities are often evaluated based on such metrics as the number of peer-reviewed articles published and grants awarded by prestigious organizations such as the National Science Foundation. Partnering with a police agency can be time consuming for the faculty member and may result in a work product that is not publishable or that is publishable only in less desirable outlets. This organizational constraint is amplified when taking into consideration the rank of a faculty member, with junior faculty members being under pressure to publish in a substantial number of peer-reviewed journals within the first five to twelve years of their career. By the time the faculty member has been promoted to full professor, when they have the greatest amount of flexibility in their workload, they have been enculturated and gained experience in writing journal articles, not in partnering with police agencies. Finding a research partner who is well trained and experienced in working with the police can be difficult.

Trust is also an essential component of successful and sustained partnerships.[26] Here, the burden is primarily on the academic researchers to demonstrate that their stated purpose is trustworthy and that their research is service oriented. This is probably why many successful research partnerships have fairly long-standing or preexisting relationships in place before collaborative research projects commence. In other words, the partnership existed before the opportunity for collaborative research presented itself.[27] Before collaborative research projects, partnerships often fall within the coordination or collaboration categories.[28] Over time, and over a history of multiple projects, researchers become the "go to" partner when collaborative research needs and opportunities, such as grant opportunities, arise.

For both parties, good communication skills, mutual respect, open-mindedness, and investment in the research questions and outcome are essential. For researchers specifically, some desirable characteristics include a genuine interest in understanding and assisting the organization involved in the collaboration as well as appreciating and being respectful of those serving the organization. Regarding practitioners, desirable characteristics include a passion for addressing the research question at hand, appreciating the need for evaluation and knowledge sharing, and having a good understanding of the subject matter underlying the question(s) being researched.[29]

The personal characteristics and prior relationship of the practitioner and researcher are also important to sustaining police-researcher partnerships. Such partnerships require building rapport and trust, mutual respect, joint learning/cross training, open communication, and participant commitment. However, factors that can facilitate partnership success and sustainability can also cripple such partnerships.[30] Facilitators of partnerships and barriers to partnerships can represent two sides of the same coin.[31] For example, trust is considered a facilitator when mutually shared; mistrust serves as a barrier to successful collaboration. Funding and providing research infrastructure are also important prerequisites for research partnership sustainability.

An assessment of Project Safe Neighborhoods by Bynum and colleagues found many of the same barriers as previously described, but they also include staff resistance to change and changing agency priorities in their list of obstacles.[32] Speaking to staff resistance to change, much of this hesitation comes from practitioners feeling as though their experience is held secondary to researcher knowledge.[33] Furthermore, a lack of past experience on the practitioner's part in terms of reading publications focused on evidence-based policing may reduce receptivity to research partnerships.[34] Given these misgivings, practitioners may perceive much of researchers' work as negative or political in nature.[35] Meanwhile, researchers' expectations regarding "evidence" may be a reason for resistance.[36] That is to say, researchers are generally interested in internal validity and other methodological concerns, whereas practitioners are focused on personal experiences in defining "evidence."[37] Importantly, in ensuring successful police-researcher partnerships, researchers must dedicate a proper amount of time to translating their findings into actionable intelligence for departments[38] as well as to upholding other tenets of action research (e.g., collaboration, transparency, etc.).[39]

■ Police Demand and University Supply of Police-Researcher Partners

So far, we have reviewed several factors influencing the growth of police-researcher partnerships and the characteristics of police-researcher partnerships, but two additional factors include the demand and use of research by the police and the availability and willingness of university researchers to partner with the police. Below we discuss these issues in the context of contemporary practices and expectations the police should hold for themselves and researchers, and we recommend ways to build effective and lasting police-researcher partnerships.

Police Demand for Research

It is not unusual for university-based researchers to gain entry into one or more law enforcement agencies to conduct dissertation-related research or research that leads to academic publication.[40] While not always the case, this research is often research "on the police" but not typically "for the police." Many of the police-research classics like Reiss and Black and Westly,[41] for example, involved gaining entrance into the world of policing to carry out research that would add to our understanding of the police as an agent of social control. This type of partnership, as noted above, involves police "cooperation" but not "coordination" or "collaboration."

Police utilization of research has a direct bearing on the demand for research, with the idea being that greater utilization leads to greater demand for both research and police-researcher partnerships. One seminal piece of research on police-researcher partnerships reported that about three-fourths of the law enforcement agencies indicated that they used research "sometimes or very often."[42] Not surprisingly, however, only about a third reported the use of academic journals as a source for identifying research findings. Most academic researchers publish their research in academic journals, which police professionals neither readily nor frequently access. Even research published in academic journals that has a direct bearing on police policy and practice is unlikely to be presented in a way that is easily consumed by a police professional audience. While publication in academic journals is good for the academic researchers involved in partnerships, those partnerships that are sustained and become true collaborations communicate research findings through means other than academic journals or even final research reports.

The utilization of research findings resulting from police-practitioner partnerships requires more than just providing them with a final project report. Instead, it requires the researcher to develop a dissemination strategy at the beginning of the project that will reach multiple audiences. During the study development phase, the researcher should meet with key stakeholders within the agency and discuss the interim and final products to be developed and their intended impact. This ensures that knowledge dissemination products are targeted for the people who have the greatest potential to influence change and gives them the information they need to achieve their goals. Additionally, these products should use nontechnical language that the target audience can understand, taking into account the amount of time they have to read these products.[43] In sum, increasing research utilization requires making sure that the information produced is in fact useful to and consumable by the agency(ies) involved in the partnership.

Academic Culture and Police-Researcher Partnership

We have already noted the importance of the expansion of criminal justice and criminology programs in higher education in the evolution of police-researcher partnerships. Growth in the number of graduate programs, especially doctoral programs, has been a major factor. From 1980 to 2018, the number of doctoral programs in criminology and criminal justice in the United States grew from six to forty-six.[44] The growth of these doctoral programs has fueled both supply and demand for police-related research and consequently police-researcher partnerships. While not limited to criminal justice and criminology, these doctoral programs created a demand for police-related research opportunities both for doctoral student dissertations and for research that leads to publication in academic journals, which is a tenure and promotion requirement for faculty in most baccalaureate and graduate criminal justice and criminology programs. The expansion of criminal justice and criminology graduate programs, especially doctoral programs, has also greatly expanded the supply of qualified researchers available to participate in police-researcher partnerships.

Most neophyte university faculty enter academia without any specific preparation for participating in police-researcher partnerships. Doctoral programs in criminal justice and criminology train students to become researchers and attach tremendous importance to research that will lead to publication, especially in highly ranked academic journals. Much, but not all, research conducted by both doctoral students and their professors involves the analysis of existing data gathered as part of research projects not specifically designed to meet agency needs. Doctoral programs in criminal justice and criminology are both formally and informally ranked, and these rankings place a lot of weight on the publication records and reputations of the faculty employed in these programs. Academic journals are also ranked using readership impact measures and perceived success in academic careers. This is not to say that research and publication are solely focused on publishing in the "right" places, but engaging in research that leads to publishing in prestigious journals is certainly a component in the socialization of people in criminal justice and criminology doctoral programs.

To be clear, not all academic programs in criminal justice and criminology focus exclusively on research that leads to publication in prestigious journals and on producing researchers and scholars capable of publishing in such journals. Many university criminal justice and criminology programs and related research centers engage in research partnerships that simultaneously meet agency needs, inform agency practice and policy, and contribute to the body of criminal justice and criminology knowledge through dissemination in academic journals. One could easily construct a list of well-known criminal justice scholars who participate in police-researcher partnerships. However, the education of future researchers (i.e., doctoral students) usually does not involve a component preparing them for participating in research collaborations with law enforcement agencies. Perhaps the best preparation strategy is for faculty researchers who are successfully involved in police-researcher partnerships to mentor students by involving them in the partnership. Such mentorship goes beyond more traditional graduate student research assistant tasks by also involving students in all facets of partnership activity. This includes involvement in partnership project planning, implementation, partnership meetings, and preparation and presentation of project results.

It is important that practitioners and academics understand the factors (several reviewed in previous sections of this chapter) that result in effective police-researcher partnerships and incorporate and promote these factors in the training of not only academic researchers but also law enforcement personnel.[45] In addressing the nature of training police researchers and scholars, Greene, citing Yin, notes, "[W]e must prepare police scholars for a future where mixed methods prevail. They should be neither armchair philosophers nor pocket-protected bean counters. Rather, to reasonably understand the police requires a balancing of quantitative and qualitative methods."[46]

The preparation of future police researchers, who are likely to become partnership participants as their careers progress, should emphasize that it is quite reasonable and feasible for both practitioners and academics to derive benefits from partnership research. Well-designed research that supplies empirical evidence informing law enforcement policy and practice will most likely find its way into academic publications that add to the scholarship on what works in policing. Police leaders need to take an active role in placing greater pressure on their local universities to be more socially embedded and requiring relevant academic units, such as departments of criminology and criminal justice, to engage in at least some use-inspired research. The academic role should not be limited to teaching and research but should also include service aimed at improving the quality of life in our communities. Police-researcher partnerships provide an excellent opportunity for researchers to serve their community.

Building Effective and Lasting Police-Researcher Partnerships

Police-researcher partnerships are an important and lasting component in the effort to continuously inform and improve the police institution. As previously stated, the IACP has set a goal of 100 percent participation of police agencies in research partnerships. Additionally, in 2017, the IACP circulated a model policy for Law Enforcement-Researcher

Collaborative Partnerships. This model policy builds on the extensive literature that exists on police-researcher partnerships and responds to the barriers to effective and sustainable partnerships. The model provides a road map to developing effective and sustainable partnerships and provides critical information on how to establish collaborative police-researcher partnerships.[47] It calls for the active participation of the agency's top leadership in establishing the partnership and the designation of a partnership manager within the agency to coordinate partnership research activity. The model provides information on identifying and selecting a research partner and developing a formal memorandum of understanding. It also calls for training agency personnel and researchers involved in the partnership and provides details on the contents of such training. Finally, the model policy includes several items related to sustaining the partnership, including such items as communication, identification of future research projects, and identification of funding sources.

■ Next Steps

We propose that police agencies should establish strong collaborative research partnerships with university-based researchers to advance police policy and practice. Not only do these partnerships provide police agencies with a feedback loop for assessing their policies and practices but they also play an important role in expanding and disseminating the body of literature on what works in policing to advance the professionalization of the police. We described how police-researcher partnerships have been examined by numerous scholars who have focused on the barriers to effective partnerships and described the solutions to these barriers to improve their effectiveness and sustainability. The lessons learned about partnerships, both barriers and solutions, have been well documented and are reflected in the model policy promulgated by the IACP, which we endorse.

The future development and use of police-researcher partnerships can benefit from the police demanding more of their local universities. Local police leaders should place greater pressure on universities to engage in use-inspired research and to be socially embedded within their communities. Police leaders should expect local universities to take greater responsibility—educationally, intellectually, and financially—in contributing to police professionalization through police-researcher partnerships. In the simplest form, this can be done by exposing undergraduate students, both in-service police and students who hope to become police officers, to partnerships to prepare them for future participation in partnership research projects. Likewise, at the graduate level, mentorship and hands-on experience in partnership research will contribute greatly to preparing academic researchers for effective participation in such arrangements. Finally, police-researcher partnerships are essential for developing critical evidence to support the development of effective local police policies and practices. Both the police and the academy benefit from effective police-researcher partnerships but more important are the benefits they produce for the community and society.

NOTES

[1] Eran Vigoda, "From Responsiveness to Collaboration: Governance, Citizens, and the Next Generation of Public Administration," *Public Administration Review* 62, no. 5 (2002): 527–540.

[2] Office of Justice Programs, *LEAA/OJP Retrospective: 30 Years of Federal Support to State and Local Criminal Justice* (Washington, DC: U.S. Department of Justice, 1996); Jeff Rojek, Hayden P. Smith, and Geoffrey P. Alpert, "The Prevalence and Characteristics of Police Practitioner–Researcher Partnerships," *Police Quarterly* 15, no. 3 (2012): 241–261.

[3] Jodi Lane, Susan Turner, and Carmen Flores, "Researcher-Practitioner Collaboration in Community Corrections: Overcoming Hurdles for Successful Partnerships," *Criminal Justice Review* 29, no. 1 (2004): 97–114; Todd Wuestewald and Brigitte Steinheider, "Practitioner–Researcher Collaboration in Policing: A Case of Close Encounters?" *Policing* 4, no. 2 (2009): 104–111.

[4] Rob Tillyer, Marie S. Tillyer, John McCluskey, Jeffery Cancino, Joseph Todaro, and Layla McKinnon, "Researcher-Practitioner Partnerships and Crime Analysis: A Case Study in Action Research," *Police Practice and Research* 15, no. 5 (2014): 404–418.

[5] John E. Eck and William Spelman, "Who Ya Gonna Call? The Police as Problem-Busters," *Crime & Delinquency* 33, no. 1 (1987): 31–52; Herman Goldstein, *Problem Oriented Policing* (New York: McGraw Hill, 1990); Herman Goldstein, "On Further Developing Problem-Oriented Policing: The Most Critical Need, the Major Impediments, and a Proposal," in *Problem-Oriented Policing: From Innovation to Mainstream*, ed. Johannes Knutsson (Monsey, NY: Criminal Justice Press, 2003), 13–48; Jerry H. Ratcliffe, *Intelligence-Led Policing* (Cullompton, UK: Willan, 2008); David Weisburd and John E. Eck, "What Can Police Do to Reduce Crime, Disorder, and Fear?" *The Annals of the American Academy of Political and Social Science* 593, no. 1 (2004): 42–65.

[6] John A. Shjarback and Michael D. White, "Departmental Professionalism and Its Impact on Indicators of Violence in Police–Citizen Encounters," *Police Quarterly* 19, no. 1 (2016): 32–62.

[7] Lois F. Mock, "Action Research for Crime Control and Prevention," in *The New Criminal Justice: American Communities and Changing World of Crime Control*, eds. John M. Klofas, Natalie K. Hipple, and Edmund F. McGarrell (New York: Routledge, 2010), 97–102.

[8] Robert F. Diegelman, "Federal Financial Assistance for Crime Control: Lessons of the LEAA Experience," *The Journal of Criminal Law and Criminology* 73, no. 3 (1982): 994–1011.

[9] James O. Finckenauer, "The Quest for Quality in Criminal Justice Education," *Justice Quarterly* 22, no. 4 (2005): 413–426, https://doi.org/10.1080/07418820500364635.

[10] David Bradley, Monique Marks, and Christine Nixon, "What Works, What Doesn't Work and What Looks Promising in Police Research Networks," in *Fighting Crime Together: The Challenges of Policing and Security Networks*, eds. Jenny Fleming and Jennifer Wood (Sydney, Australia: New South Wales Press, 2006), 170–194; Wuestewald & Steinheider, "Practitioner-Researcher Collaboration in Policing."

[11] Charles A. Murray and Robert E. Krug, *The National Evaluation of the Pilot Cities Program: Executive Summary* (Washington, DC: National Institute of Law Enforcement and Criminal Justice, Law Enforcement Assistance Administration, U.S. Department of Justice, 1975), 1.

[12] Ibid., 25.

[13] Mock, "Action Research for Crime Control and Prevention."

[14] Robin S. Engel and James L. Whalen, "Police-Academic Partnerships: Ending the Dialogue of the Deaf, the Cincinnati Experience," *Police Practice and Research: An International Journal* 11, no. 2 (2010): 105–116; Jackie Goode and Karen Lumsden, "The McDonaldization of Police-Academic Partnerships: Organisational and Cultural Barriers Encountered in Mov-

ing from Research on Police to Research with Police," *Policing & Society* 28, no. 1 (2016): 1–37; Jack R. Greene, "Collaborations Between Police and Research/Academic Organizations: Some Prescriptions from the Field," In *The New Criminal Justice: American Communities and Changing World of Crime Control*, eds. John M. Klofas, Edmund F. McGarrell, and Natalie K. Hipple, (New York: Routledge, 2010), 121–127; Daniel McCarthy and Megan O'Neill, "The Police and Partnership Working: Reflections on Recent Research," *Policing* 8, no. 3 (2014): 243–253; Edmund F. McGarrell, "Accumulating Lessons from Project Safe Neighborhoods," in *The New Criminal Justice: American Communities and Changing World of Crime Control*, eds. John M. Klofas, Natalie K. Hipple, and Edmund F. McGarrell (New York: Routledge, 2010), 136–146; Mock, "Action Research for Crime Control and Prevention."

[15] Cynthia Lum, Christopher S. Koper, and Cody W. Telep, "The Evidence-Based Policing Matrix," *Journal of Experimental Criminology* 7, no. 1 (2010): 3–26.

[16] McCarthy and O'Neill, "The Police and Partnership Working."

[17] International Association of Chiefs of Police, *Unresolved Problems and Powerful Potentials: Improving Partnerships between Law Enforcement Leaders and University Based Researchers* (Washington, DC: IACP, 2004).

[18] Geoffrey P. Alpert, Jeff Rojek, and Andrew Hansen, *Building Bridges between Police Researchers and Practitioners: Agents of Change in a Complex World* (Washington, DC: National Institute of Justice, 2013).

[19] Ibid.

[20] James M. Frabutt, M. J. Gathings, Lynn K. Harvey, and Kristen L. Di Luca, "Added Value through a Partnership Model of Action Research: A Case Example from a Project Safe Neighborhoods Research Partner," in *The New Criminal Justice: American Communities and Changing World of Crime Control*, eds. John M. Klofas, Natalie K. Hipple, and Edmund F. McGarrell (New York: Routledge, 2010), 103–113; Tami P. Sullivan, Bronwyn A. Hunter, and Bonnie S. Fisher, *Strategies for Successfully Developing and Disseminating Useful Products from Researcher–Practitioner Collaborations, Findings from the Researcher–Practitioner Partnerships Study (RPPS)* (Washington, DC: National Institute of Justice, 2013).

[21] See Alpert, Rojek, and Hansen, *Building Bridges between Police Researchers and Practitioners*, and Julie Grieco, Heather Vovak, and Cynthia Lum, "Examining Research-Practice Partnerships in Policing Evaluations," *Policing: A Journal of Policy and Practice* 8, no. 4 (2014): 368–378.

[22] Alpert, Rojek, and Hansen, *Building Bridges between Police Researchers and Practitioners*.

[23] David Canter, "A Tale of Two Cultures: A Comparison of the Cultures of the Police and of Academia," In *Policing a Safe, Just and Tolerant Society*, eds. Peter Villiers and Robert Adlam, (Winchester, UK: Waterside Press, 2004), 109–121; Jenny Fleming, "Learning to Work Together: Police and Academics," *Policing: A Journal of Policy and Practice* 4, no. 2 (2010): 139–145; Jenny Fleming, "Qualitative Encounters in Police Research," In *Qualitative Criminology*, eds. Lorana Bartels and Kelly Richards, (Sydney, Australia: Hawkins Press, 2011), 13–24; Jenny Fleming, "Changing the Way We Do Business: Reflecting on Collaborative Practice," *Police Practice and Research* 13, no. 4 (2012): 375–388; Nicholas R. Fyfe and Peter Wilson, "Knowledge Exchange and Police Practice: Broadening and Deepening the Debate Around Researcher-Practitioner Collaborations," *Police Practice and Research* 13, no. 4 (2012): 306–314; Monique Marks, Jennifer Wood, Faizel Ally, Tess Walsh, and Abbey Witbooi, "Worlds Apart? On the Possibilities of Police/Academic Collaborations," *Policing: A Journal of Policy and Practice* 4, no. 2 (2010): 112–118; Karim Murji, "Introduction: Academic-Police Collaborations—Beyond 'Two Worlds,'" *Policing: A Journal of Policy and Practice* 4, no. 2 (2010): 92–94; Sue Wilkinson, "Research and Policing—Looking to the Future," *Policing: A Journal of Policy and Practice* 4, no. 2 (2010): 146–148; Jennifer Wood, Jenny Fleming, and Monique Marks, "Building the Capacity of Police Change Agents: The Nexus Policing Project," *Policing & Society* 18, no. 1 (2008): 72–87.

[24] Greene, "Collaborations Between Police and Research/Academic Organizations."

[25] Gary Cordner and Stephen White, "The Evolving Relationship between Police Research and Police Practice," *Police Practice and Research: An International Journal* 11, no. 2 (2010): 90–94, 90.

[26] Anthony A. Braga and Marianne Hinkle, "The Participation of Academics in the Criminal Justice Working Group Process," in *The New Criminal Justice: American Communities and Changing World of Crime Control*, eds. John M. Klofas, Natalie K. Hipple, and Edmund F. McGarrell (New York: Routledge, 2010), 114–120; Engel and Whalen, "Police-Academic Partnerships"; Greene, "Collaborations Between Police and Research/Academic Organizations"; McCarthy and O'Neill, "The Police and Partnership Working."

[27] Sullivan, Hunter, and Fisher, *Strategies for Successfully Developing and Disseminating Useful Products from Researcher–Practitioner Collaborations.*

[28] Alpert, Rojek, and Hansen, *Building Bridges between Police Researchers and Practitioners.*

[29] Sullivan, Hunter, and Fisher, *Strategies for Successfully Developing and Disseminating Useful Products from Researcher–Practitioner Collaborations.*

[30] Jack McDevitt, Anthony A. Braga, Shea Cronin, Edmund F. McGarrell, and Tim Bynum, *Project Safe Neighborhoods, Strategic Interventions: Lowell, District of Massachusetts: Case Study 6* (Washington, DC: U.S. Department of Justice, Office of Justice Programs, Project Safe Neighborhoods, 2017).

[31] Alpert, Rojek, and Hansen, *Building Bridges between Police Researchers and Practitioners.*

[33] Tim Bynum, Scott H. Decker, John Klofas, Natalie K. Hipple, Edmund F. McGarrell, and Jack McDevitt, *Project Safe Neighborhoods: Strategic Interventions. Chronic Violent Offenders List: Case Study* (Washington, DC: U.S. Department of Justice, National Institute of Justice, 2006).

[33] Alpert, Rojek, and Hansen, *Building Bridges between Police Researchers and Practitioners.*

[34] Cody W. Telep, "Police Officer Receptivity to Research and Evidence-Based Policing: Examining Variability within and across Agencies," *Crime & Delinquency* 63, no. 8 (2017): 976–999.

[35] Greene, "Collaborations Between Police and Research/Academic Organizations."

[36] Michael E. Buerger, "Policing and Research: Two Cultures Separated by an Almost-Common Language," *Police Practice and Research: An International Journal* 11, no. 2 (2010): 135–143.

[37] Cody W. Telep and Cynthia Lum, "The Receptivity of Officers to Empirical Research and Evidence-Based Policing: An Examination of Survey Data from Three Agencies," *Police Quarterly* 17, no. 4 (2014): 359–385.

[38] Peter Guillaume, Aiden Sidebottom, and Nick Tilley, "On Police and University Collaborations: A Problem-Oriented Policing Case Study," *Police Practice and Research* 13, no. 4 (2012): 389–401.

[39] Mock, "Action Research for Crime Control and Prevention."

[40] Wesley G. Skogan, "The Challenge of Timeliness and Utility in Research and Evaluation," in *The New Criminal Justice: American Communities and Changing World of Crime Control*, eds. John M. Klofas, Natalie K. Hipple, and Edmund F. McGarrell (New York: Routledge, 2010), 128–131.

[41] Albert J. Reiss Jr. and Donald J. Black, "Interrogation and the Criminal Process," *The Annals of the American Academy of Political and Social Science* 374, no. 1 (1967): 47–57; William A. Westly, *Violence and the Police* (Cambridge, MA: MIT Press, 1970).

[42] Alpert, Rojek, and Hansen, *Building Bridges between Police Researchers and Practitioners*, vii.

[43] Sullivan, Hunter, and Fisher, *Strategies for Successfully Developing and Disseminating Useful Products from Researcher–Practitioner Collaborations.*

[44] Association of Doctoral Programs in Criminology and Criminal Justice, *Survey of Doctoral Programs in Criminology and Criminal Justice* (Huntsville, TX: Sam Houston State University, 2018); Richard H. Ward and Vincent J. Webb, *Quest for Quality* (New York: University Publications, 1984).

[45] Grieco, Vovak, and Lum, "Examining Research-Practice Partnerships in Policing Evaluations."

[46] Jack Greene, *What Can Criminology Do to Be More Helpful to Policing?* (Boston, MA: Northeastern University, 2017), 22, citing Robert K. Yin, *Case Study Research: Design and Methods*, 3rd ed. (Thousand Oaks, CA: Sage, 2003), and Robert K. Yin, "Mixed Methods Research: Are the Methods Genuinely Integrated or Merely Parallel," *Research in the Schools* 13, no. 1 (2006): 41–47.

[47] Jeff Rojek, Peter Martin, and Geoffrey P. Alpert, *Developing and Maintaining Police-Researcher Partnerships to Facilitate Research Use: A Comparative Analysis* (New York: Springer, 2015).

9

Response Essay

Captain Ivonne Roman
Newark Police Department, New Jersey

In February 2015, Bill Bratton spoke to a room of law enforcement officers and students gathered at Rutgers University in Newark. I was in attendance that evening as he detailed how he used disorder policing strategies, better known as the "broken windows theory," to effectively reduce crime in New York City and Los Angeles.

He also warned against the theory's misapplication. Bratton said the theory could have negative effects if the dosages or duration weren't followed as prescribed. He equated the overpolicing of New York City neighborhoods to medical malpractice, saying, "After I left New York, the police continued giving chemotherapy when the patient had improved, and the cancer was gone."

The late architect of broken windows, George Kelling, also warned about the dangers of applying his theory without careful dosage analysis or thought to possible side effects.[1] "When I would see some chief in some city say, 'Tomorrow I am going to implement a broken windows program,' my response was always 'Oh shit,'" he said.

Like broken windows, juvenile curfew laws were drafted in response to rising crime that was fueled by the crack epidemic of the 1980s.[2] Princeton professor John Dilulio's "superpredator" theory warned that the future may "unleash an army of young male predatory street criminals who will make even the leaders of the Bloods and Crips . . . look tame by comparison."[3] In response, the Clinton Administration provided the nation's mayors a framework for passing juvenile curfew laws.[4]

The superpredator prediction was enticing, but it was wrong. An extensive body of research literature deemed juvenile curfew laws ineffective and possibly harmful. A Campbell Collaboration study of the effects of these laws found that they actually slightly increased juvenile crime during curfew hours but had no significant effect on juvenile crime or juvenile victimization overall.[5] The superpredator theory was based on the use of short-term crime data projected into the future, painting an apocalyptic crisis that never materialized.

Yet the theory nonetheless led to a draconian shift in juvenile laws that was not based on evidence. These new laws were light on rehabilitation and heavy on punishment, encouraging prosecutors to charge juveniles as adults and for municipalities to enforce or enact curfew laws to control the nation's "out-of-control" youth. Mayors and police officials across America have publicly announced juvenile curfew enforcement as a summer tradition, claiming it will result in juvenile crime reduction and prevent juvenile victimization.

Juvenile justice advocates and community groups have reversed some of the 1990s "tough on juveniles" policies, but juvenile curfew laws remain ubiquitous and entrenched across the country despite evidence pointing to their ineffectiveness.

Broken windows and juvenile curfew laws are just two of many widespread policies that are based on conflicting research and evidence. Neither has been supported by a replicable body of research evidence showing that they work, as intended, without producing harm. Both are controversial theories that were not thoroughly tested and evaluated before their implementation.

Meanwhile, staples of policing such as DARE[6] and mandatory Critical Incident Stress Debriefing (CISD) have actually been proven to produce blowback effects or unintended outcomes.[7] DARE has been shown to have no effect and even to sometimes increase drug use. CISD has been shown to increase the prevalence of posttraumatic stress disorder. As a field, we have to push against this tendency to implement knee-jerk policies with no regard to the need for extensive research to inform program design, implementation, and evaluation.

Police departments and policy makers owe it to their communities and officers to create policies that protect communities from crime while ensuring that no harm is caused in the process. This can only be achieved through rigorous evaluation of police practices to identify what works, what doesn't work, and why.

I am an executive board member of the American Society of Evidence-Based Policing (ASEBP). ASEBP co-Founder Dr. Renee Mitchell often cites the seminal work of Jane McCord, "Cures that Harm: Unanticipated Outcomes of Crime Prevention Programs," as the organization's chief motivation in advocating for evidence-based poling.[8] The study evaluates criminal justice interventions that backfire to inadvertently harm the people involved.

In recognition of the value of evidence-based practices, the National Institute of Justice partnered with the International Association of Chiefs of Police to establish the Law Enforcement Advancing Data and Science (LEADS) initiative. The LEADS program supports "pracademics"—part cop, part academic—who are using the best research available to answer pressing questions for police chiefs and their departments and partnering with academics to create a form of clinical policing, experimenting with and modifying their approach based on findings.

The National Police Foundation, whose mission is to advance policing through research and science, has existed for more than fifty years. It is a pioneer in using randomized controlled trials in policing, most notably the Kansas City Preventative Patrol Experiment and the Newark Foot Patrols Experiment. These partnerships are not new, and valuable insight was gleaned from these trials.

Evidence-based policing has met both resistance and skepticism from law enforcement leaders. The LEADS program helps overcome these challenges by facilitating collaboration between police and academic researchers, thus giving police greater control of the research agenda and ensuring that research meets an agency's priorities and has practical applications in the field.

I encourage chiefs to open lines of communications with academics in their community and start conversations about how these police-academic relationships can be nurtured. By taking the lead in establishing these relationships, the chief can identify the department's priorities and address staffing constraints and work with the academic to jointly produce a research agenda that will yield actionable findings that may inform policy decisions, programs, and operational decisions. The partnership must be mutually beneficial; that is, the police cannot be passive case subjects. Without a greater role for the police, the partnership simply will not work.

Academics must value police partners' contributions to research, being ever cognizant that police officials provide limited resources and goodwill in providing access to their police departments. Without trust and mutual benefit, evidence-based policing will not extend beyond the confines of a few progressive police agencies that have successfully navigated and nurtured police/academic relationships.

Doctors take the Hippocratic Oath to "do no harm" in the name of medicine. In the same vein, police must vow to employ practices that will not place communities in more precarious situations than if no police action had been taken at all.[9] Police are working in an era of legitimacy crisis. Evidence-based policing reinforces that police department are committed to limiting harms and implementing proven strategies, so they can best serve their communities.

Doctors make life-altering decisions that directly impact a patient's health and well-being. Patients should demand that these decisions are based on thorough research and evidence. In the same vein, police officers make daily decisions that directly affect people in the communities they serve. Therefore, don't we owe it to our communities to make policies based on the best available evidence?

NOTES

[1] Simone Weichselbaum, "America's Rock-Star Cops," *The Marshall Project* (blog), October 16, 2015.

[2] Ivonne Roman, "The Curfew Myth," *The Marshall Project*, July 31, 2018.

[3] John Dilulio, "The Coming of the Super-Predators," *The Weekly Standard*, November 27, 1995.

[4] Todd S. Purdum, "Politics: Juvenile Curfews; Clinton Backs Plan to Deter Youthful Violence," *New York Times*, May 31, 1996, p. 20.

[5] David Wilson, Charlotte Gill, Ajima Olaghere, and Dave McClure, "Juvenile Curfew Effects on Criminal Behavior and Victimization," *Campbell Collaboration*, March 23, 2016.

[6] Steven L. West and Keri K. O'Neal, "Project DARE Outcome Effectiveness Revisited," *American Journal of Public Health* 94, no. 6 (2004): 1027–1029.

[7] Renee Mitchell, "The Harmful Effects of Critical Incident Stress Debriefing (CISD): Why Police Departments Should Stay Up to Date on Evidence-Based Practices," *American Society of Evidence-Based Policing,* November 29, 2018.

[8] Joan McCord, "Cures That Harm: Unanticipated Outcomes of Crime Prevention Programs," *Annals of the American Academy of Political and Social Science* 587, no. 1 (2003): 16–30.

[9] Jeremiah P. Johnson, "A Hippocratic Oath for Policing," *National Police Foundation* (blog), https://www.policefoundation.org/a-hippocratic-oath-for-policing/.

10

Build Momentum for Police Reform through Organizational Justice

Rick Trinkner
David H. Tyler
Arizona State University

Background

The history of the institution of policing is filled with efforts to reform, change, and innovate how departments serve the community.[1] Today is no different. In the wake of Ferguson, the calls for police reform from politicians, police, and community groups have been increasing.[2] History shows us, however, that lasting changes to police strategies and tactics can be hard to achieve. Many, if not most, attempts fall short of expectations.

There are numerous ways in which even the most well thought out and publicly supported police innovations can be derailed.[3] Many of these barriers emerge from within the department itself. For example, any attempts at reform are likely impossible without buy-in from the chief or head of the department. Even if the chief of the organization develops a reform plan, he or she must rely on all levels of the organizational hierarchy to effectively implement it. Mid-level management (e.g., captains, lieutenants) needs to communicate the reform plan to front-line supervisors (e.g., sergeants) so that they have a clear understanding of the vision animating the new policies and what that vision expects of officer behavior. As the link between translating command policies into street-level action, front-line supervisors must then impart the new strategy to line officers and hold them accountable for following the new policy. Finally, line officers must actually make changes to their behavior and implement the new policies out on the street. The effectiveness and institutional longevity of reforms can die at any point in this chain of command.[4]

It follows that focusing on the internal dynamics of a police department is just as important to successful police reform as determining the specific reforms to be implemented. On a broader level, this recognition is neither new nor novel. Many of the internal barriers to police reform are identical to the barriers any organization will encounter when trying to change the way its workers do business. Regardless of the institution, the question tends to be the same: how to get workers to believe in the new direction an organization is moving and encourage them to modify their behaviors accordingly.

This basic question has motivated researchers in business management and administration for decades.[5] As we discuss below, a consistent theme to emerge from this literature is that workers care about the fairness within their work environment. When workers believe their organization is fair, they are more likely to internalize the goals and norms of that organization and be more motivated to behave in a manner consistent with those ideals.[6] When workers feel they are treated unfairly and given the short end of the stick, they are more likely to have an antagonistic relationship with their organization and be cynical about policies and strategies.

Police officers are no different; they also are sensitive to organizational fairness.[7] In fact, issues of internal fairness are likely even more salient to police officers given their role as the purveyors of justice within democratic societies. Similar to any other type of worker, officers are more resistant to orders from higher-ups in the chain of command when they believe they are treated unfairly (see below). Police departments and chiefs must be cognizant of this issue for any innovation or reform effort to succeed. The purpose of this chapter is to facilitate this goal by (1) providing an overview of organizational justice theory, (2) discussing the benefits associated with organizational justice within police departments, and (3) offering a working model that departments can use to better address the fairness of their internal climate.

■ What Is Organizational Justice?

Human beings are incredibly perceptive when it comes to issues of justice, using fairness as a lens to make sense out of their social environment.[8] This sensitivity is particularly acute in the work environment, where individuals can more easily compare their effort, rewards, and experiences to those of their coworkers. Organizational justice reflects the perception of fairness within one's immediate work environment and within the broader organizational context.[9] Flowing out of research from business administration and industry management, decades of work in this area have shown the profound impact fairness has on the internal dynamics of organizations (both public and private) and the way those organizations interface with the consumers and public they serve.

The effects of fairness (and unfairness for that matter) permeate all aspects of the organizational context.[10] Workers are more satisfied with their job, their pay, their immediate supervisors, upper management, and even unions when they believe their organization is fair. They perform at a higher level, both in terms of the quality of their work and the quantity of work they produce. Workers in fair environments are more committed to the organization, feeling pride in their jobs and an emotional attachment to their coworkers and superiors. Fairness serves as a mechanism through which workers increasingly identify with their organization, internalizing the norms and standards espoused by management. Not only does this increase the likelihood of workers following organizational rules and supervisor directives, but it also encourages organizational citizenship behaviors—that is, those behaviors that increase the productivity of the workplace but are impossible to objectively require—such as altruism, courtesy, and conscientiousness.

At the same time, organizational justice guards against counterproductive work behavior and withdrawal from the work environment and responsibilities.[11] Fair organizations have lower levels of conflict among workers and less antagonism between the different levels of hierarchy (e.g., workers, supervisors, and upper management). Moreover, workers in a fair organization are less likely to report a desire to quit. Reduced turnover means better use of the money used to recruit, hire, and train workers. On a more day-to-day level, lower levels of absenteeism and job neglect have been associated with higher levels of organizational justice. Finally, and perhaps most importantly, organizational justice discourages organizational retaliatory behavior from workers, such as breaking company rules, refusing to help coworkers, purposefully working slowly or ineffectively, or stealing company property.

■ What about Organizational Justice within Police Departments Specifically?

Organizational justice has increasingly been examined within the context of police departments.[12] Just as scholars have found internal justice associated with a range of positive outcomes for business organizations, workers, and clients, policing researchers have highlighted similar benefits for police departments, their officers, and the community.

Benefits for Police Departments

Departments engaging in organizational justice practices, such as procedural and distributive fairness in decision-making, encourage their officer's loyalty and commitment to the organization.[13] When individuals feel loyal to their department, they are more willing to assume additional responsibilities beyond what their job requires to assist the department as a whole; they are also less likely to think about quitting their jobs.[14]

Internal fairness has also been linked to officers' trust in the department. For example, in a study of 510 sheriff's deputies in the southeastern United States, researchers found that respondents who felt their immediate supervisor did not treat them with respect were less likely to trust his or her decision-making and were more likely to feel department leadership did not have the agency's best interest in mind.[15] At the same time, officers are likely to feel attachment and loyalty to the organization to the extent that they believe they are treated in a fair and just manner within their department.[16] Perhaps it is not surprising then that organizational fairness has been linked to a greater willingness to engage in extra-role behaviors—that is, unrequired behaviors that improve the efficiency of the department, such as helping fellow officers with heavy workloads.[17]

Organizational justice also influences the legitimacy of supervisors, increasing the likelihood that officers will feel obligated to obey supervisor directives and department policies without direct supervision.[18] The legitimacy of management is a fundamental component of effective police organizations given the reality that officers are largely left to their own devices while patrolling. In this context, departments depend on officers following policies and exercising discretion appropriately without explicit supervision. Organizational justice facilitates this goal. For example, in their study of a large urban police department, Trinkner and his colleagues found that organizational justice was associated with a greater perception of supervisor legitimacy, which, in turn, was associated with an increased willingness to follow department rules and engage in organizational citizenship behaviors.[19] Similar results have also been found in Philadelphia[20] and Denver.[21]

Benefits for Police Officers

Organizational justice directly benefits officers as well. Several studies have demonstrated positive associations among internal justice, officer satisfaction, and motivation. For example, in their study of a specialty police unit in a large state police agency, Farmer and colleagues concluded that officers were more satisfied with their jobs to the extent that they believed their department was fair,[22] a finding also replicated outside of the United States.[23] At the same time, organizational justice has been linked to lower levels of job stress.[24] One study of officers in a large metropolitan city found that officers were less likely to be psychologically and emotionally distressed when they were treated fairly by their fellow officers and department rules were applied in an equitable manner.[25]

More recently, scholars have highlighted the potential role of organizational justice in promoting officers' beliefs in their self-legitimacy—that is, their confidence in their role as police officers and the power that comes with it.[26] Self-legitimacy has been linked to strong support for respectful citizen treatment, support for suspect's rights, and an increased ability to resolve conflicts in noncoercive ways.[27] Perhaps more important, given some of the events of the past few years, both self-legitimacy and organizational justice have been shown to be protective factors against depolicing and demotivation that can arise from negative public scrutiny.[28]

Benefits for Community Members

The possible effects of organizational justice can be felt outside the department as well. For instance, internal injustice has been shown to promote officer deviance while strengthening the "code of silence" among officers that makes it more difficult to regulate such behavior.[29] Conversely, officers in procedurally just departments have been found to be more restrained in their decisions to use force and less likely to face citizen complaints, internal investigations, and disciplinary charges.[30]

Internal organizational justice also encourages officers to adopt and support the kinds of policing strategies most likely to build trust within the community, which is direly needed in the post-Ferguson era. Trinkner and his colleagues found a link between a fair internal climate and officers' support for policing strategies emphasizing fairness, respect, and community involvement that rely on force as a last resort.[31] Similar findings have been found across the United States[32] as well as in a constabulary in Great Britain.[33] Moreover, officers tend to be more open to partnering with the surrounding community to address local problems and concerns when they work in a fair climate.[34]

■ How Can Organizational Justice Be Translated into Practice?

The importance of justice in facilitating the working relationships among members of an organization cannot be overstated. Organizational justice can be thought of like the oil in an engine, reducing friction and allowing the different mechanical parts to work harmoniously with each other.[35] Police departments, which are typically characterized by a quasi-military organizational structure, depend on a well-oiled chain of command in which policies and directives can freely flow from superordinate to subordinates who will implement those orders out on the street.[36] Organizational justice is likely just as, if not more, important within police departments as other practices attempting to change departmental behavior.

However, the question remains: how can police chiefs, administrators, and officers translate the research on organizational justice into an actionable agenda for their department? Our goal in this section is to provide a road map that distinguishes different facets of justice within any organization and the norms underlying each (see figure 1). This taxonomy is meant to be a guide to help officers at all levels of the hierarchy think about justice issues while being broad enough to fit the needs of many different departments. Given that there are approximately 18,000 police departments in the United States of various sizes policing vastly different communities,[37] it would be foolish to treat police departments as monolithic. The goal, therefore, is not to recommend specific policies that should be applied to all departments everywhere under all circumstances. Such specificity would both be unlikely to succeed and could potentially cause more problems than it would alleviate. Instead, this section offers a more general guide to the aspects of organizational justice, allowing departments to tailor their responses based on their specific needs.

Organizational justice can be split into four basic components: distributive justice, procedural justice, interpersonal justice, and informational justice.[38] Each component focuses on a different facet of the organization

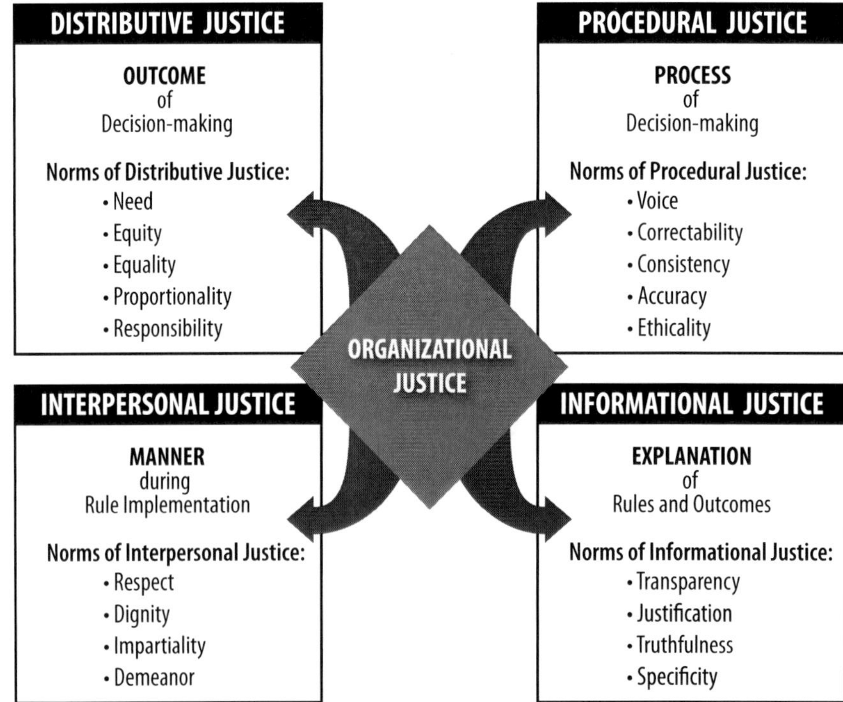

Figure 1 A Taxonomy of Organizational Justice

in terms of how decisions are made, the outcomes of those decisions, and the way workers are treated during that process. Each facet is mutually related but theoretically and empirically distinct.[39]

Distributive Justice

Distributive justice refers to the perceived fairness of resource distributions within an organization.[40] This facet of organizational justice focuses on the outcomes of the decisions by management and supervisors, such as the fairness of pay, promotions, and other rewards (and punishments). Distributive justice is fostered when outcomes are consistent with social norms of allocation, such as equity, equality, and need. From this perspective, individuals are keenly focused on their inputs at a job (e.g., effort and productivity) relative to their outputs (e.g., pay and promotion). Workers are more likely to believe their organization is distributively fair to the extent they believe their inputs match their outputs and that their input-to-output ratio is similar to that of their coworkers.

In evaluating distributive justice at the organizational level, police departments should focus on officers' outcomes (e.g., pay, raises, promotion, job assignments, and disciplinary actions) relative to their contributions. For example, they could examine the extent to which those outcomes:

1. reflect the amount of effort officers put into their work,
2. are appropriate given the work that needs to be completed to achieve it,
3. can be justified given one's performance,
4. reflect the quantity and quality of officers' contributions to the organization, and
5. consider the amount of responsibilities officers have.

Procedural Justice

Procedural justice refers to the perceived fairness of the procedures used to make decisions within an organization.[41] Rather than focusing on outcomes, procedural justice emphasizes the structural characteristics of the formal decision-making procedures that lead to those outcomes. People care about group harmony just as much as they care about outputs relative to inputs. The former promotes the solidarity that is required to achieve group goals. People use a variety of different social norms in judging the procedural justice of their organizations, including voice (e.g., degree to which they can express their concerns, opinions, and views during the decision-making process), choice (e.g., degree to which they can influence the actual outcome of the decision-making process), consistency (e.g., the degree to which the application of rules is consistent across persons/time), correctability (e.g., the existence of procedures to correct bad outcomes), accuracy (e.g., how much procedures are based on valid information), and ethicality (e.g., the degree to which procedures uphold fundamental ethical standards). Solidarity among coworkers is bolstered when they believe that the procedures governing organizational decision-making are fair and just, even in those cases where the process might result in unequal outcomes.

In evaluating procedural justice at the organizational level, police departments should focus on the actual rules in place that determine how decisions are made. For example, they could examine the extent to which the rules and procedures:

1. allow the opportunity for officers to express their views and feelings while the department is making decisions about the organization (e.g., policing strategies) and/or officers (e.g., disciplinary hearings),
2. allow the opportunity for officers to have some say in determining the outcomes of a decision-making process,
3. give their officers the ability to appeal the outcome arrived at by a set of decisional procedures,
4. are based on accurate information (including the process used to obtain that information), and
5. are available for officers to review and are written to be understandable while avoiding deception, trickery, and/or misleading information.

Interpersonal Justice

Interpersonal justice refers to the perceived fairness of interpersonal treatment during the enactment of decision-making procedures.[42] Interpersonal justice is fostered when supervisors treat their subordinates in a respectful, dignified, and impartial manner. Whereas procedural justice focuses on the structure of the actual rules themselves, interpersonal justice is concerned with the manner in which those rules are carried out. An organization can take great care to devise a set of rules that follow all the procedural justice norms described above only to have a supervisor enact them in a rude and disrespectful manner. How organizations treat their workers at the interpersonal level signals the degree to which the organization considers them valuable members of the team, thereby increasing their attachment and commitment to the organization's goals, values, and norms.

In evaluating interpersonal justice at the organizational level, police departments should focus on the relationships and communication between supervisors and their subordinates at all levels (e.g., sergeants and line officers, commanders and sergeants, etc.). For example, they could examine the extent to which:

1. subordinates feel they are treated with respect and dignity,
2. subordinates feel they are attacked or insulted by their superiors,
3. supervisors are impartial and unbiased in dealing with officers,

4. supervisors and officers behave with propriety when interacting among themselves, and
5. supervisors actually consider officers' views when given a voice.

Informational Justice

Informational justice refers to the perceived fairness of the way in which decisions are explained to employees.[43] Informational justice is fostered when organizations are transparent in their decision-making process, provide justifications for why certain decisions are made, are truthful when explaining their rationale to employees, and provide specific explanations rather than generalities. Simply treating people with respect or ensuring fair procedures will not be enough to foster a fair organizational climate if such explanations are not provided. Workers want to know *why* organizations make certain decisions and expect those explanations to be provided in an open, honest, and straightforward dialogue. Informational justice is especially pertinent when managerial decisions will negatively affect workers, effectively blunting the sting of such decisions (which may be necessary for the good of the organization).

In evaluating informational justice at the organizational level, police departments should focus on the way in which organizational procedures, decisions, and outcomes are explained to their officers. For example, they could examine the extent to which:

1. procedural rules for decision-making are explained to officers (e.g., pay rate criteria),
2. management explains to officers how they arrived at a decision,
3. decisional explanations are provided with adequate specificity and thoroughness,
4. officers feel supervisors and management are being honest and truthful in their explanations, and
5. explanations for a decision are given in a timely manner (e.g., before vs. after decision).

■ An Important Caveat

Before moving forward, a note of caution is warranted about the potential for organizational justice to change policing practices and officer behavior. While organizational justice has been linked to more support for fair and respectful policing,[44] organizational justice can also have unintended negative consequences if the department is espousing problematic strategies and policies. In this respect, increasing organizational justice within a department may actually exacerbate problems within departments that already have an antagonistic relationship with the surrounding community. To understand why this is the case, one first needs to understand the psychological mechanisms linking a fair organizational climate to worker behavior.

Organizational fairness provides vital information about group standing, essentially communicating that a person is an important and valued member of the organization.[45] As a result, people begin to identify with the group to a greater degree by incorporating facets of the group's identity into their self-concept (e.g., aligning one's personal values and goals with the group's values and goals, internalizing group norms of appropriate and proper behavior, and changing attitudes to mirror group attitudes). Such psychological engagement with the organization increases the likelihood that workers will feel obligated to follow group rules. For organizations, this is good. If an organization can get workers to follow policies and organizational norms without the need of surveillance and rewarding/punishing behavior, then the resources that would normally go to ensuring such conformity can be directed elsewhere. However, this does not mean that organizational justice will automatically encourage "good" or "bad" behavior when workers interact with customers. Instead, it will encourage commitment and adherence to group goals and norms, whatever those norms happen to be.

What does this mean within the context of a police department and the internal management of officers? As noted above, given their hierarchical structure and top-down management system, police departments depend on officers to follow policies and rules that are decided upon by those higher up the chain of command. Organizational justice is effective in meeting this need to the extent that it encourages compliance. However, it will not, in and of itself, necessarily steer officers toward one type of policing strategy over another one. Instead, it will increase the likelihood that officers will internalize the law enforcement policies that have been adopted by the department's leadership, whether that be community policing, zero tolerance law enforcement, or anything in between.

The important takeaway here is that organizational justice does not and should not subsume discussions about the appropriate strategies that police departments should use to regulate citizen behavior. If the goal of an administration is to change officers' behavior out on the street, then that administration should look at the policies and norms espoused within the department with respect to street behavior. If changes to strategies are found necessary, then organizational justice is a viable option to increase the likelihood that those changes will be implemented. Bottom line: organizational justice's ability to lead to better policing is only as good as the policies of the department dictating what is considered appropriate officer behavior.

■ Next Steps

Decades of research have shown that organizational justice is an essential human resource management tool, especially in terms of the conflicts that inevitably arise in hierarchical organizations.[46] The power of organizational justice is particularly acute in cases where organizations are attempting to change the way "they do business" through new policy and strategy implementation, encouraging workers to commit to reformulated group goals, values, and norms. In this respect, it offers a lot to the next wave of police chiefs, officers, and community members attempting to reshape American policing for the 21st century.

At the same time, organizational justice is a relatively inexpensive way to pursue police reform when compared to other more taxing strategies like body cameras, civilian review boards, or consent decrees, which often require tremendous investment and administrative support. It does not necessarily require special training programs that also can be fiscally prohibitive. It does not depend on outside forces, such as new laws or regulations, to be enacted. Any department, of any size and makeup and policing any community, can strive to monitor and evaluate its internal justice if it so chooses.

Perhaps most importantly, everyone stands to win in some capacity from an effort to increase the organizational justice within police departments. Officers would get an administration that is more responsive to their needs and better equipped to handle the internal organizational dynamics in a mutually reinforcing way. The administration would get officers more committed to the department's goals and more willing to follow orders. To the extent that the department has enforcement strategies supported by the public, citizens would get officers on the street more likely to believe in and carry out those strategies. While organizational justice does not automatically guarantee the elimination of bad policing, it is a vital tool in any efforts to make it better. If the goal is to ensure that officers behave in a fair and respectful way with citizens, it seems unlikely, if not impossible, to realize that goal if officers do not experience that same treatment within their departments.

Further Reading and Additional Resources

For departments interested in evaluating the level of justice within their organization, consult the following paper:

Jason A. Colquitt, "On the Dimensionality of Organizational Justice: A Construct Validation of a Measure," *Journal of Applied Psychology* 86, no. 3 (2001): 386–400.

For those interested in learning more about the theoretical perspectives informing our discussion above, we recommend the following two papers:

Jason A. Colquitt, Jerald Greenberg, and Cindy P. Zapata-Phelan, "What Is Organizational Justice? A Historical Overview," in *Handbook of Organizational Justice*, eds. Jerald Greenberg and Jason A. Colquitt (Mahwah, NJ: Lawrence Erlbaum Associates, Inc., 2005), 3–56.

Tom R. Tyler and Steven L. Blader, "The Group Engagement Model: Procedural Justice, Social Identity, and Cooperative Behavior," *Personality and Social Psychology Review* 7, no. 4 (2003): 349–361.

For those interested in examining the role of organizational justice within police departments specifically, we recommend the following two papers.

Ben Bradford, Paul Quinton, Andy Myhill, and Gillian Porter, "Why Do 'the Law' Comply? Procedural Justice, Group Identification, and Officer Motivation in Police Organizations," *European Journal of Criminology* 11, no. 1 (2014): 110–131.

Rick Trinkner, Tom R. Tyler, and Phillip A. Goff, "Justice from Within: The Relations between a Procedurally Just Organizational Climate and Police Organizational Efficiency, Endorsement of Democratic Policing, and Officer Well-Being," *Psychology, Public Policy, and Law* 22, no. 2 (2016): 158–172.

Notes

1 Michael S. Scott, "Which Way to Better Policing?," *Criminology & Public Policy* 16, no. 2 (2017): 607–616.

2 For example, Task Force on 21st Century Policing, *Final Report of the President's Task Force on 21st Century Policing* (Washington, D.C.: Office of Community Oriented Policing Services, 2015.

3 Wesley G. Skogan, "Why Reforms Fail," *Policing and Society* 18, no. 1 (2008): 23–34.

4 See, for example, Robert E. Worden and Sarah J. McLean, *Mirage of Police Reform: Procedural Justice and Police Legitimacy* (Oakland, CA: University of California Press, 2017).

5 Jason A. Colquitt, Jerald Greenberg, and Cindy P. Zapata-Phelan, "What Is Organizational Justice? A Historical Overview," in *Handbook of Organizational Justice*, eds. Jerald Greenberg and Jason A. Colquitt (Mahwah, NJ: Erlbaum, 2005).

6 Tom R. Tyler and Steven L. Blader, "The Group Engagement Model: Procedural Justice, Social Identity, and Cooperative Behavior," *Personality and Social Psychology Review* 7, no. 4 (2003): 349–361.

7 Rick Trinkner, Tom R. Tyler, and Phillip A. Goff, "Justice from Within: The Relations between a Procedurally Just Organizational Climate and Police Organizational Efficiency, Endorsement of Democratic Policing, and Officer Well-Being," *Psychology, Public Policy, and Law* 22, no. 2 (2016): 158–172.

8 John Rawls, *A Theory of Justice* (Cambridge, MA: Harvard University Press, 1999).

9 Jerald Greenberg, "A Taxonomy of Organizational Justice Theories," *The Academy of Management Review* 12, no. 1 (1987): 9–22.

10 Yochi Cohen-Charash and Paul E. Spector, "The Role of Justice in Organizations: A Meta-Analysis," *Organizational Behavior and Human Decision Processes* 86, no. 2 (2001): 278–321; Jason A. Colquitt, Donald E. Conlon, Michael J. Wesson, Christopher O. L. H. Porter, and K. Yee Ng, "Justice at the Millennium: A Meta-Analytic Review of 25 Years of Organizational Justice Research," *Journal of Applied Psychology* 86, no. 3 (2001): 425–445; Jerald Greenberg, "Organizational Justice: The Dynamics of Fairness in the Workplace," in *APA Handbook of Industrial and Organizational Psychology*, ed. Sheldon Zedeck (Washington, D.C.: American Psychological Association, 2011), 271–327.

11 See Cohen-Charash and Spector, "The Role of Justice in Organizations"; Colquitt et al., "Justice at the Millennium"; Greenberg, "Organizational Justice."

12 Christopher Donner, John Maskaly, Lorie Fridell, and Wesley G. Jennings, "Policing and Procedural Justice: A State-of-the-Art Review," *Policing: An International Journal of Police Strategies & Management* 38, no. 1 (2015): 153–172.

[13] Ben Bradford, Paul Quinton, Andy Myhill, and Gillian Porter, "Why Do 'the Law' Comply? Procedural Justice, Group Identification and Officer Motivation in Police Organizations," *European Journal of Criminology* 11, no. 1 (2014): 110–131.

[14] Eric G. Lambert, Nancy L. Hogan, and Marie L. Griffin, "The Impact of Distributive and Procedural Justice on Correctional Staff Job Stress, Job Satisfaction, and Organizational Commitment," *Journal of Criminal Justice* 35, no. 6 (2007): 644–656; Anne Morris, Marybeth Shinn, and Kimberly DuMont, "Contextual Factors Affecting the Organizational Commitment of Diverse Police Officers: A Levels of Analysis Perspective," *American Journal of Community Psychology* 27, no. 1 (1999): 75; Faye S. Taxman and Jill A. Gordon, "Do Fairness and Equity Matter?: An Examination of Organizational Justice among Correctional Officers in Adult Prisons," *Criminal Justice and Behavior* 36, no. 7 (2009): 695–711.

[15] Scott E. Wolfe and Justin Nix, "Police Officers Trust in Their Agency: Does Self-Legitimacy Protect against Supervisor Procedural Injustice?" *Criminal Justice and Behavior* 44, no. 5 (2017): 717–732.

[16] Ben Bradford and Paul Quinton, "Self-Legitimacy, Police Culture and Support for Democratic Policing in an English Constabulary," *British Journal of Criminology* 54, no. 6 (2014): 2013–2046.

[17] Trinkner et al., "Justice from Within"; Tom R. Tyler, Patrick E. Callahan, and Jeffery Frost, "Armed, and Dangerous(?): Motivating Rule Adherence among Agents of Social Control," *Law & Society Review* 41, no. 2 (2007): 457–492.

[18] Nicole E. Haas, Maarten Van Craen, Wesley G. Skogan, and Diego M. Fleitas, "Explaining Officer Compliance: The Importance of Procedural Justice and Trust inside a Police Organization," *Criminology & Criminal Justice: An International Journal* 15, no. 4 (2015): 442–463; Tyler et al., "Armed, and Dangerous(?)."

[19] Trinkner et al., "Justice from Within."

[20] Scott E. Wolfe and Alex R. Piquero, "Organizational Justice and Police Misconduct," *Criminal Justice and Behavior* 38, no. 4 (2011): 332–353.

[21] Joseph De Angelis and Aaron Kupchik, "Citizen Oversight, Procedural Justice, and Officer Perceptions of the Complaint Investigation Process," *Policing: An International Journal of Police Strategies & Management* 3, no. 4 (2007): 651–671.

[22] Suzanne J. Farmer, Terry A. Beehr, and Kevin G. Love, "Becoming an Undercover Police Officer: A Note on Fairness Perceptions, Behavior, and Attitudes," *Journal of Organizational Behavior* 24, no. 4 (2003): 373–387, http://doi.org/10.1002/job.196.

[23] Andy Myhill and Ben Bradford, "Overcoming Cop Culture? Organizational Justice and Police Officers' Attitudes toward the Public," *Policing: An International Journal of Police Strategies & Management* 36, no. 2 (2013): 338–356.

[24] Lambert et al., "The Impact of Distributive and Procedural Justice on Correctional Staff Job Stress, Job Satisfaction, and Organizational Commitment."

[25] Trinkner et al., "Justice from Within."

[26] Justice Tankebe, "Rightful Authority: Exploring the Structure of Police Self-Legitimacy," in *Crime, Justice, and Social Order: Essays in Honour of A. E. Bottoms*, eds. Alison Liebling, Joanna Shapland, and Justice Tankebe (Oxford, England: Oxford University Press, 2014): 1–30.

[27] Anthony Bottoms and Justice Tankebe, "Beyond Procedural Justice: A Dialogic Approach to Legitimacy in Criminal Justice," *Journal of Criminal Law & Criminology* 102, no. 1 (2013): 119–170; Bradford et al., "Self-Legitimacy, Police Culture and Support for Democratic Policing in an English Constabulary."

[28] Justin Nix and Scott E. Wolfe, "The Impact of Negative Publicity on Police Self-Legitimacy," *Justice Quarterly* 34, no. 1 (2017): 84–108; Wolfe and Nix, "Police Officers Trust in Their Agency."

[29] De Angelis et al., "Citizen Oversight, Procedural Justice, and Officer Perceptions of the Complaint Investigation Process"; Wolfe et al., "Organizational Justice and Police Misconduct."

[30] Justice Tankebe and Gorazd Meško, "Police Self-Legitimacy, Use of Force, and Pro-Organizational Behavior in Slovenia," in *Trust and Legitimacy in Criminal Justice*, eds. Gorazd Meško and Justice Tankebe (New York, NY: Springer, 2015), 261–277; Wolfe et al., "Organizational Justice and Police Misconduct."

[31] Trinkner et al., "Justice from Within."

[32] See, e.g., Maarten Van Craen and Wesley G. Skogan, "Achieving Fairness in Policing: The Link between Internal and External Procedural Justice," *Police Quarterly* 20, no. 1 (2017): 3–23.

[33] See, e.g., Bradford et al., "Self-Legitimacy, Police Culture and Support for Democratic Policing in an English Constabulary."

[34] Haas et al., "Explaining Officer Compliance."

[35] Tom R. Tyler, "Social Justice: Outcome and Procedure," *International Journal of Psychology* 35, no. 2 (2000): 117–125.

[36] James Q. Wilson, *Varieties of Police Behavior: The Management of Law and Order in Right Communities* (Cambridge, MA: Harvard University Press, 1968).

[37] Duren Banks, Joshua Hendrix, Matthew Hickman, and Tracey Kyckelhahn, *National Sources of Law Enforcement Employment Data* (Washington, D.C.: Government Printing Office, 2016).

[38] There is still some dispute in the theoretical literature about the "correct" number of organizational justice facets, although there is a fair amount of agreement about the four components presented here. For a larger discussion, please see Colquitt et al., "What Is Organizational Justice? A Historical Overview," and Greenberg, "Organizational Justice."

[39] Jason A. Colquitt, "On the Dimensionality of Organizational Justice: A Construct Validation of a Measure," *Journal of Applied Psychology* 86, no. 3 (2001): 386–400; Cohen-Charash and Spector, "The Role of Justice in Organizations"; Colquitt et al., "Justice at the Millennium."

[40] Colquitt et al., "What Is Organizational Justice? A Historical Overview."

[41] Ibid. Organizational justice scholars diverge in their conception of procedural justice from the way it is conceptualized in the literature on police legitimacy. (See Michael D. Reisig's earlier chapter in this volume entitled, "Institutionalize Procedural Justice.") In particular, the police legitimacy literature views procedural justice as an amalgam of interpersonal, informational, and procedural justice from the organizational justice framework presented here.

[42] Colquitt et al., "What Is Organizational Justice? A Historical Overview."

[43] Ibid.

[44] Trinkner et al., "Justice from Within."

[45] Tyler et al., "The Group Engagement Model."

[46] Colquitt et al., "What Is Organizational Justice? A Historical Overview"; Greenberg, "Organizational Justice."

10

Response Essay

Chief Eric Jones
Stockton Police Department

Recent policing reform initiatives have three primary shifts in common: building trust and relationships, using new metrics, and focusing more on data-driven enforcement. These policing shifts—built to address the challenges of today's complex world—follow an overarching philosophy of certain principles and values for which the industry of law enforcement must stand.

In my police department in Stockton, California, two pillars underpin these evolutionary shifts: smarter policing and principled policing. The term "smarter policing" relates to the use of intelligence-led and evidence-based strategies and is about being data driven and strategic in delivering public safety services to the community. Smarter policing includes innovation and technology to improve service delivery. If smarter policing is how we do our job, then principled policing is what our agency stands for and is the reason that the men and women in law enforcement do what they do. Smarter policing, therefore, must be driven by principled policing to ensure that the profession of law enforcement is procedurally just and legitimate.

Principled policing includes all the components used to increase the community's trust in their police department and officers. Principled policing stands upon the premise that law enforcement should be based on its founding principles. Back in 1829, the Peelian principles were developed upon the tenets of police transparency, integrity, fairness, and accountability—all critical to legitimizing policing in the eyes of the public and securing bonds of trust with the community. Arguably, these principles are even more critical—and actionable—now than they were back then. Community tensions with police are high, but by using our research and data capabilities, experts can validate not only that low community trust exists but also determine the communities where trust is low and why. This provides opportunities to better address distrust through focused deterrence crime strategies, procedural justice and implicit bias training for police officers and through racial reconciliation listening sessions.

The pillars of smarter and principled policing incorporate the three primary shifts in law enforcement: relationships, metrics, and enforcement. Much of the content of the three commonalities in recent policing reforms is contained in the California Attorney General's Principled Policing Subcommittee and Statewide Training, the National Initiative on Building Community Trust and Justice, and the President's Task Force on 21st Century Policing, all of which involved Stockton, California.

Law enforcement agencies must use effective crime-fighting strategies that also continue to build trust within the community. This link between trust and crime reduction is clear. There has also been a shift toward recognizing how best to reach out to the most disenfranchised communities. Building blocks for trust include understanding the levels and sources of mistrust, especially in our communities of color, and learning how historical acknowledgments and reconciliation can assist in meaningful dialogue. Law enforcement agencies are also beginning to recognize the importance of being trauma informed.

As far as outcomes and measurements, today's report card for police emphasizes arrests and citations less and focuses instead on trust-building metrics. Community sentiment and feedback on the policing of our communities is essential to gauging a police department's success. Promising strategies for external metrics seem to be comprehensive community surveys, while internally, we are shifting from traditional Compstat numbers to collective overviews that look at both crime-fighting and trust-building efforts in departmental meetings.

Finally, regarding enforcement, police have moved away from "blanket enforcement" toward strategic, data-driven enforcement. Instead of simply responding to high-crime areas and saturating them with zero-tolerance enforcement, police departments are targeting the tiny percentage of community members committing the vast majority of crime.

A primary hurdle that law enforcement leaders often face is steering a police department's internal culture to embrace these pillars and shifts. To succeed, departmental buy-in is required. A police chief can have great plans, but if the sergeants—arguably the most powerful or influential positions of authority for line-level staff—do not support those plans, the wheels of reform stall. If the line-level police staff do not have faith in their police department or feel there is a lack of internal procedural justice and fairness within their own agency, they may be less inclined to be procedurally just to the community during their daily contacts. The perceived procedural justice of those community contacts shapes the community's view of the legitimacy of their police department. Therefore, a "leadership sandwich" is required: both top-level command staff and line-level staff, such as informal shift/squad leadership and police union leadership, must move together in the same direction. For this to occur, both internal trust and a sense of internal organizational fairness must exist.

As Frances Frei of the Harvard Business School has observed, trust within an organization relies upon the triangle of authenticity, logic, and empathy by those in power.[1] And as suggested in chapter 10, employees are sensitive to a sense of internal fairness. If they perceive fairness within their agency, they will increasingly internalize police reforms. Internal procedural justice, known as organizational justice, guards the police agency against employee behavior that is not consistent with the standards espoused by police leadership.

The success of principled policing relies upon leadership at all levels, top to bottom, and a culture embracing change. It must be ingrained into the policing culture, which is the department's shared set of values and beliefs. The culture should be one where ideas are evaluated on merits rather than rank or politics, openness is promoted, people are held accountable, and best practices are sought. These principles must be the overarching philosophy that permeates all aspects of policy and culture. The philosophy can also be tangibly infused at the operational level through employee performance evaluations and emphasized through the behaviors the agency rewards.

In short, organizational justice that reflects a healthy internal climate is critical to moving the evolution of policing forward.

NOTE

[1] Frances Frei, "How to Build (and Rebuild) Trust," TED Talk, May 4, 2018.

11

Promoting Officer Health and Wellness

Edward R. Maguire
Logan J. Somers
Kathleen E. Padilla
Arizona State University

Police officers face a variety of risks to their health and wellness while on the job. Research has confirmed that police officers are at greater risk for adverse mental and physical health outcomes compared to the general population.[1] While the most well-known risks are those associated with intentional injuries (e.g., ambushes, assaults, etc.) and unintentional injuries (e.g., vehicle crashes and other accidental injuries), police officers also face elevated risks from less obvious sources, including stress and fatigue,[2] poor nutrition,[3] and other physical and mental health risks associated with the very nature of police work.[4] Comprehensive efforts to improve health and wellness among police officers must therefore account for a wide variety of risks. In this chapter, we focus specifically on physical and mental health risks that are not associated with intentional or unintentional injuries. We begin by reviewing the nature of these risks. We then review the effectiveness of interventions intended to reduce them. We close with a series of practical recommendations for promoting police officer health and wellness.

Occupational Health and Wellness among Police Officers

Policing involves a variety of occupational risks to the health and wellness of its workforce. Research has found elevated rates of certain types of diseases and disease-related deaths among police officers relative to the general population.[5] Police officers also have shorter life expectancies than other municipal employees.[6] Many causes contribute to the elevated rates of *morbidity* (i.e., illness, disease, or unhealthiness) and *mortality* (i.e., death) among police officers relative to the general population and other occupational groups. It is tempting to attribute the shorter life expectancy of police officers solely to the inherent dangers of the job. Indeed, the risk of death, illness, and injury due to assaults, motor vehicle accidents, and other direct threats to officer safety is a reality.[7] However, many other less obvious physiological and psychological risks increase morbidity and mortality among police officers.[8] In this section, we explore some of these issues.

Shift work is an inherent element of policing that can place a burden on an officer's psychological and physical well-being. Shift work has been shown to exert negative effects on a number of key outcomes, including a police officer's performance, physical health, and overall mood.[9] These effects may not be unique to the field of policing but rather associated with shift work more generally.[10] A systematic review of thirteen epidemiological studies examined the effects of shift work on metabolic syndrome, a set of conditions that increases the risk of cardiovascular disease, stroke, and type 2 diabetes. The review found that shift work "is significantly associated with the risk of metabolic syndrome."[11] The authors speculate that "long-term exposure to night shift work might disturb the normal circadian rhythm and may cause the imbalance of glucose and lipid metabolism," which, in turn, stimulates the onset of metabolic syndrome and its components.[12]

Many aspects of policing can also induce toxic stress among officers. For instance, police officers are often placed in situations that require rapid decision-making under duress, which can result in physical and psychological strain both during and after the event. Certain critical incidents, some of which are traumatic, can have detrimental psychological effects on officers.[13] Internal bureaucratic features of the police agency can also generate feelings of pressure, resentment, and discrimination, all of which increase stress among officers.[14] Difficult interactions with the public may stimulate feelings of resentment and isolation among officers.[15]

These and other sources of stress have led scholars to conclude that law enforcement is one of the most stressful occupations in the world.[16] Self-report surveys often identify two broad categories of stress for police officers, organizational and occupational, with organizational stressors being particularly harmful.[17] Cumulative stress over the duration of a policing career can often result in an officer experiencing burnout, which, in turn, leads to other negative health and wellness outcomes.[18] Organizational and occupational stress have been linked to a number of negative coping mechanisms, including tobacco use, excessive alcohol consumption, unhealthy diets, and a lack of exercise, all of which may coexist and which may compound health risks, especially in the context of shift work.[19]

As noted above, research on the impact of shift work in policing has reported a variety of negative health effects.[20] Shift work is thought to disrupt critical aspects of a police officer's physiological functioning and work-life balance.[21] Shift work is also thought to be associated with poor dietary choices. Police officers frequently choose to eat fast food or other unhealthy yet readily available food options. The combination of an unhealthy diet and sleep deprivation due to shift work can result in weight gain, insulin resistance, and type 2 diabetes.[22] The Buffalo Cardio-Metabolic Occupational Police Stress study (BCOPS), for example, reported that approximately 32 percent of police officers slept less than six hours in a twenty-four-hour time span and continued this trend over several days.[23] Further, the results indicated that approximately 80 percent of officers met the body mass index (BMI) criteria for being overweight or obese.[24]

In addition to having poor diets, police officers also show elevated rates of alcohol consumption, alcoholism, and binge drinking. While some police officers consume alcohol at a rate that is comparable to that of the general population,[25] a concerning percentage report alcohol consumption and abuse that exceeds that of the general public. Approximately 36 percent of officers reported episodes of binge drinking, while approximately 8 percent indicated possible alcohol abuse or dependence.[26] Furthermore, police officers are twice as likely to die from alcohol-related liver disease than is the general population.[27] Much of the link between policing and alcohol consumption is associated with exposure to critical incidents. Traumatic events observed while on the job often result in excessive drinking as a way to cope with the stress of those events. But recent research has found that social occupational stressors (e.g., difficult interactions with civilians, the loss of relationships after becoming a police officer, and the negative perceptions surrounding officers) also lead to increases in alcohol consumption.[28] Additionally, alcohol use may be associated with a police subculture that promotes after-hours drinking as both a social activity and as a coping mechanism for dealing with stress and trauma.[29]

These health-related issues often have a cumulative effect on police officers' health. For instance, the combination of shift work, stress, poor sleep quality and quantity, unhealthy diets, and a lack of exercise contribute to an increased risk of metabolic syndrome, type 2 diabetes, and, ultimately, cardiovascular disease (CVD).[30] Indeed, police officers have elevated risk factors for CVD relative to other occupations.[31] Approximately three-quarters of all first responders (including law enforcement, firefighters, and paramedics) suffer from either prehypertension or hypertension, elevating their risk for CVD.[32] Research shows that sudden cardiac deaths account for approximately 7–10 percent of on-duty deaths among police officers.[33] More specifically, bursts of increased physical stress, such as having to pursue or incapacitate a suspect at a moment's notice, can have a substantial and grave impact on the cardiovascular health of officers who already lack adequate exercise and a healthy diet.[34]

■ Research Evidence on Health and Wellness Interventions

How Do We Know Whether Interventions Are Effective?

We begin our discussion of police officer health and wellness interventions by providing a brief background on how scientists make judgments about effectiveness. Scientists evaluate the impact of interventions using various research methods, some of which are better suited than others for drawing conclusions about cause and effect. When we evaluate the impact of an intervention, we are seeking to draw conclusions about whether it *caused* a change in some outcome. For interventions covered in this chapter, the outcome is typically a psychological or physiological measure of officer health and wellness. However, some research designs are poorly suited for determining whether interventions are effective.

The best impact evaluations use research designs that enable the researcher to draw strong, confident conclusions about whether an intervention caused a change in the outcomes of interest. It is well known that randomized trials, also known as randomized experiments, enable the most confident inferences about whether an intervention is effective. However, these designs are often not feasible because they require that the units of analysis in the research (whether people, places, or organizations) be randomly allocated to treatment or control conditions. This random allocation sometimes raises ethical issues and logistical challenges. Therefore, researchers often must rely on a diverse class of research designs known as *quasi-experiments*. These can take many forms, but what they all have in common is that they do not involve the random allocation of subjects to treatment and control conditions. Very few studies that evaluate the impact of programs and practices rely on experimental or strong quasi-experimental designs. Those that do not may nonetheless be informative in certain ways, but they provide insufficient internal validity to enable clear inferences about program effectiveness and causality.

This concern about internal validity and the extent to which it allows for confident inferences about cause and effect is crucial for thinking about what works for improving officer health and wellness. Because most studies on this issue are neither experimental nor quasi-experimental, they tend to have low internal validity and therefore provide a weak basis for making inferences about an intervention's effects. In this section, we review the research evidence on two general classes of interventions (which sometime overlap in practice): those that focus on stress reduction and those that focus on diet and exercise.

Stress-Related Interventions

A systematic review of the evidence on job stress interventions outside of policing divides those interventions into three categories: primary, secondary, and tertiary.[35] Primary interventions are preventive, seeking to reduce potential stressors before they induce stress-related symptoms in employees. Secondary interventions are ameliorative, seeking to educate or otherwise equip employees to cope with stressful conditions.[36] Tertiary interventions are reactive, seeking to treat or rehabilitate employees who are already experiencing stress-related issues. The research evidence shows that primary interventions are the most effective, followed by secondary and then tertiary. Interventions that combine primary approaches with secondary and/or tertiary elements are more effective than those that rely on any one of these modalities alone. Moreover, interventions that were directed toward the organization as a whole rather than toward individual members were found to be more effective.

While the scientific literature on the effectiveness of stress-management interventions in the workplace (not specific to the police) is generally positive, the research evidence in policing is less optimistic. A recent systematic review of twelve studies concluded that stress-management interventions targeting police officers were not effective in altering physiological, psychological, or behavioral outcomes.[37] One explanation for this finding may be that the most common interventions in policing operate at the secondary or tertiary level rather than at the primary level. Another possible explanation is that "the most commonly provided interventions do not address the chronic organizational stressors that police officers experience; instead they address individual symptoms that result from stress."[38] Since the publication of that systematic review, several additional randomized trials testing stress-management interventions among police officers have become available. These studies tested different types of interventions, including imagery and skills training, resilience training, and a comprehensive team-based, health-promotion initiative. The findings from these studies provide greater room for optimism that stress-related interventions can in fact be effective in a policing setting.

Imagery and skills training involves the use of classroom-based learning and scenarios to increase a police officer's "sense of control over stress-provoking situations by rendering the incidents more predictable and by providing a psychological/tactical repertoire for the officers to utilize."[39] The proper education in and practice of relaxation techniques, guided imagery to prepare for exposure to potentially stressful scenarios, and guided imagery to master police tactical skills was shown to improve mental well-being, stomach problems, sleep quality, exhaustion, and coping skills.[40]

Resilience is "the capacity to prepare for, recover from, and adapt to stress, adversity, trauma, or tragedy."[41] Resilience training is designed to diminish the symptoms of stress by increasing physiological coherence (the ability to regulate the body's reactions to stress) and improving heart rhythm variability (the pattern of the heart's rhythm that is reflective of emotional states).[42] Analyses of officers working in different settings reveal that those who participated in resilience training show improvements in coping skills, family relationships, work performance, and interpersonal skills[43] as well as in physiological measures such as hypertension, high cholesterol, and diabetes.[44]

Researchers also tested a comprehensive team-based health-promotion program in three local law enforcement agencies using a randomized trial. Treatment group officers were provided with weekly peer-led sessions addressing a variety of health and safety issues. The intervention was associated with significant improvements in fruit and vegetable consumption, sleep quality and quantity, self-reported stress, and healthy eating after six months.[45] After twenty-four months, researchers found that all of the significant effects found at six months remained, with the exception of sleep quality and quantity.[46] This intervention is noteworthy for comprehensively focusing on a variety of health and wellness issues (such as sleep quality and healthy eating) rather than focusing on one health-related behavior intervention at a time.

Diet- and Exercise-Based Interventions

Most of the research that has tested the effects of diet- and exercise-related interventions among police officers has relied on weak methodologies with low internal validity. This makes it difficult to trust the findings and inhibits the development of scientific evidence on health and wellness in policing. However, some of the research has used stronger methodologies with sufficient internal validity to substantiate the findings. Below we provide a brief summary of this research.

Diet only. Researchers tested the effect of a low-calorie diet in which carbohydrates were eaten mostly at dinner on a sample of seventy-eight obese Israeli police officers.[47] The participants were randomly divided into two groups, both of which were assigned low-calorie diets. The control group ate carbohydrates throughout the day, while the experimental group restricted most of its carbohydrate intake to dinner. The authors hypothesized that concentrating carbohydrates at dinnertime would induce a hormonal response that would decrease hunger the next day and "improve dietary adherence."[48] Both groups experienced significant weight loss and other health benefits, but the experimental group lost significantly more weight than the control group. The authors concluded that eating carbohydrates mostly at dinner might help people who are obese or who suffer from insulin resistance or metabolic syndrome.

Exercise only. Researchers tested the effects of an inexpensive circuit-training program relative to a standard weight-training program. The circuit-training program in this study consisted of "nine exercises designed to improve muscular strength and endurance separated by 30 seconds of aerobic exercise. The exercises used chairs, tables, sawhorses, and body weight to provide the resistance."[49] The study included forty-three law enforcement trainees in North Carolina who were randomly divided into two groups, each of which completed physical training three times per week for twelve weeks. Both groups ran as part of their training program. The control group also used a standard weight-training program, while the treatment group participated in a "resistive exercise circuit training program involving the use of chairs, tables, sawhorses and body resistance" in place of weight training.[50] Both groups experienced significant improvements on several health outcomes, but the treatment group experienced greater improvements in body weight, body fat, and cholesterol levels.

Researchers in the United Kingdom conducted a quasi-experiment with 150 police officers who were divided into three groups: aerobic training, anaerobic training, and a control group.[51] Participants in the two exercise groups trained three times per week for forty-five minutes each time. The aerobic group experienced significant improvements in fitness and reductions in blood pressure compared to the control group. The anaerobic group also experienced improvements in fitness, though to a lesser degree than those in the aerobic group, and reductions in blood pressure. The authors concluded that both programs offer "substantial psychological and physiological benefits" but noted that the aerobic training program outperformed the anaerobic training program.[52]

Another group of researchers tested the effect of a four-month circuit weight-training program on forty-three Florida police officers. The officers who were randomly assigned to the treatment group exercised three times per week for twenty minutes at a time. The intervention resulted in significant reductions in stress and psychological and physical symptoms as well as increased job satisfaction. Participants also experienced some physical benefits, including an increase in bicep size and a decrease in waist size, but did not display significant changes in body weight or cardiac performance. The researchers concluded that circuit weight training produced improvements "on a variety of physical, psychological, and work-related dimensions."[53] Based on these findings, the authors recommended including circuit weight training as a part of more comprehensive stress-management interventions.

One team of researchers tested the effects of a physical conditioning program on forty-five moderately obese police officers from a large metropolitan police department.[54] The officers were randomly assigned to either a control group or a treatment group that engaged in aerobic exercise (walking and jogging) for up to forty-five minutes per session three times per week for eight weeks. Because both groups were placed on diets and received counseling on nutrition and exercise, the study only tested the exercise portion of the intervention. Both groups experienced significant increases in oxygen consumption over their baseline, but the increases were greater in the treatment group. The treatment group also experienced significantly greater improvements in self-concept. The authors concluded that "conditioning and diet were associated with greater improvements in fitness and self-concept" among obese men.[55]

Diet and exercise. Researchers in Boston used a randomized trial to test the effects of diet and resistance training on body composition among overweight but otherwise healthy police officers.[56] They found that a low-calorie, high-protein diet coupled with resistance training resulted in significant reductions in body weight and fat mass and an increase in lean muscle mass. The authors cautioned that a low-calorie diet alone "is ineffective in restoring normal body composition and can actually lead to further loss of lean mass if adequate protein is not provided."[57]

Researchers in North Carolina used a randomized trial to test the effects of a health and fitness program administered to 1,504 police trainees across twenty-five sites.[58] Participants received lectures on health, nutrition, and fitness and completed supervised workouts for one hour per day, three days per week, for nine weeks. Trainees in the experimental sites experienced significantly greater increases in cardiovascular fitness and muscular strength, and significantly greater decreases in body fat, relative to trainees in the control sites.

Researchers in Boston tested an eight-week diet and exercise program among moderately obese male members of two local police departments.[59] All participants attended weekly educational sessions on diet, nutrition, and exercise, but the experimental groups also engaged in supervised exercise three times per week, including thirty-five to sixty minutes of aerobic activity, calisthenics, and relaxation techniques. The participants were placed on two different types of diets: one focused on calorie reduction alone, while the other focused on calorie reduction plus a ketogenic diet with no carbohydrates and all fats from "lean meat, fish, and fowl."[60] The calorie-reduction diet groups "lost significantly less weight than did the other diet groups" and "those on a formula ketogenic diet containing fewer calories lost nearly twice as much weight."[61] The authors concluded that coupling diet and exercise (at least three times per week) is essential for maintaining significant reductions in body weight. Finally, the authors found that "simple instruction without supervision during weight loss is not adequate to reinforce activity changes in previously inactive subjects."[62]

The State of the Science on Diet and Nutrition

The studies above constitute the most important research on the effects of diet- and exercise-based interventions in law enforcement. They demonstrate clearly that police officers can experience significant improvements in their physical and psychological health by exercising and eating a healthy diet. While there is a much larger body of research on these health and wellness issues within the general population, it is not possible to summarize the entire scientific literature on the effectiveness of diet- and exercise-based interventions here. However, there are a few illustrative results from systematic reviews that seek to synthesize the findings of existing research on a specific issue. Below we provide a brief review of findings from systematic reviews of diet- and exercise-based interventions.

A perennial debate among diet and nutrition specialists is the proper balance between macronutrients (e.g., proteins, fats, and carbohydrates). Some experts recommend low-fat diets, while others just as enthusiastically recommend low-carbohydrate diets. Fortunately, there is a large body of research on these issues, including systematic reviews of existing research. Those reviews suggest that low-carbohydrate diets are associated with greater reductions in body weight and several other cardiovascular and metabolic risk factors.[63]

Although the research evidence on the benefits of low-carbohydrate diets is robust, much still remains to be learned. For instance, the effects of these diets on long-term health are not yet well understood because most studies have short follow-up periods.[64] One systematic review found that although low-carbohydrate diets resulted in several health-related benefits, they were also associated with increases in LDL ("bad") cholesterol.[65] Another systematic review found that diets that were high in protein and low in carbohydrates were associated with small reductions in body weight and body fat, but these effects were often temporary due to weak long-term adherence to dietary protocols.[66]

Research has also examined the effects of high- versus low-protein diets. A systematic review of seventy-four randomized trials found that high-protein diets resulted in greater reductions in body weight and other cardiac and metabolic risk factors.[67] Another systematic review of twenty-four studies examined the effects of the carbohydrate-to-protein ratio on weight loss and cardiovascular risk factors for people on low-fat, calorie-restricted diets. This review found that when fat content and overall calories were held constant, a higher-protein diet was associated with greater reductions in body weight, body fat, and triglyceride levels.[68] This underscores the fact that while much of the current debate focuses on regulating fat and carbohydrates, the research shows that optimizing protein consumption is also important.

The Mediterranean diet, which mimics the traditional food choices of people living in the Mediterranean region, has also received a lot of attention in recent years. This largely plant-based diet involves regular consumption of fruits, vegetables, healthy fats (such as olive oil), whole grains, poultry, and seafood, with only limited consumption of red meat. A systematic review of fifty studies found that the Mediterranean diet was associated with a reduced risk of metabolic syndrome and several of its individual components, including waist circumference, HDL cholesterol, triglycerides, blood pressure, and blood glucose. The authors concluded that the Mediterranean diet can serve as a cost-effective measure for preventing metabolic syndrome.[69]

In addition to the benefits of eating a healthy diet, systematic reviews have also found that exercise is associated with a variety of psychological and physical health benefits, beyond its obvious effects on physical fitness. Exercise reduces anxiety,[70] blood pressure,[71] cigarette cravings,[72] clinical depression,[73] depression resulting from mental illness, insomnia,[74] and negative affect.[75] It also improves cardio-metabolic health,[76] cognitive performance,[77] and memory.[78]

The science on the most effective types of exercise for different populations and circumstances is still developing. For instance, a recent review concluded that "further studies are still warranted to delve further into the impact that both aerobic and anaerobic exercise may have on human physiology to unequivocally determine [whether] there is superiority of one type of exercise over another."[79] However, there is growing evidence that high-intensity interval training (HIIT) outperforms lower-intensity training in diverse populations. HIIT has been shown to improve cardio-metabolic risk factors[80] and reduce fat mass[81] in overweight or obese populations. A systematic review of ten randomized trials found that HIIT outperformed moderate-intensity continuous training in improving cardiorespiratory fitness among patients with lifestyle-induced chronic diseases.[82] Another systematic review of nine randomized trials found that aerobic interval training outperformed moderate continuous training for enhancing aerobic capacity and decreasing body weight among patients with coronary artery disease.[83] Additionally, a systematic review of twenty-seven studies found that high-intensity exercise improved aerobic capacity and insulin resistance relative to low- or moderate-intensity exercise for people with type 2 diabetes.[84] Although the research evidence on the benefits of high-intensity exercise is becoming increasingly clear, much remains to be learned about its risks, long-term effects, and the extent to which these vary across different populations.

■ Next Steps

While many police agencies have adopted some type of health and wellness program, little is known about the effectiveness of these initiatives. Because the science of police health and wellness remains in its infancy, police leaders are unable to draw on a comprehensive body of police-specific scientific evidence in designing effective initiatives. As one systematic review concluded, "Empirical evidence for effective health and wellness programs in police and firefighter populations is scarce. Better evaluation and documentation of such programs is needed to advance this field of research."[85]

One systematic review of studies that tested the effects of interventions intended to reduce the risk of cardiovascular disease among emergency service workers rated fifteen of the sixteen studies as methodologically "weak." If we are serious about keeping police officers healthy, both physically and psychologically, we must invest in rigorous research that tests the effectiveness of health-related interventions in policing.

In part, this is a call to action for funding bodies (such as the National Institutes of Health and the National Institute of Justice in the United States) to invest in research on these important issues. However, it is also a call to action for police leaders. If every major police department were to collaborate with health professionals to conduct randomized trials testing interventions designed to promote physical and/or psychological wellness among police officers, the science of health and wellness in policing would progress rapidly. Police leaders must be careful to select partners with the appropriate substantive and methodological expertise to make this happen. In terms of substantive expertise, at least one partner must be knowledgeable about the content of the intervention. For instance, anyone designing a diet-related intervention for police officers must have up-to-date scientific knowledge about such interventions. At least one partner must also have the knowledge and experience to design a well-orchestrated randomized trial (or a high-quality quasi-experiment) designed to test the effectiveness of the intervention. One of the major problems with this line of research is that most studies have weak designs that result in more questions than answers. It is time to get serious about carrying out high-quality research, with strong internal validity, on health and wellness interventions in policing.

Although much remains to be learned in the context of policing, we believe there is already sufficient scientific knowledge to begin testing evidence-based health and wellness interventions in police organizations. For instance, police agencies can implement stress-reduction initiatives that combine primary, secondary, and tertiary components. These interventions can build on the evidence presented earlier on imagery and skills training, resilience training, and comprehensive team-based health-promotion initiatives. Drawing on the research evidence both inside and outside of policing, police agencies could also begin to implement diet- and exercise-related interventions for their officers. Dietary interventions could be based on the research evidence on low-carb/high-protein diets or the Mediterranean diet. Exercise interventions could be based on the research evidence on high-intensity interval training. The goal is to prevent or reverse lifestyle-related conditions such as metabolic syndrome, type 2 diabetes, and cardiovascular disease.

Police agencies could also combine these elements to develop more comprehensive initiatives that focus on a variety of physiological and psychological health and wellness issues. There is evidence to support this approach as well. For instance, a systematic review of interventions intended to reduce the risk of cardiovascular disease among emergency service workers concluded that interventions combining diet, exercise, and behavioral counseling had a stronger effect on cardiac health than interventions that implemented any one of these components alone.[86]

Police officers face a wide variety of risks to their health and wellness. Some of these risks are well known and unavoidable, including the risk of assaults, motor vehicle accidents, and other sources of intentional and unintentional injuries. Yet many other risks, though they may be less obvious, still constitute a serious threat to police officers' health and wellness. In this chapter, we have outlined the research evidence on several of these risks. We have also outlined the evidence on interventions intended to reduce these risks.

Moving forward, the challenge is twofold. First, we must build a robust body of scientific knowledge on how to improve health and wellness among police officers. Second, we must draw on the existing scientific knowledge to implement evidence-based workplace health and wellness initiatives in police agencies. We cannot leave police officers to face these issues alone.

NOTES

[1] Tara A. Hartley, Cecil M. Burchfiel, Desta Fekedulegn, Michael E. Andrew, and John M. Violanti, "Health Disparities in Police Officers: Comparisons to the U.S. General Population," *International Journal of Emergency Mental Health* 13, no. 4 (2011): 211–20; Warren D. Franke, Shannon A. Collins, and Paul N. Hinz, "Cardiovascular Disease Morbidity in an Iowa Law Enforcement Cohort, Compared with the General Iowa Population," *Journal of Occupational and Environmental Medicine* 40, no. 5 (1998): 441–44.

[2] Mark H. Anshel, "A Conceptual Model and Implications for Coping with Stressful Events in Police Work," *Criminal Justice and Behavior* 27, no. 3 (2000): 375–00; Bengt B. Arnetz, Dana C. Nevedal, Mark A. Lumley, Lena Backman, and Ake Lublin, "Trauma Resilience Training for Police: Psychophysiological and Performance Effects," *Journal of Police and Criminal Psychology* 24, no. 1 (2009): 1–9; Ronald J. Burke, "Stressful Events, Work-Family Conflict, Coping, Psychological Burnout, and Well-Being among Police Officers," *Psychological Reports* 75, no. 2 (1994): 787–00; Bernie L. Patterson, "Job Experience and Perceived Job Stress among Police, Correctional, and Probation/Parole Officers," *Criminal Justice & Behavior* 19, no. 3 (1992): 260–85; Nicole A. Roberts and Robert W. Levenson, "The Remains of the Workday: Impact of Job Stress and Exhaustion on Marital Interaction in Police Couples," *Journal of Marriage and the Family* 63, no. 4 (2001): 1052–67; Gerry M. Stearns and Robert J. Moore, "The Physical and Psychological Correlates of Job Burnout in the Royal Canadian Mounted Police," *Canadian Journal of Criminology* 35, no. 2 (1993): 127–48; Bryan Vila, Gregory B. Morrison, and Dennis J. Kenney, "Improving Shift-Schedule and Work-Hour Policies and Practices to Increase Police Office Performance, Health, and Safety," *Police Quarterly* 5, no. 1 (2002): 4–24; Hans Toch, *Stress in Policing* (Washington, DC: American Psychological Association, 2002).

[3] Robert H. Demling and Leslie DeSanti, "Effect of a Hypocaloric Diet, Increased Protein Intake and Resistance Training on Lean Mass Gains and Fat Mass Loss in Overweight Police Officers," *Annals of Nutrition and Metabolism* 44, no. 1 (2000): 21–29; Amanda V. McCormick, Irwin M. Cohen, and Darryl Plecas, *Nutrition and General Duty Police Work: The Case of Surrey RCMP Officers* (Abbotsford, British Columbia: BC Centre for Public Safety and

Criminal Justice Research, University of the Fraser Valley, 2011). https://www.ufv.ca/media/assets/ccjr/reports-and-publications/Surrey_-_Nutrition_Report.pdf

[4] A. Kim Burton, K. Malcolm Tillotson, Tara L. Symonds, Catherine Burke, and Tony Mathewson, "Occupational Risk Factors for the First-Onset and Subsequent Course of Low Back Trouble: A Study of Serving Police Officers," *Spine* 21, no. 22 (1996): 2612–20; Stefanos N. Kales, Antonio J. Tsismenakis, Chunbai Zhang, and Elpidoforos S. Soteriades, "Blood Pressure in Firefighters, Police Officers, and Other Emergency Responders," *American Journal of Hypertension* 22, no. 1 (2009): 11–20; Robyn L. Richmond, Alex Wodak, Linda Kehoe, and Nick Heather, "How Healthy Are the Police? A Survey of Lifestyle Factors," *Addiction* 93, no. 11 (1998): 1729–37; John M. Violanti, "Suicide and the Police Role: A Psychosocial Model," *Policing: An International Journal of Police Strategy and Management* 20, no. 4 (1997): 698–15; Peter C. Winwood, Michelle R. Tuckey, Roger Peters, and Maureen F. Dollard, "Identification and Measurement of Work-Related Psychological Injury: Piloting the Psychological Injury Risk Indicator among Frontline Police," *Journal of Occupational and Environmental Medicine* 51, no. 9 (2009): 1057–65; Franklin H. Zimmerman, "Cardiovascular Disease and Risk Factors in Law Enforcement Personnel: A Comprehensive Review," *Cardiology in Review* 20, no. 4 (2012): 159–66.

[5] John M. Violanti, John E. Vena, and Sandra Petralia, "Mortality of a Police Cohort: 1950–1990," *American Journal of Industrial Medicine* 33, no. 4 (1998): 366–73; Samuel Milham, Jr., "Occupational Mortality in Washington State, 1950–1979 (Cincinnati, OH: National Institute for Occupational Safety and Health, 1983); John M. Violanti, Michael E. Andrew, Cecil M. Burchfiel, Joan Dorn, Tara Hartley, and Diane B. Miller, "Posttraumatic Stress Symptoms and Subclinical Cardiovascular Disease in Police Officers, *International Journal of Stress Management* 13, no. 4 (2006): 541–54; Shantha M. W. Rajaratnam, Laura K. Barger, Steven W. Lockley, Steven A. Shea, Wei Wang, Christopher P. Landrigan, and Lawrence J. Epstein, "Sleep Disorders, Health, and Safety in Police Officers," *JAMA* 306, no. 23 (2011): 2567–78; Sandra L. Ramey, Yelena Perkhounkova, Mikyung Moon, Laura Budde, Chen Tseng, and M. Kathleen Clark, "The Effect of Work Shift and Sleep Duration on Various Aspects of Police Officers' Health," *Workplace Health & Safety* 60, no. 5 (2012): 215–22.

[6] Steven G. Brandl and Brad W. Smith, "An Empirical Examination of Retired Police Officers' Length of Retirement and Age at Death: A Research Note," *Police Quarterly* 16, no. 1 (2013): 113–23; John M. Violanti, Tara A. Hartley, Ja K. Gu, Desta Fekedulegn, Michael E. Andrew, and Cecil M. Burchfiel, "Life Expectancy in Police Officers: A Comparison with the U.S. General Population," *International Journal of Mental Health* 15, no. 4 (2013): 217–28.

[7] John M. Violanti, *Dying for the Job: Police Work Exposure and Health* (Springfield, IL: Charles C. Thomas, 2014).

[8] Tara A. Hartley, Anoop Shankar, Desta Fekedulegn, John M. Violanti, Michael E. Andrew, Sarah Knox, and Cecil M. Burchfiel, "Metabolic Syndrome and Carotid Intima Media Thickness in Urban Police Officers," *Journal of Occupational and Environmental Medicine* 53, no. 5 (2011): 553–61; Violanti et al., "Mortality of a Police Cohort," 366–73.

[9] Bryan Vila, Gregory B. Morrison, and Dennis J. Kenney, "Improving Shift Schedule and Work-Hour Policies and Practices to Increase Police Officer Performance, Health, and Safety," *Police Quarterly* 5, no. 1 (2002): 4–24; Lois James, Stephen M. James, and Bryan J. Vila, "The Impact of Work Shift and Fatigue on Police Officer Response in Simulated Interactions with Citizens," *Journal of Experimental Criminology* 14, no. 1 (2018): 111–20.

[10] Karen L. Amendola, David Weisburd, Edwin E. Hamilton, Greg Jones, and Meghan Slipka, "An Experimental Study of Compressed Work Schedules in Policing: Advantages and Disadvantages of Various Shift Lengths," *Journal of Experimental Criminology* 7, no. 4 (2011): 407–42.

[11] Feng Wang, L. Zhang, Yanfang Zhang, Bo Zhang, Yonghua He, Shao-Hua Xie, Mengjie Li, Xiaoping Miao, Emily Ying Yang Chan, J. L. Tang, Martin C. S. Wong, Zhi-Min Li, I. T. S. Yu, and Lemoxa Tse, "Meta-Analysis on Night Shift Work and Risk of Metabolic Syndrome," *Obesity Reviews* 15, no. 9 (2014): 709–20, 709.

[12] Wang et al., "Meta-Analysis on Night Shift Work and Risk of Metabolic Syndrome," 717.

[13] Joseph A. Harpold and Samuel L. Feemster, "Negative Influences of Police Stress," *FBI Law Enforcement Bulletin* 71, no. 9: 1–7, 1.

[14] John M. Violanti and Fred Aron, "Ranking Police Stressors," *Psychological Reports* 75, no. 2 (1994): 824–26.

[15] Violanti et al., "Life Expectancy in Police Officers."

[16] John M. Violanti, James R. Marshall, and Barbara Howe, "Stress, Coping, and Alcohol Use: The Police Connection," *Journal of Police Science & Administration* 13, no. 2 (1985): 106–10; Ronald J. Burke, "Work-Family Stress, Conflict, Coping, and Burnout in Police Officers," *Stress Medicine* 9, no. 3 (1993): 171–80; Chelsea Wheeler, Arianne Fisher, Andrea Jamiel, Tamara J. Lynn, and William Trey Hill, "Stigmatizing Attitudes toward Police Officers Seeking Psychological Services," *Journal of Police and Criminal Psychology* (2018): 10.1007/s11896-018-9293-x.

[17] Robyn R. M. Gershon, Briana Barocas, Allison N. Canton, Li Xianbin Li, and David Vlahov, "Mental, Physical, and Behavioral Outcomes Associated with Perceived Work Stress in Police Officers," *Criminal Justice and Behavior* 36, no. 3 (2009): 275–89.

[18] Burke, "Work-Family Stress, Conflict, Coping, and Burnout in Police Officers."

[19] Kales et al., "Blood Pressure in Firefighters, Police Officers, and Other Emergency Responders"; Sampsa Puttonen, Mikko I. Härmä, and Christer Hublin, "Shift Work and Cardiovascular Disease—Pathways from Circadian Stress to Morbidity," *Scandinavian Journal of Work, Environment & Health* 36, no. 2 (2010): 96–108; James F. Ballenger, Suzanne R. Best, Thomas J. Metzler, David A. Wasserman, David C. Mohr, Akiva Liberman, Kevin Delucchi, Daniel S. Weiss, Jeffrey A. Fagan, Angela E. Waldrop, and Charles R. Marmar, "Patterns and Predictors of Alcohol Use in Male and Female Urban Police Officers," *The American Journal on Addictions* 20, no. 1 (2011): 21–29; John M. Violanti, Desta Fekedulegn, Michael E. Andrew, Luenda E. Charles, Tara A. Hartley, Bryan Vila, and Cecil M. Burchfiel, "Shift Work and Long-Term Injury among Police Officers," *Scandinavian Journal of Work, Environment & Health* 39, no. 4 (2013): 361–68.

[20] Amendola et al., "An Experimental Study of Compressed Work schedules in Policing"; Luenda E. Charles, Cecil M. Burchfiel, Desta Fekedulegn, Bryan Vila, Tara A. Hartley, James Slaven, Anna Mnatsakanova, and John M. Violanti, "Shift Work and Sleep: The Buffalo Police Health Study," *Policing: An International Journal of Police Strategies & Management* 30, no. 2 (2007): 215–27.

[21] Vila et al., "Improving Shift Schedule and Work-Hour Policies and Practices"; Thomas C. Neylan, Thomas J. Metzler, Suzanne R. Best, Daniel S. Weiss, Jeffrey A. Fagan, Akiva Liberman, Cynthia Rogers, Kumar Vedantham, Alain Brunet, Tami L. Lipsey, and Charles R. Marmar, "Critical Incident Exposure and Sleep Quality in Police Officers," *Psychosomatic Medicine* 64, no. 2 (2002): 345–52; Kales et al., "Blood Pressure in Firefighters, Police Officers, and Other Emergency Responders"; Puttonen et al., "Shift Work and Cardiovascular Disease"; Luenda E. Charles, James E. Slaven, Anna Mnatsakanova, Claudia Ma, John M. Violanti, Desta Fekedulegn, Michael E. Andrew, Bryan J. Vila, and Cecil M. Burchfiel, "Association of Perceived Stress with Sleep Duration and Sleep Quality in Police Officers," *International Journal of Emergency Mental Health* 13, no. 4 (2011): 229–41, 229.

[22] Kales et al., "Blood Pressure in Firefighters, Police Officers, and Other Emergency Responders."

[23] Charles et al., "Association of Perceived Stress with Sleep Duration and Sleep Quality in Police Officers."

[24] Hartley et al., "Metabolic Syndrome and Carotid Intima Media Thickness in Urban Police Officers."

[25] Vicki Lindsay, "Police Officers and Their Alcohol Consumption: Should We Be Concerned?" *Police Quarterly* 11, no. 1 (2008): 74–87.

[26] Ballenger et al., "Patterns and Predictors of Alcohol Use in Male and Female Urban Police Officers."

[27] Michelle McNeill, *Alcohol and the Police Workplace-Factors Associated with Excessive Intake (Report Series No. 119.1)* (Payneham, South Australia: National Police Research Unit, 1996); Kim S. Ménard and Michael L. Arter, "Police Officer Alcohol Use and Trauma Symp-

toms: Associations with Critical Incidents, Coping, and Social Stressors," *International Journal of Stress Management* 20, no. 1 (2013): 37–56.

[28] Ménard and Arter, "Police Officer Alcohol Use and Trauma Symptoms."

[29] Jeremy D. Davey, Patricia L. Obst, and Mary C. Sheehan, "It Goes with the Job: Officers' Insights into the Impact of Stress and Culture on Alcohol Consumption within the Policing Occupation," *Drugs: Education, Prevention and Policy* 8, no. 2 (2001): 141–49.

[30] Miroslaw Janczura, Jerzy Dropinski, Andrzej Stanisz, Katarzyna Kotula-Horowitz, R. Rosa, and Teresa Domagala, "Relationship of Stress with Metabolic Syndrome and Coronary Heart Disease in Middle-Aged Police Officers," *Atherosclerosis* 252 (2016): e23; Chuan Li, Jian Cheng Liu, Xianwen Xiao, Xiao Dong Chen, S. Yue, Hui-Min Yu, Feng-shi Tian, and N. J. Tang, "Psychological Distress and Type 2 Diabetes Mellitus: A 4-Year Policemen Cohort Study in China," *British Medical Journal Open* 7, no. 1 (2017): e014235.

[31] Warren D. Franke, Sandra L. Ramey, and Mack C. Shelley, "Relationship between Cardiovascular Disease Morbidity, Risk Factors, and Stress in a Law Enforcement Cohort," *Journal of Occupational and Environmental Medicine* 44, no. 12 (2002): 1182–89; Violanti et al., "Posttraumatic Stress Symptoms and Subclinical Cardiovascular Disease in Police Officers," 541.

[32] Kales et al., "Blood Pressure in Firefighters, Police Officers, and Other Emergency Responders."

[33] Vasileia Varvarigou, Andrea Farioli, Maria Korre, Sho Sato, Issa J. Dahabreh, and Stefanos N. Kales, "Law Enforcement Duties and Sudden Cardiac Death Among Police Officers in United States: Case Distribution Study," *British Medical Journal* 349, g6534 (2014); Zimmerman, "Cardiovascular Disease and Risk Factors in Law Enforcement Personnel."

[34] Zimmerman, "Cardiovascular Disease and Risk Factors in Law Enforcement Personnel."

[35] Anthony D. Lamontagne, Tessa Keegel, Amber M. Louie, Aleck Ostry, and Paul A. Landsbergis, "A Systematic Review of the Job-Stress Intervention Evaluation Literature, 1990–2005," *International Journal of Occupational and Environmental Health* 13, no. 3 (2007): 268–80.

[36] Lamontagne et al., "A Systematic Review of the Job-Stress Intervention Evaluation Literature, 1990–2005."

[37] George T. Patterson, Irene W. Chung, and Philip W. Swan, "Stress Management Interventions for Police Officers and Recruits: A Meta-Analysis," *Journal of Experimental Criminology* 10, no. 4 (2014): 487–513.

[38] Ibid., 492.

[39] Bengt B. Arnetz, Eamonn Arble, Lena Backman, Adam Lynch, and Ake Lublin, "Assessment of a Prevention Program for Work-Related Stress among Urban Police Officers," *International Archives of Occupational and Environmental Health* 86, no. 1 (2013): 79–88, 80.

[40] Arnetz et al., "Assessment of a Prevention Program for Work-Related Stress among Urban Police Officers."

[41] Rollin McCraty and Mike Atkinson, "Resilience Training Program Reduces Physiological and Psychological Stress in Police Officers," *Global Advances in Health and Medicine* 1, no. 5 (2012): 44–66, 49.

[42] McCraty and Atkinson, "Resilience Training Program"; Sandra L. Ramey, Yelena Perkhounkova, Maria Hein, Nicole L. Bohr, and Amanda A. Anderson, "Testing a Resilience Training Program in Police Recruits: A Pilot Study," *Biological Research for Nursing* 19, no. 4 (2017): 440–49.

[43] McCraty and Atkinson, "Resilience Training Program."

[44] Ramey et al., "Testing a Resilience Training Program in Police Recruits."

[45] Kerry S. Kuehl, Diane L. Elliot, Linn Goldberg, David P. MacKinnon, Bryan J. Vila, Jennifer Smith, Milica Miočević, Holly P. O'Rourke, Matthew J. Valente, Carol DeFrancesco, Adriana Sleigh, and Wendy McGinnis, "The Safety and Health Improvement: Enhancing Law Enforcement Departments Study: Feasibility and Findings," *Frontiers in Public Health* 2 (2014): 38.

[46] Kerry S. Kuehl, Diane L. Elliot, David P. MacKinnon, Holly P. O'Rourke, Carol DeFrancesco, Milica Miočević, Matthew Valente, Adriana Sleigh, Bharti Garg, Wendy McGinnis, and Hannah Kuehl, "The SHIELD (Safety & Health Improvement: Enhancing Law Enforcement

Departments) Study: Mixed Methods Longitudinal Findings," *Journal of Occupational and Environmental Medicine* 58, no. 5 (2016): 492–98.

[47] Sigal Sofer, Abraham Eliraz, Sara Kaplan, Hillary Voet, Gershon Fink, Tzadok Kima, and Zecharia Madar, "Greater Weight Loss and Hormonal Changes after 6 Months Diet with Carbohydrates Eaten Mostly at Dinner," *Obesity* 19, no. 10 (2011): 2006–24.

[48] Sofer et al., "Greater Weight Loss and Hormonal Changes," 2007.

[49] Robert G. McMurray, Joanne S. Harrell, and Thomas R. Griggs, "A Comparison of Two Fitness Programs to Reduce the Risk of Coronary Heart Disease in Public Safety Officers," *Journal of Occupational Medicine* 32, no. 7 (1990): 616–20, 616.

[50] Ibid.," 619.

[51] Richard Norris, Douglas Carroll, and Raymond Cochrane, "The Effects of Aerobic and Anaerobic Training on Fitness, Blood Pressure, and Psychological Stress and Well-Being," *Journal of Psychosomatic Research* 34, no. 4 (1990): 367–75.

[52] Norris et al., "The Effects of Aerobic and Anaerobic Training on Fitness, Blood Pressure, and Psychological Stress and Well-Being," 373.

[53] Nancy Norvell and Dale Belles, "Psychological and Physical Benefits of Circuit Weight Training in Law Enforcement Personnel," *Journal of Consulting and Clinical Psychology* 61, no. 3 (1993): 520–27, 525–26.

[54] Margaret A. Short, Stephen DiCarlo, William P. Steffee, and Konstantin Pavlou, "Effects of Physical Conditioning on Self-Concept of Adult Obese Males," *Physical Therapy* 64, no. 2 (1984): 194–98.

[55] Short et al., "Effects of Physical Conditioning on Self-Concept of Adult Obese Males," 198.

[56] Demling and DeSanti, "Effect of a Hypocaloric Diet."

[57] Ibid., p. 26.

[58] Joanne S. Harrell, Lawrence F. Johnston, Thomas R. Griggs, Peggy Schaefer, Edward G. Carr, Jr., Robert G. McMurray, Anne R. Meibohm, Sergio Munoz, Byron N. Raines, and O. Dale Williams, "An Occupation Based Physical Activity Intervention Program," *Workplace Health and Safety* 44, no. 8 (1996): 377–84.

[59] Konstantin N. Pavlou, Suzanna Krey, and William P. Steffee, "Exercise as an Adjunct to Weight Loss and Maintenance in Moderately Obese Subjects," *American Journal of Clinical Nutrition* 49, no. 5 (1983): 1115–23.

[60] Pavlou et al., "Exercise as an Adjunct to Weight Loss and Maintenance in Moderately Obese Subjects," 1115.

[61] Ibid.

[62] Ibid., p. 1122.

[63] Tian Hu, Katherine T. Mills, Lu Yao, Kathryn Demanelis, Mohamed Eloustaz, William S. Yancy, Jr, Tanika N. Kelly, Jiang He, and Lydia A. Bazzano, "Effects of Low-Carbohydrate Diets versus Low-Fat Diets on Metabolic Risk Factors: A Meta-Analysis of Randomized Controlled Clinical Trials," *American Journal of Epidemiology* 176, no. 7 (2014): S44–54; Nadia Mansoor, Kathrine J. Vinknes, Marit B. Veierød, and Kjetil Retterstøl, "Effects of Low-Carbohydrate Diets v. Low-Fat Diets on Body Weight and Cardiovascular Risk Factors: A Meta-Analysis of Randomised Controlled Trials," *British Journal of Nutrition* 115 (2016): 466–79; F.L. Santos, Sofia S. Esteves, Alexandre da Costa Pereira, William S. Yancy, Jr., and Jonas P.L. Nunes, "Systematic Review and Meta-Analysis of Clinical Trials of the Effects of Low Carbohydrate Diets on Cardiovascular Risk Factors," *Obesity Reviews* 13, no. 11 (2012): 1048–66; Deirdre K. Tobias, Mu Chen, JoAnn E. Manson, David S. Ludwig, Walter Willett, and Frank B. Hu, "Effect of Low-Fat vs. Other Diet Interventions on Long-Term Weight Change in Adults: A Systematic Review and Meta-Analysis," *The Lancet Diabetes & Endocrinology* 3, no. 12 (2015): 968–79.

[64] Tobias et al., "Effect of Low-Fat vs. Other Diet Interventions on Long-Term Weight Change in Adults."

[65] Mansoor et al., "Effects of Low-Carbohydrate Diets v. Low-Fat Diets."

[66] Peter M. Clifton, Dominique Condo, and Jennifer B. Keogh, "Long Term Weight Maintenance after Advice to Consume Low Carbohydrate, Higher Protein Diets: A Systematic

Review and Meta-Analysis," *Nutrition, Metabolism, and Cardiovascular Diseases* 24, no. 3 (2014): 224–35.

[67] Nancy Santesso, Elie A. Akl, Marika Bianchi, Andrew Mente, Roxana Mustafa, D. Heels-Ansdell, and Holger J. Schunemann, "Effects of Higher- versus Lower-Protein Diets on Health Outcomes: A Systematic Review and Meta-Analysis," *European Journal of Clinical Nutrition* 66, no. 7 (2012): 780–88.

[68] Thomas P. Wycherley, Lisa J. Moran, Peter M. Clifton, Manny Noakes, and Grant D. Brinkworth, "Effects of Energy-Restricted High-Protein, Low-Fat Compared with Standard-Protein, Low-Fat Diets: A Meta-Analysis of Randomized Controlled Trials," *American Journal of Clinical Nutrition* 96, no. 6 (2012): 1281–98.

[69] Christina-Maria Kastorini, Haralampos J. Milionis, Katherine Esposito, Dario Giugliano, John A. Goudevenos, and Demosthenes B. Panagiotakos, "The Effect of Mediterranean Diet on Metabolic Syndrome and Its Components: A Meta-Analysis of 50 Studies and 534,906 Individuals," *Journal of the American College of Cardiology* 57, no. 11 (2011): 1299–13.

[70] Steven J. Petruzzello, Daniel M. Landers, Brad D. Hatfield, Karla A. Kubitz, and Walter Salazar, "A Meta-Analysis on the Anxiety-Reducing Effects of Acute and Chronic Exercise: Outcomes and Mechanisms," *Sports Medicine* 11, no. 3 (1991): 143–82; Bradley M. Wipfli, Chad D. Rethorst, and Daniel M. Landers, "The Anxiolytic Effects of Exercise: A Meta-Analysis of Randomized Trials and Dose-Response Analysis," *Journal of Sport and Exercise Physiology* 30, no. 4 (2008): 392–10.

[71] Seamus P. Whelton, Ashley Chin, Xue Xin, and Jiang He, "Effect of Aerobic Exercise on Blood Pressure: A Meta-Analysis of Randomized Controlled Trials," *Annals of Internal Medicine* 136, no. 7 (2002): 493–03.

[72] Marcela Haasova, Fiona C. Warren, Michael Ussher, Kate Janse Van Rensburg, Guy Faulkner, Mark Cropley, James Byron-Daniel, Emma S. Everson-Hock, Hwajung Oh, and Adrian H. Taylor, "The Acute Effects of Physical Activity on Cigarette Cravings: Systematic Review and Meta-Analysis with Individual Participant Data," *Addiction* 108, no. 1 (2012): 26–37.

[73] Lynette L. Craft and Daniel M. Landers, "The Effect of Exercise on Clinical Depression and Depression Resulting from Mental Illness: A Meta-Analysis," *Journal of Sport and Exercise Psychology* 20, no. 4 (1998): 339–57.

[74] Giselle S. Passos, Dalva Poyares, Marcos G. Santana, Silvério A. Garbuio, Sergio Tufik, and Marco Túlio Mello, "Effect of Acute Physical Exercise on Patients with Primary Insomnia," *Journal of Clinical Sleep Medicine* 6, no. 3 (2010): 270–75.

[75] Candice L. Hogan, Jutta Mata, and Laura L. Carstensen, "Exercise Holds Immediate Benefits for Affect and Cognition in Younger and Older Adults," *Psychology and Aging* 28, no. 2 (2013): 587–94.

[76] Xiaochen Lin, Xi Zhang, Jianjun Guo, Christian K. Roberts, Steve McKenzie, Wen-Chih Wu, Simin Liu, and Yiqing Song, "Effects of Exercise Training on Cardiorespiratory Fitness and Biomarkers of Cardiometabolic Health: A Systematic Review and Meta-Analysis of Randomized Controlled Trials," *Journal of the American Heart Association* 4, no. 7 (2015): e002014; Charlotte Jelleyman, Thomas Yates, Gary O'Donovan, Laura J. Gray, James A. King, Kamiesh Khunti, and Melanie J. Davies, "The Effects of High-Intensity Interval Training on Glucose Regulation and Insulin Resistance: A Meta-Analysis," *Obesity Reviews* 16, no. 11 (2015): 942–61.

[77] Yu-Kai Chang, Jeff D. Labban, Jennifer I. Gapin, and Jennifer Etnier, "The Effects of Acute Exercise on Cognitive Performance: A Meta-Analysis," *Brain Research*, 1453 (2012): 87–101.

[78] Marc Roig, Sasja Nordbrandt, Svend Sparre Geertsen, and Jens Bo Nielsen, "The Effects of Cardiovascular Exercise on Human Memory: A Review with Meta-Analysis," *Neuroscience & Biobehavioral Reviews* 37, no. 8 (2013): 1645–66.

[79] Harsh Patel, Hassan Alkhawam, Raef Madanieh, Niel Shah, Constantine E. Kosmos, and Timothy J. Vittorio, "Aerobic vs Anaerobic Exercise Training Effects on the Cardiovascular System," *World Journal of Cardiology* 9, no. 2 (2017): 134–38, 136.

[80] Romeo B. Batacan, Mitch J. Duncan, Vincent J. Dalbo, Patrick S. Tucker, and Andrew S. Fenning, "Effects of High-Intensity Interval Training on Cardiometabolic Health: A Systematic Review and Meta-Analysis of Intervention Studies," *British Journal of Sports Medicine* 51 (2017): 494–03.

[81] Florie Maillard, Bruno Pereira, and Nathalie Boisseau, "Effect of High-Intensity Interval Training on Total, Abdominal, and Visceral Fat Mass: A Meta-Analysis," *Sports Medicine* 48, no. 2 (2018): 269–88.

[82] Kassia S. Weston, Ulrik Wisloff, and Jeff S. Coombes, "High-Intensity Interval Training in Patients with Lifestyle-Induced Cardiometabolic Disease: A Systematic Review and Meta-Analysis," *British Journal of Sports Medicine* 48, no. 16 (2014): 1227–34.

[83] Nele Pattyn, Ellen Coeckelberghs, Roselien Buys, Véronique A. Cornelissen, and Luc Vanhees, "Aerobic Interval Training vs. Moderate Continuous Training in Coronary Artery Disease Patients: A Systematic Review and Meta-Analysis," *Sports Medicine*, 44, no. 5 (2014): 687–00.

[84] Aimee Grace, Erick Chan, Francesco Giallauria, Petra L. Graham, and Neil A. Smart, "Clinical Outcomes and Glycaemic Responses to Different Aerobic Exercise Training Intensities in Type II Diabetes: A Systematic Review and Meta-Analysis," *Cardiovascular Diabetology* 16, no. 1 (2017): 37.

[85] Jerome N. Rachele, Kristiann C. Heesch, and Tracy L. Washington, "Wellness Programs at Firefighter and Police Officer Workplaces: A Systematic Review," *Health Behavior and Policy Review* 1, no. 4 (2014): 302–13, 302.

[86] Alexander Wolkow, Kevin Netto, and Brad Aisbett, "The Effectiveness of Health Interventions in Cardiovascular Risk Reduction among Emergency Service Personnel," *International Archives of Occupational and Environmental Health* 86 (2013): 245–60.

11

Response Essay

Chief Steven Pitts (Ret.)
Reno Police Department

The Reno Police Department (RPD) has developed a wellness initiative that applies a comprehensive systems approach to education about, prevention of, and intervention in the many risk factors affecting RPD personnel. That work, in my view, translates well to law enforcement personnel in general. The RPD program focuses on creating an organizational culture around the concept of developing individual resiliency in personnel. The RPD program has been shown to be effective not only in improving the quality of life for its law enforcement personnel but also in generating a return on investment for law enforcement executives and local government.

Chapter 11 clearly points out the various consequences of not addressing these officer health, safety, and wellness issues in policing. Unfortunately, the real issues associated with these factors have, in most cases, fallen on deaf ears. Leadership in policing can and should work to better educate the public and local governments on how these risks affect police officers, law enforcement organizations, and the overall community. Equally importantly, the further observations and suggestions in the chapter point to a much larger challenge than simply wellness. Poor decision-making regarding these issues can lead to strategic impacts on policing as a profession.

Evidence from recent research and other sources clearly frames the pressures of a career in law enforcement, which place officers at a higher risk for cardiovascular disease, high blood pressure, diabetes, insomnia, increased levels of destructive stress hormones, post-traumatic stress disorder (PTSD), certain cancers, and, unfortunately, suicide. According to the Centers for Disease Control and Prevention's most recent vital statistics report, the average life expectancy at birth for a male is 76.1; for a female, it's 81.1 years.[1] But research conducted by Dr. John Violanti and his colleagues at the University of Buffalo has shown that the average life expectancy of a police officer is estimated to be only 66 years.[2]

Statistics like these motivated us to launch a partnership between the RPD and SpecialtyHealth, a nationally recognized health and wellness company; Robb Wolf, nationally known for his work surrounding nutrition and Paleolithic and low-carbohydrate diets; and several nationally recognized medical experts. Together, we sought to develop a wellness initiative that would address the many risk factors affecting RPD personnel. In the course of that work, we've added partnerships with Dr. Kirk Parsley on sleep disorders and processes for mitigating those disorders, Dr. Kevin Gilmartin on emotional survival, and Dr. Eric Potterat on developing healthy mental preparedness practices to aid in the management of stress, both at work and at home. The results from the RPD program have been impressive, to say the least.

I found chapter 11 to be right on target in accurately capturing the risk factors endangering law enforcement personnel. These risk factors aren't just personally costly in the quality of life for those serving and their families; they are also very costly in terms of officer health care and medical retirement costs.

At the RPD, we have seen these costs—and we have seen the savings available when officer health is improved. As early as the fall of 2008, we ran a study in which officers voluntarily participated in four to six months of evaluation and health intervention. The participating officers were selected after a review of their annual physical exams. Fifteen police officers participated in the RPD program, nine of whom were initially described as "high risk." When the officers were reevaluated following a three-month analysis and intervention, we learned that the nine high-risk officers had reduced their risk factors significantly through exercise, nutrition, and pharmacology. We estimated that this improvement, by reducing the probability of medical retirements related to heart, diabetes, and lung issues, saved the State of Nevada approximately $10.8 million, for a twenty-fold return on investment.

The program in Reno has matured significantly since 2008. It now involves the Reno Fire Department, other local public safety employees, and law enforcement agencies in Kentucky, California, and Hawaii. So far, the program has improved the lives of approximately 100 City of Reno personnel. We have also designed several new components, including advanced lipid and diabetes testing, nutrition interventions, exercise training, mental preparedness education, and treatment of sleep disorders.

Early iterations of the program followed standard American Dietetic Association guidelines that endorsed a high-carbohydrate, low-fat, and grain-based diet. Advanced testing exposed the weakness of this dietary approach, as it failed to improve blood lipid parameters and frequently worsened insulin resistance scores while elevating triglycerides and decreasing HDL cholesterol. In recent years, we have employed a Paleo/low-carb dietary intervention that has consistently improved markers of systemic inflammation, insulin resistance, and body composition. Although controversial in dietetic circles, randomized controlled trials—the gold standard of medical science—have shown a Paleo/low-carb approach to be superior in improving the health characteristics that we find most important in preventing morbidity and mortality.

When it comes to exercise, the physical demands placed on the public safety athlete can be quite variable. Exercise physiology analysis clearly illustrates that police work is anaerobic (with a power output in excess of VO_2 max) and more akin to the needs of a wrestler or football player than a marathon runner. As such, we have found significant benefit in taking a strength and conditioning approach that develops the attributes of strength and power via the conjugate periodization method. This method allows for the development of several attributes over the course of a few weeks (a mesocycle), allowing for customization based on recovery, orthopedic issues, arrest and control training, and the like. The main training attributes for officer physical fitness include functional mobility, maximum strength, rate of force production, and metabolic conditioning.

The RPD program has also implemented a component focusing on "emotional survival," a term coined by Dr. Kevin Gilmartin.[3] Dr. Gilmartin clearly pointed out that as a police officer's job takes on more and more of that officer's time and energy, it becomes not just a job but rather the central theme and defining role in their lives. Anyone who has a family member, friend, or colleague in policing has likely observed and even commented on how the job has changed that person's life and perspective.

The changes and risks observed in officers' lives are all too often associated with the inherent safety risks of policing. However, the longer-term impacts to officers' emotional and physical well-being are not being mitigated. The costs associated with this journey manifest in many ways, including substance abuse, dissatisfaction with the organization and life in general, deterioration of physical fitness and overall wellness, and the destruction of marriages and families, among other impacts. Further research by Heyman and colleagues has shown a national annual rate of 17 suicides for every 100,000 police officers.[4]

To mitigate those risks, the Reno program now includes a variety of wellness resources, including a quarterly wellness newsletter, a certification program for physical fitness specialists who are available to help officers, and a social media campaign to share education and to network with national experts. We have also developed a community connection component that works with local businesses to promote wellness within the culture of the RPD and have established annual wellness clinics for officers and immediate psychological interventions for personnel involved in traumatic incidents on the job.

Chapter 11's final recommendations clearly point out the need for collaborations like the Reno program. I agree that we must collect scientific data that will provide a better case for analysis and guide us on the road forward. But I am mindful that those endeavors can take years, even decades. As leaders in policing, we should not wait to embrace the local resources in our communities and begin to build programs that address these risks.

NOTES

1 Kenneth D. Kochanek, Sherry L. Murphy, Jiaquan Xu, and Elizabeth Arias, "Deaths: Final Data for 2017," *National Vital Statistics Report* 68, no. 9 (2019): 1-76.

2 John M. Violanti, Tara A. Hartley, Ja K. Gu, Desta Fekedulegn, Michael E. Andrew, and Cecil M. Burchfiel, "Life Expectancy in Police Officers: A Comparison with the U.S. General Population," *International Journal of Emergency Mental Health* 15, no. 4 (2013): 217–228.

3 Kevin Gilmartin, *Emotional Survival for Law Enforcement* (Tucson, AZ: E-S Press, 2002).

4 Miriam Heyman, Jeff Dill, and Robert Douglas, *The Ruderman White Paper on Mental Health and Suicide of First Responders* (Boston, MA: Ruderman Family Foundation, 2018).

12

Improve the Policing of Crowds

Edward R. Maguire
Natasha Khade
Victor Mora
Arizona State University

Background

On August 22, 2017, President Donald Trump spoke at a campaign-style rally in Phoenix, Arizona. Outside the event, Trump supporters and opponents engaged in spirited but mostly peaceful expression. Shortly after nightfall, the mood began to shift, as anarchists and protesters associated with Antifa donned masks. While thousands of protesters engaged in peaceful democratic expression, a few protesters started to throw items at police officers standing in front of the building where Trump was speaking. Police quickly changed into riot gear and formed a skirmish line. Suddenly, without warning, the police began deploying chemical munitions and firing "less lethal" projectiles at the crowd. People fled rapidly, and the protest ended abruptly. The crowd contained many vulnerable people, including children, the elderly, and people in wheelchairs. One of the attendees we interviewed later recalled that his first action after hearing a flashbang grenade and seeing tear gas deployed was to help a woman in a wheelchair escape the area safely. Numerous people were injured by the projectiles that police fired into the crowd, and hundreds (if not thousands) of people were exposed to tear gas and/or pepper spray. The vast majority of these people had not broken any law and had not been warned to disperse. Yet, the next day, Phoenix police chief Jeri Williams told a local reporter, "I absolutely give my folks an A+."[1]

The way the Phoenix police mishandled the event was not a surprise. Less than two weeks earlier, police in Charlottesville, Virginia, had underresponded in dramatic fashion to a "Unite the Right" rally at the University of Virginia led by white nationalists. Police stood by and failed to intervene as white nationalist protesters attacked counterprotesters. A thirty-two-year-old counterprotester was killed, and nineteen other people were injured when a suspected white nationalist plowed into a crowd with his car. Two Virginia state troopers were killed when their helicopter crashed while monitoring the event. An independent after-action review concluded that police had "devised a flawed Operational Plan for the Unite the Right rally" and that, as a result, they "protected neither free expression nor public safety."[2] Shortly after the events in Charlottesville, the first author of this chapter told Vice News, "No police department in the country is going to want to be accused of an underresponse."[3] Fear of underresponding may have influenced decisions by police leaders in Phoenix about how to handle the Trump rally that took place only ten days after the Charlottesville protests. As illustrated by events in Phoenix and Charlottesville, striking the right balance between underresponding and overresponding to protests can be challenging for many police leaders.

■ Police Approaches to Protests

The history of protest policing in the United States is nonlinear. During the Civil Rights movement of the 1960s and early 1970s, police relied on an approach to protests that social movement scholars refer to as the *escalated force* model. Under this approach, police ignored or disregarded the First Amendment rights of protesters, exhibited little tolerance for community disruption, communicated only minimally with protesters, and relied heavily on arrests and the use of force—often in violation of the law—as the principal tools for controlling protests. The underlying logic of this approach was that protests needed to be shut down and that police must continue to escalate their level of force until protesters complied with police requests to discontinue the protest.[4] Some of the most iconic images of the Civil Rights era depict the escalated force model in action, including the use of fire hoses and police dogs against protesters in Birmingham, Alabama, in 1963; the brutal assault of peaceful civil rights activists trying to cross the Edmund Pettus Bridge in Selma, Alabama, in 1965; and police officers beating citizens at the 1968 Democratic National Convention in Chicago.

In the 1980s and 1990s, many police agencies in the United States began to embrace a *negotiated management* approach for handling protests. Under this approach, "police negotiate with demonstrators before the demonstration so that demonstrators can exercise their First Amendment rights with minimal conflict with police."[5] A negotiated management style involves greater respect for First Amendment rights, higher tolerance for community disruption, ongoing communication between police and protesters, and less reliance on arrests and the use of force. According to social movement scholars, the negotiated management model reduced the frequency and intensity of conflict between police and protesters.[6] This approach encouraged ongoing communication between police and protesters to avoid miscommunication and to reduce the likelihood of misunderstandings about each side's expectations and intentions. Moreover, it gave a human face to both police and protesters, thereby helping to avoid harmful stereotypes that might precipitate conflict.

Unfortunately, the negotiated management approach began to fall out of favor among many U.S. police agencies in the late 1990s (while some others continued to embrace it). This shift occurred in part due to clashes between police and protesters at the 1999 World Trade Organization protest in Seattle—an episode that later became known as the "Battle in Seattle." This shift was also influenced by the 9/11 terrorist attacks, after which the nation became much more attuned to the possibility of terrorist incidents occurring on American soil. Many police agencies began to adopt significantly more aggressive and invasive approaches to protest policing that threaten the constitutional rights, and indeed the safety, of law-abiding protesters engaged in peaceful democratic expression. These newer approaches have been given several names by scholars, including the *strategic incapacitation model*, the *command and control model*, and the *Miami model*.[7] To some extent, these newer approaches resemble the escalated force model of the 1960s and 1970s. They rely heavily on arrest and the use of force as the primary tools for controlling protests. However, in certain ways, they may be even more threatening to protesters—both to their civil liberties and physical safety—than the abusive protest-policing practices that occurred in the Civil Rights era.

The strategic incapacitation model[8] is characterized by "a sense of disrespect for the exercise of First Amendment rights, an intolerance for community disruption, and unwillingness to communicate or negotiate with protesters, the use of arrests and force as primary methods for controlling protests, intensified efforts to control access to space, surveillance of protesters, and greater information sharing between law enforcement agencies."[9] Other observers divide these newer protest-policing approaches into two different categories. The first is the command and control model,[10] which emphasizes the need to micromanage all aspects of protest events, "including the use of very restrictive permitting processes [and] intense efforts to control public space through the use of barricades, police lines, and other mechanisms to surround, subdivide, and direct the flow of protesters."[11] In addition, this approach emphasizes "a willingness to use force against even minor violations of the law."[12] The command and control model is sometimes referred to as the *soft hat* model in contrast to the *hard hat* Miami model that we examine next.

The Miami model takes its name from the way that police responded to the 2003 Free Trade Area of the Americas protests in Miami. Approximately 2,500 police officers from dozens of agencies were deployed in riot gear. In an attempt to secure downtown Miami against protesters, police behaved forcefully and in a manner that one circuit court judge referred to as "a disgrace for the community."[13] An investigative panel convened after the event concluded that the Miami Police Department "was not adequately prepared to handle the intermingling of peaceful demonstrators with violent protesters."[14] The panel recommended that police receive training on the protection of First Amendment rights. Officers should be facilitators of First Amendment rights, taking enforcement action only when there is a violation of the law. The panel also encouraged dialogue between law enforcement and organizations concerned with the preservation of First Amendment rights.

In recent years, numerous police agencies across the nation have demonstrated a firm and unfortunate commitment to these newer, more aggressive, and more invasive methods for policing protests. During the Occupy movement in 2011 and 2012, many police agencies overresponded, violating people's civil rights, injuring protesters and innocent bystanders, and incurring costly civil settlements.[15] The Oakland Police Department, for instance, fired a "less lethal" beanbag round at Occupy Oakland protesters, striking Iraq war veteran Scott Olsen in the head, breaking his skull and causing permanent brain damage. He filed a federal civil rights lawsuit against the city that was settled for $4.5 million.[16] Numerous other jurisdictions also ended up paying costly civil rights settlements as a result of police use of excessive force in handling Occupy protesters.

Police handling of protests made national and international headlines once again after the shooting of an eighteen-year-old African American man named Michael Brown by a Ferguson, Missouri, police officer in August 2014. The officer was cleared of wrongdoing in both state and federal investigations, but the shooting ignited long-standing tensions between the police and the African American community and resulted in widespread protests throughout the St. Louis metropolitan area. More than fifty area police agencies responded in a manner that one observer characterized as "a mishmash of tactics and confusion."[17] Police in the area were heavily criticized for responding in a militaristic and overly forceful manner.[18] A federal judge issued a temporary restraining order against three of the police agencies, noting that they had not done a good job of distinguishing between those who were violating the law and those who were protesting peacefully. Her ruling stated that "people involved in peaceful, nonviolent political speech can do that without being lumped in with the criminals."[19] The Ferguson protests spread throughout the nation, stimulating what some have called a new civil rights movement in the

United States.[20] Today, protests continue to occur regularly across the nation in response to a variety of social and political issues. The ongoing challenge for police is learning how to ensure public safety at these events while simultaneously safeguarding people's constitutional rights and preserving police legitimacy.

It is an unfortunate reality that when police do a good job of balancing these various considerations, protests take place without incident and do not become newsworthy. Typically, the police response to protests only generates media attention when it goes wrong. Research carried out just after the Occupy movement revealed numerous instances of police behaving in a balanced, temperate manner, often under challenging circumstances. For instance, a deputy chief in Salt Lake City reported that when Occupy protesters began camping out illegally in a public park, he arranged to issue them a "conditional use" permit to allow them to camp there. He visited with protesters daily and asked them what kinds of help they needed. He would often buy them a cup of coffee while sitting and talking with them. Both he and the protesters agreed that these gestures significantly reduced the likelihood of conflict.[21] A superintendent in the Boston Police Department gave protesters his mobile phone number and visited their encampment every morning to keep the lines of communication open and to avoid conflict. Ed Davis, who served as Boston's police commissioner at the time, viewed the Occupy protests as an opportunity to continue the department's ongoing commitment to community policing. These are just two examples of communities in which thoughtful police and government officials adopted sensible strategies for handling protests. Regardless of whether these police leaders knew it, they were behaving consistently with the accumulating research evidence on protest policing.

■ Research Evidence

In this section, we review two bodies of research with direct implications for policing protests and other crowd-related events. The first is based on the study of crowd psychology and, in particular, on how crowds react to external regulation by the police and other security forces. The second is based on the notion of procedural justice and its influences on the relationships between police and those who are subject to their authority. Both bodies of research provide useful insights for thinking about policing protests in a manner that preserves public safety and police legitimacy while minimizing conflict, collateral damage, and unintended consequences.

Crowd Psychology

Historically, one of the most influential works in crowd psychology was an 1896 book entitled *The Crowd: A Study of the Popular Mind* by French scholar Gustave Le Bon. The book characterized crowds as unruly, unreasonable, and dangerous.[22] It put forth a theory that people within a crowd lose themselves and become easily swayed by influential crowd members. Le Bon wrote that when a man becomes part of a crowd, he "descends several rungs in the ladder of civilization" and becomes more capable of behaving violently; moreover, in this context, he can easily be convinced "to commit acts contrary to his most obvious interests and his best-known habits. An individual in a crowd is a grain of sand amid other grains of sand, which the wind stirs up at will."[23] At the heart of Le Bon's theory is a social contagion effect in which violent and destructive behavior spreads quickly and easily through a crowd. This pessimistic view of crowds dominated social psychology for nearly a century. It also formed the implicit basis for the development of harsh police responses to crowds. The problem is that this view is not only inaccurate, but it is also described by modern crowd psychologists as "dangerously wrong."[24]

Crowd psychologists now embrace a theory of crowd behavior that is premised on the importance of social identities. People's social identities are formed based on their understanding of "how they are positioned relative to others."[25] People can have many social identities, some of which are more permanent than others. For instance, a person can be a police officer, a Christian, a mother, and a Republican, all of which are relatively entrenched social identities. But certain events or situations—such as concerts, sporting events, reunions, or protests—may inspire more fleeting social identities. These ideas all play a central role in the elaborated social identity model (ESIM), which asserts that people may experience temporary shifts in their social identity based on the context in which they are situated.[26] ESIM is useful for thinking about crowd behavior and the factors that influence that behavior.

The ESIM emerged from observations of crowd behavior, particularly crowd conflict, by social psychologist Stephen Reicher and his colleagues. They attended various types of crowd-creating events, including protests, riots, and sporting events.[27] Reicher and his colleagues observed a consistent pattern in events that ended in violence between police and crowds. The events attracted heterogeneous crowds consisting primarily of moderates and only a handful of people with more extreme or radical orientations. However, the police treated the crowds as homogeneous and took uniform enforcement action against entire crowds rather than only those participants who were engaging in criminal or serious disorderly behavior. The moderates and the radicals were treated as equally dangerous by the police and were handled in the same manner. The behavior of the police antagonized the moderates in the crowd, who then began to side with the more radical crowd members in challenging the police.

The ESIM perspective views crowd events as intergroup encounters in which the police and other security forces can powerfully influence the crowd members' social identities.[28] Moderate crowd members may ordinarily be inclined to follow rules and laws, to respect and trust the police, and to reject the influence of those with more radical orientations who may behave in a violent, destructive, or disorderly manner. But when the police violate that trust by taking enforcement action against moderates and radicals alike, the social identities of the moderates shift toward supporting the radicals in challenging or opposing the police.

Three concepts are central to understanding the ESIM perspective.[29] The first is the idea of social context. Neither the police nor crowds exist in a vacuum. They come together in an intergroup context in which the actions of one group influence the actions of the others. When someone in a crowd throws a bottle at police, the police react. When police don riot gear or make an arrest, the crowd reacts. Understanding the social context within which the police and crowds act and react is central to thinking about how to police these events. Second is the notion of social identity. People's social identities are dynamic and can be heavily influenced by the context in which people find themselves.[30] When there is conflict between crowds and the police, how police behave can have a powerful effect on the momentary social identities of people in the crowd. Third is the relationship between identity, intention, and consequence. Regardless of a group's intentions, its actions can be interpreted differently by the other group, which may react to these actions in unanticipated ways. So, for instance, police may have good reasons to don riot gear and form a skirmish line, but regardless of whether their intentions are noble, people in a crowd are likely to perceive this approach as threatening. In these highly dynamic contexts, intentions are not always accurately recognized, which can sometimes generate unintended consequences.[31]

The ESIM perspective offers a useful framework for explaining how conflict escalates between police and protesters.[32] An asymmetry in how each side views its own actions and those of the other sets the stage for conflict. Protesters, for example, may view sitting on the road as a legitimate means of protesting, while the police may conceive of this action as threatening to public order and public safety. Conversely, police may view arrests or certain types of force in such instances as reasonable and appropriate, but the protesters may view those actions as a form of unprovoked aggression. There is also an asymmetry in power relations such that one group is able to impose its definition of legitimate action on the other. The police have the authority to impose their definitions of appropriate behavior on crowds, and they have the resources to back up their authority, even in the face of resistance. In such a context, when one group (the crowd) views the actions of the other (the police) as unilateral and illegitimate, the members of crowd may unite around a common sense of outrage and resistance against the police. This creates a common group identity in which the moderates in the crowd side with the radicals against the police.

Although researchers have observed the intergroup dynamics specified in the ESIM model in numerous types of crowd events, only one study, to our knowledge, has tested the effects of altering police practices based on

ESIM principles. The study took place during the 2004 UEFA Football European Championships in Portugal.[33] One of Portugal's two main police forces, the *Polícia de Segurança Pública* (PSP), relied on ESIM principles to develop a model of dynamic risk assessment and graded tactical intervention to reduce the likelihood of violence during the football tournament.[34] The ESIM-inspired policing model was implemented during the tournament in all the major cities of Portugal.

The strategy emphasized maintaining the perception of police legitimacy among fans. The belief was that if fans viewed the police as legitimate, the fans would self-police and enforce the maintenance of nonviolent norms within the crowd.[35] The PSP refrained from using more traditional crowd control tactics and instead worked to ensure that fans enjoyed themselves at the tournament and that police engaged in friendly and prosocial dialogue with fans.[36] Officers would often work in pairs or small groups and wear regular police uniforms. Instead of confronting fans, these officers would patrol areas where crowds were congregated and interact in a sociable manner with fans. These interactions served several purposes. They facilitated legitimate behavior, but officers were also able to monitor and gather intelligence on potential threats to public order posed by groups or individuals. Simultaneously, small teams of plainclothes officers would also be within crowds monitoring for and intervening in hostile situations likely to escalate. These tactics allowed officers to identify emerging tensions and then react swiftly and proportionately to the emergent risk. If a larger-scale problem emerged, the PSP would move to a level-two formation that involved more police in standard uniforms who would communicate with the fans and negotiate possible solutions to problems. These groups could, if necessary, escalate to a level-three formation by putting on protective equipment carried with them on their belts. Paramilitary riot police were available, but they were deliberately kept largely out of sight. The data suggest that the visibility of the paramilitary riot police was virtually zero throughout the tournament. Also, the PSP did not record an instance where they were required to draw batons for the entire tournament. Only one English fan was arrested for a violence-related offense despite the presence of approximately 150,000 fans from England attending the tournament.

Police were able to avoid the usage of indiscriminate interventions against large crowds by utilizing ESIM-inspired strategies and tactics. This resulted in widespread fan perception of police legitimacy and improved the ability of police to identify and differentiate between those within the crowd who were and were not posing a public order risk. In this context of perceived police legitimacy, the fans began to self-police by undermining individuals trying to start trouble and by cooperating with police to prevent troublemakers from gaining a foothold. Most important, however, was the almost total absence of disorder in match cities.[37]

Procedural Justice

Procedural justice refers to how authority figures treat people who are subject to their authority. It can apply to any relationship with differential levels of authority: parents and children, teachers and students, employers and employees, and police and citizens. A lengthy body of research has found that when authority figures treat subordinates in a fair and respectful manner, subordinates are more likely to view the authority figure as legitimate and to comply with his or her wishes.[38] On the other hand, those who view an authority figure as behaving in a procedurally unjust manner are more likely to defy or rebel against his or her wishes.[39] This general body of research and theory, which emerges from social psychology, has strongly influenced the study of police interactions with the public. The research shows that when police officers treat people fairly, people are not only more willing to cooperate and comply with officers, but they are also more likely to view the law and its agents as legitimate and worthy of compliance. When police treat people unfairly, people are less likely to comply with their requests and less likely to obey the law. The implications are clear. Police serve as the visible face of the law, and they must conduct themselves accordingly or risk undermining their own moral authority as well as the authority of the law and of the legal system more generally.

Several recent studies have applied procedural justice theory to the study of protest policing. Based upon a survey of Occupy protesters in Washington, D.C., researchers found that when respondents viewed the police as treating protesters in a procedurally unjust manner, they were significantly more likely to endorse the use of violence against police.[40] In New York City, where police behaved in a significantly more abusive manner toward protesters, a general measure of procedural justice that tapped into perceived police fairness, respect, and civility did not influence protesters' support for using violence against police. Instead, the key predictor of support for the use of violence against police was the extent to which protesters had experienced or observed unjust uses of force by police.[41] Moreover, observing unjust uses of force by police influenced not only protesters' *attitudes* but also their *behaviors*. Protesters who experienced or observed police using force unjustly against protesters were also more likely to report that they had physically resisted or used violence against the police.[42] Taken together, this research suggests that protesters are more likely to support the use of violence or behave violently when police use repressive tactics.[43]

■ Solutions

The two bodies of research that we have just reviewed both have key implications for policing protests. The research evidence suggests that police can reduce violence and improve both public safety and officer safety by handling protests in a manner that takes public perceptions of police seriously. When protesters perceive that police are treating them unfairly, even those who are ordinarily peaceful and law-abiding are much more likely to be defiant and to view resistance against police as reasonable. When police are perceived to behave unlawfully by violating the constitutional rights of protesters, the police undermine their own legitimacy, and therefore people are less likely to defer to police authority. Accordingly, unlawful and unnecessarily provocative behavior by the police escalates resistance and violence instead of preventing it. Based on these principles, we recommend a strategic framework for protest policing that builds on a model developed by social psychologists who study crowd behavior. That model has four components: education, facilitation, communication, and differentiation.[44]

Education refers to the need for police to educate themselves about the composition of the crowd that is expected to attend a protest. The goal is to become familiar with the nature, aims, and social identities of all groups. This goes further than gathering typical criminal intelligence in the sense that police should become familiar with those who have prosocial and those who have antisocial tendencies. Those with prosocial tendencies can serve as allies or "force multipliers" by helping to keep people calm and to prevent the onset of violence. The key is to ensure that police have the information they need about protest events and their participants as early as possible to allow for appropriate planning and preparation.

Facilitation refers to the need for police to help facilitate the constitutional rights of those who wish to engage in peaceful First Amendment expression. A key part of winning over a crowd is establishing the perception that the police are not just there to exert control over protesters but rather to *help* them engage in constitutionally protected behavior. This approach alters the psychological dynamic between police and protesters and reduces the likelihood of conflict. The idea is for police to redefine their role, and consequently their strategies and tactics, around the idea of serving as guardians to ensure public order and public safety and to safeguard the constitutional rights of those seeking to exercise those rights.[45]

Communication refers to the importance of establishing lines of communication between police and protesters before, during, and after protest events. These open lines of communication can serve as a vital de-escalation tool that enhances both public safety and officer safety. Some protest movements are described as leaderless, which can make it more challenging to establish lines of communication, but even in such movements, it is common for informal leaders or organizers to emerge. Establishing partnerships with these organizers is vital for minimizing conflict and preserving public safety. Communication problems also arise between police and their public safety partners, particularly during mutual-aid scenarios in which other law enforcement agencies are called in (or show up) to assist with mass demonstrations. After-action reviews from the 2014 Ferguson protests and the 2017 Charlottesville protests both highlighted significant communication breakdowns between police from different agencies.[46]

Differentiation refers to the need for police not to treat entire crowds as homogeneous. Protest crowds contain a mix of people, most of whom are typically peaceful and law-abiding, and some of whom may embrace violence or other forms of unlawful behavior. When a handful of people begin to behave unlawfully, the most common mistake that police make is to overreact by shutting down the protest. Even worse, some agencies immediately commence the use of riot control methods like "kettling" the crowd (detaining protesters within police cordons, often without access to food, water, or bathrooms), forming skirmish lines, making mass arrests, and using indiscriminate force against the crowd in the form of chemical agents and less lethal munitions. Instead, when the number of lawbreakers is small relative to the overall size of the crowd, the police must adopt a differentiated response, arresting the lawbreakers and allowing those who are behaving peacefully to continue doing so. This may involve the use of extraction teams who make targeted arrests of people who are violent or who are engaging in other forms of unlawful behavior. This was the approach that the Chicago police used during the mass demonstrations around the 2012 NATO Summit.

■ Next Steps

Protests are extraordinarily difficult events that challenge even the most progressive police leaders. Some agencies do an exceptional job of handing these events. Some underrespond, allowing protesters and counterprotesters to clash while police adopt an overly passive mentality. Others overrespond, adopting an overly aggressive mentality that is reminiscent of the approaches used fifty years ago during the Civil Rights movement. As a result of these overresponses, jurisdictions routinely end up settling federal civil rights lawsuits and compensating protesters (or innocent bystanders) whose rights were violated by the police. Several of these settlements have been in excess of $10 million.

There is significant room for improvement in how police handle protests. The research evidence that we reviewed in this chapter, as well as the framework that we just outlined, provide some useful ideas for reflecting on how an agency might improve its preparation for such events.

Notes

1 KTAR.com, "Phoenix Police Chief Gives Officers A+ for Conduct during Trump Rally Protest," *KTAR News*, August 23, 2017, http://ktar.com/story/1703705/phoenix-police-chief-gives-officers-a-for-conduct-during-trump-rally-protest/.

2 Hunton and Williams, *Independent Review of the 2017 Protest Events in Charlottesville* (Richmond, VA: Author, December 1, 2017, 5, 7.

[3] Sonja Sharp, "What Cops Should Do When Neo-Nazis Come to Town," *Vice.com*, August 16, 2017, https://www.vice.com/en_us/article/ywwp5v/what-cops-should-do-when-neo-nazis-come-to-town.

[4] Clark McPhail, David Schweingruber, and John McCarthy, "Policing Protests in the United States: 1990–1995," in *Policing Protest: The Control of Mass Demonstrations in Western Democracies*, eds. Donatella della Porta and Herbert Reiter (Minneapolis, MN: University of Minnesota Press, 1998), 49–69.

[5] Ibid., 51.

[6] Donatella della Porta and Herbert Reiter, eds., *Policing Protest: The Control of Mass Demonstrations in Western Democracies* (Minneapolis, MN: University of Minnesota Press, 1998); McPhail et al., "Policing Protests in the United States," 49–69.

[7] Patrick F. Gillham, Bob Edwards, and John A. Noakes, "Strategic Incapacitation and the Policing of the Occupy Wall Street Protests," *Policing and Society: An International Journal of Research and Policy* 23, no. 1 (2013): 81–102; Alex Vitale, "The Command and Control and Miami Models at the 2004 Republican National Convention: New Forms of Policing Protests," *Mobilization* 12, no 4 (2007): 403–415.

[8] Gillham et al., "Strategic Incapacitation and the Policing of the Occupy Wall Street Protests."

[9] Edward R. Maguire, "New Directions in Protest Policing," *Saint Louis University Public Law Review* 35, no. 1 (2015): 67–108, 83.

[10] Alex Vitale, "From Negotiated Management to Command and Control: How the New York Police Department Polices Protests," *Policing and Society* 15, no. 3 (2005): 283–304; Vitale, "The Command and Control and Miami Models at the 2004 Republican National Convention."

[11] Maguire, "New Directions in Protest Policing," 83.

[12] Vitale, "The Command and Control and Miami Models at the 2004 Republican National Convention," 405.

[13] Maguire, "New Directions in Protest Policing," 84.

[14] Ibid.

[15] Gillham et al., "Strategic Incapacitation and the Policing of the Occupy Wall Street Protests"; Edward R. Maguire and Megan Oakley, *Policing Protests: Lessons from the Occupy Movement and Beyond* (New York: Harry Frank Guggenheim Foundation, 2020); Traci Yoder, "A Tale of Two (Occupied) Cities: Policing Strategies at Occupy Wall Street and Occupy Philadelphia," *University of Pennsylvania Journal of Law and Social Change* 15, no. 4 (2012): 593–615.

[16] Lisa Fernandez, "Iraq War Veteran Scott Olsen Reaches $4.5M Settlement in Occupy Oakland Bean Bag Case," *NBC Bay Area*, last updated March 21, 2014.

[17] Ben Kesling and Pervaiz Shallwani, "Ferguson Police Tactics Challenged as Conflict Evolved," *Wall Street Journal*, August 21, 2014, https://www.wsj.com/articles/ferguson-police-tactics-challenged-as-conflict-evolved-1408675855.

[18] Paul D. Shinkman, "Ferguson and the Militarization of Police," *U.S. News and World Report*, August 14, 2014; Mark Thompson, "War Comes Home: The Militarization of U.S. Police Forces," *Time*, August 19, 2014.

[19] Joel Currier, "Judge Orders St. Louis Area Police to Give Protesters Tear Gas Warning and Time to Flee," *St. Louis Post-Dispatch*, December 11, 2014, http://www.stltoday.com/news/local/crime-and-courts/judge-orders-st-louis-area-police-to-give-protesters-tear/article_d93628c7-cc4e-5dfa-9873-cd4baf59ad73.html.

[20] Charlotte Alter, "The Road from Selma to Ferguson," *Time*, March 6, 2015; DeRay Mckesson, "Ferguson and Beyond: How a New Civil Rights Movement Began—and Won't End," *The Guardian*, August 9, 2015.

[21] Maguire and Oakley, *Policing Protests*.

[22] Maguire, "New Directions in Protest Policing."

[23] Gustave Le Bon, *The Crowd: A Study of the Popular Mind*, trans. (Auckland, New Zealand: The Floating Press, 2009), 38.

[24] Steven Reicher, Clifford Scott, Patrick Cronin, and Otto Adang, "An Integrated Approach to Crowd Psychology and Public Order Policing," *Policing: An International Journal of Police Strategies & Management* 27, no. 4 (2004): 558–572, p. 565.

[25] John Drury and Steven Reicher, "Collective Psychological Empowerment as a Model of Social Change: Researching Crowds and Power," *Journal of Social Issues* 65, no. 4 (2009): 707–725, 712.

[26] John Drury and Steven Reicher, "The Intergroup Dynamics of Collective Empowerment: Substantiating the Social Identity Model of Crowd Behavior," *Group Processes & Intergroup Relations* 2, no. 4 (1999): 381–402; Steven D. Reicher, "'The Battle of Westminster': Developing the Social Identity Model of Crowd Behaviour in Order to Explain the Initiation and Development of Collective Conflict," *European Journal of Social Psychology* 26, no. 1 (1996): 115–134; Clifford Stott and John Drury, "The Inter-Group Dynamics of Empowerment: A Social Identity Model," in *Transforming Politics: Power and Resistance*, eds. Paul Bagguley and Jeff Hearn (London, England: Palgrave Macmillan, 1999), 32–45; Clifford Stott and Steven Reicher, "Crowd Action as Intergroup Process: Introducing the Police Perspective," *European Journal of Social Psychology* 28, no. 4 (1998): 509–529.

[27] Stott et al., "Crowd Action as Intergroup Process"; Clifford Stott and Steven Reicher, "How Conflict Escalates: The Inter-Group Dynamics of Collective Football Crowd Violence," *Sociology* 32, no. 2 (1998): 353–377; Reicher, "'The Battle of Westminster.'"

[28] Jean-Pierre di Giacomo, "Intergroup Alliances and Rejections within a Protest Movement (Analysis of the Social Representations)," *European Journal of Social Psychology* 10, no. 4 (1980): 329–344.

[29] Drury and Reicher, "Collective Psychological Empowerment as a Model of Social Change."

[30] Reicher, "'The Battle of Westminster.'"

[31] Drury and Reicher, "Collective Psychological Empowerment as a Model of Social Change."

[32] Ibid.

[33] Reicher et al., "An Integrated Approach to Crowd Psychology and Public Order Policing"; Steven Reicher, Clifford Stott, John Drury, Otto Adang, Patrick Cronin, and Andrew Livingstone, "Knowledge-Based Public Order Policing: Principles and Practice," *Policing: A Journal of Policy and Practice* 1, no. 4 (2007): 403–415.

[34] Reicher et al., "An Integrated Approach to Crowd Psychology and Public Order Policing"; Clifford Stott and Otto Adang, *Understanding and Managing Risk-Policing Football Matches with an International Dimension in the European Union* (Copenhagen, Denmark: Bavnebanke Press, 2009); Clifford Stott and Geoff Pearson, *Football Hooliganism: Policing and the War on the English Disease* (London, England: Pennant Book, 2007).

[35] Reicher et al., "Knowledge-Based Public Order Policing"; Clifford Stott and Otto M. J. Adang, "'Disorderly' Conduct: Social Psychology and the Control of Football 'Hooliganism' at 'Euro 2004,'" *The Psychologist* 17, no. 6 (2004): 318–319; Clifford Stott, James Hoggett, and Geoff Pearson, "'Keeping the Peace': Social Identity, Procedural Justice, and the Policing of Football Crowds," *British Journal of Criminology*, 52, no. 2 (2012): 381–399.

[36] Clifford Stott, *Crowd Psychology and Public Order Policing: An Overview of Scientific Theory and Evidence.* Submission to the HMIC Policing of Public Protest Review Team (Liverpool, England: University of Liverpool, 2009).

[37] Clifford Stott, Otto Adang, Andrew Livingstone, and Martina Schreiber, "Variability in the Collective Behaviour of England Fans at Euro 2004: 'Hooliganism', Public Order Policing and Social Change," *European Journal of Social Psychology* 37, no. 1 (2007): 75–100; Clifford Stott, Andrew Livingstone, and James Hoggett, "Policing Football Crowds in England and Wales: A Model of 'Good Practice'?" *Policing & Society* 18, no. 3 (2008): 258–281.

[38] Jason Sunshine and Tom R. Tyler, "The Role of Procedural Justice and Legitimacy in Shaping Public Support for Policing," *Law & Society Review* 37, no. 3 (2003): 513–548; Tom R. Tyler, *Why People Obey the Law* (Princeton, NJ: Princeton University Press, 2006).

[39] Lawrence W. Sherman, "Defiance, Deterrence, and Irrelevance: A Theory of the Criminal Sanction," *Journal of Research in Crime and Delinquency* 30, no. 4 (1993): 445–473.

[40] Edward R. Maguire, Maya Barak, Karie Cross, and Kris Lugo, "Attitudes among Occupy DC Participants about the Use of Violence against Police," *Policing and Society* 28, no. 5 (2016): 526–540.

[41] Edward R. Maguire, Maya Barak, William Wells, and Charles Katz, "Attitudes toward the Use of Violence against Police among Occupy Wall Street Protesters," *Policing: A Journal of Police and Practice* (2018), https://doi.org/10.1093/police/pay003.

[42] David H. Tyler, Maya Barak, Edward R. Maguire, and William Wells, "The Effects of Procedural Injustice on the Use of Violence against Police by Occupy Wall Street Protesters," *Police Practice and Research* 19, no. 2 (2018): 138–152.

[43] Maguire et al., "Attitudes toward the Use of Violence against Police among Occupy Wall Street Protesters."

[44] Reicher et al., "An Integrated Approach to Crowd Psychology and Public Order Policing."

[45] Sue Rahr and Stephen K. Rice, "From Warriors to Guardians: Recommitting American Police Culture to Democratic Ideals," *New Perspectives in Policing Bulletin*, April 2015.

[46] Institute for Intergovernmental Research, *After-Action Assessment of the Police Response to the August 2014 Demonstrations in Ferguson, Missouri* (Washington, DC: Office of Community Oriented Policing Services, 2015); Hunton & Williams, LLP, *Final Report: Independent Review of the 2017 Protest Events in Charlottesville, Virginia*.

12

Response Essay

Chief Superintendent Owen West (Ret.)
West Yorkshire Police (UK)

In April 2009, Ian Tomlinson died at the hands of the police as he made his way through the police cordons and roadblocks set up to deal with serious disorder during the G20 Summit protests in London. Tomlinson was not a protester; he was simply trying to make his way through the chaos engulfing London when the protests turned into riots.

Tomlinson was forcibly struck on the leg with a baton by a police officer in full "riot gear" and, while unbalanced, was forcibly pushed to the ground. Tomlinson later died. The officer was charged and prosecuted with manslaughter but was subsequently cleared in court. The Metropolitan Police fired him at their first opportunity. There was, rightly, a national outcry that an innocent bystander could be unlawfully killed by a police service that styles itself as the most tolerant and most restrained in the world: the "British Bobbies." The incident changed the policing of protests in the United Kingdom forever.

What followed was a landmark report by the government's police watchdog: "Adapting to Protest; Nurturing the British Model of Policing."[1] The language used here is deliberate: to "nurture" something is to want to hold on to it, to protect it, and to make it stronger. In this context, it meant that the UK police service acknowledged that the covenant of consent and trust between the police and communities, between the state and its citizens—the very essence of the way of policing in the United Kingdom—was at risk and had been damaged by the police response to protest.

In a democracy, the police can only act with the citizens' consent. The use of power, force, or coercion is permitted by communities only if the state uses that power and force lawfully and proportionately and only as a last resort to protect society. Sadly, it took Tomlinson's death to remind the service of this essential contract; it was doubly sad in that the evidence about what works in crowd policing—the elaborated social identity model (ESIM)—was known to academia decades before Tomlinson died.

As we have seen, the research of Steve Reicher and others is compelling, and it has been available for years and years. However, the police in the United Kingdom and the United States have yet to realize the full potential of this work. "Classic" crowd theory—Le Bon's idea of "contagion"—remains stubbornly persistent in police training on crowds. Indeed, as recently as 2008, chunks of this book, written in 1896, were still being used to train UK police commanders.

In its response to the criticisms that followed Tomlinson's death, the UK police developed the concept of protest liaison officers. These specially trained cops have the job of using dialogue and engagement, good communication skills, and rapport building to work *with* crowds—to facilitate their lawful intention to use all in their power to avoid the use of force and coercion. In other words, the police have operationalized the principles of ESIM into a new kind of cop.

These cops wear a distinctive sky-blue vest to differentiate them from street cops, and they are now universally applied to any protest of scale in the United Kingdom. Often, a large part of their job is actually to "police the police": in other words, to help restrain their own colleagues and de-escalate situations where officers may be overreacting or being needlessly aggressive. It works, and it is now a fundamental part of the approach to protest policing in the United Kingdom.

An obvious question is why did it take the police so long to change their tactics when dealing with protest crowds? The answer is shared in both the U.S. and UK contexts. It's about fear—not so much the fear of actual disorder and violence by protesters but more about the fear of the media criticizing the police as "soft" if they try to resolve conflicts with anything other than overwhelming numbers and the availability of crowd-control munitions.

As a direct result of the media criticism in the aftermath of the UK riots of 2011, the mayor of London dashed out and bought two water cannons from Germany to placate the media that those scenes would never be tolerated again. Arguably, it was a media stunt. It certainly wasn't an evidence-based analysis of what needs to change in protest policing.

As we've seen in the policing of Phoenix after Charlottesville, no police commanders want their career blighted or their departments' reputations tarnished by appearing to be underprepared, underresourced, or soft. That renowned and sadly recently departed British scholar of public-order policing, Professor "Tank" Waddington, coined a famous phrase for this—"in the job trouble"—the idea that whatever happens on the streets during a protest is never as bad as the career-ending or career-limiting criticism by the media and others or the internal affairs investigation if the operation is perceived to have failed in some way.

Better then for the police to demonstrate control and project power, even if a judge describes a policing operation as "a disgrace for the community," as was the case in Miami, or if a police department has to pay out millions of dollars in settlements for breaching the rights of its own citizens, as we saw in the case of the "Occupy" protests.

This accountability dynamic is also the subject of research. For example, Cronin and Reicher found in their interviews with police commanders that a major fear for them was criticism by their bosses and the media more than it was in relation to anything that might happen on the streets.[2] The accountability dynamic is a major, if not *the* major factor, preventing reforms in protest policing.

That's disappointing, especially as the police on both sides of the Atlantic often talk about "evidence-based policing" (a concept invented in the United States). ESIM and everything we currently know about crowd psychology is, after all, evidence-based. It seems then that the fear of trying something new, in this context at least, is more powerful than the prize of scientifically established and tested reforms that could make protest policing safer and more legitimately conducted.

Of course, as we have seen in this chapter, there is a greater and far more serious risk for the police in the United States and United Kingdom as well as for society as a whole: the risk that a continued unchecked, unreformed, and increasingly militarized (especially in light of 9/11 and other terror threats on both sides of the Atlantic) police force may erode police legitimacy. Moreover, the principle of policing by consent may be lost—and it's a principle vital to community cohesion and democracy.

Training cops on their First Amendment rights is fine, but it's no substitute for an authentic belief that it is the fundamental job of the police in a democracy to defend and nurture that right and other universal human rights. When citizens exercise those rights as a *direct consequence* of the actions of the police themselves, as we saw in Ferguson, one would hope the police would be extra vigilant to get the balance right.

As this chapter excellently articulates, there is another way. Given current protests and activism in the United States and the United Kingdom, there has never been a more important time to implement what are, after all, evidence-based reforms.

NOTES

[1] Her Majesty's Chief Inspector of Constabulary, *Adapting to Protest: Nurturing the British Model of Policing* (London, England: HMIC, 2009), https://www.justiceinspectorates.gov.uk/hmicfrs/media/adapting-to-protest-nurturing-the-british-model-of-policing-20091125.pdf.

[2] Patrick Cronin and Stephen Reicher, "A Study of the Factors that Influence How Senior Officers Police Crowd Events: On SIDE Outside the Laboratory," *British Journal of Social Psychology* 45, no. 1 (2006): 175–196.

13

Increase Efficacy of Police Response to Sexual Assaults

Cassia Spohn
Suzanne St. George
Arizona State University

Background

In June 2010, the *Baltimore Sun* reported that the Baltimore Police Department led the country in the percentage of rape cases that were deemed to be false or baseless and thus were unfounded.[1] According to the report, from 2004 through 2009, about a third of the rapes reported to the police department were unfounded, a rate three times the national average. Also in June 2010, the *New York Times* reported that then-New York Police Commissioner Raymond W. Kelly had appointed a task force to look into the handling of rape complaints and to recommend new training protocols for dealing with victims of sexual assault. The review was prompted by complaints from rape victims, who said that their allegations of sexual assault were deemed unfounded or downgraded to misdemeanors. These news stories—along with others regarding the mishandling of rape cases in Milwaukee, Cleveland, New Orleans, and Philadelphia—culminated in a September 2010 U.S. Senate Hearing convened by then-Senator Arlen Specter to examine the systematic failure to investigate and prosecute rape on the part of police departments and prosecutors' offices nationwide. Testifying at the hearing was Carol E. Tracey, executive director of the Women's Law Project, who said, "It's clear we're seeing chronic and systemic patterns of police refusing to accept cases for investigation, misclassifying cases to noncriminal categories so that investigations do not occur, and 'unfounding' complaints by determining that women are lying about being sexually assaulted."[2]

More than three decades after the inception of the rape reform movement, which saw significant changes to the definition of rape, the elimination of resistance and corroboration requirements, the elimination of marital rape exemptions, and the enactment of rape shield laws, the response of the criminal justice system to the crime of sexual assault remains problematic. Victims are reluctant to report the crime to the police and, when they do, they are often met with skepticism and suspicion on the part of police and prosecutors. This results in a substantial number of cases being unfounded, a low arrest rate, and shockingly low rates of prosecution and conviction. In this chapter, we provide an overview of the response of the criminal justice system to the crime of sexual assault. We focus on decision-making by the police, who serve as the "gatekeepers" of the system and whose decisions determine whether the case will be investigated thoroughly and whether a suspect will be identified, arrested, and presented to the prosecutor for further processing.

■ Research on Police Decision-Making in Sexual Assault Cases

There is compelling evidence that sexual assault is a seriously underreported crime. One study that analyzed the results of the National Violence Against Women Survey found that only 19.1 percent of women who had been raped since their eighteenth birthday reported the crime; a similar survey in Canada found that only 6 percent of sexual assaults were reported to the police.[3] Even if the crime is reported to the police, the victim may decide later that they do not want to cooperate in the investigation of the crime or the prosecution of the suspect. The victim may recant or withdraw the allegations against the suspect, fail to show up for interviews with the investigating officer, or ask that the case be discontinued. Estimates of the extent to which this happens vary widely, with studies reporting that one-fourth,[4] one-third,[5] or more than 40 percent[6] of victims refuse to cooperate after reporting the crime to the police.

There is also evidence that victims of sexual assault who report the crime, and are willing to cooperate with police and prosecutors as the case moves forward, may confront criminal justice officials who are skeptical of their allegations and who question their credibility.[7] The process begins with the police, who decide whether a crime has occurred, how many investigative resources to devote to identifying the suspect and building a case, whether to arrest an identified suspect and, if so, what charges to file, and whether to refer the case to the prosecutor. These gatekeeping decisions, which largely determine the fate of the case, do not necessarily produce the outcome—arrest and successful prosecution—that the victim expected.

There is a relatively limited body of research on police decision-making in sexual assault cases. Researchers have examined the decision to unfound the charges, the decision to make an arrest, and the decision to present the case to the prosecutor for charge evaluation. These studies reveal that police decision-making is influenced by a combination of legal and extralegal factors and by police officers' beliefs in rape myths and misconceptions about sexual assault.[8] In the sections that follow, we discuss the results of this research.

Police Unfounding Decision

One of the most important, and highly criticized, decisions that police make is the decision whether to unfound the charges. If the police officer investigating the crime believes the victim's account of what happened and determines that the incident constitutes a crime, the case becomes one of the "crimes known to the police" that will be included the jurisdiction's crime statistics. If, on the other hand, the officer does not believe the victim's story and therefore concludes that a crime did not occur, the case is unfounded. Technically, cases can be unfounded only if the police determine that the allegations are false or baseless. In reality, police may use the unfounding decision to inappropriately clear cases in which they are convinced that a crime occurred but also believe that the likelihood of arrest and prosecution is low.[9] The fact that police departments are evaluated in terms of clearance rates encourages officers to unfound ambiguous or difficult cases, including those where a victim is reluctant, emotional, uncooperative, or compromised in some way (e.g., was drunk or using illegal drugs at the time of the incident, was a prostitute, had a criminal record, or had a prior sexual relationship with the accused).

There is very limited research on police unfounding decisions in sexual assault cases, and much of the research that does exist is dated.[10] An early study by the Law Enforcement Assistance Administration, in which police officers were asked to identify the factors that affected their decisions, found that the two most important predictors of whether cases would be founded or unfounded were proof of penetration and the suspect's use of physical force.[11] A later study of sexual assaults reported to the police in Chicago in 1981 differentiated between cases in which the identity of the suspect was not known and those in which the victim and the suspect were acquainted in some way.[12] In the identity cases, the most important predictors of the police founding decision were whether the complainant was willing to prosecute, whether the victim physically resisted the attack, whether a weapon was used, and whether the suspect was in custody. By contrast, in cases in which the victim and suspect were acquainted, the police were more likely to label the case a crime if the suspect was in custody, if the victim suffered collateral injury, and if there was no discrediting information (such as a pattern of alcohol or drug use, a history of mental illness, or a record of false complaints) about the victim.

A recent study of unfounding decisions made by the Los Angeles Police Department revealed a similar pattern of results.[13] This study found that the strongest predictors of unfounding were whether the victim recanted the allegations and whether the victim was assaulted by an acquaintance or intimate partner rather than a stranger, both of which had positive effects on the likelihood of unfounding. Other factors that increased the odds that the charges would be unfounded were whether the victim had a mental illness or mental health issues, whether there was information that raised questions about the victim's credibility, and whether physical evidence to corroborate the victim's allegation was lacking. As discussed in more detail below, unfounding decisions may also be based on police officers' beliefs in rape myths and misconceptions about sexual assault as well as on officers' mistaken beliefs about when unfounding is justified.

Decision to Arrest

Similar results are found in studies examining the police decision to make an arrest.[14] For example, Gary LaFree's early study of sexual assaults reported to the police in a large metropolitan jurisdiction in the Midwest revealed that the arrest decision was influenced by a combination of legal and extralegal factors: whether the victim could identify the suspect, whether the victim was willing to prosecute, whether the victim engaged in any misconduct at the time of the incident, whether the victim reported the incident promptly, whether an acquaintance rather than a stranger assaulted the victim, and whether the suspect used a weapon. On the other hand, the arrest decision was not affected by the victim's race or whether the victim resisted, where the incident occurred, whether a witness could corroborate the victim's allegations, or whether the victim was injured.[15] These findings led LaFree to conclude that, at least in this jurisdiction, the emphasis on the role played by the victim's attributes and the interpersonal context of the crime "appears to be greatly overstated."[16]

Several more recent studies call this conclusion into question. One study found that although crimes involving African American suspects and white victims were not more likely than other crimes to result in arrest, arrest was more likely if the victim and suspect had a prior relationship, if the victim agreed to undergo a sexual assault exam, and if the credibility or seriousness score of the crime (which measured whether other crimes were committed during the sexual offense, whether a weapon was used, and whether the crime occurred outdoors) was higher.[17] Alderden and Ullman similarly found that police decision-making was determined primarily by extralegal factors—the victim's preference for how the case should be handled, discrepancies in victim statements, and victim resistance,[18] while Schuller and Stewart found that police officers' responses to sexual assault vignettes were affected by the intoxication and credibility of the complainant.[19] Spohn and Tellis's study of the decision to arrest in Los Angeles also highlighted the role that victim characteristics play.[20] They examined cases with an identified suspect, finding that the case was less likely to be cleared by arrest if the case file contained information that raised questions about the victim's reputation or character, the victim had a motive to lie, or the case involved rape rather than attempted rape. The case was more likely to be cleared by arrest if the suspect used a weapon, the victim suffered collateral injuries, the victim reported the crime within one hour, and the victim was willing to cooperate in the investigation of the crime. The arrest decision, on the other hand, was not affected by the victim's age, race or ethnicity, or relationship with the suspect; by whether the victim engaged in behavior that could be perceived as risky at the time of the incident or had a mental illness or mental health issues; or by the type of resistance the victim offered.

Spohn and Tellis also analyzed whether the detective investigating the crime presented the case to the district attorney for a pre-arrest charge evaluation. They argued that the pre-arrest charge evaluation, which occurred frequently in sexual assault cases handled by the Los Angeles Police Department and the Los Angeles County Sheriff's Office, was a critical decision point in this jurisdiction, as cases that were "rejected" by the prosecutor at this stage (based on a proof beyond a reasonable doubt standard) typically did not result in the suspect's arrest (which only required probable cause). They found that only one victim characteristic—whether the victim engaged in any risky behavior at the time of the alleged assault—influenced whether the case would be presented to the district attorney for a pre-arrest charge evaluation. Cases involving victims who engaged in what could be perceived as risky behavior were 1.9 times more likely to be presented to the district attorney before the suspect's arrest. The odds of a pre-arrest charge evaluation also were affected by the seriousness of the crime and the strength of evidence in the case. Compared to cases where the most serious charge was attempted rape, cases where rape was the most serious charge were over six times more likely to be presented to the district attorney before the suspect could be arrested. The likelihood of a pre-arrest charge evaluation was significantly lower for cases where the suspect used some type of weapon, the victim reported the crime within one hour, the victim was willing to cooperate in the investigation, some physical evidence existed, and one or more witnesses were present. These results, then, suggest that detectives bring cases where the evidence is weaker or where there are questions about the victim's behavior at the time of the incident to district attorneys for a pre-arrest charge evaluation.[21]

In summary, prior research on police decisions in sexual assault cases suggests that a combination of legal and extralegal factors affect these decisions. As they evaluate cases and assess the likelihood of successful prosecution, police officers consider not only the seriousness of the offense and the strength of evidence against the defendant but also the victim's characteristics, behavior, and reputation; the relationship between the victim and the suspect; and the victim's willingness to cooperate in the investigation of the case. In the next section, we explore the role that rape myth acceptance may play in police decision-making in sexual assault cases.

■ Police Officers and Rape Myth Acceptance

Despite reforms, case attrition remains a serious problem in the criminal justice response to rape and sexual assault. The limited evidence described above suggests that police officers are influenced by rape myths—defined as "prejudicial, false, and stereotyped beliefs about rape, rape victims, and rapists"[22]—when deciding to found a case, pursue an investigation, make an arrest, and refer cases to prosecutors for charging. Although the overt endorsement of rape myths may be low,[23] rape-supportive attitudes may still affect how officers categorize rape incidents[24] and write reports,[25] assess victim credibility[26] and determine whether allegations are false.[27] These attitudes also may affect how officers treat victims and may encourage (or discourage) cooperation.[28]

Rape myths work to deny or justify rape. For example, the "real rape" myth defines rape narrowly to include only incidents involving strangers, a weapon, severe injury to the victim, and a prompt report. Incidents involving people who know each other, no injury or weapons, and delayed reports are perceived as false or less legitimate than "real rapes." "Real rapes" also involve "genuine victims" who behave according to traditional gender roles.[29] Women who violate chastity and passivity norms by dressing in revealing clothing, behaving provocatively, drinking or using drugs, or working in the sex industry are not "genuine victims" because they are perceived to precipitate their own rapes.[30] The "he didn't mean to" myth suggests that some men rape because of an uncontrollable male sex drive or mistaken consent. Finally, various myths suggest that women (and men) lie about being raped, especially to hide regrettable but consensual sex or homosexual behavior.[31] Whereas "real rape," "genuine victim," and "she lied" myths work to deny rape, "he didn't mean to" and victim-precipitation myths justify rape by shifting blame onto the victim.

Rape Myth Acceptance in Reports, Definitions, and Classifications of Rape

Generally, studies measuring overt rape myth acceptance (RMA) among police officers find that most officers do not strongly endorse rape myths. Rape myths may, however, affect officers' decisions and behavior in more subtle ways. In their content analysis of a random sample of police reports linked to rape kits that were never processed, Shaw and colleagues found rape myths manifested as three types of victim-blaming statements. Circumstantial blame, which corresponds to real rape and "she lied" myths, was evident in 25.4 percent of reports. Characterological blame statements associated with genuine victim and victim-precipitation myths, including issues of drug use, promiscuity, and being a sex worker, were evident in about 17 percent of reports. Finally, a third class of statements blamed incomplete and superficial investigations on victims for being uncooperative, lacking information, or bringing an otherwise weak case. These statements were evident in 41 percent of reports. Overall, 57 percent of reports contained at least one victim-blaming statement, indicating that RMA may manifest in reports, even if these attitudes are too subtle to be measured on a scale.[32]

Rape myths are also evident in how police officers define rape and classify sexual assault reports. Nearly 15 years after reforms, Campbell and Johnson[33] found that 50 percent of police officers sampled from two midwestern police departments defined rape according to the traditional, pre-reform definition. These officers denied the possibility of rape between nonstrangers and described many rapes as accidental ("he didn't mean to") or regrettable sex ("she lied"). The small proportion of officers who defined rape according to the reformed legal definition (19 percent) were more likely to have sexual assault case training, more experience working with rape victims, more favorable attitudes toward women, and less acceptance of interpersonal violence. A more recent study found that although 94 percent of officers in a Midwest police agency defined rape according to the current legal definition in that state, 31 percent endorsed rape myths and victim blaming in statements describing their attitudes toward rape.[34]

Even when officers *define* rape according to legal definitions, they often *evaluate* and *classify* rape reports according to rape myth criteria. For example, one study found a continuum of rape case types ranging from legitimate and serious cases to false allegations, with ambiguous cases falling between these two extremes.[35] Consistent with the "real rape" myth, legitimate and serious cases happened "in the bushes" and involved injury, weapons, a prompt report (within 24 hours), and a credible victim. These cases have a lot of evidence and are perceived (at least by some) to be the most "fun" to work. By contrast, ambiguous cases typically involve intoxicated victims and acquaintances or intimate partners in classic he said/she said scenarios, while cases identified as false allegations tended to lack evidence of force and involve a victim with a perceived motive to lie. Similar typologies have been found in Germany[36] and New Zealand.[37] Importantly, the proportion of cases perceived to be legitimate may be quite small. Among cases that New Zealand police filed across three cities, only

21 percent were classified as "genuine" or legitimate, while 38 percent were classified as ambiguous ("possibly genuine/possibly false"), and 33 percent were classified as false.

False Allegations, Victim Credibility, and Victim Cooperation

Many researchers have found that police officers overestimate the prevalence of false allegations.[38] For example, among a sample of police officers from a midsized department, estimates of false reports of sexual assault ranged from 3 percent to 90 percent with a mode of 50 percent.[39] Officers often classify reports as false if they perceive the victim has a motive to lie.[40] They also perceive high rates of false allegations among male victims, especially when the incident is interpreted as covering up consensual homosexual experimentation or "regret sex."[41] Officers with high RMA, including acceptance of real rape, victim precipitation, "she lied," and "he didn't mean to" myths, tend to estimate higher rates of false allegations than officers with low RMA.[42] Incidents are often classified as ambiguous or false if the victim deviates from the genuine victim myth, and officers with higher RMA may perceive some victims as inherently less credible. Indeed, Page found that most police officers (94 percent) agreed that any woman can be raped and, to a lesser extent, that any man can be raped (67 percent). Forty-four percent, however said they would not believe reports by prostitutes, 49 percent said they would not believe men, and 19 percent said they would not believe married women who claimed to be raped by their husbands.[43]

Officers may also question victims' credibility when they do not act the way that a genuine victim should act. Delaying incident reports, telling inconsistent stories, and concealing or lying about case details decrease perceived credibility and officers' self-perceived likelihood of moving a case forward. Victim demeanor during the reporting process is especially important in officers' credibility assessments, and myth-consistent victim demeanor often trumps other indicators of noncredibility, such as being a prostitute. In a survey of Swedish police officers and prosecutors, Ask found that police officers assume that rape and domestic violence victims, more so than victims of muggings or assault, act with expressive emotional styles (e.g., crying, despair, and signs of distress) as opposed to more controlled or neutral styles.[44] Venema also found evidence of this belief in a sample of American police officers who perceived victims as more credible when they were hysterical, panicked, or visibly shaken during the reporting process.[45]

This finding is problematic because the psychological experience of rape victims may present physically in behaviors and demeanors that police perceive as lying, which may decrease their belief in the allegation and empathy toward the victim. For example, some posttraumatic stress disorder (PTSD) symptoms (e.g., numbness and disassociation) and physical expression of shame (e.g., lack of eye contact, avoidance, and agitation) may be misperceived as signs of deception by officers expecting a hysterical victim.[46] Many officers agree that such nonverbal behavioral cues are somewhat important in assessing victim truthfulness and credibility. There is evidence, however, that the nonverbal cues people typically rely on to assess veracity are unrelated to truthfulness.[47] Given research indicating that victims of rape are equally likely to engage in expressive and controlled emotional styles immediately after a rape, police officers are at risk of misinterpreting the victim's controlled emotional style as evidence of deception in a large proportion of cases.

Misinterpreting victim demeanor as evidence of deception may cause police officers to treat victims with less sensitivity, concern, and empathy. One study found that victims who suffered more severe PTSD and shame perceived police treatment of them as less empathetic than victims with less exaggerated symptoms.[48] Another study revealed that police officers were more likely to be supportive of victims when incident and victim characteristics, including victims' demeanor, matched real rape and genuine victim stereotypes.[49] Research also reveals that positive treatment by police promotes victim cooperation with the investigation and prosecution.[50] By contrast, when police believe allegations are false, they sometimes engage in "light interrogation" of victims to identify inconsistencies in their stories.[51] These tactics make victims feel unsafe, judged, guilty, and ashamed and cause them to lose confidence in the criminal justice system, which may in turn cause victims to recant or refuse to cooperate.

Encouraging victim cooperation is important because an uncooperative victim is often the primary reason identified for ending an investigation without making an arrest.[52] Interestingly, officers may blame victims for less than thorough investigations or lack of success in a case and cite lack of cooperation, insufficient information, or disorganized demeanor as reasons that the investigation did not advance as far as it could have if the victim was genuine.[53] Additionally, officers sometimes perceive a victim's choice not to cooperate as evidence that the report was false. This creates a self-perpetuating cycle. When cases are inconsistent with rape myths, police officers perceive them as ambiguous or false and treat the "non-genuine" victims poorly; victims then respond to this "second victimization" by choosing not to cooperate further, which causes police officers to confirm their suspicions that the allegations were indeed false. Refusal to cooperate, therefore, perpetuates the tendency to overestimate the number of false allegations and to associate false allegations with cases and victims that deviate from real rape and genuine victim stereotypes.

Organizational Barriers to Reform

Clearly, RMA among police officers is a barrier to successful adjudication in cases of rape and sexual assault. As the above examples demonstrate, RMA shapes and constrains understanding of rape so that officers with high RMA define rape narrowly according to characteristics of the "real rape" stereotypes, whereas those with low RMA have more flexible and variable definitions of rape that are more inclusive across incident, victim, and assailant characteristics. Even if an individual officer does not endorse rape myths to the extent that others do, the cultural environment may affect decision-making in rape cases. For example, Venema found that patrol officers were more likely to define a depicted rape scenario as a "good case" and to indicate that they would call a detective and make an arrest in the case if they believed their *peers* also perceived the case as "good."[54] RMA, then, is not a just problem among a few high RMA officers. In fact, most officers express low levels of RMA on standardized scales. But the perception that others have high RMA may constrain officers with low RMA to conform to the perceived norms of peers. The widespread manifestation of rape myths in police decision-making, report writing, and victim treatment may result more from the normalization of rape myths in police culture than from RMA among individual officers.

This is compounded by the fact that there is evidence that the patriarchal and hypermasculinity norms common in police culture promote and perpetuate rape myths among officers. For example, Feild found that police officers' attitudes toward rape victims more closely matched those of rapists than of rape crisis counselors.[55] Officers socialized into police culture may take on these attitudes, even if they did not endorse them previously. In fact, Wentz and Archbold found that 35 percent of officers had more negative attitudes toward rape victims *after* becoming a police officer. Furthermore, a larger proportion of female officers (48 percent) than male officers (31 percent) attributed this change to a greater endorsement of rape myths, especially the belief that victims lie.[56] This finding suggests that female officers feel constrained to conform to police culture norms, even when these norms denigrate their gender. This may explain why female officers, compared to male officers, do not display the lower levels of RMA and victim blaming typically found in comparisons of female and male respondents in college and community samples. Female officers socialized into hypermasculine police culture may overcompensate for their gender identity by engaging in and perpetuating rape myths.

Patriarchal gender norms are also perpetuated in the hiring and deployment practices of police departments. Even as the gender composition in police departments changes, female officers are often relegated to undervalued "women's work," such as working with rape victims. For example, some police departments have sought to improve response to victims by employing specially trained officers or recruiting officers to sexual assault units, and women are often targeted for these positions because they are assumed to be more sensitive and empathetic toward rape victims. Victims and police officers alike use gender as a heuristic to identify sensitive and empathetic officers. Officer gender alone, however, does not guarantee better treatment, especially when selected officers lack the skills, training, and experience needed to respond effectively to sexual assault cases and victims. Although they may be well-intentioned, these practices perpetuate traditional gender role stereotypes and recreate patriarchal power hierarchies in the police organization.

Police officers also face other organizational barriers in responding empathetically to sexual assault victims. To the extent that a department officially or unofficially restricts resources to rape-myth-consistent cases, officers may be forced to dismiss or ignore ambiguous cases. Rape myths may function as a categorization tool or schema used to distinguish legitimate rapes from false allegations so as to better distribute resources. For example, officers sometimes recognize that "ambiguous" cases are legitimate, but knowing that a lack of corroborating evidence means the case will not reach reasonable doubt standards, they may choose to focus resources on cases more likely to result in charges and conviction. Page found that 47 percent of police officers sampled said anticipated decisions of prosecutors at least slightly influenced their decision to pursue a rape investigation.[57] A downstream orientation to prosecutor charging decisions and/or jury conviction decisions may also cause officers to view rape victims as witnesses to rape rather than victims of rape.[58] Framing victims in this way results in a focus on building cases, collecting evidence, and identifying false reports rather than providing victims with needed support.[59] Unfortunately, when treating victims this way is perceived as less empathetic and compassionate, victims may choose not to cooperate further.

■ Next Steps: Improving Police Response to Sexual Assault and Sexual Assault Victims

Research on the response of the criminal justice system to the crime of sexual assault consistently reveals that sexual assault cases have appallingly low rates of arrest, prosecution, and conviction. The police play an important—arguably, the most important—role in producing these high rates of case attrition. The police decide whether a victim's allegations are credible, whether allegations deemed credible should be investigated thoroughly, whether an identified suspect should be arrested, and whether the case should be forwarded to the prosecutor for a filing decision. As the gatekeepers of the criminal justice system, the police determine which sexual assault victims might eventually have their day in court.

The research reviewed above also demonstrates that police decision-making in sexual assault cases is affected by stereotypes of real rapes and genuine victims and by pervasive myths surrounding rape and its victims. Counteracting these stereotypes and myths will require ongoing, specialized training that focuses on interviewing victims, interrogating suspects, and investigating sexual assaults. Because nonstranger sexual assault is the most frequent type of case seen by law enforcement, training should specifically address investigation of this type of crime, which often is the quintessential "she said/he said" case in which the victim alleges that she was sexually assaulted and the suspect either denies the sexual activity or contends that it was consensual. These are difficult, but not impossible, cases to prosecute successfully, and officers should be trained in the use of pretext phone calls, social networking websites, and cell phone text messages to gather evidence to corroborate the victim's allegations.

Both patrol officers and detectives require specialized training because a poorly written report, an inability to build a rapport with victims to gather information, and a failure to ask appropriate questions often create the inconsistencies in victims' accounts that damage their credibility and contribute to case attrition. Officers should be taught techniques designed to engage victims as allies in the investigation and to encourage victim cooperation. This includes learning to identify, and appropriately respond to, symptoms of psychological trauma (especially PTSD), shame, and self-blame. In addition, training should emphasize that delayed reporting is the norm in sexual assault cases and that inconsistencies in the victim's account of the incident do not necessarily signal that the allegation is false.

All officers who handle sexual assault cases should receive training addressing rape myths, traditional gender role attitudes, and sexism, as the attitudes and expectations of first responders (patrol officers) may affect the decisions of better trained officers later in the case-processing pipeline. All officers should learn appropriate report writing skills, should be able to identify rape myths and victim-blaming statements in reports, and should be disciplined for using such statements in reports of their investigations. There also needs to be better communication between patrol officers, detectives, and prosecutors. Knowing that a case originally perceived as ambiguous or false resulted in a conviction can help alter officers' perceptions of "real rape." Also, learning that even weak cases can be successfully investigated and prosecuted may encourage officers to allocate resources more fairly across case types.

Law-enforcement agencies also should be encouraged to establish specialized sexual assault units that handle all sexual assault cases involving children and adults. Although this may not be feasible in smaller jurisdictions with relatively few sexual assault reports, larger jurisdictions would benefit from having a cadre of officers specifically trained in effective techniques for investigating sexual assault cases, interviewing and establishing a rapport with victims, and overcoming evidentiary issues that are common in these types of cases. These units should be staffed with officers who want to work these types of cases; moreover, selection into specialized units must be based on skill and experience, not gender.

Training alone will not improve treatment or decrease attrition without also addressing microsystem and structural barriers to reform, such as a downstream orientation to the decisions of prosecutors and juries. Officers should be encouraged to focus on conducting thorough investigations, not on future case outcomes. A probable cause standard, not a reasonable doubt standard, should guide investigations. Officers should also be trained to think about and treat victims as *victims*, not witnesses, to rape.

NOTES

[1] Cassia Spohn and Katharine Tellis, *Policing and Prosecuting Sexual Assault in Los Angeles City and County: A Collaborative Study in Partnership with the Los Angeles Police Department, the Los Angeles County Sheriff's Department, and the Los Angeles County District Attorney's Office* (Washington, DC: U.S. Department of Justice, National Institute of Justice, 2012).

[2] Ibid., 36.

[3] Janice du Mont, Karen-Lee Miller, and Terri L. Myhr, "The Role of 'Real Rape' and 'Real Victim' Stereotypes in the Police Reporting Practices of Sexually Assaulted Women," *Violence Against Women* 9, no. 4 (2003): 466–486; Patricia Tjaden and Nancy Thoennes, *Extent, Nature and Consequences of Rape Victimization: Findings from the National Violence Against Women Survey* (Washington, DC: U.S. Department of Justice, National Institute of Justice, 2006), 33.

[4] Lynda L. Holmstrom and Ann W. Burgess, *The Victim of Rape: Institutional Reactions* (New Brunswick, NJ: Transaction Publishers, 1978).

[5] Eryn N. O'Neal, "Victim Cooperation in Intimate Partner Sexual Assault Cases: A Mixed Methods Examination," *Justice Quarterly* 34, no. 6 (2017): 1014–1043; Katharine M. Tellis and Cassia C. Spohn, "The Sexual Stratification Hypothesis Revisited: Testing Assumptions about Simple Versus Aggravated Rape," *Journal of Criminal Justice* 36, no. 3 (2008): 252–261.

[6] Cassia Spohn, Nancy Rodriguez, and Mary Koss, "The 'Victim Declined to Prosecute;' Accounting for Lack of Cooperation in Sexual Assault Cases," paper presented at the annual meeting of the American Society of Criminology, St. Louis, MO, November 2008.

[7] Susan Estrich, *Real Rape* (Cambridge, MA: Harvard University Press, 1987); O'Neal, "Victim Cooperation in Intimate Partner Sexual Assault Cases"; Jessica Shaw, Rebecca Campbell, and Debi Cain, "The View from Inside the System: How Police Explain Their Response to Sexual Assault," *American Journal of Community Psychology* 58 (2016): 446–462; Cassia Spohn and Katharine Tellis, *Policing and Prosecuting Sexual Assault: Inside the Criminal Justice System* (Boulder, CO: Lynne Rienner, 2014).

[8] For two recent reviews of police officers' rape myths beliefs and perceptions of rape victims, see Kayleigh A. Parratt and Afroditi Pina, "From 'Real Rape' to 'Real Justice:' A Systematic Review of Police Officers' Rape Myth Beliefs," *Aggression and Violent Behavior* 34 (2017): 68–83; Emma Sleath and Ray Bull, "Police Perceptions of Rape Victims and the Impact on Case Decision Making: A Systematic Review," *Aggression and Violent Behavior* 34 (2017): 102–112.

[9] Amanda Konradi, *Taking the Stand: Rape Survivors and the Prosecution of Rapists* (New York: Praeger, 2007); Patricia Y. Martin, *Rape Work: Victims, Gender and Emotions in Organization and Community Context* (New York: Routledge, 2006); O'Neal, "Victim Cooperation in Intimate Partner Sexual Assault Cases."

[10] Gary LaFree, *Rape and Criminal Justice: The Social Construction of Sexual Assault* (Belmont, CA: Wadsworth, 1989); Kerstetter, "Gateway to Justice"; Thomas W. McCahill, Linda Meyer, and Arthur Fischman, *The Aftermath of Rape* (Lexington, MA: Lexington Books, 1979). For more recent research, see Megan A. Alderden and Sarah E. Ullman, "Creating a More Complete and Current Picture," *Violence Against Women* 18, no. 5 (2012): 525–551; Jeffery A. Bouffard, "Predicting Type of Sexual Assault Case Closure from Victim, Suspect and Case Characteristics," *Journal of Criminal Justice* 28, no. 6 (2000): 527–542; Liz Kelly, Jo Lovett, and Linda Regan, *Home Office Research Study 293 A Gap or Chasm? Attrition in Reported Rape Cases* (London, England: Home Office Research, Development and Statistics Directorate, 2005); Tellis and Spohn, "The Sexual Stratification Hypothesis Revisited"; Cassia Spohn,

Clair White, and Katharine Tellis, "Unfounding Sexual Assault: Examining the Decision to Unfound and Identifying False Reports," *Law & Society Review* 48, no. 1 (2014): 161–192.

11 Law Enforcement Assistance Administration, *Forcible Rape: A National Survey of the Response by Police: Police Volume I* (Washington, DC: U.S. Government Printing Office, 1977).

12 Kerstetter, "The Gateway to Justice."

13 Spohn, White & Tellis, "Unfounding Sexual Assault."

14 Alderden and Sarah E. Ullman, "Creating a More Complete and Current Picture"; Ronet Bachman, "Factors Related to Rape Reporting and Arrest: New Evidence from the NCVS," *Criminal Justice and Behavior* 25, no. 1 (1999): 8–29; Bouffard, "Predicting Type of Sexual Assault Case Closure from Victim, Suspect and Case Characteristics"; Janice Du Mont and Terri L. Myhr, "So Few Convictions: The Role of Client-Related Characteristics in the Legal Processing of Sexual Assaults," *Violence Against Women* 6, no. 10 (2000): 1109–1136; Gary LaFree, "Official Reactions to Social Problems: Police Decisions in Sexual Assault Cases," *Social Problems* 28, no. 5 (1981): 582–594; Cassia Spohn and Katharine Tellis, *Policing and Prosecuting Sexual Assault in Los Angeles City and County*; Cassia Spohn and Katharine Tellis, "Sexual Assault Case Outcomes: Disentangling the Overlapping Decisions of Police and Prosecutors," *Justice Quarterly* 36, no. 3 (2019): 383–411.

15 LaFree, "Official Reactions to Social Problems."

16 Ibid., 592.

17 Bouffard, "Predicting Type of Sexual Assault Case Closure from Victim, Suspect and Case Characteristics."

18 Alderden and Sarah E. Ullman, "Creating a More Complete and Current Picture."

19 Regina A. Schuller and Anna Stewart, "Police Responses to Sexual Assault Complaints: The Role of Perpetrator/Complainant Intoxication," *Law and Human Behavior* 24, no. 5 (2000): 535–551.

20 Spohn and Tellis, "Sexual Assault Case Outcomes."

21 Ibid.

22 Martha R. Burt and Rochelle S. Albin, "Rape Myths, Rape Definitions, and Probability of Conviction," *Journal of Applied Social Psychology* 11, no. 3 (1981): 212–230, 217.

23 Amy D. Page, "Behind the Blue Line: Investigating Police Officers' Attitudes toward Rape," *Journal of Police and Criminal Psychology* 22, no. 1 (2007): 22–32; Amy D. Page, "True Colors: Police Officers and Rape Myth Acceptance," *Feminist Criminology* 5, no. 4 (2010): 315–334; Emma Sleath and Ray Bull, "Comparing Rape Victim and Perpetrator Blaming in a Police Officer Sample: Differences between Police Officers with and without Special Training," *Criminal Justice and Behavior* 39, no. 5 (2012): 646–665; Rachel M. Venema, "Police Officers' Rape Myth Acceptance: Examining the Role of Officer Characteristics, Estimates of False Reporting, and Social Desirability Bias," *Violence and Victims* 33, no. 1 (2018): 176–200.

24 Rebecca Campbell and Camille R. Johnson, "Police Officers' Perceptions of Rape: Is There Consistency between State Law and Individual Beliefs?," *Journal of Interpersonal Violence* 12, no. 2 (1997): 255–274; Jan Jordan, "Beyond Belief? Police, Rape and Women's Credibility," *Criminal Justice* 4, no. 1 (2004): 29–59; Barbara Krahé, "Police Officers' Definitions of Rape: A Prototype Study," *Journal of Community & Applied Social Psychology* 1, no. 3 (1991): 223–244; Rachel M. Venema, "Police Officer Schema of Sexual Assault Reports: Real Rape, Ambiguous Cases, and False Reports," *Journal of Interpersonal Violence* 31, no. 5 (2016): 872–899.

25 Jessica Shaw, Rebecca Campbell, Debi Cain, and Hannah Feeney, "Beyond Surveys and Scales: How Rape Myths Manifest in Sexual Assault Police Records," *Psychology of Violence* 7, no. 4 (2017): 602–614.

26 Jordan, "Beyond Belief?"; Page, "Behind the Blue Line"; Venema, "Police Officers' Rape Myth Acceptance."

27 Jordan, "Beyond Belief?"; Venema, "Police Officer Schema of Sexual Assault Reports"; Venema, "Police Officers' Rape Myth Acceptance."

28 Aliraza Javaid, "Giving a Voice to the Voiceless: Police Responses to Male Rape," *Policing: A Journal of Policy and Practice* 11, no. 2 (2017): 146–156; Jan Jordan, "Will Any Woman Do? Police, Gender and Rape Victims," *Policing: An International Journal of Police Strategies*

& Management 25, no. 2 (2002): 319–344; Jordan, "Beyond Belief?"; Shaw et al., "Beyond Surveys and Scales."

[29] Burt et al., "Rape Myths, Rape Definitions, and Probability of Conviction"; Shaw et al., "Beyond Surveys and Scales."

[30] Menchem Amir, "Victim Precipitated Forcible Rape," *Journal of Criminal Law and Criminology* 493, no. 4 (1968): 493–502; Estrich, Real Rape.

[31] Diana L. Payne, Kimberly A. Lonsway, and Louise F. Fitzgerald, "Rape Myth Acceptance: Exploration of Its Structure and Its Measurement Using the Illinois Rape Myth Acceptance Scale," *Journal of Research in Personality* 33, no. 1 (1999): 27–68.

[32] Shaw et al., "Beyond Surveys and Scales."

[33] Campbell and Johnson, "Police Officers' Perceptions of Rape."

[34] Ericka Wentz and Carol A. Archbold, "Police Perceptions of Sexual Assault Victims: Exploring the Intra-Female Gender Hostility Thesis," *Police Quarterly* 15, no. 1 (2012): 25–44.

[35] Venema, "Police Officers' Rape Myth Acceptance."

[36] Krahé, "Police Officers' Definitions of Rape."

[37] Jordan, "Beyond Belief?"

[38] Karl Ask, "A Survey of Police Officers' and Prosecutors' Beliefs about Crime Victim Behaviors," *Journal of Interpersonal Violence* 25, no. 6 (2010): 1132–1149; Jordan, "Beyond Belief?"; Amy D. Page, "Gateway to Reform? Policy Implications of Police Officers' Attitudes toward Rape," *American Journal of Criminal Justice* 33, no. 1 (2008): 44–58; Venema, "Police Officers' Rape Myth Acceptance."

[39] Venema, "Police Officers' Rape Myth Acceptance."

[40] Jordan, "Beyond Belief?"; Venema, "Police Officer Schema of Sexual Assault Reports."

[41] Javaid, "Giving a Voice to the Voiceless," 7.

[42] Venema, "Police Officers' Rape Myth Acceptance."

[43] Page, "Behind the Blue Line."

[44] Ask, "A Survey of Police Officers' and Prosecutors' Beliefs about Crime Victim Behaviors."

[45] Venema, "Police Officers' Rape Myth Acceptance."

[46] Lucy Maddox, Deborah Lee, and Chris Barker, "Police Empathy and Victim PTSD as Potential Factors in Rape Case Attrition," *Journal of Police and Criminal Psychology* 26, no. 2 (2011): 112–117.

[47] Siegfried L. Sporer and Barbara Schwandt, "Moderators of Nonverbal Indicators of Deception: A Meta-Analytic Synthesis," *Psychology, Public Policy, and Law* 13, no. 1 (2007): 1–34.

[48] Maddox et al., "Police Empathy and Victim PTSD as Potential Factors in Rape Case Attrition."

[49] Mary C. Anders and F. Scott Christopher, "A Socioecological Model of Rape Survivors' Decisions to Aid in Case Prosecution," *Psychology of Women Quarterly* 35, no. 1 (2011): 92–106.

[50] Maddox et al., "Police Empathy and Victim PTSD as Potential Factors in Rape Case Attrition."

[51] Venema, "Police Officer Schema of Sexual Assault Reports."

[52] Spohn et al., Policing and Prosecuting Sexual Assault: Inside the Criminal Justice System.

[53] Venema, "Police Officer Schema of Sexual Assault Reports."

[54] Venema, "Police Officers' Rape Myth Acceptance."

[55] Hubert S. Feild, "Attitudes toward Rape: A Comparative Analysis of Police, Rapists, Crisis Counselors, and Citizens," *Journal of Personality and Social Psychology* 36, no. 2 (1978): 156–179.

[56] Wentz and Archbold, "Police Perceptions of Sexual Assault Victims."

[57] Page, "Behind the Blue Line"; Page, "Gateway to Reform?"

[58] Patricia Y. Martin and R. Marlene Powell, "Accounting for the 'Second Assault': Legal Organizations' Framing of Rape Victims," *Law & Social Inquiry* 19, no. 4 (1994): 853–890; Spohn et al., *Policing and Prosecuting Sexual Assault: Inside the Criminal Justice System.*

[59] Anders and Christopher, "A Socioecological Model of Rape Survivors' Decisions to Aid in Case Prosecution"; Maddox et al., "Police Empathy and Victim PTSD as Potential Factors in Rape Case Attrition."

13

Response Essay

Chief Mike Brown
Salt Lake City Police Department

Law enforcement agencies acknowledge and understand that there have been problems in the past with how police departments have responded to sexual assault victims. This includes initial response and victim interviews, follow-up victim interviews with detectives, interactions with local rape advocacy groups and forensic nurse organizations, and case screenings with local district attorneys and court procedures.

Many times, sexual assault victims felt "the system" had fallen short and let them down. And it had! The Salt Lake City Police Department (SLCPD) was no exception to this problem—but not by design or with ill intent. That was the path we had been accustomed to, and it was how we thought we could best help sexual assault victims.

So, how do you change the culture of an organization relating to how it responds to and investigates sexual assaults? How does a police department take a victim-centered, trauma-informed approach to these horrific crimes? And how does a department start the healing process and help victims put their lives back together and find closure in their darkest hours?

The SLCPD embarked on a course to change its culture. We started by contacting experts who could train our officers in best practices based on years of research in various areas of sexual assault. Dr. Rebecca Campbell shared her vast knowledge and research on violence against women and children, with an emphasis on sexual assaults, with our department. The SLCPD also contracted with Dr. David Lisak, who provided valuable insight into the false stereotypes and misconceptions about who rapists are and how rapists behave. These falsehoods continue to hamper both the criminal justice system and the institutional response to sexual violence. Dr. Lisak expounded upon the fact that historically, nonstranger rape has been one of the most difficult crimes to successfully prosecute because the nonstranger rapist presents unique challenges to those responsible for protecting the community from criminal behavior.

In 2016, the SLCPD was selected as one of four national test sites to take part in a thirty-six-month project with the Police Executive Research Forum (PERF) and the Women's Law Project (WLP). The project's purpose was to identify and examine challenges in the police response to and handling of sexual assault cases. This project included a site assessment, recommendations, and the initiation of an action plan by their team. The project culminated in the sharing of lessons learned at a national summit and a comprehensive guidebook produced by the PERF and the WLP outlining the issues, recommendations, outcomes, and promising practices identified during the project.

Through the training from Dr. Campbell and Dr. Lisak and the PERF/WLP project, the SLCPD learned where its strengths and weaknesses were and where we needed to be as an organization to better investigate and respond to sexual assaults. We needed to improve our game plan, which, in law enforcement, meant that we needed stronger policies and procedures tailored to these crimes. Our officers and detectives were investigating sexual assaults the same way as every other crime: we would show up and do our due diligence to investigate these crimes and complete our reports before signing off for the day. To improve our methods, we sought out the best practices and policies from around the country.

Based on what we learned, we carefully structured our policies, building them on a victim-centered, trauma-informed foundation. The SLCPD then sent our draft policies to local rape advocacy groups and forensic nurse organizations and sought their expertise, input, and feedback. After we incorporated that feedback, we had created a very solid policy to meet the needs of a victim-centered, trauma-informed investigation.

The first paragraph of our policy states, "Responding officer should be primarily concerned with the well-being of the victim. The initial officer shall make contact with the victim, address safety concerns, and summon emergency medical assistance if needed. It is important to remember that while taking the report from the victim, the officer must remain patient, objective, and nonjudgmental. The officer should be neutral and impartial but also compassionate and empathetic." This policy reminds our officers about how important the very first contact with a victim can be, as much of the investigative and subsequent successful prosecution rests upon this initial contact.

With this policy in hand, now the SLCPD had to roll up its sleeves and train our officers to meet this standard. The goal of this training was to improve officer responses to reports of sexual assaults through instruction in sexual assault offender behaviors, the victimology of sexual assault, and responses to traumatic experiences, including how they affect victim behavior and memory. This training consisted of the following:

- a review and working knowledge of our new rape and sexual assault policy,
- neurobiological responses to traumatic experience,
- traumatic effects on victim behavior and memory, and
- sexual-assault-specific interviewing techniques.

We completed this training, which was mandatory for all officers, in fall 2015.

The SLCPD entered into this process with the objective of improving our response to sexual assault investigations. This was a collaborative process where the SLCPD responded to and embraced recommended changes by developing new training, partnerships, and resources that resulted not only in professional guidelines for sexual assault investigations but also in a paradigm shift—a change in our department's mind-set and culture to a victim-centered, trauma-informed ideology.

How did we know whether we were moving the bar as we investigated sexual assaults? Slowly but surely, we heard from victims. Sergeant Christensen, who oversees our Special Victims Unit, recently received a letter from Trish Crump (a registered nurse and certified Sexual Assault Nurse Examiner—Adult/Adolescent with the Wasatch Forensic Nurses who also serves as a law enforcement liaison) in which she shared the following feedback from nurses:

- The officer was kind and extremely respectful to the victim.
- The officer showed compassion and empathy toward the victim.
- The officer spent time with the victim, talked to her, and walked her through the process. He spent time answering her questions.
- He treated the victim with respect, even though the victim was challenging and it was difficult to understand her train of thought.
- The officer gained the victim's trust. The victim said, "He's so nice and easy to talk to."
- The officer put the patient at ease by believing and respecting her story even though she has had trouble with the law in the past.
- The officer showed kindness and concern for the victim.
- The officer was good with the victim and family. She was sensitive. The victim stated, "She walked me into the room and introduced me to the nurses."
- Your agency is the largest in Salt Lake County and sees a high volume of sexual assault victims. We have noticed an increased desire from your officers to believe and understand the victim. They have taken the time and made victims of sexual violence a priority.

- Sexual assault is one of the most violent crimes a victim can survive, and your agency is doing what it can to help the victim through this difficult process. Thank you for your victim-centered care. We appreciate our working relationship with your agency and all that your team does for victims of sexual violence.

The investigation of sexual assaults for a law enforcement agency is never a "check the box and move on" process. It takes examining policies and procedures with an introspective, critical eye. It also requires developing partnerships as a department, collaborating with rape advocacy groups and forensic nurse organizations, and seeking feedback and input. It requires hundreds and hundreds of training hours and dedicated trainers. This training has to be ongoing, or it becomes very short-lived and "one and done." It's a journey of compassion and empathy, where the SLCPD is working to put victims first.

As chapter 13 points out, law enforcement has struggled with how it investigates sexual assaults—not intentionally but as part of a system that hasn't always recognized the intricacies and complexities of these investigations. As C. S. Lewis said, "You can't go back and change the beginning, but you can start where you are and change the ending." This is how you change police culture.